MINOR LEAGUE BASEBALL STARS

Volume III

Career Records of Players

Compiled By

The Society for American Baseball Research

Published by The Society for American Baseball Reasearch
P.O. Box 93183
Cleveland, OH 44121

ISBN 0-910137-49-8

Printed and manufactured in the United States of America
by EBSCO Media
Birmingham, Alabama

SABR's Minor League Committee is the primary sponsor of this research compilation. L. Robert Davids, 4424 Chesapeake St. NW, Washington, DC 20016, is the editor. Primary assistance has been provided by Robert C. McConnell of Wilmington, Delaware, and Robert C. Hoie of San Marino, California, and Raymond J. Nemec of Naperville, Illinois. SABR's Publications Director is Mark Alvarez.

Many SABR members contributed to this volume. The late Vern Luse made a substantial contribution, as did John Benesch, Ed Brooks, Dan Foley, Jerry Jackson, Gary Nuthals, Pat Rock, Dick Thompson, Bob Tiemann, Bill Weiss, and Gene Wood. Others asisting in various ways include the following:

Art Cantu	Ralph Horton	Bob Richardson
Bill Carle	Tom Hufford	Eves Raja
Craig Carter	Jose Jimenez	Willie Runquest
Dave Chrisman	Cliff Johnson	Steve St. Martin
Dick Clark	Lloyd Johnson	Art Schott
Merritt Clifton	David Kemp	John Schwartz
Brian Davis	Herm Krabbenhoft	Jamie Selko
Bill Deane	Bob Lindsay	Tom Shea
Harold Dellinger	Ralph LinWeber	Bernard Smith
Jack Dougherty	Jim Maywar	John Spalding
John Duxbury	Richard McBane	Renwick Speer
Willie George	Mike McCormick	Tom Strother
Bob Gerald	Jorge Menendez	Jerry Tomlinson
Ron Gersbacher	Terry O'Neil	Jerry Vaughn
Ray Gonzalez	Joe Overfield	Linda Vessa
Jerry Gregory	Frank Phelps	Frank Williams
Bill Gustafson	Jim Price	Karl Wingler
Jim Holl		Ralph Winnie

Photo and art credits: Baseball Hall of Fame Library, Cooperstown, NY; Ohio Historical Society; Joe Overfield; Bob Carroll.

Contents

Minor League Cavalcade

1 Thirty pages of anecdotes, history, and statistics, including information on Nineteenth Century Minor League baseball, black players in the Minor Leagues, father and sons in the Minors, brother combinations, and one-time Minor Leaguers who became famous in other fields.

Players

67 Frederick E. "Dutch" Dorman
68 Willie E. Duke
68 Cecil Henry "Babe" Dye
69 Charles Eugene "Truck" Eagan
69 Patrick Peter "Pete" Eagan
70 Herbert Spencer "Babe" Ellison
70 Gilbert Raymond English
71 Francisco Estrada (Soto)
72 Woodrow Clark "Woody" Fair
72 William Beattie Feathers
73 Wesley Cheek Ferrell
75 Walter Edward French
75 Delos Clinton "Del" Gainor
76 Henry Adrian Garrett
77 Joseph Clyde Glass
77 Leslie Elmer "Lon" Goldstein
78 Joseph Hall Granade
78 Pearl Zane Grey
78 Romer Carl "Reddy" Grey
80 Arthur Carle Griggs
80 Edgar Clifford Hartness
81 Charles Edwin High
81 Elmore Hill
82 Myril Oliver Hoag
84 Edward Adolph "Tex" Hoffman
85 Robert Clay Hopper
85 Arthur Leland "Mike" Hunt
86 George Christopher "Hickory" Jackson
86 Raymond F. Jacobs
87 Irvine Franklin Jeffries
87 Joseph Daniel Jenkins
88 Samuel Jethroe
89 Leonard Edward Johnston
89 Clarence Woodrow Jones
90 John William Jones
90 Walter Franklin Judnich
91 Joseph Henry Kelly
92 William Henry Kelly
92 George P. "Dummy" Kihm
93 Wescott William "Wes" Kingdon
93 John Wesley Knight
94 Charles Elmer "Punch" Knoll
95 Jesse Roy "Horse" Levan
96 Edward Clarence Levy
96 Wiliam Henry Lewis
97 Abel Lezotte
98 Howard S. Lindimore

98 Keith Edwin Little
99 Andrew David "Doc" Lotshaw
99 Michael Lutz
100 Emil Pierre "Lefty" Mailho
100 William Henry Massey
101 Horace G. "Red" McBride
101 James Ray McDaniel
102 Frank Bernard McGowan
102 Roberto Mendez (Navarro)
103 Christobal Rigoberto
        "Minny" Mendoza (Aizpuru)
103 Conklyn Wells "Al" Meriwether
104 Frank Metz
105 William Francis Mizeur
105 Peter G. Monahan
106 John Allen Monroe
106 Felipe Angel Montemayor
107 Andres Mora (Ibarra)
108 Frederick William Muller
108 William "Bade" Myers
109 Juan Navarrete (Sanchez)
109 Albert Richard Neil
110 Orville Burlin "Hank" Nesselrode
110 Frank Nesser
110 Paul Francis Owens
111 Stanley Francis Palys
111 Clarence McKay "Ace" Parker
112 Harold Robert Patchett
112 Leslie Earl Peden
113 Alonso Thomas Perry
114 Edgar Everett Pick
114 Lavern Jack Pierce
115 Alfred Frederick Joseph Platte
115 Harlin Welty Pool
116 John Calvin Powers
116 George William Quellich
117 Earl Wellington Rapp
118 George Reggis "Reg" Rawlings
118 Andrew Jackson Reese
119 Frank Reiger
119 William Joseph Rhiel
119 Kenneth Franklin Richardson
119 Virgil Donald Richardson
121 Donald Lester Richmond
121 David Leonard Roberts
122 Hector Antonio Rodriguez (Ordenana)
123 Hilario Oscar Rodriguez (Moyo)

124 Ray Rohwer
124 Harry Rosenberg
125 John William Joseph "Bunny" Roser
125 Ewell Albert "Reb" Russell
126 Robert Aloysius "Joe" Schmidt
127 John Thomas Sheehan
128 Charles Arthur "Art" Shires
128 Sylvester Adam Simon
130 Emanuel Carr Smith
130 Morris Hirsch "Moses" Solomon
131 Jesus Martin Sommers (Lopez)
131 Edward Lee Stevens
133 George Frederick Stumpf
133 Charles R. Swain
134 Douglas John "Poco" Taitt
134 Joe Cephus Taylor
135 Herbert Marx Thomas
136 Chester Julius "Chick" Tolson
136 Leonard W. Tucker
137 Jose Vidal (Nicolas)
137 Irving J. Waldron
138 Ned Waldrop
138 Frank Gray "Piggy" Ward
139 James Albert Warner
139 Arthur John "Butch" Weis
140 Stanley Aaron Wentzel
141 Lewis Whistler
141 John Wallace White
142 Solomon "Sol" White
142 Harrison P. Wickel
143 Fred "Pap" Williams
143 Marvin Williams
145 George Washington Wilson
145 John Thomas "Long Tom" Winsett
147 Burnis "Bill" Wright
147 Elmer Ellsworth Yoter
149 Andres Ayon (Garcia)
149 Edwin C. Bryan
150 Charles William Chech
151 Robert M. Couchman
151 Howard Oliver Craghead
152 William George "Wheezer" Dell
152 Carroll Phillip Dial
153 Edward Alexander Donalds
153 Gary Reese Fortune
154 Wheeler Bishop "Moose" Fuller
154 Ralph Garcia

155 Harry Ray Gardner
155 Salvador Michael Gliatto
156 Oscar M. Graham
157 Howard Watterson Gregory
157 Herbert Silas Hall
158 Luke Daniel "Hot Potato" Hamlin
158 George B. Harper
159 Bunn Hearn
160 Clarence T. "Cack" Henley
160 Carmen Proctor Hill
161 Harold Ashley Hillin
161 Roy Wesley Hitt
162 Berlyn Dale Horne
162 Edward Charles Hovlik
163 Thomas L. Hughes
164 William Elmer Jacobs
164 Earl Johnson
165 Claude Alford Jonnard
165 Charles Samuel "Rube" Kissinger
166 Frederick Augustus Klobedanz
166 Louis Paul LeRoy
168 Ray Walter Lindsay
169 Grover Cleveland Lowdermilk
169 William Francis Ludolph
170 Japhet Monroe "Red" Lynn
171 John Walter Mails
171 Leon Allen Mangum
172 John Howard Merritt
173 Otto Merz
173 George Earl Milstead
174 John Joseph Pappalau
175 Antonio Pollorena (Osuna)
175 Raymond Lee Prim
176 Francisco Ramirez (Zavala)
177 Vicente Romo (Navarro)
177 Jesse Howard "Andy" Rush
178 Norman Romaine Shope
178 Claude Alfred Thomas
179 Fay Wesley Thomas
180 John Lawrence Tillman
180 James Roy Walker
181 Thomas Royal "Goat" Walker
182 John Milton Warhop
182 William L. "Jimmy" Whelan
183 Richard Oliver Whitworth
183 Adrian Zabala (Rodriguez)

Introduction

With this third volume, which contains the records of 255 players, the Society for American Baseball Research has published the playing records of 625 minor league stars. Many of the players whose records have appeared are familiar to all fans. However, some players in this third volume are unfamiliar even to followers of the minor leagues. We feel that these players had very good careers and one of the purposes of this book is to bring their records to the attention of all fans.

This volume carries the records of a few players who made their names in other fields. Included are football stars Frank Nesser, Beattie Feathers, and Ace Parker; basketball great Benny Borgmann, and hockey hall of famer Babe Dye. Also included are novelist Zane Grey and actor Chuck Connors. This theme is carried further in the narrative section where the brief minor league records of men who became well known in other fields are carried. That section also includes a highlight history with emphasis on the 19th Century, the contribution of early black players, the role of brothers, and many other records and unusual happenings.

Attention is called to the fact that the records of five players active in 1991—all in the Mexican League—are included in this volume. They are Willie Mays Aikens, Michael Cole, Francisco Estrada, Andres Mora, and Jesus Sommers. Information on these players for the 1992 season was not available as this volume went to press.

An attempt has been made to list teams managed, where applicable, in the player records. However, this information is not necessarily complete in all cases.

It has only been in very recent years that minor league pitching records have broken innings pitched into fractions. In order to be consistent, we have rounded off *all* innings pitched to full innings. Earned run averages have been computed on this basis.

Figures in the player records in dark print indicate that the player led the league or tied in that particular category.

The History of
Minor League Baseball Stars

The Society for American Baseball Research (SABR) published the first volume of *Minor League Baseball Stars* in 1978. The book, in addition to 20 pages of photos, narrative, and charts about the best season and career records, contained the lifetime playing records of 172 of the leading minor league players of the past 100 years. It was updated and reprinted in 1984.

The positive response to the first volume resulted in the publishing of a second volume in 1985. It included the playing records of 198 additional minor league players. It also carried a section on the top 15 all-time minor league players selected by SABR, and a section on the greatest minor league managers. Copies of both early volumes can be ordered for $5 each from the SABR National Executive Office at P.O. Box 93183, Cleveland, OH 44121. Shipping is $1.50 for one book, $2.50 for two.

Minor League Cavalcade

Researching 19th Century Minor League Baseball

The National Association of Baseball Leagues was established late in 1901 and most minor league records date from the 1902 season. To mark the 50th anniversary of that organization, a monumental work by Robert Finch, L. H. Addington, and Ben Morgan entitled *The Story of Minor League Baseball, 1901-52*, was published. It carefully recorded the history of minor league play post-1900 but made no reference to the minors of the 19th century.

While SABR's 19th century committee has focused primarily on major league play, the Society's minor league committee has been making progress in researching player records of the organized leagues dating from 1877 when the International Association was established. When the first volume of *Minor League Baseball Stars* was published in 1978, the career records of only six stars who could be identified as 19th century players were included (Bud Fowler, George Hogriever, Kid Mohler, Deacon Van Buren, Moses Walker, and Perry Werden). In 1985 when the second volume was published, there were 12, including pitchers Bill Hart, Willard Mains, and George Stovey. This volume includes 16 who spent at least one-half of their time in the 19th century.

Why has it taken so long to give these players recognition? There are several reasons, but primarily it is because the minor league structure of those days was less formal than under the National Association, and some league averages were never published or published only in part with no pitching stats or no extra-base hits, etc. Researchers like Ray Nemec and the late Vern Luse were primarily responsible for putting missing league records together, and a host of members zeroed in on individual playing records. It was a difficult and time-consuming job but some interesting discoveries were made along the way.

Leagues and Teams Before 1900

The minor leagues were few but not far between in the early years. Practically all the play was concentrated in the northeastern U.S. and adjacent parts of Ontario. There was no reserve clause and no particular distinction then between what was later called the minors and the majors. It is in that context that the International Association of 1877-78 is usually referred to retroactively as the first minor league. It was organized at a meeting of team representatives in Pittsburgh on February 20, 1877. William (Candy) Cummings, the celebrated curve-ball hurler who pitched in the National League in 1876 and who would work for the Lynn, Mass., entry in 1877, was elected president. Other teams in the league were London and Guelph, Ontario; Manchester, NH; Columbus, Ohio; Rochester, NY, and the Allegheny club of Pittsburgh.

The first game was played at Lynn with Cummings losing to Manchester, 14-3. On April 30, Jim Galvin of Pittsburgh hurled the league's first shutout, defeating the Columbus Buckeyes 2-0. The final game of the season took place on October 2 with Fred Goldsmith of the London Tecumsehs defeating Galvin and Pittsburgh, 5-2, and winning the pennant. Other recognizable names in the league included King Kelly, Bobby Mathews, Jim McCormick, and Joe Hornung. Some of the teams in the International Association of 1877-78 also played in the New England Alliance, which was even less formally structured.

Two later and better organized leagues also have valid claims for being named the first minor league. The Northwestern League was started in 1879, and this did not mean the Pacific Northwest. The four cities involved were Davenport and Dubuque, Iowa; Rockford, Ill., and Omaha, Neb. Ted Sullivan, called the "Father of the Minor Leagues", was the chief organizer. He established a pre-set schedule, which the International Association lacked. League-appointed umpires were not provided, however, and there were frequent forfeits because of "hometown" umpiring. The travel distance between Rockford and Omaha and the overwhelming strength of the Dubuque club, run by Sullivan, contributed to the collapse of the league on July 7. Dubuque, whose players included Charles Comiskey and Hoss Radbourn, led with a 19-5 record.

Despite its collapse in mid-season, this circuit would set the stage for a new and expanded Northwestern League in 1883. This new league had the support of the influential former player, manager, and sporting goods dealer A. G. Spalding. An 84-game, evenly-balanced schedule was established for eight teams—Toledo, Ohio; Fort Wayne, Ind.; Grand Rapids, Bay City and East Saginaw, Mich., and Peoria, Quincy and Springfield, Ill. The stature of the team owners was such that the Northwestern League was admitted into a Tri-Partite Agreement with the National League and the American Association, which had been launched the year before.

The Interstate Association, organized in 1883 in the Philadelphia area, was accepted as an "alliance" league by the AA, and became a junior member of the Tri-Partite Agreement. The struggling Interstate, which eventually became the International League, and the Northwestern League provided many players to the 28 teams of the expanded major leagues in 1884. There also was an expansion to seven minor leagues in 1884. Overall, it was a significant growth in Organized Baseball.

Play also expanded to other regions of the country. The Southern League began in 1885, the first circuit to have a 100-game schedule. There also was a Canadian League and a short-schedule Colorado League. The California State League began in 1886, the Texas League in 1888, and the Pacific Northwest League in 1890. Throughout most of the 19th century playing era, the Eastern League and the Western League probably had the highest level of play. However, the strongest ever was the American League of 1900, which used many players from the 12-team National League of 1899, which cut back to eight teams in 1900.

In 1898 the minors started with a record 21 circuits, but, because of preoccupation with the Spanish-American War, a number of those collapsed in mid-season. In 1899 the number was down to 14. Teams dropping out and leagues falling apart was pretty standard procedure for the minors from 1877 to the end of the century.

Black Players in the Minors

At least 75 blacks played one or more games in the minors between 1878 and 1899. This does not include 61 additional blacks who played in the short-lived National Colored Baseball League of 1887, which was chartered under protection of the National Agreement. (Only 13 games were played before frequent rainouts, poor attendance, and lack of financial backing ended the unique experiment.) About one-half of the 75 played on all-black teams in otherwise white leagues. Other blacks participated on an individual basis wherever they could and usually with short tenure. Bud Fowler was the dean of 19th century blacks, breaking in with Lynn in 1878 and playing portions of ten O.B. seasons, but only one was for the full schedule.

Bud Fowler

While two blacks—Moses and Welday Walker—actually got to play briefly in the major leagues with Toledo in 1884, it is recognized that they were not the best American Negro players of that era. In addition to Fowler, more proficient players included Frank Grant, George Stovey, Sol White, and probably several members of the Cuban Giants, the top black team of that era, which played as an entry in three different leagues in 1889-90-91. Stovey won 34 games for Newark in the International League in 1887 and did not get a chance in the majors. The same applies to Grant, a second baseman, who hit .353 for Buffalo that same year, as well as leading the league in home runs. Sol White had a five-year minor league batting average of .356.

Yet with Grant and White batting .349 and .356 in the Eastern Inter-state League in 1890, it was George Williams of York (Cuban Giants) who topped the mostly white loop with a .391 mark. Teammate Arthur Thomas led in doubles and triples. The year before (1889), Trenton (Cuban Giants) pitchers William Whyte and William Selden topped the league with 26-5 and 23-6 records. In 1895, pitcher George Wilson won 29 and lost 4 for Adrian in the Michigan State League. That was his only season in O.B. as opportunities for blacks were sharply narrowed. By 1899, only one appeared in O.B. and that was Hippo Galloway, who played five games with

3

Woodstock in the Canadian League.

Here are the minor league career records of the most active black players of the 19th century. They are ranked by batting average and pitcher winning percentage. Bold face indicates leadership among black players.

Regulars	Pos.	Yrs	G	AB	R	H	2B	3B	HR	SB	BA
George Williams	Inf.	2	108	454	124	167	27	11	2	69	**.368**
Sol White	2-3	5	159	683	174	243	42	12	7	49	.356
Arthur Thomas	3-C	3	126	528	148	185	42	11	4	51	.350
Frank Grant	2-3	6	458	1879	410	**634**	**123**	34	**31**	149	.337
Bud Fowler	2-P	**10**	**466**	**2039**	**455**	628	112	**38**	8	**190**	.308
Abe Harrison	S-O	2	111	403	104	123	23	9	4	54	.305
Clar. Williams	C-O	2	102	420	98	126	17	3	1	41	.300
William Selden	P-O	3	125	478	95	142	14	8	2	47	.299
Harry Herbert	OF	5	142	565	105	162	32	2	5	26	.287
R. A. Kelley	Inf.	3	177	715	130	197	39	4	4	39	.276
Richard Johnson	C-O	4	337	1471	297	398	63	29	14	130	.271
Ben Boyd	OF	3	102	408	85	107	8	2	1	46	.266
George Stovey	P-O	6	122	464	68	121	15	3	1	26	.261
Jack Frye	1-C	5	124	446	87	113	23	7	3	27	.253
Moses Walker	C-O	5	354	1295	215	293	27	15	4	100	.226

Pitchers (T)	Yrs	G	IP	W	L	PCT.	H	R	BB	SO
William Selden (R)	3	54	460	40	11	**.784**	382	229	156	224
William Whyte (R)	3	50	429	37	11	.771	397	207	81	169
Robert Higgins (R)	2	54	473	37	14	.725	465	280	107	207
George Stovey (L)	**6**	**102**	**882**	**60**	**40**	.600	**814**	**495**	**228**	**387**

The First On-Field Player Fatality

The first and only on-field player fatality in the major leagues occurred in August 1920, when Ray Chapman of Cleveland was hit by a pitch from Carl Mays of the Yankees. This was nearly a half-century after the start of the National Association in 1871 and such an occurrence was never repeated. The minor leagues were never so fortunate, suffering more than a dozen field-related fatalities. Most of them were in the lower classifications and resulted from being hit by a pitched ball.

The first one was different. It happened in the first year of the Southern League on August 15, 1885, and involved a two-player collision. Nashville was playing league-leading Atlanta in the Georgia capital, and trailing 3-0 in the 4th. First baseman Lew Henke, batting for Atlanta, slashed a drive near third which Hillery grabbed and threw hard to first. Charles (Lefty) Marr, the regular leftfielder, who had just changed places with the injured Sowders at first base, took the throw but it popped from his hands. He lunged for it, right into the charging Henke, and both went sprawling. Marr, whose head hit Henke in the side of his stomach, recovered shortly, but Henke remained prostrate for some time. When he regained consciousness, he was attended by three doctors and transported to the club house. The game was resumed.

Henke was then moved to the team hotel where his condition seemed to improve somewhat but then deteriorated toward morning. It was determined that his liver had been ruptured with resultant internal bleeding. He became unconscious and died in late afternoon. The August 16 game had been canceled and the players hovered nearby. The funeral service was held before a large body of stunned mourners. His teammates and club officials escorted the body to the train station in Atlanta, from which it was shipped to Henke's home city of Cincinnati, where his wife lived.

An exhibition game was arranged to help pay expenses and to compensate the widow. Lefty Marr, who also was from Cincinnati and knew Henke well, would go on to spend four seasons in the majors. In 1889 he hit .306 for Columbus and led the American Association with 15 triples.

Let's Play Four—And They Did

Triple-headers—three games in one day—have been played three times in the major leagues. There was at least one instance in the minors where teams played four games in one day. That was September 15, 1889 in the Western Association. St. Joseph and Sioux City had three postponed games to make up plus one regularly scheduled game as the season neared its close. The site was Sioux City, Iowa. By agreement, the three postponed games were of five innings, two of which were played in the morning. The last game was ended after seven innings to give St. Joe time to catch the train for Milwaukee.

The Corn Huskers of Sioux City won all four games. The scores were 6-1, 12-7, 12-5, and 7-4. Pitchers Crowell and Burdick each won two. Right fielder and leadoff-man John "Monk" Cline, only five-foot-three and weighing 140 pounds, was the real star for the victors. In 12 official at bats, he scored six runs, stole three bases, and his eight hits included a double, two triples, and a home run. He would lead the Association with a .356 batting average.

St. Joe was under a handicap almost from the start when catcher Dan Mahoney broke a finger in the first inning of the first game. He was succeeded by third baseman Bill Krieg, who probably gained the distinction of being the only player in Organized Baseball to catch four games in one day. His other career distinction was to bat a record .452 in 524 at bats for Rockford in the same Western Association in 1896. Playing first base for St. Joe in all four games was Jumbo Ed Cartwright. He would get his name in the major league record book on September 23, 1890, by driving in seven runs in one inning for St. Louis in the old American Association.

The playing time for the four games at Sioux City was five hours and five minutes. Apparently no time was taken between innings for television commercials.

Looking Back at Lookabaugh

Pitchers were not pampered in the 19th century. There was no such thing as middle relief, a set-up man, or a closer. A century ago, hurlers were not only expected to go the distance but to work every second or third game. And when they pitched in the long-season California League, the workload could take its toll. This was the case with a rather obscure hurler named Jake Lookabaugh.

A native of Illinois, Lookabaugh pitched unimpressively in 1888 for Danville and Rockford before moving to Santa Fe in the New Mexico League. In 1889 he was 17-14 in three months with Pueblo in the Colorado State League. The next year he launched a three-year tour in the California League.

With San Francisco in 1890 he won 29 games and lost 26 while pitching 417 innings in 62 games. The next year with San Jose he was 43 and 25 in 68 games and 577 innings. This was a great year, but Lookabaugh was just warming up for 1892 when he worked 803 innings in 91 games, 89 of them complete. He led the league (as well as the universe) with 45 wins and 43 losses. Whet could he do for an encore? Practically nothing. He was 4-4 for Sacramento in 1893; 1-6 for Nashville in 1894; and 1-1 for Bloomington, Indiana, in 1895. His Herculean effort in 1892 apparently had done him in. In fact, his effectiveness in the second half of that season declined as San Jose, the first-half winner, slipped to fourth and last in the second half.

The decline was not so noticeable for George Harper, Lookabaugh's pitching partner in the two-man rotation for San Jose in 1891 and 1892. Harper worked 704 innings in 1891 and 697 in 1892. In the latter season, which ran 170 games, the dutiful duo labored for a combined 1500 innings. But Harper did not fade away like Lookabaugh. He won 15 games in 1893; 16 in 1894, including six with Philadelphia in the National League; and 24 with Rochester in 1895. Harper's productive career is recorded on page 158. Lookabaugh lapsed back into obscurity. His post-playing career and date and place of death are not known. However, he is remembered here, 100 years after the fact, for his incredible iron-man performance in 1892.

Jim Corbett Playing First Base

One unusual feature of minor league ball in the late 1890s was the role played by heavyweight boxing champion James J. Corbett. A national celebrity after he knocked out the great John L. Sullivan in 1892, Corbett used his great popularity and his well-rounded athletic ability to play for pay in regulation minor league games.

Corbett's manager, Billy Brady, who not only arranged his fights and his stage appearances, contacted various clubs to have Corbett play first base for as much as 40 to 50 percent of the gate. The first games were in the Eastern League in 1895. On August 12, Jim played first for Scranton against Buffalo while his brother Joe, who would later pitch in the majors for Baltimore, played shortstop. Jim had two hits and knocked in two runs and he and his brother were involved in a double play. A month later they repeated their roles for Toronto, but Jim went hitless in four trips.

Corbett did not play regulation ball in 1896, primarily because he was preparing for his title defense against the British-born Bob Fitzsimmons. Corbett was a heavy favorite when they met at Carson City, Nevada, March 17, 1897. He was leading on points when Fitz knocked him out in the 14th round with the famous solar plexus punch. Although Jim lost the crown, most boxing fans thought he was done in by a lucky punch and he was still regarded as the top fighter in the world.

Since Fitzsimmons would not give him a return bout, Corbett agreed to exploit his own popularity by playing baseball. His manager negotiated arrangements with many minor league clubs to play a game and sometimes to put on a boxing exhibition on the same day. Between June 16 and September 20, 1897, Corbett took part in 29 regulation games as well as several exhibitions. One of the latter took place August 22 when he played for the home nine of Pawtucket, RI, against the major league Louisville Colonels. The historical significance was two-fold: Pawtucket won 8-6, and the young Honus Wagner played center field for the Colonels. The box score carried the names of a charter member of the Baseball Hall of Fame and of the Boxing Hall of Fame.

Fan and press reaction to Corbett as a ballplayer was generally good. When he played for Meriden against Waterbury on July 26, for example, "Corbett surprised everyone by his good work. He made two of Meriden's four runs, got a fine hit and accepted fifteen changes without an error. The big fellow was very much in the game." However, the Youngstown (Ohio) *Vindicator* said on September 5 after a loss to Fort Wayne: "It was a big throng and an anxious crowd and they left the grounds in a disgusted mood because the game was lost and Corbett could not play marbles." (He went hitless and made two errors.)

Corbett wound up the 1897 season on a more lofty note on September 20. Playing for Milwaukee against Minneapolis, he collected two hits and was credited with knocking in the winning run 7-6. It was estimated that he made about $17,000 playing ball during the season. Attendance ranged from 2000 on a bad-weather day to 6000, a very good crowd in the minors in the 1890s.

"Gentleman Jim" had two more brief flings at the diamond game. He played three times in the New England League in June 1898, and two years later he was recruited to play two more games to help rescue the collapsing Atlantic League where he had played many of his minor league games. He had two of his most productive games, collecting seven hits in ten at bats. His final game was played in Binghamton, NY, June 27, 1900. There had been some talk that he might buy into a major league club and play first base on a regular basis, but that did not materialize. He was a great minor league attraction, but his playing record, shown here, indicates the limits to his capability on the baseball field.

Jim Corbett's Regulation Minor League Play

Date 1895	Team, Opponent & League	AB	R	H	PO	A	E	Other
Aug. 12	Scranton vs Buffalo, Eastern	4	0	2	12	0	0	2 RBI, DP
Sep. 11	Toronto vs Buffalo, Eastern	4	0	0	5	0	0	BB,DP
1897								
June 16	Scranton vs Providence, Eastern	3	0	0	10	0	0	
July 6	Rochester vs Syracuse, Eastern	4	0	0	7	0	2	
July 14	(2)Phila. vs Richmond, Atlantic	5	0	1	8	0	1	2 SO, DP
July 26	Meriden vs Waterbury, Connecticut	4	2	1	14	1	0	2 DP
July 27	(1)Hartford vs Reading, Atlantic	2	0	0	6	0	1	
	(2)Hartford vs Reading, Atlantic	4	0	1	11	0	0	RBI
July 31	Reading vs Phila., Atlantic	4	0	1	14	0	0	
Aug. 5	Reading vs Richmond*, Atlantic	3	0	0	7	1	1	HBP, DP
Aug. 6	(2)Phila. vs Norfolk*, Atlantic	3	0	0	7	0	2	DP
Aug. 7	(1)Reading vs Richmond*, Atlantic	4	0	0	10	1	1	
	(2)Reading vs Richmond*, Atlantic	3	0	0	6	0	0	
Aug. 13	#Phila. vs Reading, Atlantic	5	1	3	9	0	0	2 RBI
Aug. 14	Lancaster vs Paterson, Atlantic	3	0	0	11	0	0	

Date	Game							
Aug. 15	Paterson vs Phila., Atlantic	4	0	2	7	1	0	3B
Aug. 26	Hartford vs Reading, Atlantic	3	0	1	16	0	0	RBI
Aug. 27	Derby vs Bridgeport, Connecticut	3	1	0	12	0	0	HBP
Aug. 28	Bridgeport vs Derby, Connecticut	3	1	1	7	0	0	HBP
Sep. 4	Youngstown vs Ft. Wayne, InterSt.	2	0	0	9	0	2	BB
Sep. 6	Mansfield vs Wheeling, InterSt.	4	1	2	10	1	0	RBI
Sep. 7	Toledo vs Fort Wayne, InterState	4	0	2	4	0	0	
Sep. 8	Springfield vs Ft. Wayne, InterSt.	4	0	2	7	0	0	2 RBI, DP
Sep. 10	Wheeling vs Mansfield, InterState	5	2	3	14	1	2	2B, RBI
Sep. 11	Dayton vs Springfield, InterState	4	1	1	10	1	0	RBI
Sep. 14	Des Moines vs Burlington, West A.	6	1	2	14	2	0	SB, RBI
Sep. 15	Des Moines vs Burlington, West A.	6	1	0	9	0	1	
Sep. 16	Des Moines vs Burlington, West A.	5	1	1	12	0	0	
Sep. 17	Burlington vs Des Moines, West A.	4	0	1	11	0	2	
Sep. 18	Quincy vs St. Joseph, West Assoc.	4	2	1	9	0	0	
Sep. 20	Milwaukee vs Minneapolis, Western	5	1	2	5	1	2	RBI
1898								
June 26	Taunton vs Brockton, New England	4	1	1	7	1	0	2B, RBI
June 27	Fall River vs Taunton, New England	4	1	2	12	1	0	RBI
June 28	Fall River vs Brockton*, New Eng.	4	0	0	9	1	1	2 DP
1900								
June 11	Elmira vs Reading, Atlantic	5	2	4	5	0	0	2B, 2 SB
June 14	Allentown vs Reading, Atlantic	5	2	3	6	1	0	SB
June 27	Binghamton vs Oswego, NY State	3	0	0	10	0	2	
	Totals	**146**	**21**	**40**	**342**	**14**	**20**	**BA .274**

*Home Team. #at Harrisburg. Played 1B.

A Nine-Inning No-Hitter by a 15-Year-Old Hurler

The 1973 Baseball Research Journal carried an article on the youngest players in major league history. One of those featured was Wee Willie McGill, who was only 16 when he pitched for Cleveland of the Players League in 1890. On May 8 of that year he became the youngest hurler to pitch a complete game victory, 14-5 over Buffalo. McGill's teenage fame did not start in 1890, however. The year before, on July 26, 1889, he pitched Evansville to a 9-inning, 3-0, no-hit victory over Davenport in the Central Interstate League. This startling achievement for a 15-year-old resulted in a request for further documentation of McGill's age. A check of the Georgia census of 1880 indicated that he was six years old that summer, and his death certificate in 1944 listed his birth date as November 10, 1873. That should confirm that he really was 15 when he pitched the no-hitter.

The Evansville *Courier* gave impressive play-by-play of the July 26, 1889 game. However, it essentially ignored the special role of McGill except to say in a sidebar under the box score that "The pitching of McGill yesterday was the most wonderful on record." The explanation of this strange treatment by the *Courier* can be gleaned from earlier issues of the paper. While the "Kid" was a talented hurler for his age, he really was an undisciplined juvenile who did not have good relations with the press or the club. His erratic conduct would later develop into drinking and carousing which would hamper his great potential. In fact, only a month after his no-hitter, he was released by Evansville. Last place Burlington picked him up and—wouldn't you know—when the "Boy Wonder" faced his old teammates on September 3, he fanned eight batters in one three-inning stretch and shut them out 6-0. He won five games and lost six in his half-season of play.

Speaking of Young Players ...

Twenty years ago the *Baseball Research Journal* carried an article on the youngest person to play in an official minor league game. This was Joe Relford, the 12-year-old Negro batboy of the Fitzgerald club in the Georgia State League. On July 19, 1952, with Fitzgerald trailing Statesboro 13-0 in the eighth inning, management acquiesced to shouts from the crowd to "put in the batboy." Relford grounded out as a pinch hitter and made a sensational catch in center field.

Recent SABR research has uncovered another game which lowers the debut age of a minor league "player" to nine. The circumstances can be described briefly as follows.

On June 25, 1904, the Concord, NH, team brought ten players to Lowell, MA, for a New England League game. Ten players would have been sufficient, but catcher Diggins had to leave the game because of illness in the fourth inning, and second baseman Clark lost his temper in the sixth and was thumbed. That left Concord with only eight players and it looked like the game, 5-4 in favor of Lowell, would have to be forfeited. Up stepped the team mascot, George Diggins, the nine-year-old son of the ailing catcher, who offered to fill the gap. The Concord *Evening Standard* commented:

> "George is a right clever kid and some day will be a great ball player, but, of course, it made a farce of the game for him to play. But in he went and the nine innings were played out...He had no chances in right field and a strike out was registered against him the only time he came to bat."

The newspaper ran a photo of young Diggins in his team mascot uniform and also had a brief biographical sketch which concluded with "Some day, however, if nothing happens, George will have his picture in the paper again, and as the legitimate successor of Criger, Kling, and Diggins, Senior." There is no indication that he played in the minors again.

The Shortest and Tallest

George Diggins, Jr., would certainly be a prime candidate for the smallest player in the minors. However, he might not have been the shortest. On September 18, 1905, Buffalo manager George Stallings inserted into the lineup a music hall midget named Jerry Sullivan (shades of Eddie Gaedel) in the second game of a doubleheader at Baltimore. Wearing a cut-down uniform, he coached third base a couple of innings and then pinch hit in the ninth. Although the Baltimore pitcher had trouble getting the ball low enough for Sullivan, he finally hit one six inches off the ground that sailed over the third baseman's head for a hit. A lot of clowning took place on the bases when the Orioles tried to pick him off. When he scored on a single by Frank LaPorte, his head-first slide into home drew a tremendous ovation. More details on this offbeat episode are contained in Joe Overfield's article in *The National Pastime* of 1990.

If Jerry Sullivan was the shortest player at 3 to 3 1/2 feet, who was the tallest? It probably was not Randy Johnson, the 6-10 pitcher with Indianapolis and now with Seattle. More likely it was a turn-of-the-century hurler named Arthur Switzer. He pitched for Birmingham in 1898, and led the Southern League in wins with New Orleans when it folded in June 1899. He also pitched in the Atlantic League in 1899, and popped up in the Kansas State League after 1900. He was referred to as "the Giant" and the "seven-foot hurler." Other sources said he was 6-10 and 7-4, the latter probably an exaggeration. The Birmingham *Age-Herald* carried a stand-up photo of the local team in 1898 which had him a head-and-upper-shoulders taller than the other players.

Early Three-Base Hit Record Uncovered

Joe Delahanty was a pale imitation of his older brother Ed when it came to hitting, but he did set records for hitting triples while with Allentown in the Atlantic League in 1899. It was an individual achievement even though his brothers Jim and Tom were playing on the same team. Neither of them showed any special ability to hit three-baggers. On the other hand, Joe set OB standards in 1899 when he connected in eight consecutive games (hitting nine triples); he belted 16 in the month of July; and he hit a total of 30 in 86 games before the Atlantic League broke up on August 6. This was double the total of runner-up Frank "Piggy" Ward, who hit 15 triples in 94 games.

Delahanty was on a pace to hit 44 over the full 128-game schedule. However, he missed the opportunity taken by some other players in that circuit to expand his total by joining another minor league team. He stayed with his brothers in Allentown and played against independent teams. Joe resumed his heavy hitting when the Atlantic League reorganized in 1900. While batting .469, he hit 11 triples in 33 games before the league folded for the last time on June 14. His season mark of 30 three-base hits in 1899 was not surpassed until Jack Cross hit 32 in 1925.

Here is how Delahanty's record compares with the other minor league players who hit 29 or more triples in a season.

	G	AB	R	H	2B	3B	HR	BA
Jack Cross, 1925, London, Mich-Ont.	132	513	90	178	28	32	7	.347
Joe Delahanty, 1899, Allentown, Atl.	86	337	73	116	11	30	3	.344
Walter Shaner, 1925, Lincoln, West.	163	642	145	230	41	30	14	.358
Dusty Cooke, 1928, Asheville, Sally	146	519	112	188	30	30	13	.362
Eddie Moore, 1929, Ft. Worth, Texas	163	672	143	225	31	30	2	.335
Pete Rose, 1961, Tampa, Florida St.	130	484	105	160	20	30	2	.331
Abel Lezotte, 1895, Wil-Bar, East	111	484	110	184	31	29	5	.339
Guy Tutweiler, 1914, Prov., Inter.	148	544	74	161	21	29	5	.296
JoJo White, 1929, Ft. Smith, West A.	137	491	96	153	25	29	8	.312
Burl Horton, 1941, El Paso, Ariz-Tex	131	576	127	216	28	29	10	.375

Fathers and Sons

The dual appearance of Ken Griffey Sr., and Jr., in the majors in 1989, and playing together on the Seattle Mariners parts of 1990 and 1991 were important first achievements in major league history. The Griffeys capped those milestones by hitting back-to-back homers for the Mariners on September 14, 1990.

Father-son association on the same team has popped up several times in minor league history. One of the more interesting examples occurred in 1941 when Jim Poole, 46, was player-manager of Fort Pierce in the Florida-East Coast League and two of his players were sons, Jim, Jr., and Phil. Twelve years later, in 1953, 48-year-old Earl Caldwell, long-time major and minor league hurler, had his son Earl, Jr., as his catcher with Alexandria for part of the Evangeline League season. The father led the league with a 2.07 earned run average.

A father and son who really got to know each other on the diamond were the Jim O'Rourkes, who played together with Bridgeport in the Connecticut League 1903-08. Although referred to as Jim, Sr., and Jr., by writers of that era, the father was James Henry and the son James Stephen.

Jim the father had an unbelievably long pro career, starting with the Mansfield club in the National Association in 1872 and closing out by catching a complete game with New Haven at age 60 in 1912. That gave him a record 38 years as a player in Organized Baseball. After leaving the majors as player-manager of Washington in 1893, he umpired briefly in the National League and then began a 15-year baseball association in his native city of Bridgeport. He organized the Bridgeport Victors as an independent team in the summer of 1894, and then, as player-manager, took the team into the Connecticut State League in 1895. The next season, he led the short-schedule loop with a .437 average in 33 games, and repeated with a .405 average in 73 games in 1897. SABR member Frank Williams, who compiled the full minor league records of both O'Rourkes, notes that the "Old Man" went 6-for-6 with three homers on June 24, 1896.

In 1903, when the father was 50/51, he played in 101 games, most of them as a catcher. That was the year he brought in his 19-year-old son Jim to play third base for Bridgeport. The youngster struggled at bat, hitting under .200, but the father, now owner as well as player-manager, worked hard with him over the next couple of years. The son's performance gradually improved, particularly after being shifted to second base in 1906. He hit .274 that year, .303 in 1907, and .318 in 1908.

Father Jim, who caught a full game for the New York Giants late in 1904 (at age 51), saw his son get a shot with the New York Highlanders late in 1908. Son Jim hit .231 in 34 games and that was his only major league experience. He played for Columbus and St. Paul in the American Association in 1909-14.

In the six seasons they played together with Bridgeport, 1903-08, the father appeared in 370 games and the son 535. No tokenism there. The father made his last appearance with Bridgeport in 1909 and then sold the club. By that time he was president of the Connecticut League, a post he held through 1914, when it was called the Eastern Association. He died in Bridgeport in 1919 and was named to the Hall of Fame in 1945. His son died in 1955. It was only through the extremely long career of the influential father, who was 31 years older than his son, that the two could play together for six seasons.

By Any Other Name

James Smith, after a hitch in the U.S. Navy, reported to the Bartlesville club in the Oklahoma-Kansas League in the spring of 1908. He was an American Indian, six-feet-two and weighing

205 pounds, and hoped to get a job pitching. The only clothes he had was the Navy uniform he was wearing. The manager and players began to call him Bluejacket and the name caught on. It certainly was more colorful than Smith and he soon adopted the name as his own. It appeared that way in the box score and in the official guides.

Bluejacket won 24 games in 1912, and led the Three Eye League with 23 in 1913. He pitched for Brooklyn in the Federal League in 1914-15, and appeared in three games for Cincinnati in 1916. His 12-year career ended with Oklahoma City in the Western League in 1919.

In the same general period when Bluejacket was pitching, there was a player in the Northwestern League named Ten Million—an obvious made-up name. Actually, it wasn't! Bill Weiss, official statistician for several West Coast leagues, was in touch with the family and found that the player's father was E. C. Million, a Washington state attorney and judge. The boy, born October 14, 1889, in Mt. Vernon, Wash., was named Ten by his mother, who "had a penchant for the unusual." Her influence also caused Ten Million's daughter to be named Decillion (33 zeros) Million. The daughter, who provided this background information, uses the nickname Dixie.

A baseball star at the University of Washington in 1910, Ten Million played with Victoria in 1911, hitting .276 in 160 games. He signed with Cleveland for 1912, but was injured before he could get into a major league game. Returning to the minors, he played for Sioux City in the Western League, Spokane and Tacoma in the Northwestern, and Moose Jaw in the Western Canada League. He was a speedy outfielder and base runner and batted leadoff. On May 10, 1914, the Tacoma *Daily Ledger* reported "It is doubtful if the local fans ever saw a more brilliant day of fielding than that of Ten Million. During the afternoon he made 10 put outs in left field and fully five of them were labelled two-base hits when they left the bat. McGinnity [player-manger] pitched great ball, but he has every reason to be thankful that Ten Million was on hand to do some of the shagging."

After service in the Army in World War I, Ten Million became a Ford auto salesman in Seattle. When the 10 millionth Ford was produced in the 1920s, it was taken on a tour of the country. A public relations coup was achieved when Ten Million posed with the car.

The former ball player died June 18, 1964.

Player Released: Too Good for League

In the old days, newspaper editors were alert to "man bites dog" type of articles. The Salt Lake City *Tribune* followed that lead on July 16, 1921, when it reported that an Ogden player had been released because he was too good for the league. The player in question was Dave Davenport, former American League hurler with the Browns. In 1915, he also led the Federal League with 55 games, 393 innings, 229 strike outs, and ten shutouts.

In 1921 the six-foot-six, 220-pounder pitched for Ogden in the outlaw North Utah League. He did so well the *Tribune* stated tongue-in-cheek in a sub-headline: *Davenport Weakens and Gives One Hit. Big Dave Out of Form and Only Strikes Out 14*. Earlier he had pitched a perfect game, beating Bud Shaney of Tremonton 4-0. In his eight games with Ogden, he won seven and lost none, and had four shutouts. Davenport allowed 34 hits in his 66 innings pitched, and walked three and struck out 112—the ultimate in walk/whiff ratio!

The rival clubs complained about Davenport's overpowering performance, and league officials agreed that for the good of the circuit the big hurler would have to be released. Davenport then signed with Casper in the Midwest League, but, before he left, he stated: "Just tell the fans that I have appreciated their support and backing. They have been loyal during my stay in Ogden and I sincerely hope that they will remain loyal to the club now."

The *Tribune*, which ran a large photo of the pitcher, summed up the situation by stating: "As the record book shows, it is the first time in baseball history where a player has been released because of his winning ability."

A Double Humiliation

Pitcher Karl Black, whose record appeared in the Second Volume of *Minor League Stars* because of his 275 career wins, had his greatest season in 1923 when he won 29 games for Tulsa in the Western League. Ironically, the greatest humiliation of his career came July 1 of that year when he took the mound against Wichita. Lyman Smith, the leadoff batter, hit one of the southpaw hurler's first pitches over the fence for a home run. So did the second batter, Jocko Conlan; the third batter, Wes Griffin; and the fourth, Jim Blakesley. King Karl, a proud German whose real name was Lautenschlager, abdicated at that point. Who came in to replace him? Tulsa manager Jack Lelivelt, not wanting to waste another starter in a losing cause, brought in a semipro hurler named Wilbert Ray. He quickly retired the side on a ground out, a fly out, a harmless walk, and a strikeout. Tulsa got back into the game but eventually lost. Black apparently recovered himself and helped lead the Oilers to 101 victories and a close second-place finish.

Highest On-Base Percentage in Minors

Who had the highest career on-base percentage in the majors? It was Ted Williams at .483, followed by Babe Ruth at .474. They not only were exceptional hitters, they were the only two players to receive more than 2000 walks. When Pete Hughes' record was published in the first volume of *Minor League Stars* in 1977, on-base percentage was not the well-used stat that it is today, and he was not specifically credited with having the highest OBP in the minors.

It was fairly obvious, however, that Hughes had to be "way up there." He had that rare distinction of collecting more walks (1666) than hits (1566) in his 12-year career between 1937 and 1952. He still had enough hits to post a .350 career batting average. Although lacking hit-by-pitch data for his first two partial seasons, his total reached 49. Putting his "hits received" with his hits delivered and his walks, he was on base an average of 2.9 times for each of his 1333 games. His on-base percentage was a fantastic .530. No other seasoned minor leaguer reached the .500 mark.

Hughes also had season percentages of .577, .574, .569, and .566—well above Williams' .551 percentage in 1941. In those four seasons, Hughes had the exceedingly high walk totals of 210, 207, 193, and 180. He never became the minor league career leader primarily because he spent four years in military service in World War II. All of his O.B. career was spent in the lower classifications where he hit 284 homers and averaged almost one RBI per game.

Power and Speed in the Minors

The advent of black and Latin players in the majors in the last 40 years has placed more emphasis on the combination of power and speed. Players like Willie Mays, Bobby Bonds, and Jose Canseco immediately come to mind. Mays has the highest level of career homers (660) and stolen bases (338), and Canseco has the highest level of season homers (42) and steals (40), achieved in 1988. This feature of baseball, at least on a career basis, has not been realized in the minors primarily because players who can steal bases and also hit for power usually do not languish in the minors.

Leonard Tucker, whose record is carried on page 136, was one exception. In 1956 with Pampa in the Southwest League, he hit 51 homers and stole 47 bases. This wiped out the combined record of John Wright, who hit 52 homers and stole 42 bases with Fort Wayne in 1930. Tucker played 11 years, mostly in the lower classifications, and hit 236 career fourbaggers and stole 257 bases in only 1090 games.

Len Tucker

Who then achieved the highest level of career homers and thefts in the minors? It was Woody Fair, who wracked up 275 roundtrippers and 263 steals in 1892 games between 1934 and 1952. Most of the other career leaders, as shown below, also had long careers.

Players & Years Played	HR	SB
Woody Fair, 1934-52	275	263
Paul Easterling, 1926-51	257	265
Clarence Kraft, 1910-24	256	283
Moose Clabaugh, 1923-40	346	244
Bunny Brief, 1910-28	342	247
Spencer Harris, 1921-48	258	241
Jim Poole, 1914-46	311	240
Edward Levy, 1936-55	238	239
Leonard Tucker, 1953-63	236	257
Ken Richardson, 1934-51	222	235
Carlos Bernier, 1948-65	212	594
Earl Smith, 1911-35	212	284

Minor Leaguers with Highest Career Level of Extra-Base Hits

Charles (Count) Campau was the first minor league player to reach the 100-level in all categories of extra-base hits in his career. He got off to a good start with Savannah and New Orleans in the Southern League in 1887 when he hit 24 doubles, 18 triples, and 17 home runs. He reached the century level in 1896, and when he retired in 1905, he had 368 doubles, 172 triples, and 136 fourbaggers. He was one of only three 19th century players to reach the 100-milestone, the others being Joe Katz in 1898 and Bud Lally in 1899.

Jim Murray exceeded Campau's level of extra-base hits before he retired in 1920 with 373 doubles, a minor league record 207 triples, and 152 homers. Later in the 1920s, he in turn was succeeded by Joe Riggert with 435 doubles, 228 three-base hits (breaking Murray's mark), and 172 fourbaggers. In 1940, Stanley Keyes, who never made it to the majors, set the all-time standard with 509 doubles, 199 triples, and 343 homers. He thus became the Stan Musial (725-177-495) of the Minors.

Considering the short tenure of most minor league players in recent years, and the decline of three-base hit production, there seems no possibility that the Keyes record could be surpassed. The Mexican League, the only circuit with any substantive player continuity, has its share of home run hitters, but is not known for triple hitters or those who hit both triples and homers. Hilario Rodriguez, whose record is included in this volume and who played 16 of his 19 seasons south of the border, probably was the last minor leaguer to hit more than 100 doubles, triples, and homers. He closed out his career in 1969 with extra-base hit totals of 493-106-244.

The 32 players with the highest level of extra-base hits are shown below. The time period stretches from Campau's debut in 1887 to Carlos Bernier's close-out in 1965. Incidentally, the Latin speedster played only his final season in the Mexican League. Longevity undoubtedly played a part in the inclusion of many of the names on the list. Six of the players, led by Spencer Harris, had more than 3000 hits. On the other hand, Ben Paschal, Ray Flood, Carr Smith, and Ernie Calbert had fewer than 1900 hits.

Players & Years Played	Hits	2B	3B	HR
Stanley Keyes, 1924-40	2633	509	199	343
Lee Riley, 1927-49	2418	460	195	248
Joe Riggert, 1909-28	2717	435	228	172
George Whiteman, 1905-29	3388	671	196	162
William Mizeur, 1922-29	1942	387	157	158
Johnny Gill, 1924-47	3141	667	156	289
Bunny Brief, 1910-28	2963	594	154	342
Jim Murray, 1897-1920	2246	373	207	152
Eddie Hoffman, 1913-35	2497	487	152	191
Frank Brazill, 1918-38	2893	547	152	254
Spencer Harris, 1921-48	3617	743	150	258
Jim Blakesley, 1920-33	2338	487	148	201
Nick Cullop, 1920-44	2670	523	147	420
Ben Paschal, 1915-34	1821	319	142	152
Ray Flood, 1926-40	1785	276	173	142
Guy Sturdy, 1920-40	2545	449	140	203
Murray Howell, 1928-44	2509	459	139	229
Fred Henry, 1914-39	3384	675	200	138
Cowboy Jones, 1924-41	2347	551	138	164
Ray O'Brien, 1913-32	3152	642	186	136
Joe Bonowitz, 1918-36	2925	579	136	151
Count Campau, 1887-1905	2286	368	172	136
Frank Huelsman, 1897-1916	2180	451	149	133
Polly McLarry, 1911-28	2723	550	132	140
Buster Chatham, 1922-45	3076	506	182	132
Carr Smith, 1923-44	1798	338	145	131
Wilbur Davis, 1915-37	2690	470	130	253
Prince Oana, 1929-51	2292	428	130	261
Pete Compton, 1910-28	2547	401	147	129
Carlos Bernier, 1948-65	2374	312	129	212
Ernie Calbert, 1910-28	1883	341	128	204
Ike Boone, 1920-36	2521	477	128	217

The Non-Home Run Hitters

In 1983 Bob McConnell published an article in the *Baseball Research Journal* entitled The Non-Home Run Hitters. These were the major league players who hit the fewest fourbaggers in their careers and those who had played the most consecutive games without connecting. Bill Holbert, a catcher from 1876 to 1888, went to bat the most times—2334—without hitting a homer. Tommy Thevenow, who hit two homers, both inside-the-park, early in his career in 1926, then went from Sept. 22, 1926 to the end of his career in 1938 without hitting another. This covered 3347 at bats, a major league record.

SABR researcher McConnell now has done a similar study on minor league players. Ray Nemec provided the information that Gene Hassell, who played second and third for eight teams between 1951 and 1962, including five seasons with Denver, never hit a homer in 1058 games and 3323 at bats. He was not an automatic out, collecting 993 hits for a .299 average. His extra-base hits included 107 doubles and 34 triples.

Several minor league players, who did hit some roundtrippers, had homerless streaks of more than 4000 at bats. The longest streak was charged to John "Bunny" Griffith (see Volume II), who played in 1248 games and went to bat 4601 times between June 25, 1930, when he was with Hazelton in the New York-Penn League, and June 19, 1940. He was manager and shortstop for Salem in the Western International League when he connected in a 17-14 win at Vancouver. Ironically, one of his outfielders in that game was Moose Clabaugh, who had accumulated more than 340 homers by that time. Griffith hit 19 in his 23-year career.

Albert E. Wright, not to be confused with a contemporary slugger named Albert O. "Ab" Wright, who hit 323 homers, played in more games than Griffiths (1295), but had fewer at bats (4494). A Pacific Coast League second baseman, he homered Sept. 1, 1935 (1) for San Francisco at Seattle, and did not hit another to the end of his career in 1946.

Shortstop John O'Neil hit his last home run for Pittsfield in the Canadian-American League on June 12, 1942. He then played the rest of his career, most of it in the Pacific Coast League, through 1953 without hitting another. The streak was 1330 games and 4541 at bats. He also played in 46 games in the majors in 1946, going to bat 94 times for the Phillies without a four-base blow. This gave him an O.B. streak of 1376 games and 4635 at bats. He hit only three homers in his career.

It wasn't just middle infielders who had long homerless streaks. Les Stebbins was a first baseman in the Texas League who hit his last four-bagger for Houston on September 5, 1932. He played through 1941 and never touched home plate again on his own home run. Stebbins had 4222 at bats in 1114 games, and batted .299. It is not surprising that he never made it to the majors, which had such power-packed first sackers in the 1930s as Lou Gehrig, Jimmie Foxx, Hank Greenberg, Hal Trosky, Johnny Mize, and Dolf Camilli.

Hard to Remember and Easy to Forget

July 4, 1929, was an explosive day in the San Francisco Bay area. It was a heavy-hitting day of doubleheaders throughout the Pacific Coast League, but two examples should be sufficient. Babe Pinelli, 165-pound third baseman for San Francisco, who normally batted second, sat out the first game while slugger Smead Jolley hit two homers to lead the Seals to victory over Seattle. For some reason, probably because his name was Babe, he batted clean-up in the second game. Pinelli had six hits, including three homers, two of them grand slams, and batted in 12 runs in a romp over the Indians. Jolley, batting fifth, had four hits but knocked in only one run. In 167 games that season, Pinelli had a total of five homers (a career high), and 65 runs batted in. He undoubtedly took maximum advantage of his one opportunity to bat clean-up. In 18 seasons, 1917-32, he hit 13 homers in the minors and five in the majors.

Across the Bay in Emeryville, the home park of the Oakland Oaks, a twinbill was being played with the Missions, for whom Ike Boone hit four doubles in the first game. In the fourth inning of the second game, Roy Carlyle of Oakland, batting behind Buzz Arlett in the fifth spot, "hit a soaring drive that cleared the fence to the right of the clubhouse in centerfield." It was called a very long home run, but did not become legendary until three days later. Teammate Del

Howard, who said he saw the ball land, arranged to measure the distance.

The ball had sailed over two rooftops and landed on a third house at 1212 Park Avenue. It was found resting in a rain gutter and measured at 618 feet from home plate. This was the longest hit then recorded—except for those hit into a boxcar of a passing train! The ball was hit off pitcher Ernie Nevers, the Stanford and pro football star, who had served up a few long homers to Babe Ruth and Lou Gehrig while pitching for the St. Louis Browns in 1927.

While Pinelli's three homers and 12 RBIs were soon forgotten, Carlyle's one cannon shot was not. In fact, there was a new round of publicity describing the home run as the longest in Organized Baseball when a plaque was erected April 6, 1992, where Oaks Park stood prior to being demolished in 1955. Carlyle died in November 1956, six weeks after Pinelli gained lasting fame as the home plate umpire for Don Larsen's perfect World Series game.

Omaha Beached in Five-Game Series

In the Western League in 1931, Des Moines humiliated arch rival Omaha in a five-game series September 11-14 by scores of 16-5, 12-2, 29-6, 22-9, and 18-5. That is a cumulative score of 97 to 27, reason enough for the Omahas to slip out of the Iowa capital in the cover of darkness. Stanley Keyes was the chief exterminator, collecting 15 hits, scoring 16 runs, and knocking in 23. He hit six home runs, including four in the September 13 twin maulings of 29-6 and 22-9. He drove in eight runs in the first game and seven in the second. The next day he followed up with a grand slam and five RBI.

Why was the slugging outfielder so "Keyed-up?" Back on July 4 in Omaha, he gave Des Moines an 8-3 lead with two homers and five RBI, but the contest ended in the fifth, one out short of a regulation game. In fact, there were two outs and the count was two strikes and one ball on the batter when the umpire interrupted the play because of light rain. When it became worse he called the game. It was tough to lose those productive stats, and Keyes finished the season with *only* 144 runs, 203 hits, 36 doubles, 24 triples, 38 homers, 160 RBI, and 401 total bases in 132 games. Oh, yes, he had a batting average of .369 and a slugging percentage of .729. He led the league in all those offensive categories except doubles and triples.

Major Accidents in the Minors

The photos of the California Angels bus that crashed off the New Jersey Turnpike on May 21, 1992, brought back memories of two disastrous bus crashes in the Minors in the 1940s. While the Angels' accident resulted in serious injury to Manager Buck Rodgers, and less critical injuries to several players and club officials, the 1940s accidents took the lives of several players.

On June 24, 1946, nine players of the Spokane Western International League club were killed when their team bus, en route to Bremerton, Wash., plunged off a narrow road in the Cascade Mountains some 60 miles east of Seattle. Traveling at dusk in a drizzling rain, the bus driver veered the vehicle to avoid an oncoming auto and the bus broke through the cable-guard railing and caught fire as it hurtled 350 feet down the steep, rocky mountainside.

Eight players met instant death. They were manager-catcher Mel Cole, first baseman Victor

Picetti; pitchers Bob Kinnaman and George Lyden; shortstop George Risk; and outfielders Bob James, Fred Martinez, and Bob Paterson. A ninth player, Chris Hartje, who had played nine games with Brooklyn in 1939, died a few days later. The bus driver and six other players were injured. Included was second baseman Ben Geraghty, who became Spokane's manager in 1947 and went on to a successful career prior to his death at age 48 in 1963. (See his managing record in Volume II).

Three of Spokane's 18 players were not on the bus. Two hurlers made the trip by car and infielder Jack Lohrke left the bus at its last stop in Ellensburg, having received notice to report immediately to San Diego, which had recalled him. Henceforth, he was known as "Lucky" Lohrke. Spokane, which had a working agreement with the Brooklyn Dodgers, missed several games before it could regroup and resume play with mostly new players.

Two years later, on July 24, 1948, five players of the Duluth Northern League team lost their lives and 13 others were injured when their bus was hit head-on by a truck a few miles north of St. Paul. The team bus was en route from Eau Claire, Wisconsin, to St. Cloud, Minnesota. The truck driver and Duluth manager George Treadwell, who was driving the bus, both died in the collision and resulting fire from a ruptured gas tank. Other team members killed were outfielders Gerald Peterson and Gilbert Trible; pitcher Don Schuchmann; and second baseman Steve Lazar.

The 13 players injured, some seriously, included first baseman Mel McGaha, who later became a major league manager, and third baseman Elmer "Red" Schoendienst, brother of the St. Louis infielder, also known as Red. The accident left the Dukes with only one player—Sam Hunter—who did not make the fatal trip. The Cardinals, with whom Duluth had a working agreement, and other O.B. teams quickly helped out in stocking the Dukes with new players. Several of the injured players returned to action later in the season with other clubs. Organized Ball and fans across the nation made a substantial financial contribution to the survivors and families of the victims.

A smaller scale accident occurred near Camden, South Carolina, on September 5, 1925. The Augusta team of the Sally League, traveling in two touring cars, was en route from Charlotte, North Carolina, where it had played a 13-inning game, to the home city. It was late on Saturday night when the lead car, driven by manager-first baseman Emil Huhn, ran off the road on a curve and flipped over. Huhn, the 1923 Southern Association batting champ, who was hitting .361 at the time, and slugging catcher Frank Reiger, who was hitting .350 with 23 homers, were pinned under the wreckage and died.

Five other players were injured, including pitcher Harry Smythe, the Sally ERA leader in 1925, who had a broken collarbone. He would go on to win 301 games in the minors, plus five in the majors. His playing record is carried in Volume II. Reiger's record is carried in this volume on page 120.

Integration After World War II

Dave Hoskins was one of those special black players who helped integrate the minor leagues after World War II. Hoskins was the first black in two leagues, one in the north and the other in the south. And he played quite different positions each time.

Hoskins was an outfielder when he entered the lineup of the Grand Rapids club in the Central

League in the fifth inning of a twinbill with Saginaw August 1, 1948. He singled and scored the first run in the eighth in a 3-2 loss at Grand Rapids. The *Herald* reported that he "came up with the most spectacular catch of the night when he raced far back into deep rightfield to haul down a long blow off the bat of Everett Robinson in the ninth inning. He made the catch backhanded and received a tremendous ovation." He finished the season with a .393 average in 46 games.

Although Hoskins continued to hit well, he was gradually transformed into a pitcher. He was in that role on April 13, 1952, when he pitched Dallas to a 4-2 win over Tulsa, and he became the first black to appear in the Texas League. It was not his best-pitched game. In fact, he loaded the bases in the ninth, but, with two outs, he set the batter down on strikes and the Dallas fans gave him an ovation. On April 23 he shut out Oklahoma City and collected four hits himself. He proved to be a powerful league attraction, drawing 11,031 patrons, about one-half of them black, in a victory at Houston on April 27. The other two games in that series drew about 3000 each.

He went on to win a league-leading 22 games, had a 2.12 ERA, and batted .328 in 62 games. He moved up to Cleveland the next year, winning nine games and losing three. He was back in the minors in 1955 and wound up his career in 1960. He worked for General Motors in Flint, Michigan until his death of a heart attack at age 47 in 1970.

The Evolution of Minor League Home Run Totals

Home run hitting progressed in the minors generally on the same timetable as in the majors but individual totals of the leaders were usually higher in the minors. Part of this increase could be attributed to play in smaller parks. In a few parks a ball hit over a nearby leftfield or rightfield fence might be ruled a two-base hit. No such restriction applied to the Western Association park in St. Paul in 1889.

It was an inviting site for all the ambitious hitters in the league that year, but the Saints benefitted most. Not only did St. Paul have the top three home run hitters in the Association that year, but the Minors as well. Charlie Reilly, a switch hitter, led with 27. Joe Werrick hit 25, and John "Scrappy" Carroll 24. John Crooks of Omaha, never known as a power hitter, hit four home runs in one game at St. Paul on June 9. He was the first player in Organized Ball to achieve that distinction.

Hitting was very strong in the majors in 1894-95, primarily because of the lengthened pitching distance and other rules refinements. This also was the case in the minors, but the enhancement was reflected more in home runs. This time, Minneapolis, the other Twin City, took the lead. Perry Werden hit 43 homers in 1894 and 45 in 1895. Teammates Henry Hines and Frank Burrell joined him with 34 and 32 homers in 1894; and Bud Lally and Joe Werrick supported him with 36 and 32 in 1895. The Millers hit 219 fourbaggers in the latter year, a record that stood for decades. Even regular pitcher Chick Fraser hit 15.

Athletic Park in Minneapolis was modified the next year to cut down on home runs and then was replaced by Nicollet Field. Minneapolis would return as a home run haven a generation later. In the dead-ball era of 1900-1919, home run production was moderate. The top figures were put up by Charles Swain, who hit 39 in 1913, and Ernie Calbert with 43 in 1917. Werden's season total of 45 in 1895 remained the O.B. high until Babe Ruth hit 54 in 1920, and the minor league high until Moses Solomon hit 49 in 1923.

The situation changed dramatically in 1920, sparked primarily by Babe Ruth's 54 home runs for the Yankees. Fourbaggers rained down in minor league cities across the U.S. until 1942-45 wartime conditions reduced the deluge. Tony Lazzeri hit 60 for Salt Lake City in 1925, and Moose Clabaugh hit 62 for Tyler, Texas, the next year. Joe Hauser hit 63 for Baltimore in 1930, and 69 for Minneapolis in 1933, when all but 21 were hit at Nicollet Field. Similarly, Sulphur Dell in Nashville was the Southern Association's favorite home-run park, at least for left-handed hitters like Jim Poole, Chuck Workman, Charlie Gilbert, Carl Sawatski, Babe Barna, Jack Harshman, and Bob Lennon.

After World War II, bandbox parks in the Southwest helped such sluggers as Bob Crues, who hit 69 for Amarillo in 1948, and Joe Bauman, who belted an all-time high of 72 for Roswell, New Mexico, in 1954.

Career totals for minor leaguers leveled off after major league expansion in the 1960s and 1970s and the migration of some players to Japanese diamonds. The Mexican League became the only circuit with significant player continuity, and sluggers like Hector Espino, Jack Pierce, and Andres Mora established some noteworthy home run numbers there, as shown in the chart below.

First players to hit 20, 30, 40, 50, 60 home runs in a season, and 100, 200, 300, 400 career home runs in the minors

20 Season			30			40		
1887	Walter Andrews	28	1894	Perry Werden	43	1894	Perry Werden	43
1889	Charles Reilly	27	1894	Henry Hines	34	1895	Perry Werden	45
1889	Joe Werrick	25	1894	Joe Strauss	33	1917	Ernie Calbert	43
1889	John Carroll	24	1894	Frank Burrell	32	1920	Clarence Yaryan	41
1889	Bill Joyce	23	1894	Buck Freeman	31	1921	Bunny Brief	42
1889	Lewis Whistler	22	1894	Will Klusman	31	1922	Bunny Brief	40
1889	Elmer Cleveland	20	1895	Perry Werden	45	1923	Moses Solomon	49
1890	John Carroll	21	1895	Bud Lally	36	1923	Walter Simpson	44
1892	Ed Breckinridge	20	1895	Joe Werrick	32	1923	Paul Strand	43
1893	Abel Lezotte	25	1897	Jim Williams	31	1924	Clarence Kraft	55

50			60			100 Career	
1924	Clarence Kraft	55	1925	Tony Lazzeri	60	1895	Perry Werden
1924	Stormy Davis	51	1926	Moose Clabaugh	62	1896	Ed Breckinridge
1924	Wilbur Davis	51	1930	Joe Hauser	63	1896	Count Campau
1925	Tony Lazzeri	60	1933	Joe Hauser	69	1896	Joe Strauss
1926	Moose Clabaugh	62	1948	Bobby Crues	69	1896	Bud Lally
1929	Ike Boone	55	1954	Joe Bauman	72	1898	Joseph Katz
1929	Gus Suhr	51	1954	Bob Lennon	64	1899	Joe Werrick
1929	Ed Kallina	50	1956	Dick Stuart	66	1902	Lewis Whistler
1930	Joe Hauser	63	1956	Ken Guettler	62	1907	Buck Freeman
1930	Nick Cullop	54	1956	Frosty Kennedy	60	1907	Charles Eagan

200	**300**	**400**
1922 Bunny Brief	1926 Bunny Brief	1935 Buzz Arlett
1923 Clarence Kraft	1932 Buzz Arlett	1940 Nick Cullop
1926 Yank Davis	1934 Joe Hauser	1953 Merv Connors
1926 Ernie Calbert	1935 Nick Cullop	1975 Hector Espino
1928 Ping Bodie	1935 Moose Clabaugh	1991 Andres Mora
1929 Buzz Arlett	1936 Stanley Keyes	
1929 Stormy Davis	1940 Smead Jolley	
1930 Jim Poole	1941 Tedd Gullic	
1930 Bill Kelly	1941 Jim Poole	
1930 Fuzzy Hufft	1943 Ab Wright	

All-Time Minor League Home Run Leaders

Hector Espino	484
Buzz Arlett	432
Nick Cullop	420
Andres Mora	404
Merv Connors	400
Joe Hauser	399
Bobby Prescott	398
Jack Pierce	395
Jack Graham	384
Tedd Gullic	370

Baseball Brothers—Delahantys Were Prolific and Productive

Members of the SABR Minor League Committee have researched player records back to the 1880s and have confirmed that the Delahanty brothers were the ultimate baseball family. Not only did they play the most games and collect the most hits in the minors (5412 and 5927), but in Organized Baseball as well (9008 and 10144). All six of the sons of James and Bridget Croke Delahanty played in the minors and all but Will played in the majors. He was the youngest of the brothers, the weakest hitter in the group, and played only seven years. He was hit in the head by a pitched ball while playing with Waterbury on May 6, 1910, and missed most of that season. Although he had a fair season (for him) in the south in 1911, he was through by 1912.

The combined career records of the six brothers led the minors in games, at bats, hits, runs, doubles, and triples. Half of the contingent played together for Allentown in the Atlantic League from 1898 to 1900. Tom played second, Jim short, and Joe spent most of his time in the outfield. In a substantial way they set the precedent for Felipe, Matty, and Jesus Alou to become the first trio of brothers to appear in the same major league lineup. On September 15, 1963, the Alous formed the San Francisco Giants outfield for *one inning*!

The Cleveland-born Delahantys played in 20 different minor leagues from coast to coast. On the other hand, the Bannons of Massachusetts remained mostly in the Northeast where they became familiar names in the Connecticut, New England, and Eastern Leagues. All nine of the Bannon boys played some form of pro ball. SABR researchers Tom Shea and Dick Thompson have identified them as John, born in 1861; twins Daniel and Timothy, 1865; Thomas, 1869;

Three of the Delahanty boys, who played for Allentown in 1898

James, 1871; Patrick, 1873; William 1875; George, 1879; and Francis, 1881. John played in the Rhode Island League in 1884, and later became an umpire in the New England League. Daniel reportedly played in that league, but this could not be documented. Several members of the family played in independent leagues in Amesbury and Lynn, Mass.

Jim, Tom, Bill, and George Bannon were the only ones to have substantial records in the minors. Ironically, Jim and Tom, two of the great base stealers of that era, made their O.B. debuts with Portland in 1891 as pitcher and catcher. Jim then attended Holy Cross College in Worcester, Mass., where he became a star player who went directly to the majors. Tom had his first big season with Pawtucket in 1894, when he led the New England League in runs scored, doubles, and had 101 steals. Most of the Bannon boys were small, but this was not the case with Bill, who was 6'1" and weighed 210. That size qualified him to be an umpire in the rough-and-tumble era, and, when he wasn't playing, he called balls and strikes in several leagues between 1906 and 1914. George was the pitcher in the family. He gained his first attention as an 18-year-old by defeating the Louisville major league club in an exhibition game on August 22, 1897. He later became a hard-throwing outfielder and a good base stealer. The Bannons easily ran off with the minor league base stealing laurels, Tom, Jim, Bill, and George being credited with 1587 career thefts.

The three Boone brothers—Ike, Danny, and Bill—came up with the best totals in the "triple crown" categories of home runs, runs batted in, and batting average. First it is necessary to mention that Ronaldo Camacho and Moises Camacho, the Mexican League sluggers who sometimes played on the same teams in the 1960s and 1970s, are not believed to be brothers. A Mexican League publication indicates that they were born in different provinces of Mexico and

23

Ron's mother's surname was Duran and Moises' was Muniz. With the Camachos removed from contention, the Boones took the RBI crown from the Ferrells (Rick, Wes, George, and Marvin) by an estimated 210 runs. The Delahantys could not be considered because of the almost total lack of minor league RBI figures prior to 1920.

The Boones edged the Arletts in home runs 436 to 432. Actually, Alex Arlett was not a contributing member. Buzz hit 432 and his older brother hit none in more than 500 games. This was only the most extreme case of brothers with quite different home-run hitting ability. They include Gene Lillard, who hit 345 in the minors, and brother Bill, who hit only nine in eight seasons; Adrian Garrett, whose record is carried in this volume, hit 280 (plus 102 in Japan), and brother Wayne hit 12. Charles, a third brother, hit no homer in five years in the minors. Also, Marv Throneberry hit 201 to 49 for Faye. Finishing behind the Boones and Arletts were the three DiMaggios (Dom, 24, Joe, 74, and Vince, 273) with a total of 371.

The Boones scored best in batting average. They achieved a lively-ball-era percentage of .361, even though brother Bill hit below .300 in his short career. They were far ahead of Roy and Hiram Carlyle at .325. This is based on brothers in more than 2000 total games.

Of the hundreds of brother combinations who played in the minors in the last 115 years, only the Brashear brothers each played in 2000 games and collected 2000 hits. In the majors, Paul and Lloyd Waner came close but Lloyd finished with 1993 games. Born in Ohio, Roy and Robert, who was better known as Kitty, started their careers in the Western Association in 1898 and 1899. Roy was primarily a second baseman and Kitty a first baseman. Roy played in 2093 games and collected 2082 hits. For Kitty the numbers were 2064 and 2023. They played together only one season and that was with Vernon in the Pacific Coast League in 1910. Although neither hit for power, they had the distinction of hitting back-to-back homers in the first inning of a 3-2 win over Los Angeles on August 3. Their records are carried in this volume.

The Combined Minor League Batting Records of Brothers

Delahanty

		G	AB	R	H	2B	3B	HR	SB	BA
Ed	1887-88	104	484	110	176	28	11	10	36	.364
Tom	1894-1906	1304	5244	1001	1545	212	78	26	321	.295
Joe	1897-1912	1423	5405	832	1636	287	170	55	201	.303
Jim	1898-1916	830	3113	504	948	172	54	12	93	.305
Frank	1902-16	1189	4308	541	1095	165	54	15	260	.254
Will	1905-12	562	1994	274	527	83	29	9	122	.264
		5412	*20548*	*3262*	*5927*	*947*	*396*	*127*	*1033*	**.288**

Bannon

		G	AB	R	H	2B	3B	HR	SB	BA
Tom	1891-1910	1761	6915	1201	1888	276	63	24	823	.273
Jim	1891-1910	1620	6264	1073	1754	274	90	25	457	.280
George	1898-1911	1149	4280	602	1085	188	55	36	229	.254
Bill	1901-07	574	2162	244	525	63	19	7	78	.243
		5104	**19621**	**3120**	**5252**	**801**	**227**	**92**	*1587*	**.268**

Boone

		G	AB	R	H	2B	3B	HR	RBI	SB	BA
Danny	1919-33	1336	4627	925	1648	307	65	214	931	108	.356
Ike	1920-36	1857	6807	1362	2521	477	128	217	1473	120	.370
Bill	1925-28	160	597	92	176	30	4	5	116	19	.295
		3353	**12028**	**2379**	**4345**	**814**	**197**	*436*	*2520*	**247**	*.361*

The most active pitching brothers were Herman and Edward (Ted) Pillette. Herman, called "Old Folks," had an unusually long career which ran from 1917 to 1945. He wound up with 264 wins and 264 losses. His younger brother Ted won 116 and lost 152. That gave them 380 wins and 416 losses and ruled them out of the winning percentage sweepstakes. That title fell to Johnny and Warren (Curley) Ogden. Johnny had a spectacular 213-103 career won-lost record, the best of any 200-game winner. His brother didn't help much with a 79-73 mark, but, together, they had a creditable percentage, based on 292 wins and 176 losses.

The remaining categories of earned run average and strikeouts were captured by Enrique and Vicente Romo. Their combined ERA, compiled mostly in the Mexican League, was a fancy 2.71, and their combined 3239 strikeouts were far ahead of Grover and Louis Loudermilk's total of 2676. Grover's career record, carefully researched by Ray Nemec, includes a rookie season in 1907 when he fanned 465 batters, a minor league season record. Grover's pitching record, as well as that of Vicente Romo, are carried in this volume.

The Combined Minor League Pitching Records of Brothers

Pillette

		G	IP	W	L	Pct.	H	R	ER	BB	SO	ERA
Herman	1917-45	789	4607	264	264	.500	4973	2371	Inc.	1102	1515	Inc.
Edward	1923-34	429	2302	116	152	.433	2742	1684	Inc.	1104	696	Inc.
		1218	*6809*	*380*	*416*	*.477*	*5194*	*4055*	**Inc.**	*2206*	*2211*	**Inc.**

Romo

		G	IP	W	L	Pct.	H	R	ER	BB	SO	ERA
Vicente	1962-86	470	2896	199	134	.598	2613	1097	868	827	2109	2.68
Enrique	1966-76	332	1708	144	81	.585	1576	661	520	465	1130	2.74
		802	**4604**	**313**	**215**	**.593**	**4189**	**1758**	**1388**	**1292**	*3239*	*2.71*

Ogden

		G	IP	W	L	Pct.	H	R	ER	BB	SO	ERA
Johnny	1918-34	421	2607	213	103	.674	2682	1259	974	831	1091	3.36
Warren	1925-34	251	1299	79	73	.520	1523	735	654	403	393	4.54
		672	**3906**	**292**	**176**	*.624*	**4205**	**1994**	**1628**	**1234**	**1484**	**3.75**

Deja Vu All Over Again

Heinie Sand, shortstop for Salt Lake City, performed an unassisted triple play for the home folks against Sacramento on July 4, 1921 (second game). With Buddy Ryan the baserunner onsecond base, and Billy Orr on first, Rowdy Elliott, the batter drove a liner near second which Sand snagged. He jumped on second to retire Ryan, and tagged Orr coming down from first. Bill Rodgers, manager of Sacramento, who was coaching at third base, thought there was something familiar about this play—and there was. Five years before, on July 12, 1916, Rodgers was playing for Portland at Salt Lake City, and he pulled off an unassisted triple play. In that game, Buddy Ryan and Billy Orr, playing for Salt Lake, were the base runners on second and first. Rogers, playing second pulled down a drive from the bat of Frank Guigni, tagged Orr in the basepath, and stepped on second to retire Ryan. The circumstances, particularly those involving Ryan and Orr, were unusually similar although five years apart.

There was no five-year hiatus for Charles Reilly, who played an instrumental role in two triple plays in consecutive innings on April 23, 1903. Reilly, who had led the minors in home runs back in 1889, was captain and third baseman of Los Angeles, playing at home against Butte in the Pacific National League. In the seventh inning, Kane walked for Butte and Sam LaRoque advanced him to second with a single. McKevitt then smashed a liner toward third which Reilly brought down with a leaping catch. He threw quickly to second for another out and the ball was relayed to first for the third. "Three men were retired in about three seconds" according to the Los Angeles *Times*. The crowd roared.

The next inning, Swindells, Ward and Brockhoff all reached base for Butte. McHale, the batter, lined the ball between Reilly and third. He made a diving catch and touched third. He then whipped the ball to Messerly at first to retire Brockhoff. The crowd response was even greater than in the seventh. "Even the Butte players were warm in their praise of the plays." They could afford to be as Butte won 4-2.

They Also Played the Game

Minor League ball has been played, at least for a short time, by several men who made a mark in various fields of endeavor outside of baseball. Zane Grey and Jim Corbett were two early examples. Corbett's case was unusual because he was already famous when he began his minor league play. He also was the first of many athletes to show skill in another professional sport.

Pro football became baseball's most popular cross-over sport. In fact, about 60 athletes have been identified as playing both major league football and baseball. There were many additional NFL stars who played in the baseball minors, particularly in the 1920s and 1930s. There was at least one example of NFL stars being outfield teammates. The Jackson, Miss., *Clarion Ledger* highlighted the local Cotton States League game of June 8, 1937 as follows: "Beattie Feathers hit the fence in rightfield last night in the ninth inning to score Don Hutson with the winning run and take the second game of the series from Meridian, 8-7."

Feathers, the first NFL player to rush for 1000 yards in a season (1935), is featured in the regular records section of this volume, along with Frank Nesser and Ace Parker. Basketball star Benny Borgmann and Hockey Hall of Famer Babe Dye also are included. In this part of the book

Benny Borgman played both baseball and basketball for ten years.

we will highlight just a few celebrity types who played briefly in the minors.

This being a Presidential election year, it is appropriate to call attention to three politicians of the last half century whose names were raised as possible candidates. All three played in the minors ostensibly to raise money to go to law school. Scott Lucas of Illinois, who was to become Senate Majority Leader in 1949-50, compiled the most substantive diamond record in 1913-15. Frank Lausche, Ohio Governor and Senator, made a marvelous debut with Duluth in the

Northern League on May 4, 1916. He hit a home run, triple, and single in the season-opening victory over Superior and a large photo accompanied the description of his exploits. He was a star for about ten days and then began to fade. He could not hit the curve ball. He tried again in the Eastern League in 1917. When he was released, the U.S. had declared war, so he joined the Army. Lucas took that route about the same time.

Mario Matthew Cuomo, then known as "Matt", joined Pittsburgh's farm team at Brunswick, Georgia, after high school in 1952. A center fielder, he batted .244 in 81 games. According to *Current Biography*, "A wild pitch that hospitalized him for a month with a head injury, convinced him that the major leagues were not in his future."

Among those included in this compilation, sports entrepreneur Art Rooney probably had the best record in his brief sojourn in the minors. In his one full season with Wheeling in 1925, he batted .369 and led the Middle Atlantic League in games, hits, runs, and stolen bases. His brother and teammate Dan also had a fine year with Wheeling, hitting .359 and leading in doubles. Ironically, Dan became a Catholic priest and missionary to China while Art because a successful race tract bettor and owner and founded the NFL franchise in Pittsburgh.

Here are the minor league records, some mediocre and others fairly respectable, of a cross-section of Americans who "made it" in other fields. They are listed chronologically.

SCOTT W. LUCAS, Born Feb. 19, 1892, at Chandlerville, Ill. Died Feb. 22, 1968, at Rocky Mount, N.C. U.S. Representative from Illinois, 1935-39. Senator, 1939-51. Majority Leader, 1949-50.

			Pos	G	AB	R	H	2B	3B	HR	RBI	SB	BA
1913	Pekin	Ill-Mo	1B	34	132	24	61	13	4	1	-	12	.462
	Bloomington	Ill	OF	61	232	22	66	7	4	1	-	3	.284
1914	Bloom/Peor	Ill	1B-OF	103	369	43	89	8	3	2	-	16	.241
1915	Bloomington	Ill	OF	95	343	36	89	17	2	0	-	11	.259
				293	**1076**	**125**	**305**	**45**	**13**	**4**		**42**	**.283**

FRANK J. LAUSCHE, Born Nov. 14, 1895, at Cleveland, Ohio. Died April 21, 1990, at Cleveland, Ohio. Mayor of Cleveland, 1941-45. Governor of Ohio, 1945-47, 1949-57. Senator 1957-69.

			Pos	G	AB	R	H	2B	3B	HR	RBI	SB	BA
1916	Dul/Virg.	Northern	3B-1B	31	104	13	28	5	2	2	-	5	.269
1917	Lawrence	Eastern	3B-OF	27	84	12	13	3	0	2	-	4	.155
				58	**188**	**25**	**41**	**8**	**2**	**4**	**-**	**9**	**.218**

ARTHUR J. ROONEY, Born Jan. 27, 1901 in Coultersville, Pa. Died August 25, 1988, in Pittsburgh, Pa. Owner of race tracks, boxing promoter, and founder and long-time owner of Pittsburgh Steelers NFL franchise.

			Pos	G	AB	R	H	2B	3B	HR	RBI	SB	BA
1922	Flint	Mich-Ont	OF	10	28	5	8	2	1	0	-	0	.286
1925	Wheeling	Mid-Atl	OF	106	388	109	143	26	5	8	-	58	.369
				116	**416**	**114**	**151**	**28**	**6**	**8**	**-**	**58**	**.363**

DONALD M. HUTSON. Born Jan. 31, 1913, at Pine Bluff, Ark. College and pro football star. Premier pass receiver for Green Bay Packers, 1935-45. Led in receptions eight years; led in scoring five years. Charter member of Pro Football Hall of Fame.

		Pos	G	AB	R	H	2B	3B	HR	RBI	SB	BA
1936	Pine Bluff	Cot Sts	OF	132	536	95	167	10	10	4	43	25	.312
1937	Albany	NY-Penn	OF	14	53	8	11	2	0	0	5	3	.208
	Selma/Jack	SEastern	OF	48	195	38	58	7	4	3	13	13	.297
			194	**784**	**140**	**236**	**19**	**14**	**7**	**61**	**41**	**.301**

SAMUEL A. BAUGH. Born March 17, 1914, at Temple, Texas. College and pro football star. Outstanding quarterback for Washington Redskins, 1937-52. Led NFL in passing six years. Led in punting four years. Charter member of Pro Football Hall of Fame.

		Pos	G	AB	R	H	2B	3B	HR	RBI	SB	BA
1938	Columbus	AA	SS	16	59	3	13	2	0	0	3	0	.220
	Rochester	Int	SS	37	71	13	13	0	1	1	11	0	.183
			53	**130**	**16**	**26**	**2**	**1**	**1**	**14**	**0**	**.200**

ELIOT ASINOF. Born July 13, 1919 in New York City. Writer. Books include *Eight Men Out: The Black Sox and the 1919 World Series* (1963); *Black Men and White Law in Bedford Stuyvesant* (1970); *Bleeding Between the Lines* (1979); *Nineteen Nineteen: America's Loss of Innocence* (1990).

		Pos	G	AB	R	H	2B	3B	HR	RBI	SB	BA
1940	Moultrie	Ga-Fla	1B	15	54	8	16	2	0	0	7	1	.296
1941	Wasau	Northern	OF	41	162	39	48	4	1	0	10	5	.296
			56	**216**	**47**	**64**	**6**	**1**	**0**	**17**	**6**	**.296**

ANDREW M. "HANDY ANDY" PHILLIP. Born March 7, 1922, at Granite City, Ill. As one of Whiz Kids at Illinois, set basketball scoring record for Big Ten and was MVP in 1943. After return from military service, again made All American in 1947. Played 11 seasons in pro basketball. First NBA player to register 500 assists. Member of Naismith Basketball Hall of Fame.

		Pos	G	AB	R	H	2B	3B	HR	RBI	SB	BA
1947	Columbus	AA	PH	2	2	0	1	0	1	0	1	0	.500
	Decatur	III	OF	21	70	15	21	5	1	3	12	2	.300
1949	Win-Salem	Carol	1B	79	298	51	83	22	1	8	47	5	.279
1952	Bakersfield	Cal	OF	19	76	14	21	4	0	1	8	1	.276
	Indianapolis	AA	1B	2	3	0	0	0	0	0	0	0	.000
			123	**449**	**80**	**126**	**31**	**3**	**12**	**68**	**8**	**.281**

NATHANIEL "SWEETWATER" CLIFTON. Born Oct. 13, 1922 in Chicago. Died Aug. 31, 1990, in Chicago. Played basketball with Harlem Globetrotters in 1940s. The six-foot-seven star was first black to sign with NBA team, the New York Knicks, in 1950. Concluded career with Detroit in 1958.

			Pos	G	AB	R	H	2B	3B	HR	RBI	SB	BA
1949	Dayton	Central	1B	73	264	36	85	19	5	11	53	1	.322
	Pittsfield	Can-Am	1B	24	80	10	22	2	1	3	10	0	.275
1950	Wilkes-Bar	Eastern	1B	120	427	70	130	27	7	9	86	4	.304
				217	**771**	**116**	**237**	**48**	**13**	**23**	**149**	**5**	**.307**

THOMAS BROOKSHIER, Born in Roswell, N.M., Dec. 16, 1931. Played football at University of Colorado. Defensive back for Philadelphia Eagles 1953, and, after military service, 1956-61. Went into broadcasting and became TV football analyst for CBS.

			G	IP	W	L	H	R	ER	BB	SO	ERA
1954	Roswell	Longhorn	11	65	7	1	69	45	32	57	32	4.55

MARIO M. CUOMO, Born June 15, 1932, in Queens, N.Y. Lieutenant Governor of New York, 1979-83; Governor 1983 to present. Keynote speaker at Democratic national conventions.

			Pos	G	AB	R	H	2B	3B	HR	RBI	SB	BA
1952	Brunswick	Ga-Fla	OF	81	254	31	62	10	2	1	26	7	.244

KURT (VON VOGEL) RUSSELL. Born March 17, 1951, in Springfield, Mass. TV and movie actor. Movies included *Silkwood*, 1983; *Swing Shift*, 1984; and *Tequila Sunrise*, 1988.

			Pos	G	AB	R	H	2B	3B	HR	RBI	SB	BA
1971	Bend	NWest	2B-S	51	179	30	51	11	0	1	14	2	.285
1972	WallaWalla	NWest	2B	29	77	12	25	4	0	0	14	1	.325
1973	El Paso	Texas	2B	6	16	4	9	3	0	1	4	1	.563
				86	**272**	**46**	**85**	**18**	**0**	**2**	**32**	**4**	**.313**

RANDY MARIO POFFO. Born Nov. 15, 1952, at Columbus, Ohio. After baseball career, became professional wrestler like his father, Angelo, and brother Lanny. In the "show-biz" atmosphere of modern wrestling, he took the name of Randy "Macho Man" Savage and became a headliner. Twice held World Wrestling Federation championship.

			Pos	G	AB	R	H	2B	3B	HR	RBI	SB	BA
1971	Sarasota	Gulf Ct	C-OF	35	63	10	18	3	2	2	14	14	.286
1972	Sarasota	Gulf Ct	O-C-1	52	168	23	46	3	4	3	26	4	.274
1973	Orangeburg	W.Carol	OF-C	46	116	11	29	8	2	2	13	0	.250
	Sarasota	Gulf Ct	DH-OF	25	61	7	21	6	2	0	11	0	.344
1974	Tampa	Fla St	DH-OF	131	461	36	107	19	6	9	66	3	.232
				289	**869**	**87**	**221**	**40**	**16**	**16**	**130**	**21**	**.254**

JOHN ELWAY. Born June 28, 1960, at Port Angeles, Wash. Attended Stanford University. Quarterback for Denver Broncos, 1983 to present. Led team to NFC title, 1986, 1987, and 1989, but lost in Super Bowl.

			Pos	G	AB	R	H	2B	3B	HR	RBI	SB	BA
1982	Oneonta	NY-Penn	OF	42	151	26	48	6	2	4	25	13	.318

No Ordinary Baseball Fan

While William Howard Taft is rightly credited with initiating the practice of Presidential Openers at Washington games in 1910, an assist should be awarded to his Vice President, James Sherman. A staunch baseball fan when he was a U.S. Representative from New York, Sherman continued this interest when he served as Vice President 1909-12. After attending one of the early 1909 games, he strongly recommended that Taft spend an afternoon at the Washington ballpark. The President did so on April 17, 1909, and was caught up in the atmosphere even though the Senators lost to Boston. Taft attended a game in Pittsburgh on May 29, and another in Chicago on September 16. He participated enthusiastically in the first Presidential Opener April 19, 1910, and attended ten more games during his four-year presidency.

While the President was watching major league games, Vice President Sherman was taking in a number of minor league games around the country. Utica, N.Y., was his favorite site because it was his home town. He was there May 5, 1909, to take part in the opening of the New York State League season between Utica and Syracuse. He went back several times. On September 3, 1910, he was in Oklahoma City to try to patch up differences in both wings of the Republican Party in that election year. He had time, however, to go to the ballpark with Governor Charles Haskell to see the locals split a doubleheader with Shreveport.

One of the most interesting minor league games he attended was Minneapolis at Kansas City September 10, 1909. It was a close game with some tension. Clarence Owens was the only umpire and Sherman called him to his box between innings to protest a decision Owens had made in calling a Kansas City runner out. In a dignified way, the VP said "I believe your decision on that man was incorrect. He was safe and had he been called safe, it might have won the game for the home club. Your umpiring seems to have been good outside of that, but I believe that decision was wrong."

"Well, Mr. Sherman," Owens retorted with a smile, "possibly I did make a mistake. Even an umpire makes mistakes occasionally. I do not suppose there are any errors in judgment in Washington, but here we are liable to make all kinds of errors. You know baseball is a different vocation from making the laws of the land."

The Vice President was taken aback by the answer, but soon joined the umpire in a hearty laugh. That ended the dialogue. Minneapolis won the game, 3-2.

As he left the park with his Kansas City host, Sherman still insisted KC might have won if the umpire had made a correct call. "I hate to see the home team lose," he said. "You are used to seeing the home club lose, are you not?" said his host. "Yes," Sherman answered. "You know I live in Washington!" (The Senators won 42 and lost 110 games in 1908.)

A note on some records in this book

Player records of certain minor leagues which, for some technical or other reason did not come under the supervision of the National Association in specific years, are included in the minor league totals in this book. Some examples are the American League in 1900, the American Association in 1902 and the California League in 1902-09, the Pacific Coast League in 1903, TriState League (Penn-NY-Del) in 1904-07, Provincial League in 1937-39 and 1947-49, and the pre-1955 Mexican League.

Vince DiMaggio, an outstanding outfielder, hit for power in Minors.

Player Records (Non-Pitchers)

WILLIE MAYS AIKENS
Born October 14, 1954, at Seneca, SC.
Height 6'3", Weight 225. Bats left. Throws right.
Set Mexican League record with .454 BA in 1986

Year	Club	League	POS	G	AB	R	H	2B	3B	HR	RBI	SB	BA
1975	Quad Cities	Midwest	1B	125	443	69	126	17	1	17	**91**	6	.284
1976	El Paso	Texas	1B	133	514	**99**	163	24	4	**30**	**117**	10	.317
1977	Salt Lake City	P C	1B	77	295	62	99	23	2	14	73	4	.336
	California	American	1B	42	91	5	18	4	0	0	6	1	.198
1978	Salt Lake City	P C	1B	133	470	82	153	19	0	**29**	110	5	.326
1979	California	American	1B	116	379	59	106	18	0	21	81	1	.280
1980	Kansas City	American	1B	151	543	70	151	24	0	20	98	1	.278
1981	Kansas City	American	1B	101	349	45	93	16	0	17	53	0	.266
1982	Kansas City	American	1B	134	466	50	131	29	1	17	74	0	.281
1983	Kansas City	American	1B	125	410	49	124	26	1	23	72	0	.302
1984	Toronto	American	1B	93	234	21	48	7	0	11	26	0	.205
1985	Toronto	American	DH	12	20	2	4	1	0	1	5	0	.200
	Syracuse	Int	DH-1B	105	373	65	116	19	1	16	61	0	.311
1986	Puebla	Mexican	DH	129	445	134	**202**	38	3	46	**154**	0	**.454**
	Tidewater	Int	1B	4	15	2	2	0	0	0	0	0	.133
1987	Puebla	Mexican	DH-1B	77	268	59	95	17	2	17	67	0	.354
1988	Jalisco	Mexican	DH-1B	126	412	96	145	27	1	30	119	0	.352
1989	Leon	Mexican	1B-DH	128	423	108	167	40	1	37	**131**	1	**.395**
1990	Leon	Mexican	DH-1B	130	419	83	150	32	1	21	106	0	.358
1991	Monterrey Ind	Mexican	DH-1B	111	361	52	108	14	0	19	80	2	.299
		Majors		**774**	**2492**	**301**	**675**	**125**	**2**	**110**	**415**	**3**	**.271**
		Minors		**1278**	**4438**	**911**	**1526**	**270**	**16**	**276**	**1109**	**28**	**.344**

ANGEL LUIS ALCARAZ (ACOSTA)
Born June 20, 1941, at Humacao, Puerto Rico.
Height 5'9", Weight 165. Batted right. Threw right.
Manager: Leon-Mexican League 1979-80.

Year	Club	League	POS	G	AB	R	H	2B	3B	HR	RBI	SB	BA
1959	McCook	Neb St	PH	1	1	0	0	0	0	0	0	0	.000
1960	Orlando	Fla St	3B-2B	70	247	49	51	13	2	5	44	15	.206
1961	Artesia	Soph	2B	122	477	126	161	24	5	21	100	11	.338
1962	Salem	NWest	2B	24	67	8	17	1	0	2	7	3	.254
	Keokuk	Midwest	2B	85	268	64	78	23	1	16	59	12	.291
1963	Santa Barbara	Calif	2B	131	441	90	119	20	4	18	86	13	.270
1964	Albuquerque	Texas	2B	6	16	1	1	1	0	0	0	1	.063
	Santa Barbara	Calif	2B	42	148	22	36	7	2	6	24	7	.243
1965	Santa Barbara	Calif	2B	92	299	50	80	13	3	13	49	8	.268

Year	Club	League	POS	G	AB	R	H	2B	3B	HR	RBI	SB	BA
1966	Santa Barbara	Calif	2B-1B	113	380	68	108	22	2	22	82	7	.284
1967	Albuquerque	Texas	2-3-S	137	475	86	**156**	31	5	22	85	4	**.328**
	Los Angeles	National	2B	17	60	1	14	1	0	0	3	1	.233
1968	Los Angeles	National	2-3-S	41	106	4	16	1	0	2	5	1	.151
	Spokane	P C	2B	36	137	18	38	9	1	5	18	2	.277
1969	Omaha	AA	2B-3B	131	478	94	144	31	3	13	79	9	.301
	Kansas City	American	2-3-S	22	79	15	20	2	1	1	7	0	.253
1970	Kansas City	American	2B	35	120	10	20	5	1	1	14	0	.167
	Omaha	A A	2B-3B	77	263	30	67	11	3	6	29	1	.255
1971	Tucson	P C	2B-3B	102	303	59	88	17	2	14	65	0	.290
1972	Rich/Charles	Int	2B-3B	96	276	38	63	12	1	9	25	0	.228
1973	Puebla	Mexican	2-S-3-1	103	315	56	84	16	2	15	71	4	.267
1974	Puebla/Cord	Mexican	2B	108	352	57	99	16	3	12	69	2	.281
1975	Cordoba	Mexican	2B	113	405	49	119	18	2	12	85	1	.294
1976	Cordoba	Mexican	2B	116	385	50	117	25	1	8	54	1	.304
1977	Cordoba	Mexican	2B	38	126	16	33	5	0	4	13	2	.262
1978				Did not play in O.B.									
1979	Leon	Mexican	2B	130	446	81	134	19	2	**24**	77	2	.300
1980	Leon	Mex #1	2B	23	86	15	28	8	1	3	16	0	.326
1981	Poza Rica	Mexican	2B	91	243	16	56	6	0	2	21	2	.230
	Majors			**115**	**365**	**30**	**70**	**9**	**2**	**4**	**29**	**2**	**.192**
	Minors			**1987**	**6634**	**1143**	**1877**	**348**	**45**	**252**	**1158**	**107**	**.283**

THOMAS SAMUEL ANGLEY

Born October 2, 1904, at Baltimore, MD. Died October 26, 1952, at Wichita, KS.
Height 5'8", Weight 190. Batted left. Threw right.
Drafted by Chicago Cubs from Atlanta after 1928 season.

Year	Club	League	POS	G	AB	R	H	2B	3B	HR	RBI	SB	BA
1927	Macon	S Atl A	1B-C	87	309	46	112	19	6	3	66	6	.362
1928	Atlanta	S Atl A	C	90	235	32	76	16	6	3	28	2	.323
1929	Chicago	National	C	5	16	1	4	1	0	0	6	0	.250
	Kansas City	A A	C	76	208	31	81	15	6	6	43	1	.389
1930	KC/Indian	A A	C	116	332	47	111	21	4	6	54	3	.334
1931	Indianapolis	A A	C	115	363	68	136	16	5	18	99	1	.375
1932	Indianapolis	A A	C	95	283	45	88	15	3	9	46	0	.311
	Terre Haute	III	C	7	24	2	8	1	3	0	3	0	.333
1933	Indianapolis	AA	C	92	307	35	93	12	3	7	47	3	.303
1934	Elmira	NYPenn	C	29	90	14	33	7	3	3	24	2	.367
	Columbus	AA	C	57	136	21	46	7	0	5	31	1	.338
1935	Houston	Texas	C	41	130	8	41	8	3	0	25	0	.315
	Majors			**5**	**16**	**1**	**4**	**1**	**0**	**0**	**6**	**0**	**.250**
	Minors			**805**	**2417**	**349**	**825**	**137**	**42**	**60**	**466**	**19**	**.341**

●

On August 18, 1930, Gene Jones of Springfield pitched a nine-inning no-hitter over Decatur in the Three Eye League. The score was 4-1, the run scoring on an infield out in the ninth. The real story of the game was that Jones walked 15 batters and another one reached on an error. He was in trouble six of the nine innings. In fact, the bases were loaded in the ninth when the closest thing to a hit by Decatur occurred. It was a sharp drive back of second which the Springfield shortstop snagged and rifled the ball to first for the final out.

JAMES HENRY "FOXY" BANNON
Born May 5, 1871, at Amesbury, MA. Died March 24, 1948, at Glenbrook, NJ.
Height, 5'5", Weight 160. Batted right. Threw right.

Brother of Tom, who played in the majors, and George and William, who played in the minors.
First major leaguer to hit grand slam homers in consecutive games, August 6 and 7, 1894.
Manager: Columbus AA 1903; Montreal EL 1905-06; Binghamton NYSL 1908; Lawrence NEL
1910. Attended Holy Cross College 1892-94.

Year	Club	League	POS	G	AB	R	H	2B	3B	HR	RBI	SB	BA
1891	Portland/Lynn	New Eng	P-OF	6	19	1	2	0	0	0	-	0	.105
1892					Did not play in O.B.								
1893	St. Louis	National	OF-P	26	107	9	36	3	4	0	15	8	.336
1894	Boston	National	OF	128	494	130	166	29	10	13	114	47	.336
1895	Boston	National	OF	123	489	101	171	35	5	6	74	28	.350
1896	Boston	National	OF	89	343	52	86	9	5	0	50	16	.251
1897	Kansas City	Western	O-S-3	76	297	62	88	19	1	0	-	30	.296
	Springfield	Eastern	OF	55	235	64	86	15	7	3	-	36	.366
1898	Spring/Mont	Eastern	OF	104	438	87	122	26	8	3	-	35	.279
1899	Toronto	Eastern	O-S-2	111	454	**112**	155	**27**	9	2	-	49	**.341**
1900	Toronto	Eastern	OF	131	538	99	163	24	7	4	-	31	.303
1901	Toronto	Eastern	OF	130	520	125	177	24	13	7	-	34	.340
1902	Toronto	Eastern	OF-2B	127	516	90	150	19	12	1	-	40	.291
1903	Columbus	A A	OF	131	505	67	130	21	5	0	-	25	.257
1904	Newark	Eastern	OF	142	532	63	132	28	8	3	-	32	.248
1905	Montreal	Eastern	OF-3B	134	484	68	124	22	7	0	-	32	.256
1906	Mont/Roch	Eastern	OF	110	411	65	103	12	6	1	-	29	.251
1907	Rochester	Eastern	OF	114	418	59	97	15	2	0	-	26	.232
1908	Binghamton	NY St	OF-2B	127	479	58	118	14	4	1	-	38	.246
1909	Lynn	New Eng	OF	4	11	2	4	1	0	0	-	0	.364
	Syracuse	NY St	O-3-S	26	93	11	22	1	1	0	-	5	.237
1910	Lawrence	New Eng	OF-2B	92	314	40	81	6	0	0	-	15	.258
	Majors			**366**	**1433**	**292**	**459**	**76**	**24**	**19**	**253**	**99**	**.320**
	Minors			**1620**	**6264**	**1073**	**1754**	**274**	**90**	**25**	**-**	**457**	**.280**

THOMAS EDWARD "UNCLE TOM" BANNON
Born May 8, 1869, at South Groveland, MA. Died January 26, 1950, at Lynn, MA.
Height 5'8", Weight 175. Batted right. Threw right.

Brother of Jim, who played in the majors, and George and William who played in the minors.
Ranks second on minor league career stolen base list, with 823.
Manager: Lowell NEL in 1909; Middletown Conn A 1910; Wilmington Tri-St 1911; Haverhill
NEL 1911.
Umpire: EL 1916 and 1917.

Year	Club	League	POS	G	AB	R	H	2B	3B	HR	SB	BA
1891	Portland/Lynn	New Eng	C	2	8	2	2	1	0	0	1	.250
1892-3					Did not play in O. B.							
1894	Pawtucket	New Eng	OF	**101**	**469**	**139**	153	**39**	7	4	**101**	.326
1895	Scranton	Eastern	OF	47	209	44	68	10	3	0	25	.325
	New York	National	OF-1B	37	159	33	43	6	2	0	20	.270
1896	New York	National	OF	2	7	1	1	1	0	0	0	.143
	Metropolitan	Atlantic	OF	56	257	71	92	14	5	1	47	.358
	Syracuse	Eastern	OF-SS	54	213	46	70	10	2	1	25	.329
1897	Syra/Mont	Eastern	OF	106	401	78	110	18	9	3	39	.274

Year	Club	League	POS	G	AB	R	H	2B	3B	HR	RBI	BA
	Kansas City	Western	OF	21	85	16	17	2	1	0	12	.200
1898	Montreal	Eastern	OF	119	491	87	141	15	7	3	42	.287
1899	Montreal	Eastern	OF	117	464	82	127	23	8	3	**64**	.274
1900	Mont/Tor	Eastern	OF	125	490	93	149	18	5	2	28	.304
1901	Syra/Broc	Eastern	OF	114	459	76	109	17	5	3	25	.237
1902	New London	Conn	OF	109	440	84	132	18	3	1	**75**	.300
1903	New London	Conn	OF	110	421	68	126	21	2	0	**73**	.299
1904	Hartford/NL	Conn	OF-1B	95	374	51	92	15	0	0	46	.246
1905	Lynn	New Eng	OF	103	387	54	94	12	1	2	48	.243
1906	Lynn	New Eng	OF	105	392	47	105	14	3	0	40	.268
1907	Lynn/Lawr	New Eng	OF	86	317	39	67	7	1	0	23	.211
1908	Brockton	New Eng	OF	126	434	51	85	9	1	1	48	.196
1909	Bro/Lo/Hav	New Eng	OF	84	303	33	68	5	0	0	32	.224
1910	Middletown	Conn A	OF	46	177	30	50	5	0	0	21	.282
	Haverhill	New Eng	OF	35	124	10	31	3	0	0	8	.250
	Majors			**39**	**166**	**34**	**44**	**7**	**2**	**0**	**20**	**.265**
	Minors			**1761**	**6915**	**1201**	**1888**	**276**	**63**	**24**	**823**	**.273**

DAVID MONROE BARBEE

Born May 7, 1905, at Greensboro, NC. Died July 1, 1968, at Albermarle, NC.
Height 5'11-1/2", Weight 178. Batted right. Threw right.
Attended Oglethorpe University

Year	Club	League	POS	G	AB	R	H	2B	3B	HR	RBI	SB	BA
1925	Greensboro	Piedmont	OF	16	57	10	19	6	2	3	9	0	.333
1926	Greensboro	Piedmont	3B	90	344	79	128	26	2	**29**	85	1	.372
	Philadelphia	American	OF	19	47	7	8	1	1	1	5	0	.170
1927	Reading	Int	OF	119	413	47	108	20	3	14	52	3	.262
1928	Port/Seat	PC	OF	144	483	78	158	32	11	16	89	8	.327
1929	Seattle	PC	OF	180	613	110	194	42	10	22	118	4	.316
1930	Seat/Holl	PC	OF	149	588	132	191	30	3	**41**	155	5	.325
1931	Hollywood	PC	OF	168	650	131	216	42	2	**47**	166	4	.332
1932	Pittsburgh	National	OF	97	327	37	84	22	6	5	55	1	.257
1933	Toronto	Int	OF	87	287	43	75	15	3	5	45	0	.261
	Tulsa	Texas	OF	33	105	12	22	7	1	1	12	0	.210
1934	Minneapolis	AA	OF	25	88	12	25	7	1	0	8	0	.284
	Birmingham	S Atl A	OF	55	209	23	57	12	3	3	45	0	.273
1935	Atlanta	S Atl A	OF	12	45	7	8	1	0	0	1	0	.178
1936-41						Did not play in O.B.							
1942	Burlington	Bi-St	OF	58	196	50	59	8	0	17	50	1	.301
	Majors			**116**	**374**	**44**	**92**	**23**	**7**	**6**	**60**	**1**	**.246**
	Minors			**1136**	**4078**	**734**	**1260**	**248**	**41**	**198**	**835**	**26**	**.309**

●

Gus Schmelz, manager of Columbus, was able to get Governor William McKinley to throw out the first ball in the season-opening game against Toledo on April 16, 1892. McKinley left after two innings, missing Ed Breckinridge's home run and the 8-5 defeat of Toledo. On April 17, 1897, when Schmelz was manager of the Washington Senators, and McKinley was President, he took his team to the White House to invite the Chief Executive to the opening game. Because of other pressing business, McKinley declined. He never did attend a game while President.

CHARLES EMIL BARON
(Correct family name is BARONOVIC.)
Born November 25, 1913, at St. Louis, MO.
Height 5"10", Weight 180. Batted left. Threw left.

Manager: Fresno Cal Lg and Miami Fla Int. Lg 1947; Anniston SEL 1948-49; Jacksonville Gulf Coast Lg 1950; Port Arthur Gulf Coast Lg 1951.

Currently resides in St. Louis.

Year	Club	League	POS	G	AB	R	H	2B	3B	HR	RBI	SB	BA
1931	Elmira	NY-Penn	1B	48	179	21	54	6	2	1	15	2	.302
1932	Dayton	Central	OF-1B	52	198	28	56	8	7	4	-	5	.283
1933				Did not play in O.B.									
1934	Jacksonville	W Dixie	1B	104	388	61	131	32	9	6	59	2	.338
1935	Tyler	W Dixie	1B	126	493	98	166	30	3	3	67	12	.337
1936	Tyler	E Texas	1B	147	538	**133**	173	29	10	6	84	15	.322
1937	Tyler	E Texas	1B	138	524	122	173	30	**13**	11	119	15	.330
1938	Nashville	South A	1B	5	20	3	5	1	0	0	0	1	.250
	Pensacola	SEastern	1B	134	511	73	143	20	5	1	69	16	.280
1939	Pensacola	SEastern	1B	124	451	74	142	19	**16**	5	65	3	.315
1940	Ft. Worth	Texas	1B	21	69	4	21	7	1	0	5	1	.304
1941	Ft. Worth	Texas	1B	152	552	72	158	25	8	2	68	12	.286
1942	Ft. W/Shrev	Texas	1B	132	480	68	128	26	5	4	66	1	.267
1943	St. Paul	AA	OF-1B	118	334	41	96	18	2	2	28	8	.287
1944	St. Paul	AA	1B	148	541	100	164	29	**11**	5	73	15	.303
1945	Columbus	AA	1B	38	146	22	46	9	3	1	32	2	.315
	Rochester	Int	1B	76	235	25	52	11	4	3	33	4	.221
1946	Rochester	Int	1B	118	415	55	118	22	5	7	50	3	.284
1947	Rochester	Int	1B	21	74	6	18	5	0	0	5	0	.243
	Fresno	Calif	1B	29	105	22	41	9	2	1	33	5	.390
	Miami	Fla Int	1B	48	168	20	51	8	2	3	19	3	.304
1948	Anniston	SEastern	1B	131	538	115	171	39	10	6	67	4	.318
1949	Anniston	SEastern	1B	15	59	15	23	7	0	1	11	1	.390
1950	Jacksonville	Gulf Cst	1B	132	489	81	165	37	7	9	104	3	.337
1951	Port Arthur	Gulf Cst	1B	23	65	10	24	4	1	0	13	0	.369
		Minors		**2080**	**7572**	**1269**	**2319**	**431**	**126**	**81**	**1085**	**133**	**.306**

RICHARD DONOVAN "RICH" BARRY
Born September 12, 1940 at Berkeley, CA.
Height 6'4", Weight 205. Batted right. Threw right.

Year	Club	League	POS	G	AB	R	H	2B	3B	HR	RBI	SB	BA
1958	Modesto	Calif	OF	80	291	37	74	14	3	13	52	3	.254
1959	Modesto	Calif	OF-3B	135	505	95	135	18	4	**37**	111	8	.267
1960	Binghamton	Eastern	OF	24	85	12	23	2	3	4	17	1	.271
	Greensboro	Carolina	OF	76	230	37	45	3	1	16	42	3	.196
1961	Binghamton	Eastern	OF	128	416	52	114	27	5	23	85	2	.274
1962	Amarillo	Texas	OF	4	12	0	0	0	0	0	0	0	.000
	Augusta	Sally	OF	117	421	68	100	12	1	25	81	2	.238
1963	Augusta	Sally	1B	40	132	19	38	6	2	3	21	0	.288
1964	Richmond	Int	OF	24	82	10	17	1	0	6	15	0	.207
	Columbus	Southern	OF	89	297	59	72	19	2	21	60	2	.242
1965	Columbus	Southern	OF	31	92	9	21	5	2	4	18	0	.228
	Greensboro	Carolina	1-O-P	100	347	62	90	12	2	21	92	2	.259
1966	Macon	Southern	OF	138	488	85	142	**30**	5	16	80	5	.291

Year	Club	League	POS	G	AB	R	H	2B	3B	HR	RBI	SB	BA
1967	San Diego	PC	OF	141	490	68	130	22	2	22	73	2	.265
1968	San Diego	PC	OF-1B	130	441	55	129	21	4	9	59	3	.293
1969	Eugene	PC	OF-1B	76	270	50	83	16	3	12	59	3	.307
	Philadelphia	Nat	OF	20	32	4	6	1	0	0	0	0	.188
1970	Hawaii	PC	OF	123	435	73	120	27	4	18	85	7	.276
1971	Hawaii	PC	OF-1B	103	337	68	103	10	1	16	59	1	.306
1972	Richmond	Int	OF-1B	117	360	47	93	10	2	14	46	0	.258
		Majors		**20**	**32**	**4**	**6**	**1**	**0**	**0**	**0**	**0**	**.188**
		Minors		**1676**	**5731**	**906**	**1529**	**255**	**46**	**280**	**1055**	**44**	**.267**

CHARLES JOHN "PADDY" BAUMANN

Born December 20, 1885 at Indianapolis, IN. Died November 20, 1969 at Indianapolis, IN.
Height 5'9", Weight 170. Batted right. Threw right.
Manager: Galveston Texas Lg 1924.

Year	Club	League	POS	G	AB	R	H	2B	3B	HR	RBI	SB	BA
1908	Cedar Rapids	III	S-3-O	8	29	0	6	0	0	0	1	1	.207
1909	New Bedford	New Eng	SS-OF	123	444	58	112	19	6	1	-	25	.252
1910	New Bedford	New Eng	SS	92	313	41	88	11	15	1	-	30	.281
1911	New Bedford	New Eng	2B	77	294	58	90	14	7	4	-	14	.306
	Detroit	American	2B-OF	26	94	8	24	2	4	0	11	1	.255
1912	Detroit	American	3-2-O	13	42	3	11	1	0	0	7	4	.262
	Providence	Int	3B-SS	54	172	26	54	6	5	1	-	6	.314
1913	Providence	Int	SS	75	295	41	87	10	11	2	-	6	.295
	Detroit	American	2B	49	191	31	57	7	4	1	22	4	.298
1914	Detroit	American	2B	3	11	1	0	0	0	0	0	0	.000
	Providence	Int	3B	143	518	81	146	13	11	2	-	36	.282
1915	New York	American	2B-3B	76	219	30	64	13	1	2	28	9	.292
1916	New York	American	O-3-2	79	237	35	68	5	3	1	25	10	.287
1917	New York	American	2-O-3	49	110	10	24	2	1	0	8	2	.218
	Toledo	A A	2B	6	25	3	9	2	0	0	-	0	.360
1918	Toledo	A A	3B	32	118	14	28	2	1	0	-	4	.237
1919	Jersey City	Int	2B	136	520	74	156	20	4	1	-	22	.300
1920	Jersey City	Int	3B	95	323	51	104	12	5	1	-	12	.322
1921	Toledo	A A	3B-2B	126	432	60	121	21	7	3	55	15	.280
1922	Tulsa	Western	2B	163	650	116	219	56	5	3	-	25	.337
1923	Tulsa	Western	2B	158	611	129	229	44	3	4	-	17	.375
1924	Gal/Dallas	Texas	2B	152	574	82	193	20	4	4	77	15	.336
1925	Dallas	Texas	2B	134	563	93	175	36	2	7	64	11	.311
1926	Dallas	Texas	2B	99	395	66	117	20	1	2	32	15	.296
1927	Dallas	Texas	2B	102	365	57	98	22	1	1	49	8	.268
1928	Dallas	Texas	3B-2B	7	11	0	1	1	0	0	2	0	.091
		Majors		**295**	**904**	**118**	**248**	**30**	**13**	**4**	**101**	**30**	**.274**
		Minors		**1782**	**6652**	**1050**	**2033**	**329**	**88**	**37**	**280**	**262**	**.306**

●

Jim Thorpe had his greatest batting day ever on July 13, 1921. Playing for Toledo, he hit three home runs and a single and knocked in seven runs in a 17-4 win over Milwaukee. He didn't get all the American Association headlines that day, however, as Bunny Brief hit three homers and knocked in five runs in a Kansas City win over Columbus. Both had good season batting averages—Thorpe .358 and Brief .361—but Jim hit only nine homers, compared to 42 for the Kansas City slugger.

ERVIN THOMAS "DUTCH" BECK
Born July 19, 1878 at Toledo, OH. Died December 22, 1916 at Toledo OH.
Height 5'10", Weight 168. Batted right. Threw right.

Beck's 71 doubles in 1900 stood as the Organized Baseball record until surpassed by Les Sheehan in the PCL in 1923.

Hit the first HR in the American League on April 25, 1901 at Chicago.

Year	Club	League	POS	G	AB	R	H	2B	3B	HR	RBI	SB	BA
1895	Adrian	Mich St	2B	1	5	1	2	0	0	1	-	0	.400
1896	Toledo	Inter-St	2B-OF	130	461	101	171	30	6	2	-	30	**.371**
1897	Toledo	Inter-St	2B	119	568	122	195	39	7	14	-	13	.343
1898	Toledo	Inter-St	2B	147	634	111	188	46	4	11	-	24	.297
1899	Toledo	Inter-St	2B	132	578	104	**185**	46	8	25	-	7	.320
	Brooklyn	National	2B-SS	8	24	2	4	2	0	0	2	0	.167
1900	Toledo	Inter-St	2B	138	575	120	**207**	71	5	15	-	12	**.360**
1901	Cleveland	American	2B	135	539	78	156	26	8	6	79	7	.289
1902	Cincinnati	National	2-1-O	48	187	19	57	10	3	1	20	2	.305
	Detroit	American	1B-OF	41	162	23	48	4	0	2	22	3	.296
1903	Shreveport	South A	2B	125	495	81	**164**	26	9	3	-	15	.331
1904	Portland	P C	2B-3B	206	796	88	216	41	3	4	-	18	.271
1905	New Orleans	South A	1B	130	489	55	127	12	0	1	-	8	.260
1906	NO/Nash	South A	1B-2B	92	337	33	71	11	0	0	-	6	.211
	Augusta	Sally	1B	1	3	0	1	0	0	0	0	0	.333
		Majors		**232**	**912**	**122**	**265**	**42**	**11**	**9**	**123**	**12**	**.291**
		Minors		**1221**	**4941**	**816**	**1527**	**322**	**42**	**76**	**-**	**133**	**.309**

JUSTIN TITUS "PUG" BENNETT
Born February 20, 1874 at Ponca, NE. Died September 12, 1935 at Kirkland WA.
Height 5'6", Weight 160. Bats right. Throws right.

Year	Club	League	POS	G	AB	R	H	2B	3B	HR	SB	BA
1899	Mattoon	Ind-Ill				No record available						
1900	Toledo	Inter-St	3B-C	21	91	13	24	6	0	0	3	.264
1901						Did not play in O.B.						
1902	Shreve/NO	South A	3B-SS	110	429	80	123	16	5	4	32	.287
1903	Atlanta	South A	3B	115	446	64	120	25	3	1	18	.269
1904	Nashville	South A	2B-3B	141	518	95	**166**	23	9	0	40	.320
1905	Nashville	South A	2B	103	414	75	126	18	4	0	30	.304
	Seattle	NWestern	2B	79	330	-	101	14	3	1	18	.306
1906	St. Louis	National	2B	153	**595**	66	156	16	7	1	20	.262
1907	St. Louis	National	2B-3B	87	324	20	72	8	2	0	7	.222
1908	Seattle	NWestern	2B	154	571	81	174	20	6	12	44	.305
1909	Seattle	NWestern	2B	167	641	111	201	26	7	7	39	**.314**
1910	Seattle	NWestern	2B	158	**607**	77	145	24	5	6	30	.239
1911	Vancouver	NWestern	2B	165	601	119	180	23	4	8	**64**	.300
1912	Vancouver	NWestern	2B	168	641	107	182	27	6	6	45	.284
1913	Vancouver	NWestern	2B	157	605	92	160	17	9	6	23	.264
1914	Vancouver	NWestern	2B	149	543	89	144	26	5	1	19	.265
1915	Aberdeen	NWestern	2B	95	348	37	107	13	1	0	15	.307
1916	Great Falls	NWestern	2B	121	450	83	133	16	1	3	29	.296
1917	Vancouver	NWestern	2B	73	256	41	52	9	1	1	16	.203
		Majors		**240**	**919**	**86**	**228**	**24**	**9**	**1**	**27**	**.248**
		Minors		**1976**	**7491**	**1164**	**2138**	**303**	**69**	**56**	**465**	**.285**

LAWRENCE JOSEPH BETTENCOURT
Born September 22, 1905 at Newark, CA. Died September 15, 1978 at New Orleans, LA.
Height 5'll", Weight 195. Batted right. Threw right.
Played football for St. Mary's College. In College Football Hall of Fame. Played in the NFL in 1932 and 1933.
Managed Grand Forks, Northern Lg, in 1941

Year	Club	League	POS	G	AB	R	H	2B	3B	HR	RBI	SB	BA
1928	St. Louis	American	3-O-C	67	159	30	45	9	4	4	24	2	.283
1929	Milwaukee	A A	OF	24	74	12	19	5	1	1	-	0	.257
	Buffalo	Int	3B	20	64	10	15	4	0	1	8	2	.234
	Wichita Falls	Texas	3-O-1	47	137	25	37	10	1	6	27	1	.270
1930	Wichita Falls	Texas	OF	151	557	130	178	22	6	**43**	**145**	18	.320
1931	St. Louis	American	OF	74	206	27	53	9	2	3	26	4	.257
1932	St. Louis	American	OF-3B	27	30	4	4	1	0	1	3	1	.133
1933	Milwaukee	A A	OF	3	9	0	4	1	0	0	3	0	.444
	San Antonio	Texas	OF-1B	147	540	83	160	34	10	10	102	10	.296
1934	San Antonio	Texas	OF-1B	157	621	108	201	47	10	14	**129**	8	.324
1935	San Antonio	Texas	OF	104	372	61	99	17	3	5	53	4	.266
1936	San Antonio	Texas	OF	141	526	99	162	23	6	12	82	2	.308
1937	SA-Galveston	Texas	OF	19	75	9	18	2	0	0	11	0	.240
	New Orleans	South A	OF	85	308	37	71	9	6	6	44	2	.231
1938	Trent/Will	Eastern	O-3	138	561	69	154	32	7	6	**118**	5	.275
1939	Williamsport	Eastern	O-1-3	109	410	55	121	22	7	5	59	2	.295
1940	Springfield	Eastern	OF	118	418	72	121	23	7	7	52	2	.289
1941	Grand Forks	Northern	O-P	98	355	72	130	18	7	10	74	26	**.366**
1942-43				Did not play in O.B.									
1944	Minneapolis	A A	OF	29	69	10	17	4	0	0	7	4	.246
		Majors		**168**	**395**	**61**	**102**	**19**	**6**	**8**	**53**	**7**	**.258**
		Minors		**1390**	**5096**	**852**	**1507**	**273**	**71**	**126**	**914**	**86**	**.296**

FRED BETTS
(Listed in averages as Betz several times during early years.)
Born September, 1868 at St. Louis, MO. Died 1937 at St. Louis, MO.
Height 5'7". Weight 155. Batted left. Threw left.

Year	Club	League	POS	G	AB	R	H	2B	3B	HR	SB	BA
1889	Leadville	Colo St	3B-P	14	65	20	33	10	2	1	3	.508
1890	Spring/Wheel	Tri St	3B	81	**349**	69	**113**	20	6	8	14	.324
1891	Port/Tac	Pac NW	P-IF-OF	37	129	15	27	8	0	2	8	.209
1892	Menominee	Mich St	OF	47	203	37	57	12	4	3	8	.281
1893	Easton	Pa St	OF-3B	90	398	107	**160**	19	10	9	48	**.402**
	Wilkes-Barre	Eastern	OF	4	21	4	5	0	0	0	0	.238
1894	Wilkes-Barre	Eastern	OF	107	463	114	155	21	10	11	21	.335
1895	Wilkes-Barre	Eastern	OF-P	67	267	56	79	20	4	4	13	.296
1896	Wilkes-Barre	Eastern	OF	112	487	86	172	39	10	3	22	.353
1897	Wilkes-Barre	Eastern	OF	120	485	83	142	28	4	5	11	.293
1898	Reading	Atlantic	OF	128	548	82	156	22	7	1	20	.285
1899	Reading	Atlantic	OF	87	340	47	94	15	5	0	8	.276
1900	Utica	NY St	OF	115	456	73	151	13	5	1	26	.331
1901	Schenectady	NY St	OF	93	367	54	113	15	6	1	21	.308
1902	Schenectady	NY St	OF	108	426	89	132	26	5	0	29	.310
1903	Schenectady	NY St	OF	126	495	67	150	29	5	1	30	.303
1904	Sch/Scranton	NY St	OF	116	404	40	111	21	3	1	6	.275

Year	Club	League	POS	G	AB	R	H	2B	3B	HR	RBI	BA
1905	Scranton	NY St	OF	123	472	65	148	29	8	0	19	.314
1906	Scran/Alb	NY St	OF	111	417	43	111	20	1	1	14	.266
1907	Albany	NY St	OF	133	487	51	149	24	2	1	16	.306
1908	Grand Rapids	Central	OF	135	493	62	122	18	6	0	24	.247
1909	Freeport	Wis-Ill	OF	111	400	42	121	21	0	1	6	.303
1910	Rockford	Wis-Ill	OF-P	121	457	65	145	23	4	6	11	.317
1911	Rockford	Wis-Ill	OF-P	110	395	73	113	17	0	2	16	.286
	Minors			**2296**	**9024**	**1444**	**2759**	**470**	**107**	**62**	**394**	**.306**

WAYNE T. BLACKBURN

Born January 10, 1917, at Harmon, Ohio.
Height 5' 10-1/2", Weight 165. Batted left. Threw right.
Manager: Peoria Ill 1937; Owensboro Kitty 1951; Kinston Coastal 1952; Wausau Wis St 1953; Jamestown Pony 1954 & 1956; Augusta Sally 1958; Montgomery SL 1965 & 1966; Detroit Gulf Cst Rookie 1968.
Drew over 1400 walks during career. From 1948-56, had 715 hits and 742 walks in 711 games.

Year	Club	League	POS	G	AB	R	H	2B	3B	HR	RBI	SB	BA
1936	Paducah	Kitty	2B	116	458	**124**	158	23	6	3	82	35	.345
1937	Waterloo	Western	2B	68	275	55	70	11	0	0	28	16	.255
	Peoria	III	2B	46	167	36	66	7	5	0	-	20	.395
	Syracuse	Int	2B	3	9	1	3	0	0	0	-	0	.333
1938	Syracuse	Int	3B	4	11	3	2	0	0	0	-	0	.182
	Durham	Piedmont	2B	123	492	103	165	16	2	0	49	22	.335
1939	Durham	Piedmont	2B	126	462	104	159	22	5	2	30	29	.344
1940	Indianapolis	A A	3B	75	247	38	77	15	5	0	37	9	.312
1941	Indianapolis	A A	OF	113	428	79	134	21	4	2	32	16	.313
1942	Indianapolis	A A	OF	152	569	91	171	22	7	4	38	14	.301
1943	Indianapolis	A A	OF	153	583	**114**	169	22	7	1	50	10	.290
1944	Indianapolis	A A	OF-3B	149	535	104	180	23	7	1	65	25	.336
1945					Military Service								
1946	Indianapolis	A A	OF-3B	100	225	45	60	5	5	1	15	3	.267
1947	St. Paul	A A	-		4	7	1	2	0	0	0	1	0	.286
	Buffalo	Int	3B-OF	73	183	35	52	5	1	1	21	6	.284
1948	Little Rock	South A	3B-OF	133	466	119	152	25	3	0	41	**36**	.326
1949	Little Rock	South A	3B-OF	135	476	85	121	10	3	0	34	16	.254
1950	WPBeach	Fla Int	2B	28	102	11	19	3	0	0	10	5	.186
	Raleigh	Carolina	3B	15	50	10	10	3	0	0	2	0	.200
	Greenville	Sally	3B	25	86	25	22	4	0	0	1	2	.256
1951	Owensboro	Kitty	2-O-3	110	363	**116**	132	23	3	0	50	26	**.364**
1952	Kinston	Coast Pl	O-2-3	109	340	91	119	12	4	1	28	33	.350
1953	Wausau	Wis St	OF-2B	114	341	92	105	20	3	0	54	24	.308
1954	Jamestown	Pony	OF	23	68	24	22	4	0	0	8	2	.324
1955					Did not play in O.B.								
1956	Jamestown	Pony	OF	19	44	8	13	3	1	0	9	1	.295
	Minors			**2016**	**6987**	**1514**	**2183**	**299**	**71**	**16**	**685**	**350**	**.317**

GEORGE FRANKLIN BLACKERBY

Born November 10, 1903 at Luther, OK. Died May 30, 1987 at Wichita Falls, TX.
Height 6'1", Weight 176. Batted right. Threw right.

Year	Club	League	POS	G	AB	R	H	2B	3B	HR	RBI	SB	BA
1924	Greenville	E Texas	OF	106	416	71	133	25	1	20	-	2	.320

Year	Club	League	POS	G	AB	R	H	2B	3B	HR	RBI	SB	BA
1925	Austin	Texas A	OF	51	188	34	57	13	1	5	-	7	.303
	Greenville	E Texas	OF	38	141	20	42	9	2	1	-	5	.298
1926	Greenville	E Texas	OF	124	459	93	150	28	2	16	-	15	.327
1927	Waco	Texas	OF	141	492	89	179	36	5	17	91	16	.364
1928	Waco	Texas	OF	118	443	97	163	23	7	19	73	15	**.368**
	Chicago	American	OF	30	83	8	21	0	0	0	12	2	.253
1929	Waco	Texas	OF	158	600	132	219	45	5	**33**	115	6	.365
1930	Dal/LRock	Texas	OF	47	172	34	59	9	0	5	22	4	.343
	Birm.	South A	OF	106	385	68	131	16	2	7	83	8	.340
1931	Mobile/Knox	South A	OF	51	191	20	55	3	2	0	18	3	.288
	Oakland	P C	OF	115	435	55	127	18	5	9	61	7	.292
1932	Oakland	P C	OF-1B	167	629	74	190	25	6	4	94	11	.302
1933	Portland	P C	1B	163	614	110	209	32	3	4	92	11	.340
1934	Portland	P C	1B	170	623	65	168	31	3	8	83	6	.270
1935	Portland	P C	1B	58	217	34	62	11	2	1	34	4	.286
	Tulsa	Texas	1B	90	313	40	74	10	5	2	45	6	.236
1936	Albany/Tor	Int	OF-1B	107	299	50	98	14	6	2	56	2	.328
1937	Tor/Buf/Ro/M	Int	OF	85	236	31	62	8	1	1	24	2	.263
	Majors			**30**	**83**	**8**	**21**	**0**	**0**	**0**	**12**	**2**	**.253**
	Minors			**1895**	**6853**	**1117**	**2178**	**356**	**58**	**154**	**891**	**130**	**.318**

FRANK STEPHAN "PING" BODIE
(Correct family name is PEZZOLO.)

Born October 8, 1887 at San Francisco, CA. Died December 17, 1961 at San Francisco, CA. Height 5'8", Weight 195. Batted Right. Threw right.

Led all minor leagues in home runs in 1910 with 30.

Year	Club	League	POS	G	AB	R	H	2B	3B	HR	RBI	SB	BA
1905	San Francisco	Calif		No record available									
1906	Presidio	Calif		No record available									
1907				No record available									
1908	San Francisco	Calif	P-2-O	7	28	4	10	2	0	1	-	2	.357
	San Francisco	P C	OF	36	134	19	37	6	1	3	-	5	.276
1909	San Francisco	P C	OF	157	543	62	135	41	6	10	-	9	.249
1910	San Francisco	P C	OF	212	768	102	202	34	5	**30**	-	29	.263
1911	Chicago	American	OF-2B	145	551	75	159	27	13	4	97	14	.289
1912	Chicago	American	OF	138	472	58	139	24	7	5	72	12	.294
1913	Chicago	American	OF	127	406	39	107	14	8	8	48	5	.264
1914	Chicago	American	OF	107	327	21	75	9	5	3	29	12	.229
1915	San Francisco	P C	OF	192	720	117	234	52	3	19	-	37	.325
1916	San Francisco	P C	OF	206	769	104	233	48	5	20	-	16	.303
1917	Philadelphia	American	OF-1B	148	557	51	162	28	11	7	74	13	.291
1918	New York	American	OF	91	324	36	83	12	6	3	46	6	.256
1919	New York	American	OF	134	475	45	132	27	8	6	59	15	.278
1920	New York	American	OF	129	471	63	139	26	12	7	79	6	.295
1921	New York	American	OF	31	87	5	15	2	2	0	12	0	.172
1922	Vernon	P C	OF	145	502	69	147	33	5	6	87	7	.293
1923	Vernon	P C	OF	136	485	70	143	31	10	8	105	1	.295
1924	Des Moines	Western	OF	167	624	107	213	38	11	32	-	7	.341
1925	Wichita Falls	Texas	OF-1B	151	591	132	205	41	1	37	142	5	.347
1926	Wich Falls/SA	Texas	OF-1B	146	509	84	172	35	5	14	105	3	.338
1927	San Francisco	P C	1B-OF	109	336	55	109	16	1	12	80	5	.324
1928	S.F./Mission	P C	OF	117	333	58	116	22	1	10	62	2	.348
	Majors			**1050**	**3670**	**393**	**1011**	**169**	**72**	**43**	**516**	**83**	**.275**
	Minors			**1781**	**6342**	**983**	**1956**	**399**	**54**	**202**	**581**	**128**	**.308**

42

LUTE JOSEPH "DANNY" BOONE
Born May 6, 1890 at Pittsburgh, PA. Died July 29, 1982 at Pittsburgh, PA.
Height 5' 9", Weight 160. Batted right. Threw right.

When the Northern League began operation in 1933, Boone was League President, Crookston Manager and an active player for the Crookston team.

Manager: Des Moines, Western 1928; Crookston Northern 1933-35.

Year	Club	League	POS	G	AB	R	H	2B	3B	HR	RBI	SB	BA
1912	Steubenville	Ohio-Pa	SS		No record available								
1913	Dallas	Texas	SS	147	506	65	113	19	5	0	-	30	.223
	New York	American	SS	6	12	3	4	0	0	0	1	0	.333
1914	New York	American	2-3-OF	106	370	34	82	8	2	0	21	10	.222
1915	New York	American	2-SS-3	130	431	44	88	12	2	5	43	14	.204
1916	New York	American	3-SS-2	46	124	14	23	4	0	1	8	7	.185
	Richmond	Int	SS	11	34	5	9	1	0	0	-	3	.265
1917	Toledo	A A	2-3	111	395	39	93	6	6	0	-	25	.235
1918	Toledo	A A	2B	76	278	27	72	6	4	0	-	9	.259
	Pittsburgh	National	SS-2	27	91	7	18	3	0	0	3	1	.198
1919	St. Paul	A A	SS-2-3	115	362	39	94	15	2	1	-	13	.260
1920	St. Paul	A A	SS	153	552	80	164	33	8	2	68	29	.297
1921	St. Paul	A A	SS	129	469	71	135	28	4	2	76	19	.288
1922	St. Paul	A A	SS	167	630	104	181	36	6	8	115	20	.287
1923	St. Paul	A A	SS	162	636	124	196	42	4	10	98	32	.308
1924	St. Paul	A A	SS	134	549	79	142	31	2	4	65	26	.259
1925	St. Paul	A A	2-3-SS	149	589	90	156	34	8	5	75	31	.265
1926	KC/Louis	A A	3-SS-2	108	382	60	103	18	4	0	53	7	.270
1927	Louisville	A A	SS-2	55	188	20	51	5	2	1	18	3	.271
1928	Des Moines	Western	SS-OF	28	93	15	26	6	1	0	-	1	.280
	Columbus	A A	3B	87	302	39	78	12	3	1	30	7	.258
1929	Columbus	A A	3-SS	107	351	60	112	18	5	4	78	8	.319
1930	Columbus	A A	3-2-SS	107	319	53	94	15	6	4	57	7	.295
1931-32					Did not play in O. B.								
1933	Crookston	Northern	1B	48	142	-	55	14	1	1	-	21	.387
1934	Crookston	Northern	3B	77	268	-	77	16	1	4	-	8	.287
1935	Crookston	Northern	3B	11	29	-	7	1	0	1	1	1	.241
		Majors		**315**	**1028**	**102**	**215**	**27**	**4**	**6**	**76**	**32**	**.209**
		Minors		**1982**	**7074**	**970**	**1958**	**356**	**72**	**48**	**734**	**300**	**.277**

BERNHARD "BENNY" BORGMANN
Born November 2, 1896 at Haledon, NJ. Died November 11, 1978 at Pompton Plains, NJ.
Height 5'8", Weight 170. Batted right. Threw right.

Manager: Huntington MAL 1935 & 1936; Portsmouth MAL 1937 & 1938; Sacramento PCL 1939 & 1940, Syracuse IL 1941; Allentown Inter St 1942 & 1947; Rochester IL 1946; Houston TL 1950. Member of Naismith Memorial Basketball Hall of Fame. Led ABL in scoring in 1926-27, 1928-29, 1929-30 and 1930-31 seasons.

Year	Club	League	POS	G	AB	R	H	2B	3B	HR	RBI	SB	BA
1928	Wilkes-Barre	NY-Penn	SS	76	278	37	86	6	2	0	22	7	.309
1929	Pittsfield	Eastern	3B-SS	143	569	79	150	20	6	1	54	27	.264
1930	Pittsfield	Eastern	3B-SS	69	250	38	73	12	1	0	29	10	.292
	Harrisburg	NY-Penn	SS-2B	76	284	45	105	9	6	1	33	8	.370
1931	Wilkes-Barre	NY-Penn	2B	115	438	73	115	21	3	0	36	14	.263
1932	Greensboro	Piedmont	SS	123	489	**122**	157	29	3	2	49	**51**	.321
1933	Columbus	A A	SS	90	377	69	128	11	1	2	29	28	.340

Year	Club	League	POS	G	AB	R	H	2B	3B	HR	RBI	SB	BA
	Rochester	Int	3B	30	88	20	30	4	1	0	9	7	.341
1934	Rochester	Int	2B-3B	124	427	86	119	15	8	1	42	18	.279
1935	Huntington	Mid Atl	SS	118	476	92	146	22	5	1	61	**35**	.307
1936	Huntington	Mid Atl	2B	106	427	90	134	15	3	0	30	26	.314
1937	Portsmouth	Mid Atl	2B	128	509	114	177	24	2	1	49	22	.348
1938	Portsmouth	Mid Atl	2B	117	485	101	153	27	2	1	49	24	.315
1939	Sacramento	P C	2B	58	186	23	43	8	1	0	15	4	.231
1940	Sacramento	P C		Manager, did not play									
1941	Syracuse	Int	3B	2	5	0	0	0	0	0	1	0	.000
1942	Allentown	Inter-St	2B-SS	63	213	26	55	4	0	1	16	3	.258
	Minors			**1438**	**5501**	**1015**	**1671**	**227**	**44**	**11**	**524**	**284**	**.304**

ARTHUR BOWLAND, JR.
Born May 9, 1923 at Pawtucket, RI.
Height 6'0", Weight 180. Batted left. Threw right.
Manager: Abilene WTNM 1947 & 1948; San Angelo SWestern 1956; Plainview SWestern 1957.
Currently resides in Carthage, Texas.

Year	Club	League	POS	G	AB	R	H	2B	3B	HR	RBI	SB	BA
1942	Valdosta	Ga-Fla	OF	126	493	100	149	20	4	0	57	**26**	.302
1943-45				Military Service									
1946	Three Rivers	Can-Amer	OF-3B	114	416	96	113	18	6	2	48	18	.272
1947	Three Rivers	Can-Amer	OF	32	109	18	43	4	0	1	21	2	.394
	Abilene	WTNM	OF-2B	90	329	94	134	35	3	17	97	8	.407
1948	Abilene	WTNM	2-0-C	109	377	123	146	28	1	15	113	3	.387
	Mobile	South A	OF	32	111	15	31	3	0	0	11	1	.279
1949	St. Jean	Provincl	C	44	160	20	47	8	2	3	-	1	.294
1950	Abilene	WTNM	C-OF	95	313	62	90	19	1	5	45	1	.288
1951	Abilene	WTNM	C	136	491	115	166	37	4	11	120	12	.338
1952	Abilene	WTNM	C	123	441	96	141	33	4	8	86	11	.320
1953	Midland	Longhorn	C	120	455	91	157	23	5	9	81	11	.345
1954	Abilene	WTNM	C	120	446	113	159	28	4	14	113	8	.357
1955	San Angelo	Longhorn	C	95	351	66	118	27	2	18	88	3	.336
1956	San Angelo	SWestern	C	135	492	92	174	24	1	22	115	3	.354
1957	Plainview	SWestern	C-3B	43	153	33	52	10	0	9	25	3	.340
	Shreveport	Texas	C	72	184	16	54	9	1	2	24	0	.293
1958	Dallas	Texas	C	87	234	23	63	8	0	2	30	0	.269
	Minors			**1573**	**5555**	**1173**	**1837**	**334**	**38**	**138**	**1074**	**111**	**.331**

ROBERT NORMAN "KITTY" BRASHEAR
Born August 27, 1877 at Mansfield, OH. Died December 22, 1934 at Los Angeles, CA.
Height 5'll", Weight 205. Batted Right. Threw right.
Brother of Roy.
President, San Bernardino, So. Calif. 1913; Mgr. Tucson, RG Val. 1915.

Year	Club	League	POS	G	AB	R	H	2B	3B	HR	SB	BA
1899	Cedar Rapids	West A	P-O-2	25	86	14	24	6	1	0	5	.279
	Louisville	National	P	3	2	0	1	0	0	0	0	.500
	Ft. Wayne	Inter-St	P	19	51	10	17	3	1	0	3	.333
1900	Ft. Wayne	Inter-St	1B	138	**603**	94	154	26	4	8	18	.255
1901	Colo Spg/KC	Western	1B-O	92	388	50	93	11	4	1	5	.240
1902	St. Joseph	Western	1B	128	481	70	129	16	5	0	32	.268

Year	Club	League	POS	G	AB	R	H	2B	3B	HR	SB	BA
1903	Oak/LA	P C	1B-P	193	736	106	218	37	9	1	50	.296
1904	Sea/LA	P C	1B	142	516	80	139	34	4	2	25	.269
1905	Los Angeles	P C	SS	180	650	84	197	35	7	4	31	**.303**
1906	Los Angeles	P C	2B	65	249	48	92	10	4	0	16	.369
	Johns/Alt	Tri-St	3B-1B	89	323	30	74	12	2	0	11	.229
1907	Los Angeles	P C	2B-3B	159	581	65	157	30	3	0	36	.270
1908	Los Angeles	P C	O-2B	156	537	57	139	20	1	2	25	.259
1909	Vernon	P C	1B	201	711	82	175	37	1	2	27	.246
1910	Vernon	P C	1B-3B	185	607	46	141	32	0	5	16	.232
1911	Vancouver	NWestern	1B	130	436	75	128	21	5	4	24	.294
1912	Vancouver	NWestern	1B	122	468	45	123	18	3	7	14	.263
	Vernon	P C	1B	30	85	5	18	2	0	0	2	.212
1913	San Ber	S Calif	1B	1	4	0	1	0	0	0	0	.250
1914				Did not play in O.B.								
1915	Tucson	RG Val	1B-P	10	23	2	5	1	0	0	0	.217
		Majors		**3**	**2**	**0**	**1**	**0**	**0**	**0**	**0**	**.500**
		Minors		**2065**	**7535**	**963**	**2024**	**351**	**54**	**36**	**340**	**.269**

ROY PARKS BRASHEAR
Born January 3, 1874 at Ashtabula, OH. Died April 20, 1951 at Los Angeles, CA. Batted right. Threw right.
Brother of Kitty.
Manager: Louisville AA 1906; Mineral Wells WTexas 1921.

Year	Club	League	POS	G	AB	R	H	2B	3B	HR	SB	BA
1898	St. Joseph	West A	1B-O	10	45	6	10	2	0	0	0	.222
1899	Bloomington	West A	2B	14	51	6	8	0	0	0	7	.157
1900	Sioux City	Western	2B-SS	97	373	64	116	16	4	1	37	.311
1901	Minneapolis	Western	2B	119	463	72	140	21	2	0	28	.302
1902	St. Louis	National	1-2-O	110	388	36	107	8	2	1	9	.276
1903	Philadelphia	National	2B-1B	20	75	9	17	3	0	0	2	.227
	Louisville	A A	2B	102	502	88	129	22	5	3	28	.257
1904	Louisville	A A	2B	148	532	82	149	23	8	4	29	.280
1905	Louisville	A A	2B	130	510	90	149	24	9	10	43	.292
1906	Louisville	A A	2B	155	576	72	164	18	**19**	3	34	.285
1907	Louisville	A A	2B	158	600	81	157	18	7	0	42	.262
1908	Kansas City	A A	2B	156	555	73	164	32	8	3	30	.295
1909	Kansas City	A A	2B	159	529	53	115	20	4	1	15	.217
1910	Vernon	P C	2B	223	762	94	180	22	3	18	37	.236
1911	Vernon	P C	2B	197	679	125	202	37	7	13	36	.297
1912	Vernon	P C	2B	192	692	108	217	43	6	11	27	.314
1913	Venice	P C	2B-1B	148	504	51	130	17	5	1	13	.258
1914	Portland/LA	P C	1B	49	92	7	21	5	0	1	1	.228
	Seattle	NWestern	2B	36	134	17	31	10	0	0	1	.231
		Majors		**130**	**463**	**45**	**124**	**11**	**2**	**1**	**11**	**.268**
		Minors		**2093**	**7599**	**1089**	**2082**	**330**	**87**	**69**	**408**	**.274**

●

Clyde Barfoot won 314 games in the minors. He won a career high of 25 for Vernon in the Pacific Coast League in 1925. But they all didn't come easy. On October 15, 1925, he had to pitch 15 innings before he was returned a 6-5 victor over Los Angeles. It was his own homer in the 15th that did it. And that was his second roundtripper of the game.

JOSEPH WARLICK BRATCHER
Born July 22, 1898 at Grand Saline, TX. Died October 13, 1977 at Fort Worth, TX.
Height 5' 8-1/2", Weight 140. Batted left. Threw right.
Manager: Lake Charles Evang 1937-39; Sweetwater Longhorn 1951.
Umpired in W Dixie League 1934.

Year	Club	League	POS	G	AB	R	H	2B	3B	HR	RBI	SB	BA
1920	Cisco/East	W Texas	OF	105	394	57	**126**	19	**14**	3	-	16	.320
1921	Cisco/Abil	W Texas	OF	43	154	-	51	-	-	-	-	-	.331
	Ft. Worth	Texas	OF	19	55	8	15	3	0	0	10	3	.273
1922	Paris	Tex-Okla	OF	108	**421**	**100**	**138**	20	7	9	-	33	.328
	Ft. Worth	Texas	OF	2	5	1	0	0	0	0	0	0	.000
1923	Ardmore	West A	OF	145	605	113	198	35	7	27	-	18	.327
1924	Okmulgee	West A	OF	130	564	140	216	44	11	23	114	11	.383
	St. Louis	National	OF	4	1	1	0	0	0	0	0	0	.000
	Oakland	P C	OF	49	200	29	53	12	4	2	34	1	.265
1925	Oakland	P C	OF	85	286	38	85	19	1	0	17	6	.297
	Peoria	III	OF	55	214	57	95	15	9	**20**	-	8	.444
1926	Oakland	P C	OF	138	435	69	141	17	3	4	45	9	.324
1927	Oakland	P C	OF	171	602	108	193	38	12	12	101	11	.321
1928	Oakland	P C	OF	38	105	12	25	3	0	2	13	0	.238
	Denver	Western	OF	71	290	63	101	16	4	9	-	2	.348
1929	Denver	Western	OF	154	624	142	226	39	18	12	-	10	.362
1930	Chattanooga	South A	OF	26	85	8	19	3	0	1	13	0	.224
	Denver	Western	OF	81	332	64	111	11	4	3	49	3	.334
1931	Galveston	Texas	OF	18	54	4	4	1	1	0	3	0	.074
	Omaha	Western	OF	8	30	3	8	2	0	0	-	0	.267
		Majors		**4**	**1**	**1**	**0**	**0**	**0**	**0**	**0**	**0**	**.000**
		Minors		**1446**	**5455**	**1016**	**1805**	**297**	**95**	**127**	**399**	**131**	**.331**

EDWARD L. "HOME RUN" BRECKINRIDGE
Born 1869 at Cleveland, OH.
Height 6'2", Weight 195. Batted right. Threw right.
Umpire: New Eng League 1897-98. Baseball coach at Amherst College 1906-10.
Led all minor leagues in home runs with 20 in 1892, and 25 in 1896. Tied for lead in 1891 with 18.

Year	Club	League	POS	G	AB	R	H	2B	3B	HR	SB	BA
1888	Ft. Way/Log	Ind St	P-OF	20	89	19	33	12	1	0	2	.371
	Canton	Tri-St	2B-P	3	11	3	2	0	0	0	1	.182
1889	Colo. Spgs.	Colo St	1B	27	118	33	34	6	0	2	4	.288
1890	Burlington	Cen In-St	1B	84	331	74	94	13	3	11	11	.284
	Dubuque	Ill Iowa	1B	7	29	9	12	6	0	1	0	.414
	Portland	Pac NW	1B	20	65	13	22	4	1	1	6	.338
1891	Gr. Rapids	NWestern	1B	**71**	256	53	81	**20**	2	**16**	12	.316
	Oshkosh	Wis St	1B	24	88	22	25	3	1	2	13	.284
1892	Columbus	Western	1B	**59**	201	49	60	**15**	3	**18**	7	.299
	Troy	Eastern	1B	50	172	27	44	13	3	2	1	.256
1893	Troy/Wil-Bar.	Eastern	1B	105	375	95	115	23	4	10	14	.307
1894	Troy/Spring.	Eastern	1B	113	440	98	146	26	17	9	11	.332
1895	Johnstown	NY St	1B	29	116	32	43	12	5	1	1	.371
	Rochester	Eastern	1B	87	325	77	110	24	6	7	6	.338
1896	Brockton	New Eng	1B	99	350	84	142	23	4	**25**	13	.406
1897	Syracuse	Eastern	1B	12	47	6	6	3	1	0	0	.128
1898	Taunton	New Eng	1B	11	50	17	17	3	1	3	0	.340

| 1899 | Brockton | New Eng | 1B | 72 | 274 | 70 | 88 | 13 | 3 | 12 | 9 | .321 |
| | **Minors** | | | **893** | **3337** | **781** | **1074** | **219** | **55** | **120** | **111** | **.322** |

JOSEPH JOHN BROVIA
Born February 18, 1922 at Davenport, CA.
Height 6'3", Weight 200. Batted left. Threw right.

Year	Club	League	POS	G	AB	R	H	2B	3B	HR	RBI	SB	BA
1940	El Paso	Ariz-Tex	OF	104	415	73	159	21	19	3	**103**	4	**.383**
1941	San Francisco	P C	OF	92	195	20	62	6	3	0	27	0	.318
1942	San Francisco	P C	OF	24	36	4	6	2	0	0	4	0	.167
	Tacoma	West Int	OF	78	310	54	90	17	3	6	52	2	.290
1943-45						Military Service							
1946	Salt Lake City	Pioneer	OF	47	183	30	62	16	5	2	27	3	.339
	San Francisco	P C	OF	9	9	0	1	0	0	0	0	0	.111
1947	San Francisco	P C	OF	114	359	45	111	29	4	10	63	1	.309
1948	San Francisco	P C	OF	127	444	53	143	28	4	9	89	0	.322
1949	Portland	P C	OF	117	364	59	114	21	2	11	51	2	.313
1950	Portland	P C	OF	193	649	88	182	28	0	39	114	1	.280
1951	Portland	P C	OF	161	574	76	174	25	2	32	133	2	.303
1952	Portland	P C	OF	170	551	78	160	25	1	21	85	0	.290
1953	Sacramento	P C	OF	165	526	76	165	36	1	20	97	1	.314
1954	Sacramento	P C	OF	149	504	59	152	32	0	13	91	0	.302
1955	Oakland	P C	OF	114	372	59	121	19	4	19	73	0	.325
	Cincinnati	National	PH	21	18	0	2	0	0	0	4	0	.111
1956	Buffalo	Int	OF	46	122	12	28	7	0	6	28	0	.230
	San Jose	Calif	OF	71	252	67	91	18	0	22	90	0	.361
1957	Veracruz	Mexican	OF	23	80	13	25	6	0	1	16	1	.313
	Majors			**21**	**18**	**0**	**2**	**0**	**0**	**0**	**4**	**0**	**.111**
	Minors			**1804**	**5945**	**866**	**1846**	**336**	**48**	**214**	**1143**	**17**	**.311**

EDWARD WILLIAM BROWN
Born July 17, 1891 at Milligan, NE. Died September 10, 1956 at Vallejo, CA.
Height 6'3", Weight 190. Batted right. Threw right.
Set an NL record, since surpassed, by playing 618 consecutive games for Dodgers and Braves between June 5, 1924, and June 8, 1928.
Manager: Omaha WL 1932; Fairbury Neb St 1936.

Year	Club	League	POS	G	AB	R	H	2B	3B	HR	RBI	SB	BA
1913	Superior	Neb St	SS-OF	18	68	-	29	7	4	0	-	0	.426
1914	Superior	Neb St	OF	113	439	59	131	22	7	3	-	20	.298
1915	Fairbury	Neb St	OF	35	137	-	43	8	0	4	-	2	.314
	Mason City	Cent A	OF	78	293	44	86	24	5	0	-	19	.294
1916	Mason City	Cent A	OF	129	495	63	145	28	10	9	-	24	.293
1917	Mason City	Cent A	OF	81	308	31	83	13	7	1	-	14	.269
1918						Military Service							
1919	San Antonio	Texas	OF	155	547	57	153	31	3	5	-	10	.280
1920	San Antonio	Texas	OF	153	**615**	77	**200**	34	3	8	83	24	.325
	New York	National	OF	3	8	1	1	1	0	0	0	0	.125
1921	New York	National	OF	70	128	16	36	6	2	0	12	1	.281
1922	Indianapolis	A A	OF	161	633	110	214	44	16	12	133	4	.338
1923	Indianapolis	A A	OF	156	620	96	224	37	19	8	104	6	.361
1924	Indianapolis	A A	OF	40	171	23	56	9	2	3	32	2	.327

Year	Club	League	POS	G	AB	R	H	2B	3B	HR	RBI	SB	BA
	Brooklyn	National	OF	114	455	56	140	30	4	5	78	3	.308
1925	Brooklyn	National	OF	153	618	88	189	39	11	5	99	3	.306
1926	Boston	National	OF	153	612	71	**201**	31	8	2	84	5	.328
1927	Boston	National	OF-1B	155	558	64	171	35	6	2	75	11	.306
1928	Boston	National	OF-1B	142	523	45	140	28	2	2	59	6	.268
1929	Toledo	A A	OF	155	599	86	188	44	12	3	71	15	.314
1930	Dal/Hou/FW	Texas	OF	142	551	91	197	37	4	12	101	7	.358
1931	Ft. Worth	Texas	OF	161	628	90	199	42	4	7	109	22	.317
1932	Omaha	Western	OF	147	579	110	204	52	5	1	96	9	.352
1933-35				Did not play in O.B.									
1936	Fairbury	Neb St	OF	31	59	10	19	4	0	2	7	1	.322
		Majors		**790**	**2902**	**341**	**878**	**170**	**33**	**16**	**407**	**29**	**.303**
		Minors		**1755**	**6742**	**947**	**2171**	**436**	**101**	**78**	**736**	**179**	**.322**

JOSEPH MILTON BROWN
Born September 17, 1902 at Buffalo, NY.
Height 5'9", Weight 160. Batted right. Threw right.
Manager: Springfield West A 1936; Rome Can-Amer 1937.
1929 Rochester infield of Brown, Sand, Toporcer, Collins participated in 223 D.P.s.

Year	Club	League	POS	G	AB	R	H	2B	3B	HR	RBI	SB	BA
1924	Reading	Int	3-2-S	152	568	74	181	31	8	2	59	14	.319
1925	Reading	Int	3B	145	503	80	138	36	9	4	57	9	.274
1926	Newark	Int	3B	160	539	98	165	44	4	10	95	18	.306
1927	Syracuse	Int	3B-2B	164	575	125	178	34	3	14	97	34	.310
1928	Rochester	Int	3B-2B	164	638	137	200	29	11	6	74	20	.313
1929	Rochester	Int	3B	157	619	116	176	27	16	4	81	16	.284
1930	Rochester	Int	3B	162	661	153	207	37	12	10	68	17	.313
1931	Jersey City	Int	3B	130	495	69	151	25	2	1	36	12	.305
1932	J.C./Rochester	Int	3B	148	575	94	159	34	6	4	60	17	.277
1933	Roch/J.C./Buf	Int	3B	145	533	83	154	29	2	3	48	18	.289
1934	Toronto	Int	3B	28	72	15	24	4	0	0	8	2	.333
1935	Dallas	Texas	3B	3	9	0	1	0	0	0	0	0	.111
	Knoxville	South A	3B-2B	105	346	58	105	29	5	2	27	13	.303
1936	Springfield	West A	3B-2B	114	387	82	132	33	5	2	69	15	.341
1937	Rome	Can-Amer	3B	68	210	34	57	14	0	0	37	6	.271
		Minors		**1845**	**6730**	**1218**	**2028**	**406**	**83**	**62**	**816**	**211**	**.301**

PAUL SAMUEL BRUNO
Born June 14, 1915 at New Orleans, LA.
Height 5'10-1/2", Weight 180.
Batted left. Threw left.
Manager: Hammond Evang 1947-49; Baton Rouge Evang 1950.

Year	Club	League	POS	G	AB	R	H	2B	3B	HR	RBI	SB	BA
1934	New Iberia	Evang	P-UT	59	121	10	26	3	1	3	18	0	.215
1935	New Iberia	Evang	P-UT	58	152	19	46	10	0	6	23	2	.303
	Asheville	Piedmont	P	10	17	2	4	0	0	1	2	0	.235
1936	Jacksonville	E Texas	P-UT	18	44	4	9	2	0	0	4	0	.205
	New Iberia	Evang	P	13	55	5	19	4	0	1	11	0	.345
1937	Abbeville	Evang	IF-OF	109	404	70	155	36	6	18	104	7	**.384**
1938	Evansville	III	OF-P	49	196	16	48	9	3	3	35	0	.245

	Greenville	Cottn St	OF	64	261	46	97	26	4	6	75	2	.372
1939	Memphis	South A	OF	73	182	21	57	7	0	4	27	2	.313
1940	Montgomery	SEastern		On suspended list									
1941	Memphis	South A	OF	9	8	0	3	1	0	0	1	0	.375
	Durham	Piedmont	OF-P	123	465	57	141	27	6	10	89	6	.303
1942-43				Did not play in O.B.									
1944	New Orleans	South A	OF	122	462	57	150	22	2	3	73	3	.325
1945				Military service									
1946	New Orleans	South A	OF	110	355	43	109	16	4	6	64	3	.307
	Hammond	Evang	OF	3	7	0	2	0	0	0	0	-	.286
1947	Hammond	Evang	1B-P	110	389	86	129	30	3	18	91	10	.332
1948	Hammond	Evang	1B-P	103	315	67	106	18	0	16	77	9	.337
1949	Hammond	Evang	1B-P	58	171	19	59	11	0	5	38	2	.345
1950	Baton Rouge	Evang	P-UT	19	47	8	19	4	0	1	10	1	.404
1951	Houma	Evang	1B-P	39	101	17	27	3	0	6	26	0	.267
	Minors			**1149**	**3752**	**547**	**1206**	**229**	**29**	**107**	**768**	**47**	**.321**

Pitching Record

Year	Club	League	G	IP	W	L	H	R	ER	BB	SO	ERA
1934	New Iberia	Evang	41	222	13	14	209	105	-	92	177	-
1935	New Iberia	Evang	34	272	15	14	231	115	-	71	167	-
	Asheville	Piedmont	6	29	1	2	31	16	12	12	13	3.72
1936	Jacksonville	E Texas	9	44	3	4	44	27	24	13	14	4.91
	New Iberia	Evang	14	83	6	4	89	37	33	34	34	3.58
1938	Evansville	III	-	-	0	0	-	-	-	-	-	-
1941	Durham	Piedmont	3	11	0	1	10	10	-	4	5	-
1944	New Orleans	South A	4	8	0	0	-	-	-	-	-	-
1946	New Orleans	South A	1	4	0	0	-	-	-	-	-	-
1947	Hammond	Evang	**47**	253	**25**	5	214	81	55	45	**260**	1.96
1948	Hammond	Evang	**45**	248	**22**	5	240	97	79	55	228	2.87
1949	Hammond	Evang	22	121	9	3	110	47	33	29	86	2.45
1950	Baton Rouge	Evang	11	78	7	2	47	21	15	16	59	1.73
1951	Houma	Evang	10	75	7	2	74	34	29	12	58	3.48
	Minors		**247**	**1448**	**108**	**56**	**1299**	**590**	**280**	**383**	**1101**	**2.71**

GLENN CHARLES BURNS
Born September 10, 1928, at New Salem, PA.
Height 6'1", Weight 200. Batted right. Threw right.
Knocked in 197 runs in 141 games in 1951

Year	Club	League	POS	G	AB	R	H	2B	3B	HR	RBI	SB	BA
1947	Niagara Falls	Mid Atl	3B-OF	11	30	4	7	1	0	0	7	0	.233
1948	New Castle	Mid Atl	OF-3B	97	395	61	117	21	6	4	71	0	.296
	Danville	Carolina	OF	18	31	5	6	1	0	0	1	1	.194
1949	Longview	E Texas	OF	135	**561**	101	186	39	12	18	**136**	5	.332
1950	Gladewater	E Texas	OF-3B	32	128	27	37	6	2	8	35	0	.289
	Gainesville	Big St	OF	93	372	70	117	21	5	12	70	2	.315
1951	Lamesa	WTNM	OF-3B	141	587	125	230	**55**	7	27	**197**	6	**.392**
1952	Wichita Falls	Big St	OF	42	166	34	49	7	2	10	44	1	.295
	San Angelo	Longhorn	OF	77	299	61	107	19	2	18	68	3	.358
1953	San Angelo	Longhorn	OF	127	495	113	171	36	5	38	121	3	.345

Year	Club	League	POS	G	AB	R	H	2B	3B	HR	RBI	SB	BA
1954	Abilene	WTNM	OF-P	134	526	109	152	35	6	27	**137**	4	.289
1955	Midland	Longhorn	OF-P	132	492	127	197	36	3	34	130	8	.400
		Minors		**1039**	**4082**	**837**	**1376**	**277**	**50**	**196**	**1017**	**33**	**.337**

RUSSELL GEORGE BURNS

Born June 17, 1920 at Independence, KS. Died about 1980 at Independence, KS.
Height 6'2", Weight 215. Batted right. Threw right.

Year	Club	League	POS	G	AB	R	H	2B	3B	HR	RBI	SB	BA
1940	Joplin	West A	OF	6	20	4	4	1	0	0	1	0	.200
	Norfolk	Western	OF	113	437	93	144	25	13	17	87	25	.330
1941	Joplin	West A	OF	136	513	99	160	26	15	20	103	28	.312
1942-45		Military Service											
1946	Kansas City	A A	OF	78	263	40	62	10	5	8	44	1	.236
	Beaumont	Texas	OF	24	79	10	19	5	1	1	9	0	.241
1947	Beau/Tulsa	Texas	OF	88	303	36	66	11	6	11	48	2	.218
	Des Moines	Western	OF	43	153	38	63	7	3	10	47	5	.412
1948	Tulsa	Texas	OF	132	494	88	153	34	5	**26**	**113**	9	.310
1949	Tulsa	Texas	OF	154	580	125	197	39	3	27	**153**	4	.340
1950	Syracuse	Int	OF	71	262	42	75	11	2	2	36	0	.286
	Tulsa	Texas	OF	59	218	24	51	9	1	2	32	4	.234
1951	Tulsa/Dallas	Texas	OF	145	531	67	151	33	4	11	108	8	.284
1952	Okla City	Texas	OF	149	541	79	160	34	2	23	**120**	2	.296
1953	Okla City	Texas	OF	153	562	87	154	34	2	29	**124**	1	.274
1954	Okla City	Texas	OF	152	524	89	167	37	0	24	110	2	.319
1955	Okla City	Texas	OF	151	507	74	136	25	1	18	70	1	.268
1956	Little Rock	South A	OF	8	28	3	5	1	0	1	3	0	.179
	Plainview	SWestern	OF	108	419	119	153	30	3	38	124	0	.365
		Minors		**1770**	**6434**	**1117**	**1920**	**372**	**66**	**268**	**1332**	**92**	**.298**

HOWARD LEE CAMP

Born July 1, 1893 at Munford, AL. Died May 8, 1960 at Eastaboga, AL.
Height 5'9", Weight 169. Batted left. Threw right.
Manager: Meridian Cottn St 1928; Talladega Ga-Ala 1929.

Year	Club	League	POS	G	AB	R	H	2B	3B	HR	RBI	SB	BA
1913	Talladega	Ga-Ala	OF	90	347	44	109	16	1	1	-	17	.314
1914	Talladega	Ga-Ala	OF	57	300	35	85	16	2	2	-	11	.283
1915	Talladega	Ga-Ala	OF	57	209	35	68	14	4	1	-	18	.325
1916	Talladega	Ga-Ala	OF	59	230	34	71	12	2	2	-	17	.309
	Charleston	S Atl A	OF	42	156	10	32	4	1	2	-	7	.205
1917	Charleston	S Atl A	OF	77	294	43	**105**	15	6	3	-	15	**.357**
	New York	American	OF	5	21	3	6	1	0	0	0	0	.286
	Newark	Int	OF	50	192	25	58	10	4	0	-	4	.302
1918		Did not play in O.B.											
1919	Toledo	A A	OF	123	481	56	121	16	8	1	-	13	.252
1920	Dallas	Texas	OF	110	426	55	142	23	5	1	46	18	.333
	Vernon	T C	OF	13	33	5	9	0	2	1	-	1	.273
1921	Memphis	Sally	OF	156	632	100	218	34	8	5	99	23	.345
1922	Memphis	Sally	OF	149	556	82	173	20	5	10	-	17	.311
1923	Memphis	Sally	OF	149	596	82	182	31	9	2	60	17	.305
1924	Birmingham	Sally	OF	158	609	84	190	36	10	6	86	7	.312
1925	Reading	Int	OF	75	279	51	82	18	7	8	37	4	.294

Year	Club	League	POS	G	AB	R	H	2B	3B	HR	RBI	SB	BA
	Nashville	Sally	OF	65	288	67	106	22	8	9	53	6	.368
1926	Nashville	Sally	OF	129	476	84	155	29	7	9	82	8	.326
1927	Charlotte	S Atl A	OF	150	564	99	172	26	8	20	79	10	.305
1928	Meridian	Cottn St	OF	121	459	86	152	31	2	4	-	26	.331
1929	Talladega	Ga-Ala	OF	85	306	60	100	25	8	9	-	22	.327
1930	Pine Bluff	Cottn St	OF	39	150	22	40	11	0	2	21	5	.267
		Majors		**5**	**21**	**3**	**6**	**1**	**0**	**0**	**0**	**0**	**.286**
		Minors		**1954**	**7583**	**1159**	**2370**	**409**	**107**	**98**	**563**	**266**	**.313**

BEN HOWARD "ROSIE" CANTRELL
Born August 20, 1918 at Knoxville, TN.
Height 5'10", Weight 165. Batted right. Threw right.

Year	Club	League	POS	G	AB	R	H	2B	3B	HR	RBI	SB	BA
1937	Tarboro	Coast Pl	3B	16	59	10	17	4	0	1	8	1	.288
1938	Eliz/Green	Appalach	OF	85	326	66	102	19	10	5	55	14	.313
1939	Pine Bluff	Cottn St	OF	84	338	58	120	26	8	8	52	7	.355
	Dayton	Mid Atl	OF	50	204	26	56	11	3	3	29	3	.275
1940	Anniston	SEastern	OF	50	208	28	55	9	2	5	37	1	.264
	Green/Clark	Cottn St	OF	70	272	44	82	14	9	1	39	5	.301
1941	Clark/Hel	Cottn St	OF	133	538	97	187	38	13	16	133	14	.348
1942	Little Rock	South A.	OF	142	519	70	156	34	6	5	86	11	.301
1943	Little Rock	South A.	OF	138	535	82	170	30	9	3	101	4	.318
1944	Little Rock	South A.	OF	111	449	76	150	30	8	6	113	4	.334
1945	Hollywood	P C	OF	148	502	63	141	20	3	3	69	1	.281
1946	Atlanta	South A.	OF	5	20	1	5	1	0	0	1	0	.250
1947	Little Rock	South A.	OF	153	555	79	179	33	10	6	94	4	.323
1948	L. R./Bgham	South A.	OF	135	476	60	149	28	5	6	98	5	.313
1949	Pine Bluff	Cottn St	OF	136	492	89	158	31	3	12	102	0	.321
1950	Pine Bluff	Cottn St	OF	132	521	112	**189**	35	4	16	**144**	4	**.363**
1951	Pine Bluff	Cottn St	OF	128	479	80	145	25	1	10	101	6	.303
1952	Greenville	Cottn St	OF	83	303	36	87	14	4	0	40	2	.287
1953	Houston	Texas	OF	29	75	3	15	3	0	0	5	0	.200
		Minors		**1828**	**6871**	**1080**	**2163**	**405**	**98**	**106**	**1307**	**86**	**.315**

CHARLES "CHICK" CARGO
Born August 14, 1875 at Pittsburgh, PA.
Height 5'6", Weight 148. Batted right. Threw right.

Brother of Robert Cargo, major league player.

Hit 4 triples and a home run in a game on May 4, 1905 while playing for York.

Year	Club	League	POS	G	AB	R	H	2B	3B	HR	SB	BA
1896	Wash (PA)	Inter-St	3-2-C	60	230	31	64	12	6	3	11	.278
1897	Dayton	Inter-St	3B	66	275	40	83	17	2	0	12	.302
1898	Oswego	NY St	3B-2B	94	355	44	85	20	7	0	11	.239
1899	Oswego	NY St	SS	116	**475**	76	128	25	13	4	35	.269
1900	Oswego	NY St	SS	66	276	47	82	13	1	0	19	.297
	Springfield	Eastern	3B-SS	49	192	26	46	8	2	0	6	.240
1901	Albany	NY St	SS	115	**469**	**110**	125	12	4	0	21	.267
1902	Albany	NY St	SS	116	449	94	119	15	9	1	23	.265
1903	Albany	NY St	SS	124	508	76	143	20	7	1	25	.281
1904	Albany	NY St	SS	131	507	71	135	17	2	0	24	.266
1905	York	Tri-St	SS	55	212	39	60	7	9	2	7	.283

	Albany	NY St	SS	68	258	34	65	8	3	0	15	.252
	Jersey City	Eastern	SS	10	29	3	8	1	0	0	4	.276
1906	New Orleans	South A	2B-SS	131	471	35	116	12	2	0	19	.246
1907	Troy	NY St	SS	134	471	74	132	24	2	0	27	.280
1908	Troy	NY St	SS	139	517	72	143	18	6	1	43	.277
1909	Troy	NY St	SS	125	442	43	101	14	3	0	28	.229
1910	Lynn	New Eng	SS	125	458	64	104	14	4	0	42	.227
1911	Lynn	New Eng	3B-SS	125	446	80	124	18	5	1	22	.278
1912	Lynn/Law	New Eng	S-O-3	120	401	52	101	21	3	1	14	.252
1913	Law/NB/FR	New Eng	SS	103	378	53	88	12	0	2	15	.233
1914	Hav/Lowell	New Eng	SS-2B	66	240	25	65	6	2	3	9	.271
	Minors			**2138**	**8059**	**1189**	**2117**	**314**	**92**	**19**	**432**	**.263**

EDWIN ELLIOTT CARNETT
Born October 21, 1916, at Springfield, MO.
Height 6', Weight 185. Batted left. Threw left.
Manager: Vancouver W Int 1946; Borger WTNM 1948-49, 51; Ponca City West A 1954;
Gainesville/Ponca City Sooner St 1955.

Year	Club	League	POS	G	AB	R	H	2B	3B	HR	RBI	SB	BA
1935	Ponca City	WestA	P-OF	57	170	15	46	9	2	0	19	0	.271
1936	Ponca City	WestA	P-OF	77	244	41	63	14	6	2	33	5	.258
	Los Angeles	P C	P	7	4	0	1	0	0	0	0	0	.250
1937	Tulsa	Texas	P-1B	66	168	28	51	11	4	0	26	2	.304
1938	Los Angeles	P C	P	21	31	4	8	1	0	0	1	0	.258
1939	Milwaukee	A A	P	53	106	11	29	3	2	1	11	1	.274
1940	Kansas City	A A	P	8	11	3	5	0	1	0	5	0	.455
	Newark	Int	P	5	4	1	1	0	0	0	0	0	.250
	Binghamton	Eastern	P	22	34	4	7	2	0	0	3	0	.206
1941	Boston	National	P	2	0	0	0	0	0	0	0	0	.000
	Kansas City	A A	P	49	48	15	16	4	0	0	11	0	.333
1942	Binghamton	Eastern	1B	14	53	5	9	0	2	1	3	0	.170
	Seattle	P C	P	42	62	6	16	1	0	0	4	1	.258
1943	Seattle	P C	OF-P	121	403	44	121	12	4	2	28	21	.300
1944	Chicago	American	O-1-P	126	457	51	126	18	8	1	60	5	.276
1945	Cleveland	American	OF-P	30	73	5	16	7	0	0	7	0	.219
1946	Seattle	P C	OF-1B	52	181	17	37	2	3	1	13	1	.204
	Vancouver	West Int	1B	36	141	25	39	7	2	3	18	3	.277
1947	Tulsa	Texas	1B	16	29	4	7	1	1	0	4	0	.241
	W. Falls/Paris	Big St	OF-1B	105	389	89	132	23	4	9	69	17	.339
1948	Borger	WTNM	OF-1B	135	563	158	230	59	10	33	161	9	.409
1949	Borger	WTNM	OF-1B	96	338	81	112	21	6	13	79	5	.331
1950	Borger	WTNM	OF-1B	144	538	126	194	47	6	24	135	13	.361
1951	Borger/Albuq.	WTNM	OF-1B	111	366	44	115	22	5	1	60	4	.314
1952	Borger	WTNM	1B-OF	125	475	83	151	36	1	16	107	0	.318
1953	Abilene	WTNM	OF-1B	63	247	23	84	22	0	0	37	0	.340
1954	Ponca City	West A	OF	100	304	38	86	20	6	4	64	1	.283
1955	Gaines/P. City	Sooner St	OF	93	282	39	68	11	0	4	41	7	.241
	Majors			**158**	**530**	**56**	**142**	**25**	**8**	**1**	**67**	**5**	**.268**
	Minors			**1618**	**5191**	**904**	**1628**	**328**	**65**	**114**	**932**	**90**	**.314**

Pitching Record

Year	Club	League	G	IP	W	L	H	R	ER	BB	SO	ERA
1935	Ponca City	WestA	34	256	19	11	264	124	91	94	160	3.20
1936	Ponca City	WestA	31	215	16	10	217	127	91	84	155	3.81
	Los Angeles	P C	6	17	0	3	25	15	15	6	3	7.94
1937	Tulsa	Texas	33	177	15	6	196	105	81	53	110	4.12
1938	Los Angeles	P C	21	91	3	6	110	63	42	30	54	4.15
1939	Milwaukee	A A	26	138	4	11	158	81	67	58	76	4.37
1940	Kansas City	A A	8	28	2	2	24	14	12	15	7	3.86
	Newark	Int	4	7	1	1	9	8	8	4	1	10.29
	Binghamton	Eastern	13	65	6	3	59	24	20	30	17	2.77
1941	Boston	National	2	1	0	0	4	3	3	3	2	27.00
	Kansas City	A A	26	77	4	2	88	53	42	32	26	4.91
1942	Seattle	P C	22	84	4	6	85	37	33	37	26	3.54
1943	Seattle	P C	11	63	4	4	62	33	22	22	18	3.14
1944	Chicago	American	2	2	0	0	3	2	2	0	1	9.00
1945	Cleveland	American	2	2	0	0	0	0	0	0	1	0.00
1946	Vancouver	West Int	2	9	0	1	15	8	8	3	6	8.00
1947	Tulsa	Texas	2	3	0	0	5	7	6	4	1	18.00
	WF-Paris	Big St	7	36	3	2	-	-	-	-	-	4.75
1948	Borger	WTNM	27	86	5	2	118	63	54	25	71	5.65
1949	Borger	WTNM	18	67	0	2	121	68	61	30	38	8.19
1950	Borger	WTNM	25	137	13	6	148	69	48	38	81	**3.15**
1951	Borger/Albuq.	WTNM	23	121	9	7	177	87	63	42	47	4.69
1952	Borger	WTNM	19	135	10	6	150	90	60	45	42	4.00
1953	Abilene	WTNM	12	104	4	7	110	58	47	34	41	4.07
1954	Ponca City	West A	14	80	7	3	82	44	36	37	51	4.05
1955	Gaines/P. City	Sooner St	7	-	0	1	-	-	-	-	-	-
		Majors	**6**	**5**	**0**	**0**	**7**	**5**	**5**	**3**	**4**	**9.00**
		Minors	**391**	**1996**	**129**	**102**	**2223**	**1178**	**907**	**723**	**1031**	**4.16**

ARNOLDO LAVAGNINO CASTRO
Born January 11, 1939 at Guasave, Sinaloa, Mex.
Height 5'9", Weight 170. Bats right. Throws right.

Manager: Tabasco Mexican 1980; Chihuahua Mexican 1982.

Year	Club	League	POS	G	AB	R	H	2B	3B	HR	RBI	SB	BA
1957	Aguascal	Cent Mex	2B-SS	101	418	65	109	17	11	3	32	15	.261
1958	Chihuahua	Ariz-Mex	SS	37	170	45	56	21	1	4	20	11	.329
1959					Did not play in O.B.								
1960	Aguascal	Cent Mex	3B-1B	49	157	28	52	10	3	5	26	7	.331
	MC Reds	Mexican	3B	30	49	6	10	1	0	1	8	0	.204
1961	Aguascal	Cent Mex	2B-1B	46	166	26	52	10	2	0	22	7	.313
1962	MC Tigers	Mexican	SS-3B	123	459	49	130	17	5	0	40	8	.283
1963	MC Tigers	Mexican	3-S-2	102	297	40	95	19	6	4	43	9	.320
1964	MC Tigers	Mexican	2B-SS	134	543	90	173	38	5	5	73	7	.319
1965	MCTigers	Mexican	2B	141	559	87	190	28	9	8	69	10	.340
1966	Morelia	Cent Mex	2B	3	11	5	5	2	0	0	2	0	.455
	MC Tigers	Mexican	2B-SS	134	501	79	147	26	3	4	47	15	.293
1967	MC Tigers	Mexican	2B	118	439	76	144	21	6	6	40	5	.328
1968	MC Tigers	Mexican	2-S-3	123	398	38	122	15	2	6	55	5	.307

Year	Club	League	POS	G	AB	R	H	2B	3B	HR	RBI	SB	BA
1969	Caboria	Mex N	2B	2	7	1	0	0	0	0	1	0	.000
	MC Tigers	Mexican	2-S-3	109	377	45	111	19	6	3	47	2	.294
1970	MC Tigers	Mexican	2-S-3	137	437	50	106	20	0	5	45	2	.243
1971	Sabinas	Mexican	2B-3B	143	505	62	142	31	2	12	68	9	.281
1972	Sabinas	Mexican	2B	129	471	47	134	15	1	9	59	2	.285
1973	Sabinas	Mexican	2-3-S	125	437	38	138	19	2	1	58	10	.316
1974	Coahuila	Mexican	3-2-S	135	532	52	145	21	0	6	58	12	.273
1975	Coahuila	Mexican	2B-3B	106	400	39	118	18	2	2	34	9	.295
1976	Coahuila	Mexican	2-3-1	115	400	37	104	15	1	4	45	3	.260
1977	MC Tigers	Mexican	2-3-S	106	342	41	94	13	3	5	29	4	.275
1978	MC Tigers	Mexican	2B-1B	131	391	41	110	19	1	4	46	9	.281
1979				Did not play in O.B.									
1980	MC Tigers	Mex #1	2B-1B	15	36	4	11	0	0	0	2	1	.306
1981				Did not play in O.B.									
1982	Chihuahua	Mexican		Manager, did not play									
1983	Veracruz	Mexican	SS	5	6	0	0	0	0	0	0	0	.000
		Minors		**2399**	**8508**	**1091**	**2498**	**415**	**71**	**97**	**969**	**162**	**.294**

JAMES CHRISTOPHER "IKE" CAVENEY

Born December 10, 1894 at San Francisco, CA. Died July 6, 1949 at San Francisco, CA.
Height 5'9", Weight 165. Batted right. Threw right.
Manager: San Francisco P C 1932-34.

Year	Club	League	POS	G	AB	R	H	2B	3B	HR	RBI	SB	BA
1914	Murray/SLC	Utah St	SS-2B	69	268	46	82	10	7	10	35	4	.306
	Chattanooga	South A	SS	32	74	9	14	2	2	0	-	1	.189
1915	Chattanooga	South A	SS	124	415	37	88	18	0	1	-	7	.212
1916	Springfield	Central	SS	132	490	62	129	19	7	1	-	15	.263
1917	Springfield	Central	SS	126	479	80	141	26	9	7	-	14	.294
1918	Columbus	A A	SS	72	251	23	51	6	4	0	-	5	.203
1919	San Francisco	P C	S-2-3	170	654	87	178	29	5	8	-	20	.272
1920	San Francisco	P C	SS-2B	191	723	82	202	41	8	1	-	27	.279
1921	San Francisco	P C	SS	173	689	118	224	58	5	11	76	29	.325
1922	Cincinnati	National	SS	118	394	41	94	12	9	3	54	6	.239
1923	Cincinnati	National	SS	138	488	58	135	21	9	4	63	5	.277
1924	Cincinnati	National	SS-2B	95	337	36	92	19	1	4	32	2	.273
1925	Cincinnati	National	SS	115	358	38	89	9	5	2	47	2	.249
1926	Seat/Oak	P C	S-2-3	177	654	73	202	29	5	7	81	10	.309
1927	Oakland	P C	3B	169	588	69	164	33	7	5	71	2	.279
1928	Oakland/SF	P C	3B-2B	125	457	51	120	22	3	6	47	1	.263
1929	San Francisco	P C	2B	148	530	67	177	30	3	9	87	6	.334
1930	San Francisco	P C	2B-3B	169	575	87	193	39	1	8	84	4	.336
1931	San Francisco	P C	2B-3B	115	407	48	136	26	8	3	55	3	.334
1932	San Francisco	P C	2B	43	76	8	22	5	0	0	10	1	.289
1933	San Francsico	P C	2B-3B	29	60	4	20	3	1	0	8	0	.333
1934	San Francisco	P C	2B-3B	21	19	0	5	0	1	0	1	0	.263
		Majors		**466**	**1577**	**173**	**410**	**61**	**24**	**13**	**196**	**15**	**.260**
		Minors		**2085**	**7409**	**951**	**2148**	**396**	**76**	**77**	**555**	**149**	**.290**

HARRY "PEP" CLARK
Born March 20, 1883 at Union City, OH. Died June 8, 1965 at Milwaukee, WI.
Height 5'7-1/2", Weight 175. Batted right. Threw right.
Manager: Milwaukee A A 1913-16, 1922-25. Set record for most games played in AA with 1834.

Year	Club	League	POS	G	AB	R	H	2B	3B	HR	SB	BA
1903	Dallas	Texas	3B	99	411	50	131	19	3	11	21	.319
	Chicago	American	3B	15	65	7	20	4	2	0	5	.308
1904	Milwaukee	A A	3B	137	554	68	141	22	5	1	28	.255
1905	Milwaukee	A A	3B	143	492	79	120	22	6	2	14	.244
1906	Milwaukee	A A	3B	125	450	71	115	17	8	1	21	.256
1907	Milwaukee	A A	3B	136	450	55	88	9	3	3	16	.196
1908	Milwaukee	A A	3B	112	374	54	95	16	6	5	12	.254
1909	Milwaukee	A A	3B	173	548	78	141	25	8	4	28	.257
1910	Milwaukee	A A	3B	164	525	69	131	22	7	4	20	.250
1911	Milwaukee	A A	3B	162	540	82	141	20	7	6	14	.261
1912	Milwaukee	A A	3B	138	473	74	138	24	13	4	17	.292
1913	Milwaukee	A A	3B	165	556	85	159	16	19	3	25	.286
1914	Milwaukee	A A	3B	150	478	108	144	25	4	4	16	.301
1915	Milwaukee	A A	3B	130	358	59	97	13	6	1	12	.271
1916	Milwaukee	A A	3B	89	243	36	50	6	3	1	10	.206
1917-21						Did not play in O.B.						
1922	Milwaukee	A A	3B	5	13	2	2	0	0	0	0	.154
1923	Milwaukee	A A	3B	5	11	2	2	1	0	0	0	.182
		Majors		**15**	**65**	**7**	**20**	**4**	**2**	**0**	**5**	**.308**
		Minors		**1933**	**6476**	**972**	**1695**	**257**	**98**	**50**	**254**	**.262**

JAMES BUSTER "BUS" CLARKSON
Born March 13, 1989 at Hopkins, SC. Died January 18, 1989 at Jeannette, PA.
Height 5'11", Weight 200. Batted right. Threw right.
Attended Wilberforce University.

Year	Club	League	POS	G	AB	R	H	2B	3B	HR	RBI	SB	BA
1937	Pittsburgh	Neg. Nat.				No record available							
1938	Pittsburgh	Neg. Nat.				No record available							
1939	Toledo	Neg. Nat.	-	5	19	-	8	-	-	-	-	-	.421
1940	Ind/Newark	Neg. Am.	SS	11	45	-	18	1	0	5	-	-	.400
	Nuevo Laredo	Mexican	SS	19	80	12	27	4	3	1	13	1	.338
1941	Tampico	Mexican	SS	82	326	67	109	23	3	19	83	7	.334
1942	Newark	Neg. Am.	-	2	7	-	2	2	0	0	-	-	.286
1943-45						Military Service							
1946	Vera Cruz	Mexican	3B-SS	37	131	29	39	8	1	9	32	7	.298
	Philadelphia	Neg. Am.	-	38	146	26	45	7	2	2	34	-	.308
1947	Vera Cruz	Mexican	SS	112	390	75	118	19	7	17	68	20	.303
1948	St. Jean	Provincl	-	80	276	93	110	12	0	**28**	68	-	.399
1949	Philadelphia	Neg. Am.	3B-SS	56	192	32	60	-	-	-	-	-	.313
1950	Baltimore	Neg. Am.	SS-3B	33	108	21	32	10	1	4	18	-	.296
	Milwaukee	A A	3B	59	205	34	62	11	1	7	33	0	.302
1951	Milwaukee	A A	SS	97	283	52	97	12	4	5	49	6	.343
1952	Boston	National	SS-3B	14	25	3	5	0	0	0	1	0	.200
	Milwaukee	A A	SS-3B	74	242	49	77	14	2	12	68	10	.318
1953	Dallas	Texas	3B	137	445	91	147	32	1	18	87	11	.330
1954	Beau/Dallas	Texas	SS-3B	157	543	109	176	21	2	**42**	135	7	.324
1955	Los Angeles	P C	3B	100	316	40	93	8	0	13	46	1	.294

Year	Club	League	POS	G	AB	R	H	2B	3B	HR	RBI	SB	BA
1956	Los Angeles	P C	3B	8	11	2	3	1	0	0	0	0	.273
	Tulsa	Texas	3B	48	137	24	35	4	0	5	19	1	.255
	Des Moines	Western	3B	60	205	45	57	11	0	13	50	3	.278
	Majors			**14**	**25**	**3**	**5**	**0**	**0**	**0**	**1**	**0**	**.200**
	Minors			**1070**	**3590**	**722**	**1150**	**180**	**24**	**189**	**751**	**74**	**.320**
	Negro Lg			**145**	**517**	**79**	**165**	**20**	**3**	**11**	**52**	**-**	**.319**

JOHN PAUL COBB

(Known by middle name.)
Born February 23, 1888 at Royston, GA. Died October 27, 1964 at Sarasota, FL.
Height 6' 0", Weight 165. Batted right. Threw right.
Brother of Ty Cobb.
Attended Georgia Tech in spring of 1906. Returned in 1916.
Drafted by St. Louis Browns after 1908 season. Served in U.S. Marines during WWI.

Year	Club	League	POS	G	AB	R	H	2B	3B	HR	RBI	SB	BA
1907	Kalamazoo	S Mich	OF	34	128	11	31	3	1	0	-	6	.242
	Leavenworth	West A	OF	52	192	9	48	-	-	-	-	-	.250
1908	Enid/Joplin	West A	OF	140	479	81	131	15	10	10	-	34	.273
1909	Memphis	South A	OF	5	14	1	5	1	0	0	-	2	.357
	Fresno	Calif	OF	36	130	16	27	5	1	9	-	4	.208
1910	Lincoln	Western	OF	167	613	92	190	25	12	6	-	37	.310
1911	Lincoln	Western	OF	168	620	94	190	36	5	9	59	48	.306
1912	Lincoln	Western	OF	144	567	73	150	39	9	2	-	22	.265
1913	Lincoln	Western	OF	82	292	40	74	20	1	2	-	7	.253
	Ogden	Utah St	OF	36	141	29	47	15	3	0	19	5	.333
1914	Ogden	Utah St	OF	108	430	83	131	43	4	5	67	23	.305
1915				Did not play in O.B.									
1916	Terre Haute	Central	OF	5	18	1	5	1	0	0	0	0	.278
	Newp News	Virginia	OF	6	21	2	3	0	1	0	-	0	.143
	Jacksonville	Sally	1B	18	62	11	18	3	2	1	-	1	.290
	Minors			**1001**	**3707**	**543**	**1050**	**206**	**49**	**44**	**145**	**189**	**.283**

ANDREW HOWARD COHEN

Born October 25, 1904 at Baltimore, MD. Died October 29, 1988 at El Paso, TX.
Height 5' 8", Weight 155. Batted right. Threw right.
Brother of Syd, major league pitcher. Attended University of Alabama.
Manager: Pine Bluff CSL and Dayton MAL 1939; Dayton MAL 1940; El Paso Mex Nat 1946; Eau Claire Northern 1948-50; Denver Western 1951-54; New Orleans South A 1955-56; Indianapolis AA 1957.

Year	Club	League	POS	G	AB	R	H	2B	3B	HR	RBI	SB	BA
1925	Waco	Texas	SS	106	417	60	130	18	1	6	51	8	.312
1926	Waco	Texas	SS	30	114	15	26	6	0	3	14	1	.228
	New York	National	S-2-3	32	35	4	9	0	1	0	8	0	.257
1927	Buffalo	Int	SS-2B	150	555	90	196	34	5	14	118	3	.353
1928	New York	National	2-S-3	129	504	64	138	24	7	9	59	3	.274

Year	Club	League	POS	G	AB	R	H	2B	3B	HR	RBI	SB	BA
1929	New York	National	2-S-3	101	347	40	102	12	2	5	47	3	.294
1930	Newark	Int	3-2-S	106	386	42	100	9	4	6	56	2	.259
1931	Newark	Int	2B	131	539	81	171	23	9	10	65	2	.317
1932	Newark	Int	2B	51	216	30	61	4	2	4	26	1	.282
	Minneapolis	A A	2B	93	420	66	122	16	3	1	41	0	.290
1933	Minneapolis	A A	2B	123	545	70	149	29	2	3	49	4	.273
1934	Minneapolis	A A	2B	145	666	106	207	33	4	0	62	0	.311
1935	Minneapolis	A A	2B	153	665	90	182	30	7	2	55	0	.274
1936	Minneapolis	A A	2B	112	485	76	147	23	5	7	65	0	.303
1937	Minneapolis	A A	2B	131	497	76	159	28	12	11	82	3	.320
1938	Minneapolis	A A	2B	145	597	66	150	24	4	4	55	4	.251
1939	Minneapolis	A A	2B	2	1	0	0	0	0	0	1	0	.000
	Pine Bluff	Cottn St	2B	75	276	30	77	17	3	6	48	3	.279
	Dayton	Mid Atl	2B	50	187	19	64	6	4	1	25	4	.342
1940	Dayton	Mid Atl	2B	120	455	39	116	20	2	0	56	6	.255
1941	Elmira	Eastern	2B	132	459	27	99	19	4	0	50	2	.216
1942	Elmira	Eastern	2B	25	89	7	22	2	1	0	6	0	.247
1943-45			Military Service										
1946	El Paso	Mex Nat	2B	14	51	8	21	4	2	0	9	0	.412
	Majors			**262**	**886**	**108**	**249**	**36**	**10**	**14**	**114**	**6**	**.281**
	Minors			**1894**	**7620**	**998**	**2199**	**345**	**74**	**78**	**934**	**43**	**.289**

MICHAEL DEWAYNE COLE
Born September 30, 1960 at San Diego, CA.
Height 5' 9", Weight 160. Bats left. Throws right.
Ranks 4th on career minor league SB list.

Year	Club	League	POS	G	AB	R	H	2B	3B	HR	RBI	SB	BA
1980	Elizabethton	Appalach	2B-OF	54	212	41	61	6	1	0	20	14	.288
1981	Wisc.Rapids	Midwest	2B	114	414	75	103	8	3	1	22	32	.249
1982	Visalia	Calif	2B-OF	114	381	86	110	15	4	1	40	71	.289
1983	Savannah	Southern	OF-3B	137	470	87	134	21	4	1	36	75	.285
1984	Greenville	Southern	OF-2B	137	502	105	153	11	6	2	38	85	.305
1985	Green/Memp	Southern	OF	40	150	27	42	5	3	1	13	22	.280
	Omaha	A A	OF	69	227	41	77	7	5	0	19	28	.339
1986	Cordoba	Mexican	OF	45	156	40	58	3	5	0	17	25	.372
1987	Campeche	Mexican	OF	116	438	101	157	20	7	4	41	66	.358
1988	Campeche	Mexican	OF	124	480	109	159	17	14	2	42	80	.331
1989	Tabasco	Mexican	OF	127	459	108	172	16	10	0	37	100	.375
1990	Campeche	Mexican	OF	123	452	91	152	15	2	0	34	56	.336
1991	San Luis Pot	Mexican	OF	70	240	61	89	6	3	3	37	24	.371
	Minors			**1270**	**4581**	**972**	**1467**	**150**	**67**	**15**	**396**	**678**	**.320**

JIMMIE COLLINS
(Jimmie is correct first name and has no middle name)
Born November 19, 1948 at Canton, MS.
Height 6' 2", Weight 185. Bats left. Throws left.

Year	Club	League	POS	G	AB	R	H	2B	3B	HR	RBI	SB	BA
1971	Wytheville	Appalach	1B-OF	33	56	7	19	4	2	1	7	3	.339
1972	Greenwood	W Carol	OF	112	371	62	104	12	2	0	32	25	.280
	Savannah	Southern	OF	3	2	1	0	0	0	0	0	0	.000
1973	Savannah	Southern	OF	19	42	7	6	1	0	0	4	3	.143

Year	Club	League	POS	G	AB	R	H	2B	3B	HR		SB	BA
	Kinston	Carolina	OF-P	100	363	62	118	18	5	4	41	15	.325
1974	Savannah	Southern	OF	138	521	64	135	11	5	4	60	16	.259
1975	Savannah	Southern	OF	131	470	55	139	16	5	2	43	16	.296
1976	Richmond	Int	OF	80	266	35	78	11	5	2	29	7	.293
	Savannah	Southern	OF-1B	5	17	1	2	0	0	1	3	1	.118
1977	Richmond	Int	OF	111	344	30	83	12	1	0	36	6	.241
1978	Chihuahua	Mexican	OF	136	528	87	185	28	12	11	67	22	.350
1979	Chihuahua	Mexican	OF	124	470	95	**206**	**35**	10	6	60	33	**.438**
1980	Chihuahua	Mex #1	OF	91	346	62	131	19	13	4	52	19	.379
	Saltillo	Mex #2	OF	39	137	25	**52**	8	3	2	**31**	5	**.380**
1981	Chih/Salt	Mexican	OF	123	446	73	144	25	12	5	48	19	.323
1982	Coatzacualcos	Mexican	OF	108	397	66	128	19	3	0	49	15	.322
1983	Coatzacualcos	Mexican	OF	117	432	52	128	18	3	2	46	39	.296
1984	MC Reds/Cord	Mexican	OF	109	403	81	166	35	4	6	59	12	.412
1985	Cord/Vera	Mexican	OF	124	445	72	141	30	2	6	56	14	.317
1986	Leon/SanLuis	Mexican	OF	126	474	102	174	**41**	8	7	73	7	.367
1987	Tabasaco	Mexican	OF-1B	122	428	67	141	22	5	10	67	5	.329
		Minors		**1951**	**6958**	**1106**	**2280**	**365**	**100**	**73**	**863**	**282**	**.328**

FRANK HENRY CONNAUGHTON

Born January 1, 1869, at Clinton, MA. Died December 1, 1942, at Boston, MA.
Height 5' 9", Weight 165. Batted right. Threw right.

Manager: Haverhill New Eng 1909; New Bedford New Eng and Bangor-New Brunswick Maine St 1913.

Basically a catcher at start of career. Used catcher's mitt when shifted to infield. This may have led to rule prohibiting the use of large gloves by infielders. Ill with malaria late in 1898. This may be reason that he did not play in 1899.

Died when struck by automobile on Boston Street.

Year	Club	League	POS	G	AB	R	H	2B	3B	HR	SB	BA
1891	Woonsocket	New Eng	C-O-1	37	154	27	44	8	3	1	9	.286
1892	Paw/Lewis	New Eng	C	87	396	92	122	**34**	1	1	**44**	.308
1893	Savannah	Southern	O-C-2-S	82	292	55	80	6	1	0	-	.274
	Lewiston	New Eng	C	11	39	6	11	2	0	0	2	.282
1894	Brockton	New Eng	C-S-1	20	91	30	31	5	1	2	5	.341
	Boston	National	S-C-O	46	171	42	59	9	2	2	3	.345
1895	Kansas City	Western	SS	115	493	118	177	36	12	9	20	.359
1896	New York	National	SS-OF	88	315	53	82	3	2	2	22	.260
1897	Kansas City	Western	SS	137	563	95	157	18	12	0	26	.279
1898	Kansas City	Western	SS	106	434	83	120	11	6	1	20	.276
1899					Did not play in O.B.							
1900	Worcester	Eastern	2B	100	393	52	103	14	4	0	13	.262
1901					Did not play in O.B.							
1902	Buf/Worc	Eastern	SS-2B	119	448	52	118	17	7	1	10	.263
1903	Montreal	Eastern	SS-2B	123	476	58	121	23	7	0	19	.254
1904	Haverhill	New Eng	SS	114	442	66	127	35	4	2	27	.287
	Toledo	A A	SS-2B	5	19	1	7	0	0	0	0	.368
1905	Nashua	New Eng	SS	27	106	14	22	6	0	0	9	.208
	Harrisburg	Tri-St	SS-C	41	145	15	34	4	2	0	9	.234
1906	Law/Hav	New Eng	2B-SS	109	414	43	106	15	6	1	30	.256
	Boston	National	SS-2B	12	44	3	9	0	0	0	1	.205
1907	Lynn	New Eng	2B	108	390	46	97	23	2	1	38	.249
1908	Lawrence	New Eng	2B	84	318	30	80	16	3	1	21	.252

Year	Club	League	POS	G	AB	R	H	2B	3B	HR	RBI	SB	BA
1909	Haverhill	New Eng	2B	124	480	73	141	**34**	4	0	18		.294
1910	Waterbury	Conn	2B	124	491	74	123	31	10	0	18		.251
1911	Brockton	New Eng	2B	119	474	75	148	26	6	2	19		.312
1912	New Bedford	New Eng	2B	113	400	46	97	18	1	0	9		.243
1913	New Bedford	New Eng	2B	27	98	15	27	9	0	0	5		.276
	Bangor	NB-Maine	2B	45	189	40	63	10	7	3	13		.333
		Majors		**146**	**530**	**98**	**150**	**12**	**4**	**4**	**26**		**.283**
		Minors		**1977**	**7745**	**1206**	**2156**	**401**	**99**	**25**	**384**		**.278**

KEVIN JOSEPH ALOYSIUS "CHUCK" CONNORS
Born April 10, 1921 at Brooklyn, NY.
Height 6' 5-1/2", Weight 212. Batted left. Threw left.
Attended Seton Hall College.
Played pro basketball for Rochester 1945-46 and for Boston 1946-47 and 1947-48.
Became television/movie actor after baseball career.

Year	Club	League	POS	G	AB	R	H	2B	3B	HR	RBI	SB	BA
1940	Newport	NEastern	1B	4	11	1	1	0	0	0	1	-	.091
1941						Did not play in O.B.							
1942	Norfolk	Piedmont	1B	72	250	28	66	9	6	5	45	2	.264
1943-45						Military Service							
1946	Newp News	Piedmont	1B	119	430	72	126	29	6	**17**	68	19	.293
1947	Mobile	Sally	1B	145	514	65	131	29	6	15	82	10	.255
1948	Montreal	Int	1B	147	512	79	157	36	5	17	88	9	.307
1949	Montreal	Int	1B	133	477	90	152	25	5	20	108	6	.319
	Brooklyn	National	PH	1	1	0	0	0	0	0	0	0	.000
1950	Montreal	Int	1B	121	407	69	118	26	4	6	68	14	.290
1951	Chicago	National	1B	66	201	16	48	5	1	2	18	4	.239
	Los Angeles	P C	1B	98	390	75	125	28	2	22	77	8	.321
1952	Los Angeles	P C	1B	113	406	50	105	27	2	6	51	4	.259
		Majors		**67**	**202**	**16**	**48**	**5**	**1**	**2**	**18**	**4**	**.238**
		Minors		**952**	**3397**	**529**	**981**	**209**	**36**	**108**	**588**	**72**	**.289**

HERBERT LEROY CONYERS
Born January 8, 1921 at Cowgill, MO. Died September 16, 1964 at Cleveland OH.
Height 6' 5", Weight 210. Batted left. Threw right.
Won batting titles in four different leagues.

Year	Club	League	POS	G	AB	R	H	2B	3B	HR	RBI	SB	BA
1941	Appleton	Wis St	1B	110	407	87	126	25	4	10	73	12	.310
1942	Wausau	Northern	1B	115	436	92	158	**37**	8	7	79	10	**.362**
1943-45						Military service							
1946	Harrisburg	Inter-St	1B	91	341	54	115	25	3	9	67	1	.337
	Wilkes-Barre	Eastern	1B	36	116	15	28	3	1	1	26	1	.241
1947	Harrisburg	Inter-St	1B	135	543	109	**194**	29	10	17	118	4	**.357**
1948	Baltimore	Int	1B	28	108	5	25	4	0	1	15	2	.231
	Dayton	Central	1B	113	461	83	163	43	8	14	96	0	**.354**
1949	Okla City	Texas	1B	147	603	101	**214**	**52**	5	8	134	5	**.355**
1950	Cleveland	American	1B	7	9	2	3	0	0	1	1	1	.333
	San Diego	P C	1B	66	220	20	49	11	1	1	24	2	.223
	Okla City	Texas	1B	29	111	17	32	9	1	2	25	0	.288
1951	San Diego	P C	1B	35	122	15	27	8	3	0	17	1	.221

	Dallas	Texas	1B	115	440	67	129	24	7	2	47	1	.293
1952	Indianapolis	A A	1B	48	168	14	39	4	0	4	25	3	.232
	Birmingham	South A	1B	78	285	22	76	8	6	4	43	1	.267
	Majors			**7**	**9**	**2**	**3**	**0**	**0**	**1**	**1**	**1**	**.333**
	Minors			**1146**	**4361**	**701**	**1375**	**282**	**57**	**80**	**789**	**43**	**.315**

CLIFFORD RANKIN "PAT" CRAWFORD
Born January 28, 1902 at Society Hill, SC.
Height 5' 11", Weight 170. Batted left. Threw right.

Year	Club	League	POS	G	AB	R	H	2B	3B	HR	RBI	SB	BA
1924	Charlotte	Sally	3B-1B	95	376	65	114	23	7	7	44	6	.303
1925	Greenville	Sally	3B-1B	89	329	68	113	27	6	11	44	4	.343
1926	Greenville	Sally	3B	111	445	77	146	27	4	21	93	4	.328
1927	Greenville	Sally	3B	118	443	85	148	26	4	24	90	13	.334
1928	Toledo	A A	1B-3B	113	429	58	149	27	10	2	70	9	.347
1929	New York	National	1B-3B	65	57	13	17	3	0	3	24	1	.298
1930	NY/Cinci	National	2B-1B	101	300	35	86	10	3	6	43	2	.287
1931	Columbus	A A	1B	157	633	142	237	41	13	**28**	**154**	18	.374
1932	Columbus	A A	1B	160	640	116	236	34	5	30	140	14	.369
1933	St. Louis	National	1-2-3	91	224	24	60	8	2	0	21	1	.268
1934	St. Louis	National	3B-2B	61	70	3	19	2	0	0	16	0	.271
	Majors			**318**	**651**	**75**	**182**	**23**	**5**	**9**	**104**	**4**	**.280**
	Minors			**843**	**3295**	**611**	**1143**	**205**	**49**	**123**	**635**	**68**	**.347**

VICTOR JOSE DAVALILLO
Born July 31, 1939 at Cabinas, Venezuela
Height 5' 7", Weight 150. Bats left. Trows left.
Brother of Pompeyo, major league player. Minor league pitching record was 33-27 in 187 games.

Year	Club	League	POS	G	AB	R	H	2B	3B	HR	RBI	SB	BA
1958	Visalia	Calif	P	19	15	4	5	0	0	1	2	0	.333
	Palatka	Fla St	P	15	6	3	1	0	0	0	1	0	.167
1959	Palatka	Fla St	P	73	79	16	23	3	2	2	10	2	.291
1960	Topeka	III	P-OF	84	155	19	42	5	3	3	23	5	.271
1961	Columbia	Sally	P-OF	34	46	2	9	1	0	1	8	0	.196
	Topeka	III	P	14	21	5	6	1	0	1	3	0	.286
	Jersey City	Int	P	33	59	7	15	3	1	0	1	0	.254
1962	Jacksonville	Int	OF-P	150	578	99	**200**	27	**18**	11	69	**24**	**.346**
1963	Cleveland	American	OF	90	370	44	108	18	5	7	36	3	.292
1964	Cleveland	American	OF	150	577	64	156	26	2	6	51	21	.270
1965	Cleveland	American	OF	142	505	67	152	19	1	5	40	26	.301
1966	Cleveland	American	OF	121	344	42	86	6	4	3	19	8	.250
1967	Cleveland	American	OF	139	359	47	103	17	5	2	22	6	.287
1968	Cle.-Cal.	American	OF	144	519	49	144	17	7	3	31	25	.277
1969	California	American	OF-1B	33	71	10	11	1	1	0	1	3	.155
	St. Louis	National	OF-P	63	98	15	26	3	0	2	10	1	.265
1970	St. Louis	National	OF	111	183	29	57	14	3	1	33	4	.311
1971	Pittsburgh	National	OF-1B	99	295	48	84	14	6	1	33	10	.285
1972	Pittsburgh	National	OF-1B	117	368	59	117	19	2	4	28	14	.318
1973	Pittsburgh	National	OF-1B	59	83	9	15	1	0	1	3	0	.181
	Oakland	American	OF-1B	38	64	5	12	1	0	0	4	0	.188
1974	Oakland	American	OF	17	23	0	4	0	0	0	1	0	.174

	Cordoba	Mexican	O-1-P	71	249	46	82	9	5	4	27	3	.329
1975	Cordoba	Mexican	OF-1B	114	408	70	145	21	3	9	70	7	.355
1976	Puebla	Mexican	OF-1B	123	501	84	167	23	1	8	63	5	.333
1977	Aguascal	Mexican	O-1-P	135	516	87	198	30	8	6	78	20	**.384**
	Los Angeles	National	OF	24	48	3	15	2	0	0	4	0	.313
1978	Los Angeles	National	OF-1B	75	77	15	24	1	1	1	11	2	.312
1979	Los Angeles	National	OF	29	27	2	7	1	0	0	2	2	.259
	Albuquerque	P C	OF-P	51	139	27	44	6	0	3	19	3	.317
1980	Aguascal	Mex #1	OF-P	94	363	67	**143**	15	5	6	50	1	.394
	Albuquerque	P C	OF-P	36	108	13	31	7	1	2	19	1	.287
	Los Angeles	National	1B	7	6	1	1	0	0	0	0	0	.167
1981	Aguascal	Mexican	OF-1B-P	40	153	21	47	10	3	2	14	0	.307
		Majors		**1458**	**4017**	**509**	**1122**	**160**	**37**	**36**	**329**	**125**	**.279**
		Minors		**1086**	**3396**	**570**	**1158**	**161**	**50**	**59**	**457**	**71**	**.341**

CECIL AUSTIN "STORMY" DAVIS

Born October 10, 1900 at Corbin, KY. Died May 26, 1957 at Mobile, AL.
Height 5' 10", Weight 165. Batted right. Threw right.

Father of James who played for Ballinger-Longhorn League in 1947. James was hit by a pitch in a game against Sweetwater on July 3 and he died 7 days later.

Manager: Jacksonville E Texas 1940.

Year	Club	League	POS	G	AB	R	H	2B	3B	HR	RBI	SB	BA
1921	Cleveland	Appalach	OF	91	346	56	87	8	2	9	-	3	.251
	Little Rock	South A	OF	27	80	13	28	1	5	1	14	2	.350
1922	Joplin	West A	OF	132	485	76	166	35	20	9	-	24	.342
1923	Okmulgee	West A	OF	144	539	105	183	28	8	34	-	9	.340
1924	Okmulgee	West A	OF	160	**676**	**187**	246	48	10	**51**	162	9	.364
1925	Ft. Worth	Texas	OF	153	**669**	141	183	50	3	29	99	2	.274
1926	Waco	Texas	OF	94	355	47	109	20	1	16	55	3	.307
	Okla City	Western	OF	54	227	48	76	12	7	5	-	8	.335
1927	Omaha/Amar	Western	OF	148	603	103	201	49	10	13	-	8	.333
1928	Augusta	Sally	OF	141	534	97	168	36	7	27	**125**	9	.315
1929	Lake Charles	Cottn St	OF	122	478	81	156	25	3	**28**	-	15	.326
1930	Pine Bluff	Cottn St	OF	93	365	74	117	33	6	12	73	13	.321
1931	Pine Bluff	Cottn St	OF	125	505	83	152	32	6	12	**100**	28	.301
1932	Pine Bluff	Cottn St	OF	70	284	43	86	17	0	7	-	9	.303
1933	Wac/PB/Long	Dixie	OF	100	376	60	114	13	4	**17**	86	3	.303
		Minors		**1654**	**6522**	**1214**	**2072**	**407**	**92**	**270**	**714**	**145**	**.318**

EDWARD JAMES DELAHANTY

Born October 30, 1867 at Cleveland, OH. Died July 2, 1903 at Niagara Falls, NY.
Height 5' 11", Weight 170 Batted right. Threw right.

Brother of Frank, Jim, Joe, Tom and Will; all professional players.
Elected to Baseball Hall of Fame in 1945.

Year	Club	League	POS	G	AB	R	H	2B	3B	HR	RBI	SB	BA
1887	Mansfield	Ohio St	2B-C	83	387	90	136	19	7	5	-	21	.351
1888	Wheeling	Tri-St	2B	21	97	20	40	9	4	5	-	15	.412
	Philadelphia	National	2B-OF	74	290	40	66	12	2	1	31	38	.228
1889	Philadelphia	National	O-2-1	56	246	37	72	13	3	0	27	19	.293
1890	Cleveland	Players	S-2-0-3	115	517	107	154	26	13	3	64	25	.298

1891	Philadelphia	National	O-1-2	128	543	92	132	19	9	5	86	25	.243
1892	Philadelphia	National	OF-3B	123	477	79	146	30	**21**	6	91	29	.306
1893	Philadelphia	National	O-2-1	132	595	145	219	35	18	**19**	**146**	37	.368
1894	Philadelphia	National	O-1-3-S	114	489	147	199	39	18	4	131	21	.407
1895	Philadelphia	National	O-S-2-3	116	480	149	194	**49**	10	11	106	46	.404
1896	Philadelphia	National	O-1-2	123	499	131	198	**44**	17	**13**	**126**	37	.397
1897	Philadelphia	National	OF-1B	129	530	109	200	40	15	5	96	26	.377
1898	Philadelphia	National	OF	144	548	115	183	36	9	4	92	**58**	.334
1899	Philadelphia	National	OF	146	581	135	**238**	**55**	9	9	**137**	30	**.410**
1900	Philadelphia	National	1B	131	539	82	174	32	10	2	109	16	.323
1901	Philadelphia	National	OF-1B	139	542	106	192	**38**	16	8	108	29	.354
1902	Washington	American	OF-1B	123	473	103	178	**43**	14	10	93	16	**.376**
1903	Washington	American	OF-1B	42	156	22	52	11	1	1	21	3	.333
		Majors		**1835**	**7505**	**1599**	**2597**	**522**	**185**	**101**	**1464**	**455**	**.346**
		Minors		**104**	**484**	**110**	**176**	**28**	**11**	**10**	**-**	**36**	**.364**

FRANK GEORGE "PUDGIE" DELAHANTY
Born January 29, 1883 at Cleveland, OH. Died July 22, 1966 at Cleveland, OH.
Height 5' 9", Weight 160. Batted right. Threw right.
Brother of Ed, Jim, Joe, Tom and Will; all professional players.

Year	Club	League	POS	G	AB	R	H	2B	3B	HR	RBI	SB	BA
1902	Atl/Birm	South A	OF	71	167	29	45	8	10	0	-	12	.269
1903	Syracuse	NY St	OF	118	462	59	112	26	6	2	-	17	.242
1904	Montgomery	South A	O-S-2	128	475	42	116	18	6	2	-	17	.244
1905	Birmingham	South A	OF	88	330	47	102	18	2	1	-	14	.309
	New York	American	1B-OF	9	27	0	6	1	0	0	2	0	.222
1906	New York	American	OF	92	307	37	73	11	8	2	41	11	.238
1907	Cleveland	American	OF	15	52	3	9	0	1	0	4	2	.173
1908	New York	American	OF	37	125	12	32	1	2	0	10	9	.256
	New Orleans	South A	OF	64	250	25	62	14	1	0	-	16	.248
1909	Louisville	A A	OF	134	503	53	119	22	3	3	-	31	.237
1910	Indianapolis	A A	OF	100	391	47	90	5	9	3	-	26	.230
1911	St. Paul	A A	OF	147	576	74	159	23	7	3	-	46	.276
1912	Minneapolis	A A	OF	146	511	75	136	11	5	0	-	36	.266
1913	Minneapolis	A A	OF	136	442	70	106	10	4	1	-	31	.240
1914	Buff/Pitt	Federal	OF-2B	120	433	54	93	8	11	3	34	28	.215
1915	Pittsburgh	Federal	OF	14	42	3	10	1	0	0	3	0	.238
1916	Erie	Inter-St	OF	57	201	20	48	10	1	0	-	14	.239
		Majors		**287**	**986**	**109**	**223**	**22**	**22**	**5**	**94**	**50**	**.226**
		Minors		**1189**	**4308**	**541**	**1095**	**165**	**54**	**15**	**-**	**260**	**.254**

JAMES CHRISTOPHER DELAHANTY
Born June 20, 1879 at Cleveland, OH. Died October 17, 1952 at Cleveland, OH.
Height 5' 10-1/2", Weight 170. Batted right. Threw right.
Brother of Ed, Frank, Joe, Tom and Will; all professional players.
Manager: Beaumont TL 1916.
Broke knee on May 23, 1901. Out for balance of season.
Leading batter for Detroit in 1909 World Series with .346 average.

Year	Club	League	POS	G	AB	R	H	2B	3B	HR	RBI	SB	BA
1898	Montgomery	Southern	3B	23	92	19	22	4	2	0	-	1	.239

Year	Club	League	POS	G	AB	R	H	2B	3B	HR	RBI	SB	BA
	Allentown	Atlantic	SS	96	365	39	73	15	7	1	-	4	.200
1899	Allentown	Atlantic	OF	59	216	33	54	6	2	1	-	7	.250
1900	Allentown	Atlantic	SS-3B	33	147	40	44	9	4	1	-	4	.299
	Worcester	Eastern	3B	80	317	55	89	14	2	3	-	18	.281
1901	Chicago	National	3B-2B	17	63	4	12	2	0	0	4	5	.190
1902	New York	National	OF	7	26	3	6	1	0	0	3	0	.231
	Little Rock	South A	3B	101	381	82	125	27	**19**	0	-	17	.328
1903	Little Rock	South A	3B	90	345	69	132	32	6	1	-	16	**.383**
1904	Boston	National	3-2-O-P	142	499	56	142	27	8	3	60	16	.285
1905	Boston	National	OF-P	125	461	50	119	11	8	5	55	12	.258
1906	Cincinnati	National	3-S-O	115	379	63	106	21	4	1	39	21	.280
1907	SL/Wash	American	2-3-O-1	142	499	52	139	21	7	2	60	24	.279
1908	Washintgon	American	2B	83	287	33	91	11	4	1	30	16	.317
1909	Wash/Detroit	American	2B	136	452	47	105	23	6	1	41	13	.232
1910	Detroit	American	2B	106	378	67	111	16	3	2	45	15	.294
1911	Detroit	American	1-2-3	144	542	83	184	30	14	3	94	15	.339
1912	Detroit	American	2B-OF	78	266	34	76	14	1	0	41	9	.286
	Minneapolis	A A	1B-OF	27	96	18	43	7	2	0	-	1	.448
1913	Minneapolis	A A	1B-OF	157	610	81	181	25	4	4	-	5	.297
1914	Brooklyn	Federal	2B-1B	74	214	28	62	13	5	0	15	4	.290
1915	Brooklyn	Federal	2B	17	25	0	6	1	0	0	2	1	.240
	Hartford	Colonial	2B	76	256	33	97	19	2	0	-	14	**.379**
1916	Beaumont	Texas	2B	88	288	35	88	14	4	1	-	6	.306
Majors				**1186**	**4091**	**520**	**1159**	**191**	**60**	**18**	**489**	**151**	**.283**
Minors				**830**	**3113**	**504**	**948**	**172**	**54**	**12**	-	**93**	**.305**

JOSEPH NICHOLAS DELAHANTY

Born October 18, 1875 at Cleveland, OH. Died Janury 9, 1936 at Cleveland, OH.
Height 5' 9", Weight 168. Batted right. Threw right.

Brother of Ed, Frank, Jim, Tom and Will; all professional players.
Hit 30 triples in 86 games in 1899.

Year	Club	League	POS	G	AB	R	H	2B	3B	HR	RBI	SB	BA
1897	FR/Newport	New Eng	3B-2B	25	93	18	32	8	0	0	-	5	.344
1898	Pat/Allentown	Atlantic	OF-3B	85	322	43	100	11	12	2	-	10	.311
1899	Allentown	Atlantic	SS	86	337	73	116	11	**30**	3	-	25	.344
1900	Allentown	Atlantic	2B	33	143	44	**67**	8	**11**	1	-	2	**.469**
	Montreal	Eastern	2B	54	206	22	51	10	7	2	-	2	.248
1901	Montreal	Eastern	OF	131	517	78	151	31	17	4	-	19	.292
1902	Worcester	Eastern	3B	135	545	86	151	24	13	8	-	18	.277
1903	Worcester	Eastern	OF	40	165	24	43	4	3	3	-	6	.261
	NO/Memp	South A	2B-OF	48	197	34	73	18	3	6	-	4	.371
1904	Buffalo	Eastern	OF	132	475	77	134	**31**	11	1	-	33	.282
1905	Buffalo	Eastern	OF-1B	104	396	50	124	22	9	5	-	18	.313
1906	Williamsport	Tri-St	OF	113	423	56	118	23	**17**	5	-	13	.279
1907	Williamsport	Tri-St	OF	108	380	65	135	24	14	4	-	16	**.355**
	St. Louis	National	OF	6	21	3	7	0	0	1	2	3	.333
1908	St. Louis	National	OF	140	499	37	127	14	11	1	44	11	.255
1909	St. Louis	National	OF-2B	123	411	28	88	16	4	2	54	10	.214
1910	Toronto	Eastern	OF	144	522	60	150	29	10	2	-	10	.287
1911	Toronto	Eastern	OF	125	472	69	125	19	10	5	-	11	.265
1912	Cleveland	United St	OF	16	58	12	24	5	0	3	-	3	.414
	Wilkes-Barre	NY St	OF	44	154	21	42	9	3	1	-	6	.273
Majors				**269**	**931**	**68**	**222**	**30**	**15**	**4**	**100**	**24**	**.238**
Minors				**1423**	**5405**	**832**	**1636**	**287**	**170**	**55**	-	**201**	**.303**

THOMAS JAMES DELAHANTY

Born March 9, 1872 at Cleveland, OH. Died January 10, 1951 at Sanford, FL.
Height 5' 8", Weight 175. Batted left. Threw right.
Brother of Ed, Frank, Jim, Joe and Will, all professional players.
Manager: Denver WL 1903.

Year	Club	League	POS	G	AB	R	H	2B	3B	HR	SB	BA
1894	Peoria	West A	2B	101	437	91	130	16	13	10	18	.297
	Philadelphia	National	2B	1	4	0	1	0	0	0	0	.250
1895	Atlanta	Southern	2B	104	455	112	132	29	8	3	65	.290
	Detroit	Western	2B	16	66	21	27	0	0	1	4	.409
1896	Cleve/Pitt	National	3B-SS	17	59	12	14	4	0	0	4	.237
	Toronto	Eastern	SS	99	383	86	94	10	5	2	40	.245
1897	Louisville	National	2B	1	4	1	1	1	0	0	0	.250
	Mil/KC/Det	Western	2B-SS	94	381	92	114	20	6	2	25	.299
	Newark	Atlantic	2B	22	86	20	27	6	1	0	4	.314
1898	Allen/New	Atlantic	2B	118	420	77	121	16	6	0	25	.288
1899	Allentown	Atlantic	2B	54	210	38	70	6	3	0	12	.333
1900	Allentown	Atlantic	2B	19	82	18	26	7	2	0	1	.317
	Cleveland	American	2B	3	10	0	2	0	0	0	0	.200
	Young/Mar	Inter-St	2B	52	193	21	52	9	0	0	8	.269
1901	Col/Mar	West A	2B	61	224	36	70	11	0	1	5	.313
	Denver	Western	2-S-O-1	18	65	6	10	1	1	0	1	.154
1902	Denver	Western	2B	137	554	118	194	19	13	4	38	.350
1903	Denver	Western	2B-OF	113	461	82	143	13	7	1	19	.310
1904	Seattle	P C	3B	194	830	117	229	36	9	2	36	.276
1905	Pueb/Co Sps	Western	3B-1B	72	286	51	87	10	3	0	13	.304
1906	Williamsport	Tri-St	OF	27	101	15	17	3	1	0	7	.168
		Majors		**19**	**67**	**13**	**16**	**5**	**0**	**0**	**4**	**.239**
		Minors		**1304**	**5244**	**1001**	**1545**	**212**	**78**	**26**	**321**	**.295**

WILLIAM JOHN "WILL" DELAHANTY

Born February 28, 1886 at Cleveland, OH. Died October 16, 1957 at Cleveland, OH.
Height 5' 9", Weight 165. Batted right. Threw right.
Brother of Ed, Frank, Jim, Joe and Tom; all professional players. On June 28, 1905, hit 2-run
homer in 18th to beat Zanesville 5-4.

Year	Club	League	POS	G	AB	R	H	2B	3B	HR	SB	BA
1905	Niles	Ohio-Pa	OF-2B	49	186	27	52	9	2	2	11	.280
1906	Mansfield	Ohio-Pa	SS	134	523	59	130	15	6	0	39	.249
1907	Mansfield	Ohio-Pa	SS	103	355	49	94	12	9	1	23	.265
1908	Wilkes-Barre	NY St	SS	84	296	46	81	8	5	4	10	.274
1909	W-B/Bing	NY St	SS-2-3	25	71	8	16	6	0	0	2	.225
1910	Waterbury	Conn	OF	8	21	3	6	2	1	0	1	.286
	Ashland	Vir Val	OF	8	22	0	7	5	0	0	0	.318
1911	Cmbus/Cmbia	Sally	2B-3B	138	475	75	131	26	5	2	0	.276
1912	Zanesville	Central	2B	13	45	7	10	0	1	0	6	.222
		Minors		**562**	**1994**	**274**	**527**	**83**	**29**	**9**	**122**	**.264**

OTTO GEORGE DENNING
Born December 28, 1912 at Hays, KS. Died May 25, 1992 at Chicago, IL.
Height 5' 11", Weight 180. Batted right. Threw right.
Manager: Pensacola SEastern and Oil City MAL 1948; Oil City MAL 1949; Waterloo III 1950; Waterloo III and Colorado Springs WL 1951.

Year	Club	League	POS	G	AB	R	H	2B	3B	HR	RBI	SB	BA
1932	Davenport	Miss Val	OF	31	78	9	15	3	2	0	7	1	.192
1933	Davenport	Miss Val	C	96	356	67	113	27	4	5	72	4	.317
1934	Davenport	Western	C-1B	100	376	53	117	30	3	1	72	10	.311
1935	Davenport	Western	C-OF	90	320	51	85	21	2	2	54	3	.266
1936	Davenport	Western	1B-C	114	432	73	128	34	3	5	74	9	.296
1937	Elmira	NY-Penn	C-1-O	111	370	55	125	25	3	5	64	13	.338
1938	Minneapolis	A A	C-1B	81	228	34	78	18	4	9	42	1	.342
1939	Minneapolis	A A	C-OF	71	195	31	59	10	2	13	47	1	.303
1940	Minneapolis	A A	C-1B	130	410	59	135	22	8	11	74	6	.329
1941	Minneapolis	A A	C-1B	144	510	85	168	34	4	17	105	4	.329
1942	Cleveland	American	C-OF	92	214	15	45	14	0	1	19	0	.210
1943	Cleveland	American	1B	37	129	8	31	6	0	0	13	3	.240
	Buffalo	Int	C-1B	112	376	52	107	17	5	9	58	8	.285
1944	Buffalo	Int	O-1-C	142	527	100	152	34	3	21	99	16	.288
1945	Milwaukee	A A	1B	143	483	79	148	21	5	9	92	15	.306
1946	Toronto	Int	1B-C	33	120	16	28	11	0	2	19	0	.233
	Mil/Louis	A A	1B-C	40	60	8	19	3	0	0	9	1	.317
1947	Louis/Mil	A A	C-1B	34	41	8	12	3	0	0	3	0	.293
1948	Pensacola	SEastern	1B	6	10	0	0	0	0	0	0	0	.000
	Oil City	Mid Atl	1B	34	117	30	43	6	0	6	37	0	.368
1949	Oil City	Mid Atl	C-1B	77	205	51	79	21	0	11	62	1	.385
1950	Waterloo	III	C-1B	12	14	0	2	1	0	0	1	1	.143
	Majors			**129**	**343**	**23**	**76**	**20**	**0**	**1**	**32**	**3**	**.222**
	Minors			**1601**	**5228**	**861**	**1613**	**341**	**48**	**126**	**991**	**94**	**.309**

GEORGE FRANCIS DETORE
Born November 11, 1906 at Utica, NY.
Height 5' 8", Weight 170. Batted right. Threw right.
Manager: San Diego P C 1943-44; Toledo A A 1946; Williamsport EL 1947; Toledo A A 1948; Salisbury NCSL 1950-51; Bristol Appalach 1952-53; St. Jean Provincl 1954; Salem Appalach 1964-66.

Year	Club	League	POS	G	AB	R	H	2B	3B	HR	RBI	SB	BA
1929	Decatur	III	3B-SS	135	488	106	167	16	18	10	93	29	.342
1930	New Orleans	South A	3B	126	430	74	143	27	9	3	79	13	.333
	Cleveland	American	3B	3	12	0	2	1	0	0	2	0	.167
1931	Cleveland	American	3-S-2	30	56	3	15	6	0	0	7	2	.268
	New Orleans	South A	3B	28	112	17	34	3	3	1	22	3	.304
1932	Buffalo	Int	3B	157	590	132	187	39	4	24	97	8	.317
1933	Toledo	A A	2-3-C	137	508	103	179	37	7	11	82	16	.352
1934	Louis/Mil	A A	1-2-3	113	380	51	102	18	5	6	45	8	.268
1935	Milwaukee	A A	3B-C	120	375	65	107	23	5	7	68	11	.285
1936	Milwaukee	A A	C	89	264	46	87	10	5	6	38	10	.330
1937	San Diego	P C	C	133	434	70	145	22	8	3	72	16	**.334**
1938	San Diego	P C	C-3B	109	296	48	77	12	4	3	40	8	.260
1939	San Diego	P C	C-1B	129	411	59	146	28	5	4	72	12	.355
1940	San Diego	P C	C	90	265	45	85	18	5	2	35	3	.321

1941	San Diego	P C	C-1B	118	378	61	121	26	6	5	61	9	.320
1942	San Diego	P C	C-1B	106	303	37	76	12	3	2	38	3	.251
1943	San Diego	P C	C	73	187	26	60	12	1	1	29	1	.321
1944	San Diego	P C	C	32	48	8	14	3	1	0	4	1	.292
1945	Indianpolis	A A	C	78	186	19	44	5	0	1	22	2	.237
1946	Toledo	A A		Manager and coach; did not play									
1947	Williamsport	Eastern	C	1	1	0	1	0	0	0	2	0	1.000
		Majors		**33**	**68**	**3**	**17**	**7**	**0**	**0**	**9**	**2**	**.250**
		Minors		**1774**	**5656**	**967**	**1775**	**311**	**89**	**89**	**899**	**153**	**.314**

VINCENT PAUL DI MAGGIO

Born September 6, 1912 at Martinez, CA. Died October 3, 1986 at North Hollywood, CA.
Height 5' 11", Weight 183. Batted right. Threw right.
Brother of Joe and Dom. Hit home run in first O.B. at bat April 7, 1932.
Manager: Stockton Calif 1948; Pittsburg Far West 1949-51.

Year	Club	League	POS	G	AB	R	H	2B	3B	HR	RBI	SB	BA
1932	Tucson	Ariz-Tex	IF-OF	94	398	90	138	22	9	**25**	81	14	.347
	San Francisco	P C	OF	59	200	35	54	13	2	6	31	2	.270
1933	SF/Holly	P C	OF	96	339	54	113	24	4	11	65	7	.333
1934	Hollywood	P C	OF	166	587	89	169	25	3	17	91	7	.288
1935	Hollywood	P C	OF	174	659	107	183	36	4	24	112	15	.278
1936	San Diego	P C	OF	176	641	109	188	43	14	19	102	22	.293
1937	Boston	National	OF	132	493	56	126	18	4	13	69	8	.256
1938	Boston	National	OF-2B	150	540	71	123	28	3	14	61	11	.228
1939	Kansas City	A A	OF	154	544	122	158	32	9	**46**	**136**	21	.290
	Cincinnati	National	OF	8	14	1	1	1	0	0	2	0	.071
1940	Cinci/Pitt	National	OF	112	360	61	104	26	0	19	54	11	.289
1941	Pittsburgh	National	OF	151	528	73	141	27	5	21	100	10	.267
1942	Pittsburgh	National	OF	143	496	57	118	22	3	15	75	10	.238
1943	Pittsburgh	National	OF-SS	157	580	64	144	41	2	15	88	11	.248
1944	Pittsburgh	National	OF-3B	109	342	41	82	20	4	9	50	6	.240
1945	Philadelphia	National	OF	127	452	64	116	25	3	19	84	12	.257
1946	Phil/NY	National	OF	21	44	3	4	1	0	0	1	0	.091
	San Francisco	P C	OF	43	129	19	34	10	2	1	21	3	.264
1947	Oakland	P C	OF	140	473	80	114	20	4	22	81	7	.241
1948	Stockton	Calif	OF	127	420	108	119	24	1	**30**	100	15	.283
1949	Pittsburg	Far West	OF	101	362	108	133	19	1	37	117	11	.367
1950	Pittsburg	Far West	OF	125	434	105	153	28	6	26	129	15	.353
1951	Pittsburg	Far West	OF	44	127	32	33	9	1	4	29	4	.260
	Tacoma	West Int	OF	74	236	35	53	12	2	5	44	6	.225
		Majors		**1110**	**3849**	**491**	**959**	**209**	**24**	**125**	**584**	**79**	**.249**
		Minors		**1573**	**5549**	**1093**	**1642**	**317**	**62**	**273**	**1139**	**149**	**.296**

CARL HENRY DITTMAR

Born March 21, 1901 at Baltimore, MD.
Height 5' 9", Weight 168. Batted right. Threw right.
Manager: Bisbee Ariz-Tex 1939-41.
Currently resides in Laguna Hills, CA.

Year	Club	League	POS	G	AB	R	H	2B	3B	HR	RBI	SB	BA
1922	Crisfield	E Shore	SS	69	230	38	59	8	2	3	-	7	.257

1923	Crisfield	E Shore	SS	58	221	31	58	5	4	7	-	4	.262
1924	Muskogee	West A	SS	163	567	104	176	36	8	17	114	17	.310
1925	Muskogee	West A	SS	150	561	110	160	34	4	24	95	8	.285
1926	Augusta	Sally	SS	139	473	66	118	21	5	2	63	7	.249
1927	San Francisco	P C	SS	164	570	86	153	32	3	4	71	5	.268
1928	Los Angeles	P C	SS	180	626	71	159	22	6	2	63	15	.254
1929	Los Angeles	P C	SS	154	505	83	153	30	4	5	43	14	.303
1930	Los Angeles	P C	SS	166	622	94	193	39	5	14	125	13	.310
1931	Los Angeles	P C	SS	139	470	78	134	25	5	8	95	11	.285
1932	Los Angeles	P C	SS	174	583	86	174	40	3	4	78	9	.298
1933	Los Angeles	P C	SS	149	478	61	126	19	2	5	49	2	.264
1934	Los Angeles	P C	SS	151	517	75	152	33	2	3	73	7	.294
1935	Los Angeles	P C	SS	78	215	21	56	6	1	0	36	2	.260
1936	Los Angeles	P C	SS-2B	125	427	47	122	16	2	1	44	5	.286
1937	Los Angeles	P C	2B	72	228	20	63	8	1	0	37	1	.276
1938	Los Angeles	P C	3-S-2	11	19	1	4	2	0	0	2	0	.211
1939	Bisbee	Ariz-Tex	2B	19	38	8	14	2	0	0	4	0	.368
	Minors			**2161**	**7350**	**1080**	**2074**	**378**	**57**	**99**	**992**	**127**	**.282**

FREDERICK E. "DUTCH" DORMAN

Born June 6, 1902, at Carlstadt, NJ. Died April 5, 1988, at York, PA.
Height 5' 9-1/2", Weight 155. Batted right. Threw right.

Manager: Johnsown Mid Atl 1936; York NYPL 1936; Duluth Northern 1937-39; Cooleemee NCSL 1940; Hagerstown Inter-St 1941-43; Wilmington Inter-St 1944; Hagerstown Inter-St 1945; Hartford EL 1946-47; Pawtucket NEL 1949; Hagerstown Inter-St 1950-52; Hagerstown Piedmond 1953; Allentown EL 1954; Waterloo III 1955; Sunbury Piedmont 1955.

While managing Wilmington on July 8, 1944, attacked umpire Hal Lyons and was suspended for remainder of season.

Year	Club	League	POS	G	AB	R	H	2B	3B	HR	RBI	SB	BA
1922	Winston	Piedmont	SS	105	338	34	77	14	0	0	-	11	.228
1923	Danville	Piedmont	SS	126	493	**107**	154	30	6	5	-	33	.312
1924	Williamsport	NY-Penn	SS	134	514	115	158	24	6	3	-	28	.307
1925	Wichita Falls	Texas	3B	127	454	68	124	24	5	0	59	6	.273
1926	Wichita Falls	Texas	3B-SS	11	38	8	11	4	0	0	8	1	.289
1927	Beaumont	Texas	3B	153	565	79	155	29	6	2	49	22	.274
1928	Williamsport	NY-Penn	3B	78	299	50	90	13	5	0	23	7	.301
1929	Manchester	New Eng	SS	105	404	84	128	19	6	1	51	6	.317
	Springfield	Eastern	3B-SS	11	28	3	8	1	0	0	2	2	.286
1930	WB/Wp/El/Y	NY-Penn	2B-3B	111	376	75	110	11	10	1	46	13	.293
1931	York	NY-Penn	2B-3B	131	465	96	146	19	3	1	37	16	.314
1932	York	NY-Penn	2B	81	315	56	102	9	2	0	48	14	.324
1933	Scran/York	NY-Penn	3B-2B	141	507	79	139	26	3	0	54	18	.274
1934	Hazleton	NY-Penn	3B	133	496	102	141	26	8	2	52	17	.284
1935	Hazleton	NY-Penn	2B	132	494	103	137	19	6	1	41	4	.277
1936	York/W-B	NY-Penn	3B-2B	85	340	75	108	19	5	0	35	5	.318
	Johnstown	Mid Atl	OF	41	149	37	54	9	0	0	16	6	.362
1937	Duluth	Northern	2B	123	453	**124**	153	**32**	2	0	58	14	.338
1938	Duluth	Northern	2B	120	440	98	132	32	3	0	53	20	.300
1939	Duluth	Northern	2B	120	422	91	123	20	1	0	36	25	.291
1940	Portsmouth	Mid Atl	2B	43	124	42	26	7	2	0	16	3	.210
	Cooleemee	N Car St	2B	18	67	12	23	2	0	0	7	2	.343
	Sunbury	Inter-St	3B	44	163	37	49	9	2	2	15	1	.301
1941	Hagerstown	Inter-St	3B	122	398	79	97	17	2	0	28	7	.244

1942	Hagerstown	Inter-St	3B-OF	95	254	44	68	9	0	0	23	8	.268
1943	Wilmington	Inter-St	3B-SS	108	335	62	92	14	3	0	29	8	.275
1944	Wilmington	Inter-St	2B-OF	7	25	1	4	0	0	0	3	1	.160
1945	Hagerstown	Inter-St	3-S-P	16	32	11	5	2	1	0	2	1	.156
1946	Hartford	Eastern	3B-SS	7	16	2	4	1	0	0	1	0	.250
1947	Hartford	Eastern	3B-SS	12	21	7	5	2	0	0	3	1	.238
		Minors		**2540**	**9025**	**1781**	**2623**	**443**	**87**	**18**	**795**	**300**	**.291**

WILLIE ELEANOR DUKE
Born July 5, 1909 at Franklinton, NC.
Height 5' 9", Weight 175. Batted left. Threw right.
Graduated from North Carolina State University in 1933 with a degree in business administration.
Manager: Clinton Tobac St 1946; Durham Carolina 1947-48; Winston-Salem Carolina 1949.
Currently resides in Raleigh, NC

Year	Club	League	POS	G	AB	R	H	2B	3B	HR	RBI	SB	BA
1934	Nash/Memp	South A	OF	74	273	39	88	16	8	3	53	6	.322
	Jackson	E Dixie	OF	75	294	79	102	26	8	7	46	13	.347
1935	Memphis	South A	OF	157	603	91	190	26	12	13	100	20	.315
1936	Memphis	South A	OF	137	505	84	174	25	18	17	102	6	.345
1937	Nashville	South A	OF	126	448	86	139	32	5	**19**	94	9	.310
1938	Minneapolis	A A	OF	15	28	6	7	1	1	1	2	0	.250
	Nashville	South A	OF	62	199	32	57	9	1	4	28	3	.286
1939	NO/Atlanta	South A	OF	141	496	81	158	34	8	12	101	6	.319
1940	Little Rock	South A	OF	151	573	111	207	39	6	8	93	7	.361
1941	Little Rock	South A	OF	36	122	25	41	10	2	2	18	0	.336
	Elmira	Eastern	OF	109	394	64	109	23	2	5	45	5	.277
1942	Knox/Memp	South A	OF	68	239	39	74	20	2	7	37	2	.310
	Wilmington	Inter-St	OF	33	130	13	29	9	1	3	22	1	.223
	Portsmouth	Piedmont	OF	31	86	9	18	4	1	0	10	0	.209
1943-45					Military Service								
1946	Clinton	Tobac St	OF	96	328	106	129	29	6	27	109	15	**.393**
1947	Durham	Carolina	OF	122	439	104	169	**42**	4	13	117	2	.385
1948	Durham	Carolina	OF	110	346	104	123	36	7	12	89	3	.355
1949	WS/Danville	Carolina	OF	119	413	80	144	37	1	22	106	3	.349
1950	Green/Ral	Carolina	OF	53	154	30	47	6	1	5	36	0	.305
	Rockingham	Tobac St	OF	38	138	37	48	11	3	4	35	2	.348
		Minors		**1753**	**6208**	**1220**	**2053**	**435**	**97**	**184**	**1243**	**103**	**.331**

CECIL HENRY "BABE" DYE
Born May 13, 1898 at Hamilton, Ont. Died January 2, 1962 at Chicago, IL.
Height 5' 8", Weight 155. Batted left. Threw left.
In National Hockey League Hall of Fame. Led NHL in goals three times and in scoring twice.

Year	Club	League	POS	G	AB	R	H	2B	3B	HR	RBI	SB	BA
1920	Tor/Syra	Int	OF	3	9	0	1	0	0	0	0	0	.111
	Brantford	Mich-Ont	OF	75	260	37	85	11	2	1	20	17	.327
1921	Brantford	Mich-Ont	OF	104	436	67	153	20	10	8	87	26	.351
1922	Buffalo	Int	OF	134	468	88	146	26	12	4	67	18	.312
1923	Buffalo	Int	OF	155	619	133	197	40	13	16	87	29	.318
1924	Buffalo	Int	OF	164	650	114	202	43	7	10	75	20	.311
1925	Buffalo	Int	OF	125	443	77	130	21	7	5	46	5	.293
1926	Tor/Balt	Int	OF	51	181	26	39	5	1	1	20	3	.215
		Minors		**811**	**3066**	**542**	**953**	**166**	**52**	**45**	**402**	**118**	**.311**

CHARLES EUGENE "TRUCK" EAGAN

Born August 10, 1877 at Oakland, CA. Died March 19, 1949 at San Francisco, CA.
Height 5' 11", Weight 190. Batted right. Threw right.
Led all minor leagues in home runs in 1904 and in 1905.

Year	Club	League	Pos	G	AB	R	H	2B	3B	HR	SB	BA
1898	SF/San Jose	PC	2B-SS	42	172	26	41	9	1	1	8	.238
1899	Sacramento	Calif	SS	81	333	58	92	19	2	7	27	.276
1900	Sacramento	Calif	SS	88	327	70	90	18	3	11	23	.275
1901	Pittsburgh	National	SS	4	12	0	1	0	0	0	1	.3
	Cleveland	American	2B-3B	5	18	2	3	0	1	0	0	.167
	Oakland	Calif	1-3-S	114	435	64	106	22	1	8	14	.244
1902	Sacramento	Calif	S-1B	159	653	70	168	29	5	4	18	.257
1903	Los Angeles	P C	SS	206	818	137	262	56	24	13	56	.320
1904	Tacoma	P C	IF	191	736	121	229	52	7	25	29	11
1905	Tacoma	P C	SS	210	774	104	215	49	3	21	29	.278
1906	Fresno	P C	SS	167	652	70	170	18	12	2	22	.261
1907	Oakland	P C	SS	194	708	96	237	45	2	10	31	.335
1908	Oakland	P C	S-1B	184	687	81	180	28	2	9	17	.262
1909	Vernon	P C	2B-SS	188	647	65	144	27	2	9	14	.223
1910	Sacramento	Calif	SS	36	130	13	38	7	2	0	0	.292
1911	Richmond	Virginia	2B	61	216	38	66	19	6	3	8	.306
		Majors		**9**	**30**	**2**	**4**	**0**	**1**	**0**	**1**	**.133**
		Minors		**1921**	**7288**	**1013**	**2038**	**398**	**72**	**123**	**296**	**.280**

PATRICK PETER "PETE" EAGAN

Year	Club	League	POS	G	AB	R	H	2B	3B	HR	SB	BA
1890	Troy	NY St	OF	74	326	78	109	11	7	2	48	.334
1891	Troy	East A	OF	27	119	14	23	4	0	0	12	.193
1892	Rochester	Eastern	OF	1	4	1	1	0	0	0	1	.250
	Danville	Pa St	OF	29	115	21	32	3	1	0	1	.278
1893	Harrisburg	Pa St	OF	74	322	65	108	19	8	0	25	.335
1894	Harrisburg	Pa St	OF-2B	87	377	93	126	18	8	3	-	.334
1895	Harrisburg	Pa St	OF	30	136	42	51	12	2	0	9	.375
	Scranton	Eastern	OF	74	328	57	100	22	5	0	10	.305
1896	Scranton	Eastern	OF	101	431	91	145	26	8	3	39	.336
1897	Scranton	Eastern	OF	98	420	77	127	21	2	5	14	.302
1898	Roch-Buf	Eastern	OF	24	92	9	23	4	0	0	3	.250
	Utica	NY St	OF	64	282	51	103	20	4	2	10	.365
1899	Scranton	Atlantic	OF	63	238	30	74	15	3	1	5	.311
	Utica	NY St	OF	64	250	52	87	7	5	0	17	.348
1900	Cortland	NY St	OF	109	466	89	163	25	3	1	11	.350
1901	Montreal	Eastern	OF	10	43	6	13	1	0	0	0	.302
	Schenectady	NY St	OF	102	437	57	128	15	2	0	25	.293
1902	Ilion	NY St	OF	105	421	41	118	16	1	0	13	.280
1903	Albany	NY St	OF	112	453	48	123	15	0	0	17	.272
1904	JAG	NY St	OF	108	450	54	135	18	8	2	12	.300
1905	JAG	NY St	OF	99	409	49	119	19	5	1	18	.291
1906	JAG	NY St	OF	132	528	60	136	14	6	0	25	.258
1907	Troy	NY St	OF	115	466	46	131	15	3	0	14	.281
1908	Troy	NY St	OF	124	484	44	130	16	1	1	12	.269
		Minors		**1828**	**7608**	**1178**	**2309**	**336**	**82**	**21**	**343**	**.303**

HERBERT SPENCER "BABE" ELLISON
Born November 15, 1895 at Rutland, AR. Died August 11, 1955 at San Francisco, CA.
Height 5' 11", Weight 170. Batted right. Threw right.
Attended University of Arkansas.
Manager: San Francisco P C 1923-26; Dallas T L 1928.
Served in the U.S. Army for most of 1918 season. Hit three home runs in consecutive games against Salt Lake City, May 24 and 25, 1924.

Year	Club	League	POS	G	AB	R	H	2B	3B	HR	RBI	SB	BA
1915	Clinton	Cent A	SS	112	398	49	100	18	2	2	-	17	.251
1916	Muscatine	Cent A	3B	127	493	103	**178**	**46**	**16**	4	-	19	**.361**
	Detroit	American	3B	2	7	0	1	0	0	0	1	0	.143
1917	St. Paul	A A	2B-OF	139	528	72	147	15	22	5	-	19	.278
	Detroit	American	1B	9	29	2	5	1	2	1	4	0	.172
1918	Detroit	American	OF-2B	7	23	1	6	1	0	0	2	1	.261
1919	Detroit	American	2-O-S	56	134	18	29	4	0	0	11	4	.216
1920	Detroit	American	1-0-3	61	155	11	34	7	2	0	21	4	.219
1921	San Francisco	P C	0-2-1	171	634	124	197	46	4	18	102	10	.311
1922	San Francisco	P C	1B	187	718	116	220	30	10	16	**141**	20	.306
1923	San Francisco	P C	1B-2B	192	757	145	271	67	10	23	139	12	.358
1924	San Francisco	P C	1B	**201**	805	142	**307**	68	11	33	**188**	10	.381
1925	San Francisco	P C	1B-2B	174	708	122	230	38	7	22	160	8	.325
1926	San Francisco	P C	1-2-3	105	321	36	97	28	0	3	48	1	.302
1927	San Francisco	P C	OF-1B	12	28	5	7	1	1	1	5	0	.250
	Minneapolis	A A	1B	52	149	20	37	5	0	4	29	2	.248
1928	Dallas	Texas	1B-2B	79	255	41	76	16	0	7	39	0	.298
		Majors		**135**	**348**	**32**	**75**	**13**	**4**	**1**	**39**	**9**	**.216**
		Minors		**1551**	**5794**	**975**	**1867**	**378**	**83**	**138**	**851**	**118**	**.322**

GILBERT RAYMOND ENGLISH
Born July 2, 1909 at Glenola, NC.
Height 5'11", Weight 180. Batted right. Threw right.

Year	Club	League	POS	G	AB	R	H	2B	3B	HR	RBI	SB	BA
1930	Durham	Piedmont	3B-OF	130	485	67	137	28	5	11	73	6	.282
1931	Durham	Piedmont	3B	127	486	82	167	35	6	19	106	6	.344
	New York	National	3B	3	8	0	0	0	0	0	0	0	.000
1932	Bridgeport	Eastern	3B	72	291	46	91	16	4	5	44	1	.313
	New York	National	3B-SS	59	204	22	46	7	5	2	19	0	.225
1933	Buffalo/JC	Int	3B	134	467	64	130	21	4	13	76	1	.278
1934	Portland	P C	3B-OF	167	634	75	177	33	5	9	73	11	.279
1935	Portland	P C	3B	171	675	107	221	35	8	8	118	9	.327
1936	Detroit	American	3B	1	1	0	0	0	0	0	0	0	.000
	Buffalo	Int	3B	19	66	6	13	2	0	0	10	0	.197
	Toledo	A A	3B	102	412	74	138	21	15	5	78	4	.335
1937	Detroit	American	2B	18	65	6	17	1	0	1	6	1	.262
	Boston	National	3B	79	269	25	78	5	2	2	37	3	.290
1938	Boston	National	3-O-S-2	53	165	17	41	6	0	2	21	1	.248
	Kansas City	A A	3B	20	58	5	9	2	0	0	7	0	.155
1939	St. Paul	A A	3B	139	501	96	172	35	7	19	92	4	**.343**
1940	St. Paul	A A	3B	127	480	65	152	15	9	19	89	6	.317
1941	St. Paul	A A	3B-OF	152	551	84	174	32	5	13	93	9	.316
1942	St. Paul/Ind.	A A	OF-3B	134	475	48	120	27	6	4	57	0	.253
1943	Indianapolis	A A	OF-3B	141	543	80	175	26	3	3	83	0	.322

Year	Club	League	POS	G	AB	R	H	2B	3B	HR	RBI	SB	BA
1944	Brooklyn	National	S-3-2	27	79	4	12	3	0	1	7	0	.152
	Indianapolis	A A	3-O-1	91	332	59	107	18	6	4	47	2	.322
1945	Indianapolis	A A	3B-OF	137	504	81	144	26	6	9	97	2	.286
1946	Indianapolis	A A	3B	58	135	16	41	7	0	3	17	2	.304
	Majors			**240**	**791**	**74**	**194**	**22**	**7**	**8**	**90**	**5**	**.245**
	Minors			**1921**	**7095**	**1055**	**2168**	**379**	**89**	**144**	**1160**	**63**	**.306**

FRANCISCO "PAQUIN" ESTRADA (SOTO)
Born February 12, 1948 at Navojoa, Sonora, Mexico.
Height 5' 8", Weight 182. Bats right. Throws right.
Probably holds O. B. record for most games caught in career.

Year	Club	League	POS	G	AB	R	H	2B	3B	HR	RBI	SB	BA
1964	San L. Potosi	Mex Cent	C-OF	73	172	20	37	8	0	5	21	0	.215
1965	San L. Potosi	Mex Cent	C	128	438	76	111	18	7	10	64	1	.253
1966	MC Reds	Mexican	C	74	160	20	38	11	0	3	12	0	.238
1967	MC Reds	Mexican	C	136	469	57	132	22	2	8	72	4	.281
1968	MC Reds	Mexican	C	140	425	48	105	15	2	7	44	5	.247
1969	MC Reds	Mexican	C-1B	116	318	32	83	12	4	3	34	3	.261
1970	MC Reds	Mexican	C-1-3	138	442	83	134	24	11	18	85	1	.303
1971	Memphis	Texas	C	51	159	22	40	8	0	7	28	1	.252
	Tidewater	Int	C	58	192	20	50	7	0	6	21	0	.260
	New York	National	C	1	2	0	1	0	0	0	0	0	.500
1972	Salt L City	P C	C	21	41	2	11	2	0	0	4	0	.268
	Rochester	Int	C	65	202	23	51	5	1	6	15	0	.252
1973	Midland	Texas	C	67	212	30	63	13	0	6	25	2	.297
	Wichita	A A	C	2	9	0	2	1	0	0	2	0	.222
1974	Puebla	Mexican	C-1B	125	443	72	138	19	2	8	54	5	.312
1975	Puebla	Mexican	C-3B	122	442	50	139	17	1	5	64	4	.314
1976	Puebla	Mexican	C	110	350	30	90	8	2	1	35	0	.257
1977	Puebla	Mexican	C-1B	137	439	50	124	15	1	5	59	2	.282
1978	Puebla	Mexican	C-1B	140	460	55	147	18	3	3	61	6	.320
1979	Puebla	Mexican	C	112	399	54	129	19	1	2	69	4	.323
1980	Puebla	Mex #1	C	84	307	38	83	13	0	2	46	3	.270
1981	Campeche	Mexican	C	112	389	29	98	7	1	0	34	1	.252
1982	Campeche	Mexican	C	119	362	27	90	7	1	2	39	6	.249
1983	Campeche	Mexican	C	81	245	23	61	9	0	1	24	3	.249
1984	Toluca/Leon	Mexican	C	86	284	33	70	12	0	0	23	2	.246
1985	Campeche	Mexican	C	77	213	24	49	9	0	2	20	2	.230
1986	Campeche	Mexican	C	88	286	30	87	14	1	3	32	7	.304
1987	Campeche	Mexican	C	87	246	32	64	15	0	4	30	4	.260
1988	Campeche	Mexican	C	57	150	14	46	3	0	2	10	2	.307
1989	Leon	Mexican	C	43	121	14	31	4	0	0	8	3	.256
1990	Leon	Mexican	C	23	57	3	11	1	0	0	4	0	.193
1991	Leon	Mexican	C	75	229	23	64	8	1	1	36	0	.279
	Majors			**1**	**2**	**0**	**1**	**0**	**0**	**0**	**0**	**0**	**.500**
	Minors			**2747**	**8661**	**1034**	**2378**	**344**	**41**	**120**	**1075**	**71**	**.275**

●

The Cleveland Plain Dealer *made this comment on July 4, 1897: "There is a Texas League twirler of the name of Drinkwater. He is safe from any possible draft by the Louisville club. Such a name as his would at once make enemies of the Kentucky bleachers, to say nothing of driving them to drink."*

WOODROW CLARK "WOODY" FAIR
Born April 11, 1914 at Turner, WA.
Height 5' 10", Weight 170. Batted right. Threw right.
Manager: New Iberia Evang 1942; Carthage KOM 1947; Danville Carolina 1948-49; Iola KOM 1952.

Year	Club	League	POS	G	AB	R	H	2B	3B	HR	RBI	SB	BA
1934	Rogers	Ark St	OF	55	212	36	51	6	2	7	46	10	.241
1935	Rogers/Cass	Ark St	OF-3B	100	402	80	113	21	10	20	75	30	.281
1936	Monett	Ark-Mo	SS-OF	102	409	104	127	23	6	21	84	39	.311
1937	Springfield	West A	C-OF	13	37	9	9	2	2	0	4	4	.243
	New Iberia	Evang	O-2-S	90	333	57	101	23	11	8	40	7	.303
1938	New Iberia	Evang	OF	75	290	42	82	23	6	7	50	6	.283
1939	New Iberia	Evang	O-S-C	121	457	89	141	34	8	16	83	19	.309
1940	New Iberia	Evang	O-2-S	135	510	101	162	26	6	**24**	**125**	27	.318
1941	New Iberia	Evang	OF-3B	131	502	95	154	29	8	**13**	**113**	13	.307
1942	New Iberia	Evang	OF-SS	31	108	18	36	6	2	1	9	2	.333
	Memphis	South A	SS-OF	19	71	9	20	4	2	0	12	1	.282
1943	Memphis	South A	OF-SS	24	85	9	13	0	1	0	11	1	.153
	Utica	Eastern	2B-OF	97	361	59	109	21	8	3	71	12	.302
	Toronto	Int	OF	6	24	3	7	1	0	0	0	1	.292
1944-5					Did not play in O.B.								
1946	Durham	Carolina	OF-SS	139	569	**161**	198	**51**	7	24	**161**	7	.348
1947	Carthage	KOM	2B	73	274	67	104	19	4	11	63	17	.380
	Winston-Sal	Carolina	2-S-3	46	184	44	65	24	3	7	43	9	.353
1948	Danville	Carolina	OF	96	378	104	127	24	2	29	110	13	.336
1949	Danville	Carolina	OF-SS	134	523	109	170	32	4	38	117	11	.325
1950	Danville	Carolina	OF-3B	142	540	92	162	22	2	23	**103**	5	.300
1951	Raleigh	Carolina	OF	44	165	18	42	7	0	2	25	1	.255
	Lakeland	Fla Int	OF	89	328	41	93	24	2	8	68	5	.284
1952	Lakeland	Fla Int	OF	62	228	27	55	4	6	4	23	1	.241
	Iola	KOM	3B	68	265	67	79	12	3	9	57	22	.298
	Minors			**1892**	**7255**	**1441**	**2220**	**438**	**105**	**275**	**1493**	**263**	**.306**

WILLIAM BEATTIE FEATHERS
(Known by middle name.)
Born August 4, 1908 at Bristol, VA. Died March 11, 1979 at Winston-Salem, NC.
Height 5' 10", Weight 185. Batted right. Threw right.
All-American football player at University of Tennessee in 1933. Played in NFL for Chicago Bears, 1934-37, Brooklyn 1938-39, and Green Bay 1940. Selected to All-Pro team in 1934 season. Head baseball and football coach at North Carolina State 1944-51.
Manager: Kingsport Appalach 1943.

Year	Club	League	POS	G	AB	R	H	2B	3B	HR	RBI	SB	BA
1936	Greenville	Cottn St	OF	4	11	4	3	0	0	0	2	2	.273
	Americus	Ga-Fla	OF	61	240	58	95	11	4	9	52	4	.396
	Knoxville	South A	OF	19	77	16	32	4	4	5	20	0	.416
1937	Jackson	SEastern	OF	83	302	42	81	8	4	6	48	14	.268
	Knoxville	South A	OF	36	131	13	37	6	1	0	19	0	.282
1938	Jackson	SEastern	OF	119	411	73	120	23	7	9	77	12	.292
1939	Jackson	SEastern	OF	7	4	1	0	0	0	0	0	0	.000
	Palatka	Fla St	OF	25	91	17	24	6	1	1	15	1	.264
	Pen. Gap	Appalach	OF	66	236	49	76	13	8	3	47	8	.322
1940-41					Did not play in O.B.								

Year	Club	League	POS	G	AB	R	H	2B	3B	HR	RBI	SB	BA
1942	Statesville	N Car St	OF	87	338	51	100	15	**15**	9	68	2	.296
1943	Kingsport	Appalach	OF	108	382	79	132	20	10	**9**	87	16	.346
	Minors			**615**	**2223**	**403**	**700**	**106**	**54**	**51**	**435**	**59**	**.315**

WESLEY CHEEK FERRELL

Born February 2, 1908 at Greensboro, NC. Died December 9, 1976 at Sarasota, FL.
Height 6' 2", Weight 195. Batted right. Threw right.
Brother of Rick, HOF Catcher; George and Marv, minor league players.
Manager: Leakesville Bi-St 1941; Lynchburg Virginia 1942; Greensboro Carolina 1945;
Lynchburg Piedmont 1946; Marion W Carol 1948; Greensboro Carolina 1949; Tampa Fla Int 1949;
Rock Hill W Carols 1963; Shelby W Carols 1965.
Outstanding major league pitcher with 193 wins. Won 20 or more games six times. Holds major league record for most HR in a season by a pitcher with 9 in 1931. Holds major league record for most HR in a career by a pitcher with 37 (plus 1 as a pinch hitter).

Year	Club	League	POS	G	AB	R	H	2B	3B	HR	RBI	SB	BA
1927	Cleveland	American	P	1	0	0	0	0	0	0	0	0	.000
1928	Terre Haute	III	P	49	105	12	28	1	1	2	19	1	.267
	Cleveland	American	P	2	4	0	1	0	1	0	0	0	.250
1929	Cleveland	American	P	47	93	12	22	5	3	1	12	1	.237
1930	Cleveland	American	P	53	118	19	35	8	3	0	14	0	.297
1931	Cleveland	American	P	48	116	24	37	6	1	9	30	0	.319
1932	Cleveland	American	P	55	128	14	31	5	2	2	18	0	.242
1933	Cleveland	American	P-OF	61	140	26	38	7	0	7	26	0	.271
1934	Boston	American	P	34	78	12	22	4	0	4	17	1	.282
1935	Boston	American	P	75	150	25	52	5	1	7	32	0	.347
1936	Boston	American	P	61	135	20	36	6	1	5	24	0	.267
1937	Boston/Wash	American	P	71	139	14	39	7	0	1	25	0	.281
1938	Wash/NY	American	P	31	61	7	13	3	0	1	7	0	.213
1939	New York	American	P	3	8	0	1	1	0	0	1	0	.125
1940	Brooklyn	National	P	2	2	0	0	0	0	0	0	0	.000
1941	Boston	National	P	4	4	2	2	0	0	1	2	0	.500
	Leak-Spr-Dra	Bi-St	OF	74	253	58	84	13	2	20	70	0	.332
1942	Lynchburg	Virginia	2B-OF	123	410	92	148	18	9	**31**	99	4	**.361**
1943-44					Did not play in O. B.								
1945	Greensboro	Carolina	1B-OF	8	29	11	7	1	0	3	9	0	.241
1946	Lynchburg	Piedmont	OF-P	18	36	2	3	1	0	0	2	0	.083
1947					Did not play in O. B.								
1948	Marion	W Carol	OF-P	104	381	99	162	30	14	24	119	3	**.425**
1949	Greensboro	Carolina	OF	20	69	8	25	2	0	3	9	0	.362
	Tampa	Fla Int	1B-OF-P	30	92	9	23	2	0	1	8	0	.250
	Majors			**548**	**1176**	**175**	**329**	**57**	**12**	**38**	**208**	**2**	**.280**
	Minors			**426**	**1375**	**291**	**480**	**68**	**26**	**84**	**335**	**8**	**.349**

●

Jack Taylor, the iron-man National League hurler who pitched 188 consecutive complete games from June 20, 1901 through August 9, 1906, still had something on the ball when he was working in the minors in 1909. Hurling for Grand Rapids in the Central League on June 4, he tossed a 1–0 no-hitter over Fort Wayne. Pitching for Dayton in the same circuit on August 21, 1909, he shut out Terre Haute 4–0 on two hits in the first game, and then won 1–0 in 11 innings in the nightcap.

Wes Ferrell.
When his pitching career was over, he started a new career in the Minors as
a hard-hitting outfielder and manager.

WALTER EDWARD FRENCH
Born July 12, 1899 at Moorestown, NJ. Died May 13, 1984 at Mountain Home, AR.
Height 5' 7-1/2", Weight 155. Batted left. Threw right.

All American football player at West Point. Played in NFL for Rochester in 1922 and Pottsville in 1925.

Won MVP award in the Southern Association in 1933.

Year	Club	League	POS	G	AB	R	H	2B	3B	HR	RBI	SB	BA
1923	Philadelphia	American	OF	16	39	7	9	3	0	0	2	0	.231
	Williamsport	NY-Penn	OF	112	465	126	169	23	15	8	-	46	.363
1924	Shreveport	Texas	OF	117	526	107	184	34	11	0	44	26	.350
1925	Philadelphia	American	OF	67	100	20	37	9	0	0	14	1	.370
1926	Philadelphia	American	OF	112	397	51	121	18	7	1	36	2	.305
1927	Philadelphia	American	OF	109	326	48	99	10	5	0	41	9	.304
1928	Philadelphia	American	OF	49	74	9	19	4	0	0	7	1	.257
1929	Philadelphia	American	OF	45	45	7	12	1	1	1	9	0	.267
1930	Portland	P C	OF	160	644	103	199	21	4	0	49	9	.309
1931	Little Rock	South A	OF	155	674	133	235	25	9	3	56	51	.349
1932	Little Rock	South A	OF	152	628	102	211	25	8	3	59	26	.336
1933	LR/Knoxville	South A	OF	153	612	116	215	42	13	10	59	29	.351
1934	Knoxville	South A	OF	145	579	80	180	28	3	3	53	34	.311
1935	Williamsport	NY-Penn	OF	133	557	76	171	16	8	0	48	32	.307
		Majors		**398**	**981**	**142**	**297**	**45**	**13**	**2**	**109**	**13**	**.303**
		Minors		**1127**	**4685**	**843**	**1564**	**214**	**71**	**27**	**368**	**253**	**.334**

DELOS CLINTON "DEL" GAINOR
Born November 10, 1886 at Montrose, WV. Died January 29, 1947 at Elkins, WV.
Height 6' 00", Weight 180. Batted right. Threw right.

Brother of Dee, minor league player.

Manager: Fairmont MAL 1930.

Year	Club	League	POS	G	AB	R	H	2B	3B	HR	RBI	SB	BA
1909	Grafton	Pa-WV	1B	74	284	59	90	9	6	6	-	31	.317
	Detroit	American	1B	2	5	0	1	0	0	0	0	0	.200
1910	Ft. Wayne	Central	1B	136	489	72	152	29	5	4	-	28	.311
1911	Detroit	American	1B	70	248	32	75	11	4	2	25	10	.302
1912	Detroit	American	1B	51	179	28	43	5	6	0	20	14	.240
1913	Detroit	American	1B	104	363	47	97	16	8	2	25	10	.267
1914	Det/Boston	American	1B-2B	39	84	11	20	9	2	2	13	2	.238
1915	Boston	American	1B-OF	82	200	30	59	5	8	1	29	7	.295
1916	Boston	American	1B-2B	56	142	14	36	6	0	3	18	5	.254
1917	Boston	American	1B	52	172	28	53	10	2	2	19	1	.308
1918				Military Service									
1919	Boston	American	1B-OF	47	118	9	28	6	2	0	13	5	.237
1920	Milwaukee	A A	1B-OF	37	127	25	49	6	2	5	29	9	.386
1921	Milwaukee	A A	OF	135	529	107	180	32	16	9	124	24	.340
1922	St. Louis	National	1B-OF	43	97	19	26	7	4	2	23	0	.268
1923				Did not play in O.B.									
1924	Houston	Texas	1B	135	497	112	174	44	11	15	117	9	.350
1925	Houston	Texas	1B	115	442	107	145	31	3	15	77	3	.328
1926	Houston	Texas	1B	39	142	16	42	10	2	0	24	1	.296
	Syracuse	Int	1B	4	13	0	5	0	0	0	2	0	.385
1927	Syracuse	Int	1B	40	76	18	25	4	1	2	9	1	.329
1928	Rochester	Int	1B	52	61	3	20	2	1	0	8	0	.328

1929	Baltimore	Int	1B	33	32	3	11	3	1	2	9	0	.344
1930	Fairmont	Mid Atl	1B	21	39	7	17	3	0	0	5	0	.436
		Majors		**546**	**1608**	**218**	**438**	**75**	**36**	**14**	**185**	**54**	**.272**
		Minors		**821**	**2731**	**529**	**910**	**173**	**48**	**58**	**404**	**106**	**.333**

HENRY ADRIAN GARRETT
(Known by middle name.)
Born January 3, 1943 at Brooksville, FL.
Height 6' 3", Weight 185. Batted left. Threw right.
Brother of Wayne, major leaguer, and Charles, who played in minors. Manager: Appleton Midwest 1982; Glens Falls EL 1983.

Year	Club	League	POS	G	AB	R	H	2B	3B	HR	RBI	SB	BA
1961	Palatka	Fla St	OF	68	218	34	54	4	7	2	31	4	.248
	Davenport	Midwest	OF	10	26	7	5	0	0	0	3	1	.192
1962	Cedar Rapids	Midwest	OF	124	429	81	109	19	3	19	87	11	.254
1963	Boise	Pioneer	OF	32	123	37	39	10	0	9	43	1	.317
	Austin	Texas	OF	55	154	13	30	7	1	4	21	2	.195
1964	Austin	Texas	OF	123	421	57	118	23	11	7	48	3	.280
1965	Atlanta	Int	OF	128	411	72	92	17	3	20	63	3	.224
1966	Atlanta	National	OF	4	3	0	0	0	0	0	0	0	.000
	Richmond	Int	OF	114	342	47	67	9	3	16	40	4	.196
1967	Richmond	Int	OF	8	29	5	9	0	1	1	2	1	.310
	Austin	Texas	O-2-3	126	449	73	114	15	3	27	90	10	.254
1968	Richmond	Int	OF-3B	70	226	19	48	10	0	5	20	1	.212
	Evansville	Southern	OF	42	137	19	29	2	1	7	17	7	.212
1969	Richmond	Int	OF	12	38	3	7	1	1	0	2	2	.184
	Shreveport	Texas	O-3-1	107	352	67	92	10	4	**24**	75	3	.261
1970	San Antonio	Texas	O-3-1	128	448	82	124	21	3	**29**	86	4	.277
	Chicago	National	PH	3	3	0	0	0	0	0	0	0	.000
1971	Tacoma	P C	OF-1B	131	450	97	130	17	8	**43**	119	1	.289
	Oakland	American	OF	14	21	1	3	0	0	1	2	0	.143
1972	Iowa	A A	OF	62	220	33	61	9	3	12	32	2	.277
	Oakland	American	OF	14	11	0	0	0	0	0	0	0	.000
1973	Wichita	A A	1B	15	53	15	20	3	1	8	20	0	.377
	Chicago	National	OF-C	36	54	7	12	0	0	3	8	1	.222
1974	Wichita	A A	O-C-1	92	318	75	89	13	3	**26**	83	3	.280
	Chicago	National	C-O-1	10	8	0	0	0	0	0	0	0	.000
1975	Chicago	National	1B	16	21	1	2	0	0	1	6	0	.095
	Wichita	A A	OF-1B	52	212	41	68	17	3	12	48	2	.321
	California	American	1-O-C	37	107	17	28	5	0	6	18	3	.262
1976	California	American	C-1B	29	48	4	6	3	0	0	3	0	.125
	Hawaii	P C	1B	31	126	20	39	3	0	9	31	0	.310
1977	Hiroshima	Jap Cent	OF	128	445	64	124	19	0	35	91	1	.279
1978	Hiroshima	Jap Cent	OF	130	462	76	125	9	0	40	97	2	.271
1979	Hiroshima	Jap Cent	OF	126	395	53	89	9	2	27	59	3	.225
		Majors		**163**	**276**	**30**	**51**	**8**	**0**	**11**	**37**	**4**	**.185**
		Minors		**1530**	**5182**	**897**	**1344**	**210**	**59**	**280**	**961**	**65**	**.259**
		Japan		**384**	**1302**	**193**	**338**	**37**	**2**	**102**	**247**	**6**	**.260**

JOSEPH CLYDE GLASS
(Known by middle name.)
Born August 18, 1902 at Gentry, AR. Died September 13, 1975 at Siloam Springs, AR.
Height 5' 7-1/2", Weight 165. Batted left. Threw right.
Manager: Lake Charles CSL 1930; Siloam Springs Arkansas 1934.

Year	Club	League	POS	G	AB	R	H	2B	3B	HR	RBI	SB	BA
1923	Coffeyville	SWestern	SS-OF	125	448	44	122	17	3	1	-	14	.272
1924	Coffeyville	SWestern	3B	47	169	27	51	5	2	3	13	5	.302
1925	Mexia	Texas A	3B	126	487	96	169	**48**	6	14	-	7	.347
	Waco	Texas	3B	12	41	4	9	1	0	0	4	0	.220
1926	Waco	Texas	3B	34	100	11	35	6	1	2	25	3	.350
	Mexia	Texas A	3B	109	385	79	139	35	7	8	-	4	**.361**
1927	Waco	Texas	3B	5	16	1	3	1	0	1	-	0	.188
	Mexia	LoneStar	3-S-O	99	351	57	123	18	8	1	-	13	.350
1928	Meridian	Cottn St	OF-3B	106	354	62	108	24	2	3	-	10	.305
1929	Lake Charles	Cottn St	3B	123	466	95	163	32	3	3	-	14	.350
1930	LC/Bat Rouge	Cottn St	OF-3B	127	446	**109**	152	**43**	11	11	106	18	.341
1931	Vicksburg	Cottn St	OF	118	423	94	135	21	8	4	41	24	.319
1932	Jackson	SEastern	OF-3B	32	114	28	35	4	6	3	-	2	.307
	El Dorado	Cottn St	3B	52	173	55	72	15	6	6	-	10	**.416**
1933	Musko/DM	Western	OF	123	427	96	142	20	2	6	-	17	.333
1934	Siloam Spr.	Ark St	OF-3B	67	230	46	86	12	**12**	7	**67**	7	.374
	Minors			**1305**	**4630**	**904**	**1544**	**302**	**77**	**73**	**256**	**148**	**.333**

LESLIE ELMER "LON" GOLDSTEIN
Born May 13, 1918 at Austin, TX.
Height 6' 2-1/2", Weight 190. Batted left. Threw left.
Manager: Greenville Big St 1949; Temple Big St 1953.
Currently resides in Fort Worth, TX.

Year	Club	League	POS	G	AB	R	H	2B	3B	HR	RBI	SB	BA
1940	Columbia	Sally	1B	147	586	117	194	39	13	12	118	8	.331
1941	Columbia	Sally	1B	140	536	98	179	**48**	6	6	86	7	.334
1942	Birmingham	South A	1B	153	563	77	164	27	7	15	114	10	.291
1943	Syracuse	Int	1B	42	121	16	29	8	1	1	15	2	.240
	Birmingham	South A	1B	56	202	27	68	13	7	3	38	9	.337
	Cincinnati	National	1B	5	5	1	1	0	0	0	0	0	.200
1944	Syracuse	Int	1B	28	102	4	25	4	0	1	22	0	.245
1945						Military Service							
1946	Cincinnati	National	PH	6	5	1	0	0	0	0	0	0	.000
1947	Gainesville	Big St	1B	85	332	93	133	19	2	33	122	5	.401
1948	Gainesville	Big St	1B	143	543	116	196	**58**	1	16	138	6	.361
1949	Gainesville	Big St	1B	147	535	81	187	38	3	15	130	8	.350
1950	Gainesville	Big St	1B	142	534	85	169	38	5	8	92	11	.316
1951	Temple	Big St	1B	104	412	68	155	33	5	7	90	6	**.376**
1952	Temple	Big St	1B	124	496	78	163	38	1	12	97	5	.329
1953	Temple	Big St	1B	117	446	52	124	25	0	4	60	10	.278
1954	Corpus Christi	Big St	1B	82	313	47	101	16	1	6	66	3	.323
1955	Yuma	Ariz-Mex	1B	61	242	50	78	22	0	7	72	5	.322
	Majors			**11**	**10**	**2**	**1**	**0**	**0**	**0**	**0**	**0**	**.100**
	Minors			**1571**	**5963**	**1009**	**1965**	**426**	**52**	**146**	**1260**	**95**	**.330**

JOSEPH HALL GRANADE
Born December 9, 1902 at Frankville, AL.
Height 5' 10-1/2", Weight 165. Batted left. Threw right.
Manager: El Dorado Dixie 1933.

Year	Club	League	POS	G	AB	R	H	2B	3B	HR	RBI	SB	BA
1925	Texark/Tyler	E Texas	OF	120	529	109	**182**	28	9	14	-	**47**	.344
	Shreveport	Texas	OF	13	48	4	12	0	0	0	2	0	.250
1926	Texarkana	E Texas	OF	112	**494**	105	**180**	21	6	13	-	32	.364
1927	Monroe	Cottn St	OF	124	**515**	93	**180**	28	12	4	-	**55**	.350
1928	Monroe	Cottn St	OF	125	**521**	**96**	**174**	30	6	8	-	**51**	.334
1929	Monroe	Cottn St	OF	118	457	76	168	31	5	4	-	29	**.368**
	Ft. Worth	Texas	OF	14	51	4	13	3	0	0	8	0	.255
1930	Denver	Western	OF	137	540	105	176	28	10	4	72	28	.326
1931	Jacks/Monroe	Cottn St	OF	20	76	10	21	2	0	0	10	3	.276
	San Antonio	Texas	OF	3	9	0	2	0	0	0	0	0	.222
	Durham	Piedmont	OF	10	42	2	9	1	0	0	-	3	.214
1932	Musk/Hutch	West A	OF	112	440	93	148	23	13	3	65	19	.336
1933	El Dorado	Dixie	OF	117	483	84	162	23	12	1	58	16	.335
		Minors		**1025**	**4205**	**781**	**1427**	**218**	**73**	**51**	**215**	**283**	**.339**

PEARL ZANE GREY
(Known by middle name.)
(Played under name Pearl Zane in 1895 to protect eligibility at University of Pennsylvania.)
Born January 31, 1872 at Zanesville, OH. Died October 23, 1939 at Altadena, CA.
Height 5' 8", Weight 150. Batted right. Threw right.
Brother of Romer Grey.

Famous writer, particularly of western adventure stories. Wrote several baseball novels including *The Redheaded Outfield*.

Year	Club	League	POS	G	AB	R	H	2B	3B	HR	SB	BA
1895	Findlay	Inter-St	OF	21	88	22	26	5	0	2	13	.295
	Jackson	Mich St	OF	27	123	38	49	8	4	3	19	.398
1896-98				Played for independent clubs								
1898	Newark	Atlantic	OF	38	148	18	41	7	1	0	7	.277
		Minors		**86**	**359**	**78**	**116**	**20**	**5**	**5**	**39**	**.323**

ROMER CARL "REDDY" GREY
Born January 4, 1875 at Zanesville, OH. Died Novmeber 9, 1934 at Altadena, CA.
Height 5' 10", Weight 170. Batted left. Threw left.
Brother of Zane. Was one of the outfielders upon which the novel *The Redheaded Outfield* by Zane Grey was based.

Scored 8 runs in game for Ft. Wayne May 9, 1896.

Year	Club	League	POS	G	AB	R	H	2B	3B	HR	SB	BA
1895	Findlay	Inter-St	OF	52	233	**64**	80	15	4	**14**	19	.343
	Jackson	Mich St	OF	31	152	57	69	10	10	2	11	.454
1896	Ft. Wayne	Inter-St	OF	61	273	68	102	19	20	1	6	.374
1897	Buffalo	Eastern	OF	133	563	118	174	29	11	2	19	.309
1898	Toronto	Eastern	OF	122	**543**	110	**174**	25	7	5	21	.320
1899	Toronto	Eastern	OF	112	458	90	145	15	9	9	33	.317

Zane Grey.
Made his minor league debut as left fielder with Findley, Ohio, in the Inter-State League June 15, 1895. He went hitless but walked and scored on a grand-slam homer by his brother Romer. During 1895, he played under the name of Pearl Zane (his real first and middle name) to protect his eligibility at the University of Pennsylvania, where he was a pitcher before graduating in 1896 with a D.D.S. degree. When not playing in O.B., Grey played independent ball with various Ohio teams and for the Orange, N.J., Athletic Club.

Year	Club	League	POS	G	AB	R	H	2B	3B	HR	RBI	SB	BA
1900	Toronto	Eastern	OF	89	356	66	104	9	5	4	18		.292
1901	Buff/Roch.	Eastern	OF	124	473	72	145	18	11	**12**	36		.307
1902	Rochester	Eastern	OF	46	196	30	49	5	5	0	4		.250
1903	Pittsburgh	National	OF	1	3	1	1	0	0	0	0		.333
	Wor/Mont.	Eastern	OF	56	226	25	70	9	3	0	1		.310
	Majors			**1**	**3**	**1**	**1**	**0**	**0**	**0**	**0**		**.333**
	Minors			**826**	**3473**	**700**	**1112**	**154**	**85**	**49**	**168**		**.320**

ARTHUR CARLE GRIGGS

Born December 10, 1883 at Topeka, KS. Died December 19, 1938 at Los Angeles, CA.
Height 5' 11", Weight 185. Batted right. Threw right.
Starred as a football player at the University of Kansas and at the University of Pittsburgh.
Manager: Omaha WL 1924-25; Wichita WL 1928-31; Tulsa TL 1932-33 and 35.

Year	Club	League	POS	G	AB	R	H	2B	3B	HR	RBI	SB	BA
1906	Little Rock	South A	P	2	4	1	0	0	0	0	-	0	.000
	Lake Charles	S Texas	C-P	11	32	2	11	3	0	2	-	0	.344
1907	San Antonio	Texas	P-2-O	62	185	23	52	14	4	4	-	6	.281
1908	San Antonio	Texas	2B-C	118	435	60	132	12	12	11	-	19	.303
1909	St. Louis	American	1-O-2-S	108	364	38	102	17	5	0	43	11	.280
1910	St. Louis	American	O-2-1-S	123	416	28	98	22	5	2	30	11	.236
1911	Cleveland	American	2-O-3-1	27	68	7	17	3	2	1	7	1	.250
	Toledo	A A	1B-OF	21	52	8	15	4	0	0	-	5	.288
1912	Toledo	A A	OF	14	41	5	9	0	0	0	-	2	.220
	Cleveland	American	1B	89	273	29	83	16	7	0	39	10	.304
1913	Montreal	Int	1B	40	144	21	42	7	4	0	-	5	.292
1914	Brooklyn	Federal	1B-OF	40	112	10	32	6	1	1	15	1	.286
1915	Brooklyn	Federal	1B-OF	27	38	4	11	1	0	1	2	0	.289
1916	Vernon	P C	OF	127	386	48	106	26	5	7	-	9	.275
1917	Vernon/Port	P C	1B-OF	186	684	88	213	44	6	10	-	31	.311
1918	Sacramento	P C	1B-OF	89	344	49	130	16	4	**12**	-	22	**.378**
	Detroit	American	1B	28	99	11	36	8	0	0	16	2	.364
1919	Sacramento	P C	1B	148	545	55	157	34	8	9	-	7	.288
1920	Los Angeles	P C	1B	94	373	54	114	17	7	2	-	1	.306
1921	Los Angeles	P C	1B	177	678	105	199	45	14	10	119	6	.294
1922	Los Angeles	P C	1B	175	639	95	216	49	5	20	129	10	.338
1923	Los Angeles	P C	1B	153	495	84	163	28	5	21	88	1	.329
1924	Omaha	Western	1B	50	171	22	49	16	0	1	-	0	.287
1925	Omaha	Western	1B	134	508	108	171	39	6	28	-	3	.337
1926	Seattle	P C	1B	89	234	27	81	16	3	5	36	0	.346
	Majors			**442**	**1370**	**127**	**379**	**73**	**20**	**5**	**152**	**36**	**.277**
	Minors			**1690**	**5950**	**855**	**1860**	**370**	**83**	**142**	**372**	**127**	**.313**

EDGAR CLIFFORD HARTNESS

Born March 12, 1920 at Murphy, NC.
Height 5' 11", Weight 180. Batted left. Threw left.
Manager: Eastman Ga St 1949-50; Macon Sally 1951-52; Tifton Ga-Fla 1953-54; Sherbrooke Provincl 1955.

Year	Club	League	POS	G	AB	R	H	2B	3B	HR	RBI	SB	BA
1938	Americus	Ga-Fla	1B	108	443	66	123	16	**14**	8	69	2	.278
1939	Americus	Ga-Fla	OF	129	491	89	175	27	9	1	69	20	**.356**
1940	Macon	Sally	1B-OF	150	625	111	198	25	14	4	62	28	.317

Year	Club	League	POS	G	AB	R	H	2B	3B	HR	RBI	SB	BA
1941	Macon	Sally	OF-1B	136	516	103	162	27	11	5	64	23	.314
1942	Macon	Sally	1B	95	368	72	120	15	4	3	49	15	.326
1943-45					Military Service								
1946	Los Angeles	P C	PH	4	3	0	1	0	0	0	2	0	.333
	Nashville	South A	OF	11	27	0	9	2	0	0	4	0	.333
	Macon	Sally	OF	98	373	62	110	13	5	2	49	15	.295
1947	Macon	Sally	OF-1B	128	494	90	148	24	8	3	68	25	.300
1948	Macon	Sally	OF-1B	150	547	93	178	41	10	3	81	14	.325
1949	Eastman	Ga St	1B	139	486	119	177	41	12	13	**136**	27	**.364**
1950	Eastman	Ga St	1B	142	503	**137**	**201**	48	11	20	**134**	25	**.400**
1951	Macon	Sally	1B-OF	127	458	78	143	29	8	0	43	9	.312
1952	Macon	Sally	OF	114	398	49	104	21	5	1	40	2	.261
1953	Tifton	Ga-Fla	1B	135	491	94	158	25	6	6	83	15	.322
1954	Tifton	Ga-Fla	1B-OF	113	365	68	133	27	2	4	56	6	**.364**
1955	Sherbrooke	Provincl	1B-OF	67	210	32	74	22	0	2	37	3	.352
	Minors			**1846**	**6798**	**1263**	**2214**	**403**	**119**	**75**	**1046**	**229**	**.326**

CHARLES EDWIN HIGH
Born December 1, 1898 at Ava, IL. Died September 11, 1960 at Oak Grove, OR.
Height 5' 9", Weight 170. Batted left. Threw right.
Brother of Andy and Hugh, major league players.

Year	Club	League	POS	G	AB	R	H	2B	3B	HR	RBI	SB	BA
1919	Evansville	III	OF	119	434	64	143	15	10	3	-	21	.329
	Philadelphia	American	OF	11	29	2	2	0	0	0	1	2	.069
1920	Atlanta	South A	OF	142	525	52	151	31	12	2	-	8	.288
	Philadelphia	American	OF	17	65	7	20	2	1	1	6	0	.308
1921	Columbus	A A	OF	140	505	97	167	31	12	13	75	17	.331
1922	Portland	P C	OF	178	649	103	205	35	5	24	107	12	.316
1923	Portland	P C	OF	156	558	98	189	34	5	20	94	8	.339
1924	Portland	P C	OF	165	612	94	197	31	7	20	139	4	.322
1925	Portland	P C	OF	162	608	118	205	36	3	20	107	9	.337
1926	Buffalo	Int	OF	137	482	97	154	29	9	13	82	5	.320
1927	Buffalo/Tor	Int	OF	70	191	30	49	6	2	4	31	3	.257
1928	Columbus	A A	OF	80	268	47	92	16	5	9	38	7	.343
1929	Colum/Minn	A A	OF	113	323	75	98	15	0	28	87	5	.303
1930	Minneapolis	A A	OF	104	275	79	105	18	2	25	82	2	.382
1931	Minn/Ind	A A	OF	84	249	44	73	13	2	14	58	0	.293
1932	Seattle	P C	OF	25	88	8	21	1	1	0	8	0	.239
	Majors			**28**	**94**	**9**	**22**	**2**	**1**	**1**	**7**	**2**	**.234**
	Minors			**1675**	**5767**	**1006**	**1849**	**311**	**75**	**195**	**908**	**101**	**.321**

ELMORE HILL
Born June 27, 1947 at Gastonia, NC.
Height 6' 2", Weight 190. Batted right. Threw right.

Year	Club	League	POS	G	AB	R	H	2B	3B	HR	RBI	SB	BA
1965	Fox Cities	Midwest	OF	107	396	38	109	18	2	7	51	3	.275
1966	Stockton	Calif	OF	21	44	6	7	2	1	1	4	1	.159
	Batavia	NY-Penn	OF	28	79	13	29	11	0	1	20	2	.367
	Miami	Fla St	OF	29	89	10	12	2	0	2	10	1	.135
1967	Miami	Fla St	OF	114	350	40	82	15	4	9	37	8	.234
1968	Miami	Fla St	OF	123	372	46	97	23	**13**	10	65	5	.261

Year	Club	League	POS	G	AB	R	H	2B	3B	HR	RBI	SB	BA
1969					Did not play in O. B.								
1970	Orlando	Fla St	O-3-1	129	485	68	133	19	6	**22**	84	18	.274
1971	Charlotte	Southern	OF	11	36	0	5	1	0	0	2	0	.139
	Lynchburg	Carolina	O-3-1	76	208	20	46	9	3	7	28	1	.221
	Wisc. Rapids	Midwest	1B	20	78	11	18	4	2	8	16	1	.231
1972	Wisc. Rapids	Midwest	OF-1B	101	359	71	88	9	2	20	69	10	.245
1973	Wisc. Rapids	Midwest	OF-1B	112	424	62	115	26	4	7	76	8	.271
1974	Wisc. Rapids	Midwest	OF-1B	121	443	95	**150**	25	2	**32**	113	11	.339
1975	Wisc. Rapids	Midwest	OF-1B	126	404	71	111	13	1	**31**	86	2	.275
1976	Wisc. Rapids	Midwest	D-1-O	128	486	**112**	132	**30**	4	30	**103**	1	.272
1977	Wisc. Rapids	Midwest	1B	137	477	104	145	17	3	**41**	**112**	6	.304
1978	Wisc. Rapids	Midwest	D-1-O	117	416	62	116	25	0	25	94	8	.279
1979	Jacksonville	Southern	DH	45	182	19	33	3	0	8	20	0	.181
1980	Fort Myers	Fla St	OF-1B	18	44	9	16	2	1	2	6	0	.364
	Minors			**1563**	**5372**	**857**	**1444**	**254**	**48**	**263**	**996**	**86**	**.269**

MYRIL OLIVER HOAG

Born March 9, 1908 at Davis, CA. Died July 28, 1971 at High Springs, FL.
Height 5' 11", Weight 180. Batted right. Threw right.
Manager: Palatka Fla St 1946; Gainesville Fla St 1947-48 & 51; St. Petersburg Fla Int 1949; Valley and Rome Ga-Ala 1950. Fanned 280 batters for Gainesville at age 41 in 1949.

Year	Club	League	POS	G	AB	R	H	2B	3B	HR	RBI	SB	BA
1926	Sacramento	P C	OF	2	3	0	1	0	0	0	2	0	.333
1927	Sacramento	P C	OF	4	16	0	3	1	0	0	-	0	.188
	Twin Falls	Utah-Ida	OF	55	226	36	69	12	3	7	-	2	.305
1928					Did not play in O. B.								
1929	Sacramento	P C	OF	116	414	47	116	25	2	6	54	5	.280
1930	Sacramento	P C	OF	188	725	148	244	57	9	17	121	19	.337
1931	New York	American	OF	44	28	6	4	2	0	0	3	0	.143
1932	New York	American	OF	46	54	18	20	5	0	1	7	1	.370
1933	Newark	Int	OF	150	565	86	168	31	8	21	106	9	.297
1934	New York	American	OF	97	251	45	67	8	2	3	34	1	.267
1935	New York	American	OF	48	110	13	28	4	1	1	13	4	.255
1936	New York	American	OF	45	156	23	47	9	4	3	34	3	.301
1937	New York	American	OF	106	362	48	109	19	8	3	46	4	.301
1938	New York	American	OF	85	267	28	74	14	3	0	48	4	.277
1939	St. Louis	American	OF-P	129	482	58	142	23	4	10	75	9	.295
1940	St. Louis	American	OF	76	191	20	50	11	0	3	26	2	.262
1941	SL/Chicago	American	OF	107	381	30	97	13	3	1	44	6	.255
1942	Chicago	American	OF	113	412	47	99	18	2	2	37	17	.240
1943					Military Service								
1944	Chi/Clev	American	OF	84	325	38	90	10	3	1	31	7	.277
1945	Cleveland	American	OF-P	40	128	10	27	5	3	0	3	1	.211
1946	Palatka	Fla St	OF-P	121	403	79	138	37	4	**8**	96	21	**.342**
1947	Gainesville	Fla St	OF-P	102	323	72	113	18	5	4	75	21	**.350**
1948	Gainesville	Fla St	P-OF	59	135	27	44	8	2	2	21	7	.326
1949	St.Petersburg	Fla Int	P	4	4	0	0	0	0	0	0	0	.000
	Gainesville	Fla St	P-OF	62	164	22	52	7	2	1	26	8	.317
1950	Valley/Rome	Ga-Ala	P-OF	56	107	15	31	6	0	1	18	10	.290
1951	Gainesville	Fla St	P	30	68	6	14	2	0	0	5	3	.206
	Majors			**1020**	**3147**	**384**	**854**	**141**	**33**	**28**	**401**	**59**	**.271**
	Minors			**949**	**3153**	**538**	**993**	**204**	**35**	**67**	**524**	**105**	**.315**

Luis Alcaraz (record on page 33)

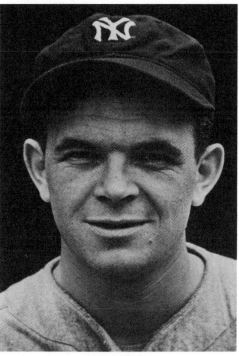

Myril Hoag

Sam Jethroe (Record on page 88)

Bill Kelly (Record on page 92)

Pitching Record

Year	Club	League	G	IP	W	L	H	R	ER	BB	SO	ERA
1939	St. Louis	American	1	1	0	0	0	0	0	0	0	0.00
1945	Cleveland	American	2	3	0	0	3	0	0	1	0	0.00
1946	Palatka	Fla St	19	87	6	8	80	58	35	54	79	3.62
1947	Gainesville	Fla St	32	173	17	3	143	53	35	51	115	**1.82**
1948	Gainesville	Fla St	34	239 ·	24	4	154	59	35	84	149	**1.32**
1949	St. Petersburg	Fla Int	4	12	0	1	11	7	4	7	3	3.33
	Gainesville	Fla St	36	271	24	9	227	110	88	97	**280**	2.92
1950	Valley/Rome	Ga-Ala	36	208	15	11	191	105	60	73	137	2.60
1951	Gainesville	Fla St	21	137	5	10	126	84	63	51	76	4.14
	Majors		**3**	**4**	**0**	**0**	**3**	**0**	**0**	**1**	**0**	**0.00**
	Minors		**182**	**1127**	**91**	**46**	**932**	**476**	**320**	**417**	**839**	**2.56**

EDWARD ADOLPH "TEX" HOFFMAN

Born November 30, 1893 at San Antonio, TX. Died May 19, 1947 at New Orleans, LA.
Height 6' 1", Weight 200. Batted left. Threw right.
Manager: Tallahassee Ga-Fla 1935.

Year	Club	League	POS	G	AB	R	H	2B	3B	HR	RBI	SB	BA
1913	Chattanooga	South A	3B	1	4	1	1	0	0	0	0	0	.250
	Charleston	Sally	2B	23	83	8	16	4	1	2	9	3	.193
1914	Flint	S Mich	3B	147	559	65	147	27	11	12	-	11	.263
1915	Flint	S Mich	2-O-S	70	256	36	73	10	4	7	-	10	.285
	Cleveland	American	3B	9	13	1	2	0	0	0	2	0	.154
	Cleveland	A A	3B	63	225	24	52	11	4	0	-	6	.231
1916	Springfield	Central	3B	130	465	49	123	16	12	9	-	33	.265
	Toledo	A A	3B	11	26	0	3	1	0	0	-	1	.115
1917	San Antonio	Texas	3B	43	137	16	32	7	2	0	-	4	.234
	SB/FtWayne	Central	3B-1B	99	356	40	101	18	4	7	-	20	.284
1918	Waco	Texas	2B-3B	88	315	36	83	18	1	6	-	21	.263
1919	Waco/FtWorth	Texas	2B	155	551	60	127	27	5	7	-	34	.230
1920	Fort Worth	Texas	2B	149	543	86	175	29	9	10	77	23	.322
1921	Fort Worth	Texas	2B	129	504	75	157	27	9	7	72	11	.312
1922	Fort Worth	Texas	2B	149	600	104	183	40	12	12	113	14	.305
1923	Fort Worth	Texas	2B	136	496	73	147	32	3	13	96	5	.296
1924	New Orleans	South A	2B	154	530	77	149	27	19	11	94	8	.281
1925	New Orleans	South A	2B	155	575	96	163	30	23	16	111	10	.283
1926	Shreveport	Texas	2B	158	549	100	158	34	1	21	94	8	.288
1927	Selma	SEastern	2B	126	424	62	126	29	7	9	-	6	.297
1928	Albany	SEastern	2B-1B	120	416	75	132	29	5	15	90	6	.317
	Macon	Sally	2B	25	89	17	20	5	0	4	11	1	.225
1929	Mob/Memp	South A	2B-1B	14	37	4	8	2	0	0	4	1	.216
	Canton	Central	2B	102	367	71	112	30	9	11	61	13	.305
1930	Mob/NO	South A	2B	64	210	26	50	9	2	4	35	3	.238
	Spring/TH	III	2B	48	181	35	58	10	3	3	26	4	.320
1931	Baton Rouge	Cottn St	2B	62	212	33	55	8	2	4	23	2	.259
1932-34	Did not play in O. B.												
1935	Tallahassee	Ga-Fla	INF	62	185	34	46	7	4	1	31	0	.249
	Majors			**9**	**13**	**1**	**2**	**0**	**0**	**0**	**2**	**0**	**.154**
	Minors			**2483**	**8895**	**1303**	**2497**	**487**	**152**	**191**	**947**	**258**	**.281**

ROBERT CLAY HOPPER
(Known by middle name.)
Born October 3, 1902 at Porterville, MS. Died April 17, 1976 at Greenwood, MS.
Height 5' 11", Weight 175. Batted right. Threw right. Manager: Laurel CSL 1929; Scottdale MAl 1931; Mobile SEL 1932; Elmira NYPL 1932; Springfield MissVall 1933; Greensburg PSA 1934; Greenwood E Dixie 1935; Greensburg PSA 1936; Springfield WA 1937-38; Columbus SAL 1939-41; Houston TL 1942; Mobile SA 1945; Montreal IL 1946-49; St. Paul AA 1950-51; Portland PCL 1952-55; Hollywood PCL 1956. His 27-year managing record totaled 1916 wins and 1675 losses.

Hit 4 HR in a game against Quincy on July 17, 1927 (1st G).

Year	Club	League	POS	G	AB	R	H	2B	3B	HR	RBI	SB	BA
1926	Ft. Smith	West A	OF	104	423	96	158	36	12	13	-	13	.374
1927	Danville	III	OF	127	463	81	146	20	16	13	80	21	.315
1928	Rochester	Int	OF	9	19	5	8	1	0	1	7	1	.421
	Laurel	Cottn St	OF	45	165	34	53	8	2	8	-	1	.321
1929	Laurel	Cottn St	OF	16	58	5	15	2	0	0	-	3	.259
1930	Greensboro	Piedmont	OF	140	521	121	185	37	15	23	121	17	.355
1931	Scottdale	Mid Atl	OF	126	449	117	159	26	18	24	102	17	.354
1932	Mobile	SEastern	OF	13	36	4	15	3	3	0	12	3	.417
	Elmira	NY-Penn	OF	52	150	17	34	4	3	0	18	1	.227
1933	Springfield	Miss Val	OF	103	347	74	121	20	12	8	92	12	.349
1934	Greensburg	Pa St A	OF	94	307	73	100	18	13	13	66	15	.326
1935	Greenwood	E Dixie	OF	123	408	68	131	25	11	7	60	10	.321
1936	Greensburg	Pa St A	1B	88	279	58	101	18	7	6	62	18	.362
1937	Springfield	West A	OF	108	337	56	101	23	5	5	65	6	.300
1938	Springfield	West A	OF-1B	97	278	65	78	16	7	3	45	10	.281
1939	Columbus	Sally	OF	17	22	4	6	4	0	0	6	0	.273
1940	Columbus	Sally	OF	12	17	2	7	1	0	1	7	0	.412
1941	Columbus	Sally	PH	6	6	0	0	0	0	0	0	0	.000
	Minors			**1280**	**4285**	**880**	**1418**	**262**	**124**	**125**	**743**	**148**	**.331**

ARTHUR LELAND "MIKE" HUNT
Born October 12, 1907 at Santa Clara, CA.
Height 6' 3-1/2", Weight 205. Batted right. Threw right.
On spring training roster of Boston Braves in 1933.
Currently resides in Ephrata, Washington.

Year	Club	League	POS	G	AB	R	H	2B	3B	HR	RBI	SB	BA
1927	Poca/Ogden	Utah-Ida	P	10	21	0	4	2	0	0	-	0	.190
1928					Did not play in O.B.								
1929	San Bernar.	Calif St	OF	56	208	37	75	16	1	2	40	1	.361
	Tucson	Ariz St	OF	31	122	24	40	7	0	4	-	0	.328
1930	Globe/Miami	Ariz St	OF-P	104	418	85	145	23	11	21	82	3	.347
	San Francisco	P C	OF	19	70	14	21	2	3	0	7	0	.300
1931	San Francisco	P C	OF	76	228	34	69	14	1	5	43	1	.303
1932	San Francisco	P C	OF	151	529	84	167	26	8	14	84	2	.316
1933	Mission/SF	P C	OF	60	168	28	51	5	0	6	42	3	.304
	Atlanta	South A	PH	2	2	0	0	0	0	0	0	0	.000
1934	Seattle	P C	OF	175	644	125	223	42	5	30	128	8	.346
1935	Seattle	P C	OF	163	639	122	211	45	6	25	112	12	.330
1936	Seattle	P C	OF	169	670	116	212	50	6	**30**	**135**	6	.316
1937	Seattle	P C	OF	172	647	129	202	43	3	**39**	**131**	2	.312
1938	Seattle	P C	OF	157	539	98	157	26	6	13	77	1	.291
1939	Seattle	P C	OF	121	371	57	96	26	3	15	76	3	.259
	Minors			**1466**	**5276**	**953**	**1673**	**327**	**53**	**204**	**957**	**42**	**.317**

GEORGE CHRISTOPHER "HICKORY" JACKSON
Born January 2, 1882 at Springfield, MO. Died November 25, 1972 at Cleburne, TX.
Height 6' 0-1/2", Weight 180. Batted right. Threw right.
Manager: Tyler Lone Star1927-28; El Dorado CSL 1929-32.

Year	Club	League	POS	G	AB	R	H	2B	3B	HR	RBI	SB	BA
1906	Jackson	Cottn St	P	3	8	1	2	0	0	0	-	0	.250
1907	Lake Charles	Gulf Cst	1B	44	153	31	43	6	2	1	-	16	.281
1908	Lake Charles	Gulf Cst	3B-SS-P	28	108	25	28	6	1	3	-	6	.259
	Dallas	Texas	OF	74	219	31	53	11	3	0	-	21	.242
1909	Dallas	Texas	OF	129	431	65	117	21	3	6	-	53	.271
1910	Dallas	Texas	OF	144	515	80	144	17	7	5	-	**55**	.280
	Memphis	South A	OF	5	18	1	3	2	0	0	-	0	.167
1911	Memphis	South A	OF	85	300	29	78	17	4	2	-	13	.260
	Boston	National	OF	39	147	28	51	11	2	0	25	12	.347
1912	Boston	National	OF	110	397	55	104	13	5	4	48	22	.262
1913	Boston	National	OF	3	10	2	3	0	0	0	0	0	.300
	Buffalo	Int	OF	116	423	72	110	15	7	3	-	29	.260
1914	Buffalo	Int	OF	97	312	54	84	17	4	4	-	12	.269
1915	Buffalo	Int	OF	78	200	31	51	10	1	1	-	7	.255
1916	Buffalo	Int	OF	116	449	80	146	**34**	9	2	-	11	.325
1917	Buffalo	Int	OF	112	404	46	111	20	3	3	-	7	.275
1918	Fort Worth	Texas	OF-1B	69	243	25	74	16	1	3	-	6	.305
1919	San Antonio	Texas	OF	81	284	31	75	10	1	3	-	8	.264
1920	Shreveport	Texas	OF-1B	133	493	87	164	31	9	6	37	31	.333
1921	Shreveport	Texas	OF	160	**625**	109	194	31	11	10	98	39	.310
1922	Shreveport	Texas	OF	111	410	64	141	28	2	10	74	14	.344
1923	Shrev/Beau	Texas	OF-1B	82	256	35	64	11	3	4	40	10	.250
1924	Tyler	E Texas	1B-OF	110	415	**103**	154	31	0	26	-	20	.371
1925	Tyler	E Texas	1B-OF	92	351	91	127	28	0	16	-	20	.362
1926	Greenville	E Texas	OF-1B	90	336	55	97	17	0	10	-	14	.289
1927	Tyler	Lone Star	1B	115	428	71	126	21	0	21	-	14	.294
1928	Tyler	Lone Star	1B-OF	87	317	58	105	17	1	13	-	12	.331
1929	Laurel/El Dor	Cottn St	1B	71	231	40	64	14	0	5	-	6	.277
1930	El Dorado	Cottn St	1B	72	240	41	69	9	3	1	36	11	.288
1931	El Dorado	Cottn St	1B	55	125	16	37	8	0	0	14	0	.296
1932	El Dorado	Cottn St	1B	34	87	11	20	1	0	1	-	4	.230
		Majors		**152**	**554**	**85**	**158**	**24**	**7**	**4**	**73**	**34**	**.285**
		Minors		**2393**	**8381**	**1383**	**2481**	**449**	**75**	**159**	**299**	**439**	**.296**

RAYMOND F. JACOBS
Born January 2, 1902 at Salt Lake City, UT. Died April 4, 1952 at Los Angeles, CA.
Height 6' 00", Weight 160. Batted right. Threw right.
Manager: Yakima Western Int 1937-39; Twin Falls Pioneer 1940; Spokane Pioneer 1941-42.

Year	Club	League	POS	G	AB	R	H	2B	3B	HR	RBI	SB	BA
1923	Los Angeles	P C	SS	15	45	6	16	3	0	1	8	1	.356
1924	Los Angeles	P C	3B	147	517	73	143	44	0	9	76	2	.277
1925	Los Angeles	P C	S-3-1	150	539	116	167	53	3	13	75	18	.310
1926	Los Angeles	P C	1B	178	580	92	148	39	6	21	102	13	.255
1927	Los Angeles	P C	1-2-S	97	359	70	116	25	7	13	64	9	.323
1928	Los Angeles	P C	1B	36	111	8	23	5	0	0	11	1	.207
	Chicago	National	PH	2	2	0	0	0	0	0	0	0	.000
	Toledo/Minn	A A	SS-2B	40	141	23	47	5	4	4	-	2	.333

Year	Club	League	POS	G	AB	R	H	2B	3B	HR	RBI	SB	BA
1929	Los Angeles	P C	2-1-3	178	591	84	196	40	8	20	118	11	.332
1930	Los Angeles	P C	1B	196	710	128	216	41	8	20	130	11	.304
1931	Los Angeles	P C	1B-3B	124	386	78	115	29	3	18	73	5	.298
1932	Portland	P C	1B	40	149	15	43	5	1	5	34	2	.289
	Galveston	Texas	1B	27	88	7	11	3	0	1	5	1	.125
1933	Hollywood	P C	1B	159	564	107	160	35	0	36	125	9	.284
1934	Hollywood	P C	1B-2B	178	597	93	172	28	1	24	112	9	.288
1935	Hollywood	P C	1B	115	402	62	119	17	3	13	69	11	.296
1936	San Diego	P C	1B	106	332	42	93	23	1	5	46	8	.280
1937	Yakima	West Int	1B-3B	118	432	82	139	37	3	8	78	4	.322
1938	Yakima	West Int	1B	90	291	48	88	24	3	5	44	9	.302
1939	Yakima	West Int	1B	95	321	49	78	15	0	14	48	4	.243
1940	Twin Falls	Pioneer	1B	13	31	2	6	0	0	2	8	0	.194
1941	Spokane	West Int	1B	24	37	4	9	3	0	0	3	1	.243
1942	Spokane	West Int	1B	24	39	6	11	2	0	1	9	1	.282
	Majors			**2**	**2**	**0**	**0**	**0**	**0**	**0**	**0**	**0**	**.000**
	Minors			**2150**	**7262**	**1195**	**2116**	**476**	**51**	**233**	**1238**	**132**	**.291**

IRVINE FRANKLIN JEFFRIES

Born September 10, 1905 at Louisville, KY. Died June 8, 1982 at Louisville, KY.
Height 5' 10", Weight 175. Batted right. Threw right.
Manager: Kingsport Appalach 1949.

Year	Club	League	POS	G	AB	R	H	2B	3B	HR	RBI	SB	BA
1928	Akron	Central	SS	57	219	26	62	10	9	3	-	2	.283
	Dallas	Texas	SS	17	72	6	22	4	0	0	7	0	.306
1929	Dallas	Texas	3B-SS	168	630	86	192	37	9	10	89	11	.305
1930	Toledo	A A	SS	45	185	27	61	13	3	5	-	5	.330
	Chicago	American	SS-3B	40	97	14	23	3	0	2	11	1	.237
1931	Chicago	American	3-2-S	79	223	29	50	10	0	2	16	3	.224
1932	St. Paul	A A	2B	166	690	106	213	52	8	20	82	7	.309
1933	St. Paul	A A	2B	**153**	686	125	**236**	45	11	17	102	4	.344
1934	Philadelphia	National	2B-3B	56	175	28	43	6	0	4	19	2	.246
	Baltimore	Int	2B	79	302	52	91	15	2	8	50	4	.301
1935	Baltimore	Int	2B-3B	154	638	111	181	44	3	19	68	15	.284
1936	Balt/Montreal	Int	2B-3B	113	367	73	115	25	4	5	55	5	.313
1937	Montreal	Int	3B	138	500	78	154	36	2	6	65	11	.308
1938	Portland	P C	3B	177	687	74	195	42	1	5	78	6	.284
1939	Portland	P C	2B	167	645	93	204	34	1	5	69	2	.316
1940	Fort Worth	Texas	3B-1B	135	494	54	119	14	7	3	45	5	.241
	Majors			**175**	**495**	**71**	**116**	**19**	**0**	**8**	**46**	**6**	**.234**
	Minors			**1569**	**6115**	**911**	**1845**	**371**	**60**	**106**	**710**	**77**	**.302**

JOSEPH DANIEL JENKINS

Born October 12, 1890 at Shelbyville, TN. Died June 21, 1974 at Fresno, CA.
Height 5' 11", Weight 170. Batted right. Threw right.

Year	Club	League	POS	G	AB	R	H	2B	3B	HR	RBI	SB	BA
1912	Rome	SEastern	C-OF	51	156	13	27	4	3	1	-	8	.173
1913	Keokuk	Cent A	C	121	413	55	117	-	-	-	-	14	.283
1914	St. Louis	American	C	19	32	0	4	1	1	0	0	2	.125
1915	Atlanta	South A	C	96	262	24	66	9	5	1	-	7	.252
1916	Houston	Texas	C	113	329	35	105	24	10	3	-	3	.319

Year	Club	League	POS	G	AB	R	H	2B	3B	HR	RBI	SB	BA
1917	Chicago	American	PH	10	9	0	1	0	0	0	2	0	.111
1918		Military Service											
1919	Chicago	American	C	11	19	0	3	1	0	0	1	1	.158
1920	Salt Lake	P C	C	107	289	35	75	13	2	6	-	3	.260
1921	Salt Lake	P C	C	94	184	27	62	14	0	11	37	2	.337
1922	Salt Lake	P C	C	125	351	36	105	17	1	8	40	1	.299
1923	Salt Lake	P C	C	104	303	51	106	23	1	9	51	5	.350
1924	Salt Lake/LA	P C	C	117	333	44	96	12	2	9	66	2	.288
1925	Atlanta	South A	C	91	247	34	75	13	7	2	38	2	.304
1926	Seattle	P C	C	104	247	18	70	11	0	4	45	1	.283
1927	Seattle	P C	C	81	198	24	64	8	1	3	22	0	.323
1928	Newark	Int	C	97	259	32	82	15	3	5	45	2	.317
1929	Newark/Buff.	Int	C	45	96	11	32	4	1	3	24	1	.333
	Elmira	NY-Penn	C	35	103	16	34	4	3	2	18	1	.330
1930	Elmira	NY-Penn	C	102	337	43	108	18	6	3	53	0	.320
	Majors			**40**	**60**	**0**	**8**	**2**	**1**	**0**	**3**	**3**	**.133**
	Minors			**1483**	**4107**	**498**	**1224**	**189**	**45**	**70**	**439**	**52**	**.298**

SAMUEL JETHROE

Born January 20, 1922 at East St. Louis, IL.
Height 6' 1", Weight 178. Batted both. Threw right.
Set International League record with 89 stolen bases in 1949.

Year	Club	League	POS	G	AB	R	H	2B	3B	HR	RBI	SB	BA
1942	Cincinnati	Neg Nat	OF	10	39	-	19	5	1	0	-	1	.487
1943	Cleveland	Neg Nat	OF	25	98	-	28	8	4	2	-	0	.286
1944	Cleveland	Neg Nat	OF	68	275	-	97	14	2	2	-	18	.353
1945	Cleveland	Neg Nat	OF	56	214	-	84	10	10	3	-	21	.310
1946	Cleveland	Neg Nat	OF	62	226	-	70	-	-	6	-	20	.310
1947	Cleveland	Neg Nat	OF	70	288	-	98	5	0	2	-	3	.340
1948	Montreal	Int	OF	76	292	52	94	19	11	1	25	18	.322
1949	Montreal	Int	OF	153	635	154	207	34	19	17	83	89	.326
1950	Boston	National	OF	141	582	100	159	28	8	18	58	35	.273
1951	Boston	National	OF	148	572	101	160	29	10	18	65	35	.280
1952	Boston	National	OF	151	608	79	141	23	7	13	58	28	.232
1953	Toledo	A A	OF	145	543	137	168	32	10	28	74	27	.309
1954	Pittsburgh	National	OF	2	1	0	0	0	0	0	0	0	.000
	Toronto	Int	OF	154	593	113	181	36	8	21	84	23	.305
1955	Toronto	Int	OF	145	485	88	127	16	4	16	66	24	.262
1956	Toronto	Int	OF	149	567	105	163	25	4	19	68	22	.287
1957	Toronto	Int	OF	130	451	83	125	16	6	15	39	24	.277
1958	Toronto	Int	OF	68	184	20	43	11	0	2	18	5	.234
	Majors			**442**	**1763**	**280**	**460**	**80**	**25**	**49**	**181**	**98**	**.261**
	Minors			**1020**	**3750**	**752**	**1108**	**189**	**62**	**119**	**457**	**232**	**.295**
	Negro Lg			**291**	**1140**	**-**	**396**	**42**	**17**	**15**	**-**	**63**	**.347**

●

It was not uncommon for a minor leaguer to attempt to play an inning at each of the nine positions in a late-season game. One of the most unusual and well played was by pitcher Red Lucas with Seattle on October 18, 1925. A good hitter who played occasionally in the infield, he was without error at each position, pitched well, and hit a homer and single in a 2-0 win over Portland.

LEONARD EDWARD JOHNSTON
Born March 15, 1929 at Pontiac, MI.
Height 5' 10", Weight 175. Batted left. Threw left.

Manager: Burlington Carolina 1967-68; Sumter W. Carolinas 1970; Sarasota Gulf Cst 1971; Elmira EL 1972; Cleveland Gulf Cst Rookie 1973; Newport News Carolina 1974; Miami Fla St 1976-77; Hagerstown Carolina 1984.

Year	Club	League	POS	G	AB	R	H	2B	3B	HR	RBI	SB	BA
1952	Madisonville	Kitty	OF	61	204	45	72	15	2	1	16	29	.353
1953	Colorado Spr	Western	OF	155	**626**	133	199	26	6	2	68	**60**	.318
1954	Memphis	South A	OF	136	511	82	151	21	5	1	49	**39**	.295
1955	Memphis	South A	OF	44	134	24	34	8	0	0	13	13	.254
	Charleston	A A	OF	104	410	65	118	19	3	0	24	**25**	.288
1956	Richmond	Int	OF	153	**619**	83	**182**	26	5	1	43	**40**	.294
1957	Richmond	Int	OF	151	593	85	168	21	9	3	41	**26**	.283
1958	Richmond	Int	OF	135	474	81	118	18	9	2	38	**37**	.249
1959	Houston	A A	OF	58	173	27	41	7	4	0	15	3	.237
	Charleston	Sally	OF	56	204	35	52	5	4	0	14	8	.255
1960	Asheville	Sally	OF	52	213	51	68	14	4	5	22	10	.319
	Indianapolis	A A	OF	76	270	43	82	11	5	1	35	23	.304
1961	Indianapolis	A A	OF	113	370	69	110	20	6	1	22	25	.297
1962	Indianapolis	A A	OF	113	352	59	95	13	2	1	45	16	.270
1963	Indianapolis	Int	OF	115	305	58	80	14	3	4	30	12	.262
1964	Indianapolis	P C	OF	127	412	75	130	22	7	4	67	11	.316
1965	Indianapolis	P C	OF	81	175	20	36	2	1	2	14	2	.206
1966	Indianapolis	P C	OF	94	235	29	59	7	4	1	19	6	.251
1967	Burlington	Carolina	OF	2	5	0	1	0	0	0	2	0	.200
		Minors		**1826**	**6285**	**1064**	**1796**	**269**	**79**	**29**	**577**	**385**	**.286**

CLARENCE WOODROW JONES
Born November 7, 1941 at Zanesville, OH
Height 6' 2", Weight 185. Batted left. Threw left.

Only player to hit 200+ homers in minors and in Japanese leagues.

Year	Club	League	POS	G	AB	R	H	2B	3B	HR	RBI	SB	BA
1959	Johnson City	Appalac	1B	3	7	2	0	0	0	0	0	0	.000
1960						Did not play in O.B.							
1961	Kokomo	Midwest	OF	51	160	28	34	6	0	8	27	2	.213
	Artesia	Soph	OF	36	118	37	43	10	0	9	32	2	.364
1962	Great Falls	Pioneer	OF-1B	114	347	77	97	16	0	25	89	3	.280
1963	Santa Barb	Calif	OF	98	319	56	86	13	2	20	66	5	.270
	Albuquerque	Texas	1B-OF	12	30	5	3	0	0	2	6	1	.100
1964	Salem	NWest	OF	139	489	**114**	**168**	30	5	33	**120**	13	.344
1965	Albuquerque	Texas	1B	121	416	76	117	24	2	18	79	4	.281
1966	Tacoma	PC	1B	26	69	11	12	1	0	1	7	0	.174
	Dallas-FtW	Texas	1B	82	270	39	66	17	0	13	43	1	.244
1967	Chicago	National	OF-1B	53	135	13	34	7	0	2	16	0	.252
	Tacoma	PC	1B	61	211	34	60	11	2	14	52	1	.284
1968	Tacoma	PC	1B	146	523	79	140	21	5	**24**	76	5	.268
	Chicago	National	1B	5	2	0	0	0	0	0	0	0	.000
1969	Indianapolis	AA	1B-OF	129	447	68	110	20	4	21	82	3	.246
1970	Nankai	Jap Pac	1B	128	443	69	108	16	0	33	88	9	.244
1971	Nankai	Jap Pac	1B	125	412	62	95	11	0	35	73	4	.231
1972	Nankai	Jap Pac	1B	126	452	65	132	19	1	32	70	4	.292

1973	Nankai	Jap Pac	1B	126	410	75	100	9	0	32	76	1	.244
1974	Kintetsu	Jap Pac	1B	130	411	66	93	12	1	**38**	90	5	.226
1975	Kintetsu	Jap Pac	1B	130	429	54	98	12	0	29	73	3	.228
1976	Kintetsu	Jap Pac	1B	114	377	54	92	12	1	**36**	68	0	.244
1977	Kintetsu	Jap Pac	1B	82	248	30	44	8	1	11	24	0	.177
1978	Aguascal	Mexican	DH-1B	134	424	78	132	27	1	23	88	3	.311
		Majors		**58**	**137**	**13**	**34**	**7**	**0**	**2**	**16**	**0**	**.248**
		Minors		**1152**	**3830**	**704**	**1068**	**196**	**21**	**211**	**767**	**43**	**.279**
		Japan		**961**	**3182**	**475**	**762**	**99**	**4**	**246**	**562**	**26**	**.239**

JOHN WILLIAM JONES
Born May 13, 1901 at Coatesville, PA. Died November 3, 1956 at Baltimore, MD.
Height 5' 11", Weight 195. Batted left. Threw left.

Year	Club	League	POS	G	AB	R	H	2B	3B	HR	RBI	SB	BA
1923	Montreal	E Canada	OF-P	82	300	60	111	16	8	9	-	14	**.370**
	Philadelphia	American	OF	1	4	0	1	0	0	0	1	0	.250
1924	Portland	P C	OF	36	114	12	38	3	2	1	10	1	.333
	Denver	Western	OF	50	179	32	55	9	4	9	-	4	.307
	Williamsport	NY-Penn	OF	18	68	14	18	3	1	3	-	1	.265
1925	Spartanburg	Sally	OF	125	519	112	183	37	15	25	105	7	.353
1926	Memphis	South A	OF	68	259	36	66	17	6	4	27	2	.255
	Knoxville	Sally	OF	77	270	42	88	16	5	8	27	4	.326
1927	Charl/Ash	Sally	OF	145	539	84	163	24	**22**	18	87	3	.302
1928	Bridgeport	Eastern	OF	17	59	11	18	5	2	0	12	0	.305
	Wilkes-Barre	NY-Penn	OF	6	20	4	2	0	0	1	2	0	.100
	Charlotte	Sally	OF	98	349	51	106	18	3	15	61	1	.304
1929	Charlotte	Sally	OF	14	45	4	7	1	0	0	0	0	.156
	HighPt/Hend	Piedmont	OF	113	397	87	130	21	4	31	75	4	.327
1930	Henderson	Piedmont	OF	142	542	114	187	43	10	28	124	7	.345
	Hollywood	P C	OF	25	89	17	24	5	1	0	16	0	.270
1931	Hollywood	P C	OF	3	7	1	1	0	0	0	0	0	.143
	Dallas	Texas	OF	2	4	0	0	0	0	0	0	1	.000
	HighPt/Green	Piedmont	OF	40	158	25	36	9	3	3	24	0	.228
	Danville	III	OF	21	84	10	19	5	2	1	10	0	.226
1932	Rich/Albany	Eastern	OF	75	314	55	110	34	5	4	57	0	.350
	Philadelphia	American	OF	4	6	0	1	0	0	0	0	0	.167
1933	JC/Albany	Int	OF	49	175	24	50	7	0	8	27	0	.286
	Durham	Piedmont	OF	40	154	20	55	6	2	1	22	0	.357
	Charleston	Mid Atl	OF	12	48	3	16	3	0	0	8	0	.333
1934	Seattle	P C	OF	9	35	5	10	1	1	0	3	0	.286
	Sprg/Wor/Wat	NEastern	OF	87	316	61	114	25	4	9	-	8	**.361**
1935	Elmira	NY-Penn	OF	10	35	1	6	2	0	0	4	0	.171
		Majors		**5**	**10**	**0**	**2**	**0**	**0**	**0**	**1**	**0**	**.200**
		Minors		**1364**	**5079**	**885**	**1613**	**310**	**100**	**178**	**701**	**57**	**.318**

WALTER FRANKLIN JUDNICH
Born January 24, 1917 at San Francisco, CA. Died July 12, 1971 at Glendale, CA.
Height 6' 01", Weight 205. Batted left. Threw left.

Year	Club	League	POS	G	AB	R	H	2B	3B	HR	RBI	SB	BA
1935	Akron	Mid Atl	OF-1B	109	398	57	107	24	7	8	61	7	.269
1936	Norfolk	Piedmont	OF	143	565	100	171	26	11	24	108	5	.303

Year	Club	League	POS	G	AB	R	H	2B	3B	HR	RBI	SB	BA
1937	Oakland	P C	OF	175	651	107	206	42	14	11	81	21	.316
1938	Kansas City	A A	OF	150	557	94	152	34	10	22	104	8	.273
1939	Newark	Int	OF	149	538	95	153	23	13	21	105	8	.284
1940	St. Louis	American	OF	137	519	97	157	27	7	24	89	8	.303
1941	St. Louis	American	OF	146	546	90	155	40	6	14	83	5	.284
1942	St. Louis	American	OF	132	457	78	143	22	6	17	82	3	.313
1943-45					Military Service								
1946	St. Louis	American	OF	142	511	60	134	23	4	15	72	0	.262
1947	St. Louis	American	1B-OF	144	500	58	129	24	3	18	64	2	.258
1948	Cleveland	American	OF-1B	79	218	36	56	13	3	2	29	2	.257
1949	Pittsburgh	National	OF	10	35	5	8	1	0	0	1	0	.229
	San Francisco	P C	OF	116	379	75	102	15	2	18	63	0	.269
1950	Seattle	P C	OF-1B	166	505	91	144	22	1	19	84	3	.285
1951	Seattle	P C	OF	147	517	93	170	35	8	21	102	4	.329
1952	Seattle	P C	OF	177	668	93	192	**41**	5	15	105	4	.287
1953	Seattle	P C	OF-1B	163	583	81	174	26	4	16	101	0	.298
1954	Portland	P C	OF	156	547	70	149	26	2	18	81	1	.272
1955	Port/SF	P C	OF	137	451	67	126	30	2	9	60	2	.279
	Majors			**790**	**2786**	**424**	**782**	**150**	**29**	**90**	**420**	**20**	**.281**
	Minors			**1788**	**6359**	**1023**	**1846**	**344**	**79**	**202**	**1055**	**63**	**.291**

JOSEPH HENRY KELLY

Born September 23, 1886 at Weir City, KS. Died August 16, 1977 at St. Joseph, MO.
Weight 5' 9", Weight 175. Batted right. Threw right.

Manager: St. Joseph WL 1926; Amarillo WL 1927; Columbia S Atl A 1928-29; Oklahoma City WL 1930.

Year	Club	League	POS	G	AB	R	H	2B	3B	HR	RBI	SB	BA
1908	Tulsa	Kan-Ok	OF	65	242	49	73	18	6	1	-	4	.302
1909	Pittsburg	West A	OF-2B	120	457	66	111	38	13	4	-	20	.243
1910	Joplin	West A	2B	115	450	90	135	20	11	7	-	51	.300
1911	St. Joseph	Western	OF	166	632	115	171	29	9	2	51	63	.271
1912	St. Joseph	Western	OF-2B	168	**682**	137	196	38	15	4	-	46	.287
1913	St. Joseph	Western	OF	161	658	136	209	28	13	6	-	**68**	.318
1914	Pittsburgh	National	OF	141	508	47	113	19	9	1	48	21	.222
1915	Indianapolis	A A	OF	147	550	107	165	20	5	1	76	**61**	.300
1916	Indianapolis	A A	OF	35	121	15	36	4	2	1	-	8	.298
	Chicago	National	OF	54	169	18	43	7	1	2	15	10	.254
1917	Boston	National	OF	116	445	41	99	9	8	3	36	21	.222
1918	Boston	National	OF	47	155	20	36	2	4	0	15	12	.232
1919	Boston	National	OF	18	64	3	9	1	0	0	3	2	.141
	Toledo	A A	OF	128	505	71	127	18	9	2	-	23	.251
1920	Toledo	A A	OF	166	**695**	100	207	25	10	3	92	29	.298
1921	San Francisco	P C	OF	168	619	86	176	39	8	4	83	23	.284
1922	San Francisco	P C	OF	156	573	114	191	32	8	5	68	32	.333
1923	San Francisco	P C	OF	107	443	86	154	38	3	5	41	15	.348
1924	San Francisco	P C	OF	149	638	117	192	55	3	8	65	21	.301
1925	SF/Vernon	P C	OF	24	71	11	19	1	0	0	5	1	.268
	Omaha	Western	OF	95	406	84	131	22	2	2	-	8	.323
1926	St. Joseph	Western	OF	141	535	113	167	22	10	1	-	22	.312
1927	Amarillo	Western	OF	116	394	78	133	23	11	5	-	17	.338
1928	Columbia	S Atl A	OF	137	508	90	166	14	11	3	56	15	.327
1929	Columbia	S Atl A	OF	147	542	97	158	22	6	2	43	28	.292
1930	Oklahoma C	Western	OF	16	33	2	2	0	1	0	0	0	.061
	Majors			**376**	**1341**	**129**	**300**	**38**	**22**	**6**	**117**	**66**	**.224**
	Minors			**2527**	**9754**	**1764**	**2919**	**506**	**156**	**66**	**580**	**555**	**.299**

WILLIAM HENRY KELLY
Born December 28, 1898 at Syracuse, NY. Died April 8, 1990 at Syracuse, NY.
Height 6', Weight 190. Batted right. Threw right.
Umpired in the NYPL, EL, IL, PCL and AA from 1932 to 1941. In military service 1941-43.
Manager: Elizabethton Appalach 1945; Davenport III 1946; Los Angeles P C 1947-50; Springfield IL 1951-52; Joplin WA 1954.
Elected to International League Hall of Fame in 1954.

Year	Club	League	POS	G	AB	R	H	2B	3B	HR	RBI	SB	BA
1920	Philadelphia	American	1B	9	13	0	3	1	0	0	0	0	.231
1921	Bay City	Mich-Ont	1B	104	355	65	113	34	7	4	77	15	.318
1922	Buffalo	Int	1B	115	377	61	115	23	10	12	54	4	.305
1923	Buffalo	Int	1B	164	620	123	217	49	9	15	128	8	.350
1924	Buffalo	Int	1B	165	629	108	204	40	9	**28**	**155**	3	.324
1925	Buffalo	Int	1B	162	629	131	200	28	12	26	**125**	0	.318
1926	Buffalo	Int	1B	165	612	135	202	38	7	**44**	**151**	4	.330
1927	Minneapolis	A A	1B	52	187	26	43	5	0	10	24	0	.230
	Newark	Int	1B	78	297	42	86	11	4	8	49	4	.290
1928	Philadelphia	National	1B	23	71	6	12	1	1	0	5	0	.169
	Roch/Buff	Int	1B	136	473	63	132	31	4	18	73	3	.279
1929	Buffalo	Int	PH	5	5	1	1	0	0	1	3	0	.200
	Beaumont	Texas	1B	127	451	77	142	31	7	13	86	11	.315
1930	Fort Worth	Texas	1B	97	349	59	100	17	2	23	70	3	.287
	Buffalo	Int	1B	39	133	22	34	4	1	5	22	2	.256
1931	Mobile	South A	1B	37	138	12	27	5	2	0	15	0	.196
	Majors			**32**	**84**	**6**	**15**	**2**	**1**	**0**	**5**	**0**	**.179**
	Minors			**1446**	**5255**	**925**	**1616**	**316**	**74**	**207**	**1032**	**57**	**.308**

GEORGE P. "DUMMY" KIHM
Born August 2, 1873 at New Washington, OH. Died October 10, 1936 at Delphos, OH.
Height 5' 11", Weight 178. Batted right. Threw right.
Kihm was a deaf mute. Led AA first basemen in putouts 1903-08.

Year	Club	League	POS	G	AB	R	H	2B	3B	HR	SB	BA
1895	Findlay	Int	C-1-O-P	37	169	45	57	5	7	1	27	.337
	Jackson	Mich St	1B	31	141	41	57	14	2	8	8	.404
1896	Tacoma	Pac NW	1B	34	122	41	43	10	4	7	13	.352
	Toledo	Int	1B-C	58	200	44	60	17	8	4	22	.300
1897	Ft. Wayne	Int	1B	124	440	129	154	31	12	17	31	.350
1898	FtW/NCastle	Int	1B	148	585	96	169	27	18	9	36	.289
1899	Wheel/Mans	Int	1B	27	104	15	25	3	0	1	2	.240
1900	Troy	NY St	1B	110	417	77	122	10	11	4	15	.293
1901	Troy	NY St	1B	78	299	54	99	12	7	1	9	.331
	Los Angeles	Calif	1B	49	163	35	43	7	6	2	10	.264
1902	Indianapolis	A A	1B	134	514	99	152	36	11	5	16	.296
1903	Indianapolis	A A	1B	124	463	93	148	28	12	3	14	.320
1904	Columbus	A A	1B	**154**	575	93	179	38	10	4	23	.311
1905	Columbus	A A	1B	143	508	71	145	29	6	3	15	.285
1906	Columbus	A A	1B	148	514	72	143	17	6	2	11	.278
1907	Columbus	A A	1B	158	573	81	165	17	10	0	22	.288
1908	Columbus	A A	1B	154	533	60	128	17	5	0	16	.240
1909	Grand Rapids	Central	1B	128	416	35	108	10	3	4	6	.260
1910	Grand Rapids	Central	1B	141	488	54	120	21	9	3	20	.246
1911	GRapids/Nwk	Central	1B	135	437	64	128	21	6	1	15	.293
	Minors			**2115**	**7661**	**1299**	**2245**	**370**	**153**	**79**	**331**	**.293**

WESCOTT WILLIAM "WES" KINGDON
Born July 4, 1900 at Los Angeles, CA. Died April 19, 1975 at Capistrano, CA.
Height 5' 8", Weight 148. Batted right. Threw right.
Manager: Bartlesville West A 1937; Dover and Pocomoke City E Shore 1938; Pocomoke City E Shore 1939; Selma SEastern 1940.

Year	Club	League	POS	G	AB	R	H	2B	3B	HR	RBI	SB	BA
1919	Portland	P C	SS-2B	47	149	16	26	3	0	0	-	3	.174
1920	Portland	P C	SS	126	388	39	76	15	3	0	-	5	.196
1921	Bridgeport	Eastern	SS	150	509	71	138	25	16	3	-	5	.271
1922	Bridgeport	Eastern	SS	147	512	77	148	19	10	3	-	17	.289
1923	Buffalo	Int	2-3-S	144	475	66	126	31	9	5	-	4	.265
1924	Buffalo	Int	SS-2B	168	546	78	152	24	8	7	-	4	.278
1925	Buffalo	Int	SS	158	527	80	139	25	5	11	86	0	.264
1926	Buff/Newark	Int	SS	148	526	115	157	26	4	13	70	8	.298
1927	Newark	Int	S-3B	159	514	82	162	26	5	8	80	15	.315
1928	Newark	Int	SS	162	566	106	167	32	4	7	62	11	.295
1929	Newark	Int	2B-3B	118	366	49	84	15	1	2	45	9	.230
1930	Columbus	A A	SS	108	392	60	105	23	9	3	-	15	.268
	Houston	Texas	SS	18	50	9	11	1	0	0	7	0	.220
1931	Chattanooga	Sally	SS	155	603	96	167	18	14	3	54	8	.277
1932	Washington	American	3B-SS	18	34	10	11	3	1	0	3	0	.324
	Chattanooga	Sally	2-S	64	228	49	75	14	7	0	34	5	.329
1933	Chattanooga	Sally	SS	120	442	62	124	20	4	5	70	6	.281
	Minneapolis	A A	-	11	26	5	5	1	0	1	-	0	.192
1934	Memphis	Sally	SS	68	240	46	68	20	3	2	42	0	.283
1935-36				Did not play in O. B.									
1937	Bartlesville	West A	3-S	41	143	25	34	4	1	0	12	3	.238
	Sanford	Fla St	2B	29	105	17	28	3	0	0	13	8	.267
1938	Pocomoke C	E Shore	2B	54	179	37	59	14	1	4	28	3	.330
1939	Pocomoke C	E Shore	-	14	43	7	14	3	0	2	7	0	.326
1940	Selma	SEastern	SS	19	52	6	16	4	0	0	10	0	.308
		Majors		**18**	**34**	**10**	**11**	**3**	**1**	**0**	**3**	**0**	**.324**
		Minors		**2228**	**7581**	**1198**	**2081**	**366**	**104**	**79**	**620**	**129**	**.275**

JOHN WESLEY KNIGHT
Born October 6, 1885 at Philadelphia, PA. Died December 19, 1965 at Walnut Creek, CA.
Height 6' 02-1/2", Weight 180. Batted right. Threw right.
Manager: Cleveland AA 1914-15; Denver WL 1928.

Year	Club	League	POS	G	AB	R	H	2B	3B	HR	RBI	SB	BA
1905	Philadelphia	American	SS-3B	88	325	28	66	12	1	3	29	4	.203
1906	Philadelphia	American	3B-2B	74	253	29	49	7	2	3	20	6	.194
1907	Phil/Boston	Ameican	3B-SS	138	499	37	107	16	4	2	41	9	.214
1908	Baltimore	Eastern	SS-3B	140	495	62	113	10	12	9	-	16	.228
1909	New York	American	S-1-2	116	360	46	85	8	5	0	40	15	.236
1910	New York	American	IF-OF	117	414	58	129	25	4	3	45	23	.312
1911	New York	American	INF	132	470	69	126	16	7	3	62	18	.268
1912	Washington	American	2B-1B	32	93	10	15	2	1	0	9	4	.161
	Jersey City	Eastern	1B	78	257	33	54	10	7	1	-	9	.210
1913	Jersey City	Int	2B	77	300	40	81	9	6	1	-	16	.270
	New York	American	1B-2B	70	250	24	59	10	0	0	24	7	.236
1914	Cleveland	A A	SS	135	530	75	163	26	13	3	58	13	.308
1915	Cleveland	A A	SS-2B	131	440	61	124	26	5	4	39	12	.282

1916	Minneapolis	A A	1B-2B	164	592	89	151	27	9	1	-	22	.255
1917	Minneapolis	A A	1B-3B	151	563	75	154	32	8	6	-	16	.274
1918	Minneapolis	A A	1B	27	107	6	30	6	0	0	-	5	.280
1919	Seattle	P C	1-2-3	146	523	54	157	35	8	2	8	8	.300
1920	Oakland	P C	INF	188	693	86	196	53	5	6	-	9	.283
1921	Oakland	P C	2B-1B	179	667	109	228	62	11	15	129	10	.342
1922	Oakland	P C	2B-1B	80	262	31	70	15	1	1	30	5	.267
1923	Oakland	P C	2B-1B	127	378	56	127	24	0	6	58	4	.336
1924	Denver	Western	1B-2B	157	610	114	193	56	12	6	-	10	.316
1925	Denver	Western	1B	169	645	151	227	56	16	19	-	8	.352
1926	Sacramento	P C	1-3-S	96	324	52	91	19	2	5	50	3	.281
1927	Sacramento	P C	1B	87	270	36	84	14	2	10	46	5	.311
1928	Denver	Western	1B	103	341	42	103	22	6	6	-	3	.302
	Majors			**767**	**2664**	**301**	**636**	**96**	**24**	**14**	**270**	**86**	**.239**
	Minors			**2235**	**7997**	**1172**	**2346**	**502**	**123**	**101**	**418**	**174**	**.293**

CHARLES ELMER "PUNCH" KNOLL

Born October 7, 1881 at Evansville, IN. Died February 8, 1960 at Evansville, IN.
Height 5' 7-1/2", Weight 170. Batted right. Threw right.

Brother of Julius "Hub" Knoll, a well known minor league player.

Father-in-law of Sylvester Simon (see playing record elsewhere in this section).

Manager: Evansville 1908-09; Dayton 1910-12 and part of 1913; Evansville 1913-17; Ludington 1920; Bay City 1921-24; Danville 1925-26; Quincy part of 1927; Fort Wayne 1928; Wilkes-Barre part of 1929; Fort Wayne 1930.

Year	Club	League	POS	G	AB	R	H	2B	3B	HR	RBI	SB	BA
1901	Evansville	III	OF	43	170	24	40	8	3	1	-	6	.235
	Memphis	South A	OF	48	184	37	51	11	3	0	-	3	.277
1902	Nashville	South A	OF	129	**497**	83	133	18	8	1	-	28	.268
1903	Nashville	South A	OF	122	488	64	137	27	5	2	-	28	.281
1904	Nashville	South A	OF-C	101	365	64	98	15	11	3	-	22	.268
1905	Washington	American	OF	85	244	24	52	10	5	0	29	3	.213
1906	New Orleans	South A	OF	135	486	60	117	25	5	0	-	28	.241
1907	Evansville	Central	OF-C	122	389	37	88	17	2	2	-	18	.226
1908	Evansville	Central	OF	140	506	85	157	28	6	**12**	-	30	.310
1909	Evansville	Central	OF	125	450	63	142	18	9	**11**	-	31	.316
1910	Dayton	Central	OF	139	477	79	130	18	10	5	-	27	.273
1911	Dayton	Central	OF	132	478	85	143	26	12	**11**	-	23	.299
1912	Dayton	Central	OF	117	356	46	100	17	4	0	-	14	.281
1913	Evansville	Central	OF	127	441	64	126	29	6	5	-	14	.281
1914	Evansville	Central	OF	125	453	82	139	25	9	9	-	18	.307
1915	Evansville	Central	OF	122	431	58	113	18	2	3	-	17	.262
1916	Evansville	Central	OF	131	446	50	123	20	9	2	-	14	.276
1917	Evansville	Central	OF	107	395	42	91	16	3	3	-	9	.230
1918					Did not play in O. B.								
1919	Evansville	III	OF	52	172	21	40	7	2	2	-	2	.233
1920	Ludington	Central	OF	116	408	69	117	28	4	7	-	3	.287
1921	Bay City	Mich-Ont	OF	100	392	76	121	35	9	0	59	11	.309
1922	Bay City	Mich-Ont	OF	119	444	70	130	27	12	4	67	11	.293
1923	Bay City	Mich-Ont	OF	64	188	34	61	10	3	1	32	1	.324
1924	Bay City	Mich-Ont	OF	31	58	5	15	8	1	0	9	0	.259
1925	Danville	III	OF	35	67	13	22	1	2	1	-	0	.328
1926	Danville	III	OF	25	32	3	8	1	0	0	-	1	.250
1927	Quincy	III	OF	9	21	1	4	2	0	0	1	0	.190

Year	Club	League	POS	G	AB	R	H	2B	3B	HR	RBI	SB	BA
1928	Fort Wayne	Central	P-C	3	3	0	1	0	0	0	0	0	.333
1929	Wilkes-Barre	NY-Penn					Manager, did not play.						
1930	Fort Wayne	Central	OF	3	3	0	1	0	0	0	1	0	.333
	Majors			**85**	**244**	**24**	**52**	**10**	**5**	**0**	**29**	**3**	**.213**
	Minors			**2522**	**8800**	**1315**	**2448**	**455**	**140**	**85**	**169**	**359**	**.278**

JESSE ROY "HORSE" LEVAN
Born July 15, 1926 at Reading, PA.
Height 6', Weight 205. Batted left. Threw right.
Placed on permanently suspended list of Organized Ball, July 3, 1959, for cooperating with gamblers in "foul ball hitting" scandal in Southern Association.

Year	Club	League	POS	G	AB	R	H	2B	3B	HR	RBI	SB	BA
1944	Wilmington	Inter-St	OF	136	522	111	165	28	8	4	71	28	.316
1945-46							Military Service						
1947	Wilmington	Inter-St	OF	139	**570**	106	176	19	20	19	109	14	.309
	Philadelphia	National	OF	2	9	3	4	0	0	0	1	0	.444
1948	Toronto	Int	OF	31	106	14	28	3	0	3	22	3	.264
	Wilmington	Inter-St	OF	113	439	85	151	34	8	7	106	12	.344
1949	Milwaukee	A A	OF	12	29	5	3	0	0	0	2	0	.103
	Hartford	Eastern	OF	18	60	9	13	4	0	0	9	1	.217
	Bluefield	Appachal	OF	5	16	3	3	0	0	1	3	0	.188
	Sunbury	Inter-St	OF	57	223	31	65	12	3	5	31	2	.291
1950	Hagerstown	Inter-St	OF-1B	130	512	92	**171**	34	8	13	102	10	**.334**
1951	Raleigh	Carolina	1B	5	18	3	4	1	0	1	4	0	.222
	St. Hyacinthe	Provincl	1B-OF	120	472	73	164	**36**	6	17	93	4	.347
1952	Miami Beach	Fla St	1B	152	574	**93**	**192**	**35**	3	10	87	13	**.334**
1953	Atlanta	South A	1B	3	14	2	3	0	0	0	1	0	.214
	Ft.Lauderdale	Fla St	OF-1B	138	**542**	96	**175**	31	9	16	97	20	.323
1954	Miami Beach	Fla St	1B-P	101	374	83	**130**	21	5	**23**	89	18	**.348**
	Charlotte	Sally	1B	29	114	23	47	11	3	7	41	2	.412
	Washington	American	3B-1B	7	10	1	3	0	0	0	0	0	.300
1955	Charlotte	Sally	1B-OF	87	329	35	92	17	3	7	37	2	.280
	Washington	American	PH	16	16	1	3	0	0	1	4	0	.188
1956	Chattanooga	Sally	1B	150	543	91	169	28	3	25	114	1	.311
1957	Chattanooga	Sally	1B	153	**588**	89	169	**38**	9	25	**114**	8	.287
1958	Chattanooga	Sally	1B	153	558	99	163	15	4	26	90	2	.292
1959	Chattanooga	Sally	1B	75	279	38	94	13	2	7	43	1	.337
	Majors			**25**	**35**	**5**	**10**	**0**	**0**	**1**	**5**	**0**	**.286**
	Minors			**1807**	**6882**	**1181**	**2177**	**380**	**94**	**216**	**1265**	**141**	**.316**

●

Lincoln and Omaha were deadlocked at 10-10 in a long Western League game on July 5, 1916. It was the 18th inning and Lincoln manager Ducky Holmes, who had played in the majors many years before, felt he had to do something desperate before the curtain of darkness fell. Although 47 years old, he inserted himself as a pinch hitter and singled in the winning run.

EDWARD CLARENCE LEVY
(Real name Whitner. Levy was name of step-father.)
Born October 28, 1916 at Birmingham, AL.
Height 6' 5 1/2", Weight 190. Batted right. Threw right.
Manager: Sanford Fla St 1946 & 50; Orlando Fla St 1951-52; Daytona Beach Fla St 1953-54;
Vidalia Ga St 1955.

Year	Club	League	POS	G	AB	R	H	2B	3B	HR	RBI	SB	BA
1936	Norfolk	Piedmont	1B	26	96	10	25	4	0	2	13	1	.260
	Augusta	Sally	1B	38	146	31	52	11	6	1	25	2	.356
	Newark	Int	1B	2	2	0	0	0	0	0	0	0	.000
	Binghamton	NY-Penn	1B	17	55	7	12	4	3	0	7	0	.218
1937	Norfolk	Piedmont	1B	136	524	94	164	40	12	14	88	18	.313
1938	Binghamton	Eastern	1B	134	509	81	162	35	14	12	81	23	.318
1939	Newark	Int	1B	95	348	50	91	22	3	11	47	5	.261
	Oakland	P C	1B	53	191	14	41	6	5	4	26	6	.215
1940	Philadelphia	Naitonal	PH	1	1	0	0	0	0	0	0	0	.000
	Newark	Int	1B	137	536	87	154	26	4	20	87	19	.287
1941	Newark	Int	1B	23	86	11	22	5	0	1	11	2	.256
	Kansas City	A A	1B	64	233	32	72	10	3	4	30	11	.309
1942	New York	American	1B	13	41	5	5	0	0	0	3	1	.122
	Kansas City	A A	1B	139	503	63	154	37	7	8	70	21	.306
1943	Newark	Int	OF	144	512	75	165	31	8	12	81	15	.322
1944	New York	American	OF	40	153	12	37	11	2	4	29	1	.242
	Milwaukee	A A	OF-3B	46	126	17	36	5	2	1	15	3	.286
1945					Did not play in O. B.								
1946	Sanford	Fla St	1B	129	462	86	147	30	8	2	97	30	.318
1947	Toronto	Int	1B-OF	126	425	47	122	26	5	13	71	7	.287
1948	Baltimore	Int	1B	121	408	56	99	19	5	22	79	1	.243
1949	San Antonio	Texas	1B	57	184	21	49	8	0	8	35	2	.266
	Springfield	III	OF	37	112	21	35	11	0	3	23	3	.313
1950	Sanford	Fla St	1B	128	406	87	136	33	1	**33**	105	15	.335
1951	Orlando	Fla St	1B	128	437	87	134	29	2	17	89	17	.307
1952	Orlando	Fla St	1B	133	435	88	143	33	3	19	84	14	.329
1953	Day Beach	Fla St	1B-P	116	440	95	133	33	2	14	99	8	.302
1954	Day Beach	Fla St	1B-P	119	415	66	116	27	2	16	98	13	.280
1955	Vidalia	Ga St	1B-P	28	45	7	13	1	0	1	7	3	.289
	Majors			**54**	**195**	**17**	**42**	**11**	**2**	**4**	**32**	**2**	**.215**
	Minors			**2176**	**7636**	**1233**	**2277**	**486**	**95**	**238**	**1368**	**239**	**.298**

WILIAM HENRY LEWIS
Born October 15, 1904 at Ripley, TN. Died October 24, 1977 at Mamphis, TN.
Height 5' 9", Weight 165. Batted right. Threw right.

Year	Club	League	POS	G	AB	R	H	2B	3B	HR	RBI	SB	BA
1924	Vicks/Hattie	Cottn St	2B-SS	75	253	27	49	7	1	2	-	1	.194
1925	Corinth	Tri-St	SS-2B	101	371	63	110	20	9	6	-	3	.296
1926	Blackwell	SWestern	O-S-3	88	306	52	97	18	6	12	-	5	.317
1927	Laredo	Tex Val	SS	74	262	56	101	25	1	11	-	7	.385
	Wichita Falls	Texas	INF	11	29	3	5	3	1	0	6	0	.172
1928					Did not play in O.B.								
1929	Springfield	West A	INF-O	129	425	83	136	31	11	5	67	13	.320
1930	Augusta	Sally	3B	29	103	13	27	6	1	0	4	0	.262
	Independence	West A	SS	87	307	86	122	34	13	4	62	8	.397

1931	Greensboro	Piedmont	3-C-2	128	450	106	144	31	8	12	98	17	.320
1932	Greensboro	Piedmont	C-3-1	115	402	85	132	26	10	12	114	14	.328
1933	St. Louis	National	C	15	35	8	14	1	0	1	8	0	.400
1934	Rochester	Int	C	116	382	55	121	26	7	3	69	2	.317
1935	Montreal	Int	C	87	232	27	61	10	3	0	33	0	.263
	Boston	National	C	6	4	1	0	0	0	0	0	0	.000
1936	Boston	National	C	29	62	11	19	2	0	0	3	0	.306
1937	Indianapolis	A A	C	78	232	27	67	8	3	0	25	1	.289
1938	Indianapolis	A A	C	92	255	31	71	14	2	1	42	5	.278
1939	Indian/Louis	A A	C	83	246	30	72	7	2	0	24	2	.293
1940	Louisville	A A	C	69	179	28	49	5	5	0	28	1	.274
1941	Chattanooga	South A	C	113	345	43	106	19	5	0	51	2	.307
1942	Knoxville	South A	C	120	324	59	104	27	0	2	74	2	.321
1943	Knoxville	South A	C	59	111	19	30	3	1	1	17	0	.270
1944	Mobile	South A	C	80	217	44	73	14	5	1	41	4	.336
1945	St. Paul	AA	C	90	195	24	57	7	3	1	30	0	.292
	Majors			**50**	**101**	**20**	**33**	**3**	**0**	**1**	**11**	**0**	**.327**
	Minors			**1824**	**5626**	**961**	**1734**	**341**	**97**	**73**	**785**	**87**	**.308**

ABEL LEZOTTE
Born April 13, 1870 at Lewiston, ME. Died December 4, 1926 at Wilkes-Barre, PA.
Height 5'8", Weight 174.
Manager: Wilkes-Barre East 1907-08.
Hit 29 triples in 1895, then a record.

Year	Club	League	POS	G	AB	R	H	2B	3B	HR	SB	BA
1891	Lewiston	New Eng	C-O-1-3	31	132	19	39	10	1	1	6	.295
1892	Lewiston	New Eng	OF	66	314	53	85	19	1	**10**	8	.271
1893	Lewiston	New Eng	OF	92	**403**	100	**144**	25	3	25	16	.357
1894	Wilkes-Barre	Eastern	OF	78	336	73	108	21	15	5	8	.321
	Lewiston	New Eng	OF	2	8	0	0	0	0	0	0	.000
1895	Wilkes-Barre	Eastern	OF-C	111	484	110	164	31	**29**	5	9	.339
1896	Wilkes-Barre	Eastern	OF	112	500	97	**195**	33	18	3	13	**.390**
	Pittsburgh	National	1B	7	29	3	3	0	0	0	1	.103
1897	Syracuse	Eastern	OF-1B	136	548	90	177	40	9	5	21	.323
1898	Syracuse	Eastern	OF-1B	115	442	47	121	13	6	3	16	.274
1899	Syracuse	Eastern	OF-1B	73	300	50	91	18	2	1	12	.303
1900	Montreal	Eastern	OF	127	522	67	140	27	5	4	8	.268
1901	GR/Wheeling	West A	OF	127	512	101	169	40	8	2	8	.330
1902	Peoria	Western	OF	143	541	58	157	23	12	1	16	.290
1903	Peoria	Western	OF-1B	126	497	51	148	14	12	1	11	.298
1904	St. Joseph	Western	OF-1B	130	505	57	132	26	4	0	15	.261
1905	St. Jopseh	Western	OF	41	155	24	35	5	4	0	3	.226
	Topeka	West A	OF	64	228	31	78	20	0	0	7	.342
1906	Mansfield	Ohio-Pa	OF	71	272	19	69	11	3	1	7	.254
1907	Wilkes-Barre	NY St	PH	1	1	0	0	0	0	0	0	.000
	Majors			**7**	**29**	**3**	**3**	**0**	**0**	**0**	**1**	**.103**
	Minors			**1646**	**6700**	**1047**	**2052**	**376**	**132**	**67**	**184**	**.306**

HOWARD S. LINDIMORE
Born December, 1893. Died November 16, 1933 at Oklahoma City, OK.
Height 5' 11", Weight 160. Batted left. Threw right.

Year	Club	League	POS	G	AB	R	H	2B	3B	HR	RBI	SB	BA
1916	Topeka	Western	SS	22	81	13	23	3	1	1	-	0	.284
1917	Joplin	Western	SS	90	295	48	75	13	3	1	-	3	.254
	Ok City/Tulsa	West A	2-3-O	38	126	18	37	10	1	2	-	3	.294
	Mason City	Cent A	SS	12	42	3	8	1	0	0	-	2	.190
1918					Military Service								
1919	Ok City	Western	SS-3B	135	497	78	157	28	15	2	-	16	.316
1920	Ok City	Western	3B-SS	149	572	104	189	25	12	2	-	20	.330
1921	Los Angeles	P C	3B	132	457	41	123	19	8	1	51	4	.269
1922	Los Angeles	P C	2B-3B	190	672	75	182	25	11	1	71	18	.271
1923	Los Angeles	P C	2B	121	407	52	118	15	4	1	35	7	.290
1924	Salt Lake C	P C	2B	184	764	**183**	259	58	9	15	114	6	.339
1925	Salt Lake City	P C	2B-3B	138	566	96	188	42	3	6	70	5	.332
1926	Hallywood	P C	2B	16	41	7	12	1	0	0	3	2	.293
	Fort Worth	Texas	2B	99	328	55	96	20	3	2	33	7	.293
1927	Fort Worth	Texas	2B	127	450	55	119	15	1	2	52	6	.264
1928					Did not play in O.B.								
1929	Wichita	Western	2B	142	510	93	147	28	3	8	-	4	.288
1930	Wichita	Western	2B	144	572	126	195	28	7	11	77	9	.341
1931	St. Joseph	Western	2B	132	502	81	166	21	6	2	58	5	.331
1932	St. Joseph	Western	2B	142	565	82	176	34	12	1	93	6	.312
1933	Jop/Musk/Bart	Western	2B-3B	98	379	62	122	19	3	4	-	18	.322
		Minors		**2111**	**7826**	**1272**	**2392**	**405**	**102**	**62**	**657**	**141**	**.306**

KEITH EDWIN LITTLE
Born August 16, 1929 at Grandville, MI.
Height 6' 2-1/2", Weight 210. Batted right. Threw right.
Hit four home runs in one game for Corpus Christi, May 22, 1955.

Year	Club	League	POS	G	AB	R	H	2B	3B	HR	RBI	SB	BA
1948	Thomasville	Ga-Fla	1B	131	500	67	133	16	8	7	73	2	.266
1949	Rome	Can-Amer	1B-OF	125	479	73	162	31	8	19	110	1	.338
	Toledo	A A	PH	1	0	1	0	0	0	0	0	0	.000
1950	Flint	Central	1B	116	469	79	144	**41**	3	17	115	5	.307
1951-52					Military Service								
1953	Buffalo	Int	1B	14	46	9	12	2	0	6	17	0	.261
	Montgomery	Sally	1B	91	303	35	72	24	1	8	45	0	.238
1954	Charleston	A A	1B	24	87	9	15	3	1	4	13	0	.172
	Galveston	Big St	1B	112	400	97	122	21	1	37	113	1	.305
1955	Corpus Christi	Big St	1B	97	364	83	112	16	1	**47**	116	2	.308
	Columbus	Int	1B	8	18	4	3	2	0	1	3	0	.167
1956	Monterrey	Mexican	1B	53	186	22	41	6	2	14	42	0	.220
	Ok City	Texas	1B	82	313	59	83	8	0	28	61	0	.265
1957	Ok City/Hous	Texas	1B	127	441	69	107	24	1	30	64	1	.243
1958	Dallas	Texas	1B	138	480	70	128	26	1	25	95	1	.267
1959	Dallas	Texas	1B	117	397	51	105	15	2	21	65	2	.264
		Minors		**1236**	**4483**	**728**	**1239**	**235**	**29**	**264**	**932**	**15**	**.276**

ANDREW DAVID "DOC" LOTSHAW
Born January 27, 1880 at Cold Springs, IN. Died February 21, 1953 at Indianapolis, IN.
Height 5' 11", Weight 180. Batted left. Threw right.

Led league in home runs six years.

Served the Chicago Bears football team and the Chicago Cubs baseball team as trainer for many years. He actually started as a trainer for the A. E. Staley team before they became the Chicago Bears. He was with the Cubs from 1922 through 1952.

Year	Club	League	POS	G	AB	R	H	2B	3B	HR	SB	BA
1906	Jacksonville	Kitty	O-C-IF	127	475	70	112	14	**24**	**11**	24	.236
1907	Charleston	East Ill	O-2-1	73	270	42	75	9	**9**	**10**	9	.278
1908	Marion/Ports	Ohio St	1-O-2	76	240	28	55	7	6	5	17	.229
1909	Bearstown	Ill-Mo	1B-OF	126	444	72	146	32	**14**	5	39	**.329**
1910	Galesburg	Cent A	1B	134	469	47	91	9	6	4	18	.194
1911	Canton	Ill-Mo	1B-OF	122	451	93	**160**	28	11	**29**	17	**.355**
1912	Canton	Ill-Mo	OF-1B	103	332	76	116	20	11	**11**	32	.349
1913	Covington	Federal	OF	1	3	0	0	0	0	0	0	.000
1914	Champaign	Ill-Mo	1B	89	337	61	80	21	**14**	**10**	15	.237
1915-16			Did not play in O.B.									
1917	Indianapolis	A A	OF-1B	5	19	2	8	0	0	0	0	.421
1918	Indianapolis	A A	OF	9	20	1	2	0	0	0	0	.100
1919	Flint/Brant	Mich-Ont	1B	84	296	59	79	14	4	**13**	11	.267
1920-21			Did not play in O. B.									
1922	Indianapolis	A A	OF	1	1	0	0	0	0	0	0	.000
		Minors		**950**	**3357**	**551**	**924**	**154**	**99**	**98**	**182**	**.275**

MICHAEL LUTZ
Born August 29, 1927 at Leavittsburg, OH.
Height 6' 1", Weight 205. Batted right. Threw right.

Year	Club	League	POS	G	AB	R	H	2B	3B	HR	RBI	SB	BA
1948	Burlington	Cent A	OF	129	471	90	130	32	3	21	100	3	.276
1949	Spartanburg	Tri-St	OF	139	461	85	125	27	5	22	98	10	.271
1950	Dayton	Central	OF	133	473	90	153	35	2	14	86	9	.323
1951	Dallas	Texas	OF	42	126	19	30	6	0	5	21	2	.238
	Wichita	Western	OF	90	299	53	74	13	0	19	55	0	.247
1952	Wichita	Western	OF	19	54	16	14	1	1	2	15	0	.259
	Reading	Eastern	OF	116	390	71	125	26	4	23	**93**	4	**.321**
1953	Indianapolis	A A	OF	15	50	6	6	2	1	1	3	0	.120
	Tulsa	Texas	OF	89	293	49	79	17	0	11	68	3	.270
1954	Tulsa	Texas	OF	133	411	62	114	19	2	13	57	0	.277
1955	Tulsa	Texas	OF	147	475	91	130	13	4	25	90	6	.274
1956	Shreveport	Texas	PH	4	3	0	0	0	0	0	0	0	.000
	Nashville	South A	OF	104	303	39	83	20	3	6	45	1	.274
1957	Shrev/Tuls/SA	Texas	OF	147	481	66	124	11	0	26	83	3	.258
1958	CorpusChristi	Texas	OF	152	546	**114**	**171**	31	3	**39**	111	8	.313
1959	CC/Austin	Texas	OF	117	350	57	88	9	0	12	46	1	.251
1960	Austin	Texas	OF	15	45	4	13	2	0	2	9	0	.289
		Minors		**1591**	**5231**	**912**	**1459**	**264**	**28**	**241**	**980**	**50**	**.279**

EMIL PIERRE "LEFTY" MAILHO
Born December 16, 1909 at Berkeley, CA.
Height 5' 10", Weight 165. Batted left. Threw left.

Year	Club	League	POS	G	AB	R	H	2B	3B	HR	RBI	SB	BA
1930	Phoenix	Ariz St	OF-P	86	323	77	106	9	2	11	52	17	.328
1931	Phoenix	Ariz St	OF-P	95	397	**108**	144	21	6	14	-	20	.363
	Oakland	P C	OF	10	15	3	5	0	1	0	1	0	.333
1932	Oakland	P C	OF	135	456	83	144	23	5	2	42	16	.316
1933	Oakland	P C	OF	180	690	142	209	34	12	4	58	52	.303
1934	Oakland	P C	OF	58	96	14	19	4	0	0	8	4	.198
1935	Oakland	P C	OF	172	652	117	230	42	17	2	88	36	.353
1936	Philadelphia	American	OF	21	18	5	1	0	0	0	0	0	.056
	Atlanta	South A	OF	94	368	64	116	17	9	5	44	10	.315
1937	Atlanta	South A	OF	153	569	108	196	32	10	5	88	13	.344
1938	Atlanta	South A	OF	148	519	99	158	33	9	10	79	21	.304
1939	Atlanta	South A	OF	146	498	**122**	171	38	8	9	83	23	.343
1940	Atlanta	South A	OF	152	555	**144**	202	56	8	10	77	14	.364
1941	Atlanta	South A	OF	128	430	112	128	30	5	4	40	10	.298
1942	Oakland	P C	OF-1B	155	599	91	178	29	3	1	42	15	.297
1943	Oakland	P C	OF	155	598	100	188	37	8	2	46	13	.314
1944	Oakland	P C	OF	123	465	64	129	20	3	0	27	16	.277
1945	San Francisco	P C	OF	149	484	80	148	20	6	1	69	9	.306
1946	Ok City	Texas	OF	55	177	27	40	4	3	0	9	4	.226
	Majors			**21**	**18**	**5**	**1**	**0**	**0**	**0**	**0**	**0**	**.056**
	Minors			**2194**	**7891**	**1555**	**2511**	**449**	**115**	**80**	**853**	**293**	**.318**

WILLIAM HENRY MASSEY
Born January 1871 at Philadelphia, PA. Died October 9, 1940 at Manila, Philippines.
Height 5' 11", Weight 168. Batted right. Threw -.
Umpired in United States League in 1912.

Year	Club	League	POS	G	AB	R	H	2B	3B	HR	SB	BA
1893	Reading	Pa St	1B	32	148	33	51	15	3	3	2	.345
1894	Scran/Phil	Pa St	1B	102	461	101	**176**	27	16	9	14	.382
	Scranton	Eastern	1B	6	22	4	6	1	0	0	0	.273
	Cincinnati	National	1-2-3	13	53	7	15	3	0	0	0	.283
1895	Carbondale	Pa St	1B-C	94	425	120	174	26	14	8	14	.409
1896	Carb/Potts	Pa St	1B	56	249	65	**110**	**22**	5	6	7	**.442**
	Scranton	Eastern	1B	40	172	19	57	9	2	0	0	.331
1897	Scranton	Eastern	1B	114	463	69	145	23	10	3	14	.313
1898	Roch/Spring	Eastern	1B	113	471	71	142	16	11	6	16	.301
1899	Buffalo	Western	1B	59	231	33	67	14	3	3	5	.290
	Hartford	Eastern	1B	47	186	37	67	11	4	0	4	.360
1900	Hartford	Eastern	1B	127	472	70	122	27	**16**	6	7	.258
1901	Hartford	Eastern	1B	115	438	59	122	21	13	3	6	.279
1902	Toronto	Eastern	1B	128	521	77	162	31	10	5	18	.311
1903	Toronto	Eastern	1B	121	461	66	139	**33**	5	3	19	.302
1904	San Francisco	P C	1B	66	240	24	54	8	2	1	6	.225
	Toronto	Eastern	1B	24	79	7	19	3	1	0	3	.241
	Kansas City	A A	1B	55	205	34	71	13	0	0	5	.346
1905	KC/Indian	A A	1B	140	527	67	152	33	3	0	9	.288
1906	Montreal	Eastern	1B	50	178	15	36	4	0	0	8	.202
	Holyoke	Conn	1B	65	255	37	74	13	0	3	12	.290

Year	Club	League	POS	G	AB	R	H	2B	3B	HR	RBI	SB	BA
1907	Holyoke	Conn	1B	123	473	64	132	20	4	1	17		.279
1908	Holyoke	Conn	1B	127	455	52	120	21	2	2	17		.264
1909	Lowell/Law	New Eng	1B	99	351	25	92	14	5	2	8		.262
		Majors		**13**	**53**	**7**	**15**	**3**	**0**	**0**	**0**		**.283**
		Minors		**1903**	**7483**	**1149**	**2290**	**405**	**129**	**64**	**211**		**.306**

HORACE G. "RED" MCBRIDE
Born August 9, 1908 at Bloomsburg, PA.
Height 5' 11", Weight 185. Batted left. Threw left.

Year	Club	League	POS	G	AB	R	H	2B	3B	HR	RBI	SB	BA
1926	Parksley	E Shore	OF	39	141	22	39	8	1	8	-	7	.277
1927	Harrisburg	NY-Penn	OF	140	497	83	152	23	13	7	99	18	.306
1928	Harrisburg	NY-Penn	OF	134	478	64	152	30	18	3	80	12	.318
1929	Harrisburg	NY-Penn	OF	122	434	70	138	21	**18**	7	78	12	.318
1930	Harrisburg	NY-Penn	OF	136	524	115	198	40	**21**	11	97	4	**.378**
1931	Harrisburg	NY-Penn	OF	135	521	92	**181**	37	13	10	100	10	.347
	Montreal	Int	OF	8	31	5	8	1	0	0	3	1	.258
1932	Harrisburg	NY-Penn	OF	3	11	1	3	1	0	0	2	0	.273
	Norfolk	Eastern	OF	15	38	1	11	1	2	0	9	0	.289
1933	Williamsport	NY-Penn	OF	136	503	84	161	29	9	10	**103**	10	.320
1934	Williamsport	NY-Penn	OF	139	536	**114**	**197**	37	12	**26**	**129**	10	.368
1935	Williamsport	NY-Penn	OF			On suspended list							
1936	Williamsport	NY-Penn	OF	125	496	89	163	30	6	**19**	102	7	.329
		Minors		**1132**	**4210**	**740**	**1403**	**258**	**113**	**101**	**802**	**91**	**.333**

JAMES RAY MCDANIEL
Born December 14, 1932 at Marshall, MO.
Height 6' 1", Weight 185.
Batted right. Threw right.
Hit 3 HR on last day of 1958 season to beat out George Freese for HR title, 37 to 35.

Year	Club	League	POS	G	AB	R	H	2B	3B	HR	RBI	SB	BA
1950	Reno	Far West	P	5	4	2	0	0	0	0	0	0	.000
	Riverside	Sunset	P-OF	7	17	5	4	0	0	0	1	0	.235
1951	Tacoma	West Int	P	3	0	0	0	0	0	0	0	0	.000
	Bakersfield	Calif	P	5	6	1	1	0	0	0	0	0	.167
	Yuma	SW Int	P	4	6	3	3	2	0	0	2	0	.500
1952	Visalia	Calif	OF-P	134	518	93	152	30	9	23	134	6	.293
1953	Des Moines	Western	OF	126	422	49	95	12	2	12	56	9	.225
1954	Des Moines	Western	OF	121	357	63	89	16	0	19	67	4	.249
1955	Des Moines	Western	OF-P	133	439	89	103	21	2	24	80	10	.235
1956	DM/Topeka	Western	OF-P	136	488	96	145	31	6	26	95	19	.297
1957	Topeka	Western	OF-P	141	490	122	153	26	4	36	116	10	.312
1958	Salt Lake C.	P C	OF	131	467	92	137	22	6	**37**	100	3	.293
1959	Columbus	Int	OF	64	216	33	54	6	3	9	33	7	.250
	Denver	A A	OF	81	300	61	86	18	0	24	79	2	.287
1960	Denver	A A	OF	134	475	97	137	37	6	19	92	7	.288
1961	Denver	A A	OF	150	554	101	156	27	3	30	114	10	.282
1962	Denver/OK C	A A	OF	126	379	77	94	14	4	17	70	5	.248
1963	Ok City	A A	OF	46	148	23	34	9	1	4	19	2	.230
		Minors		**1547**	**5286**	**1007**	**1443**	**271**	**46**	**280**	**1058**	**94**	**.273**

FRANK BERNARD MCGOWAN

Born November 8, 1901 at Branford, CT. Died May 6, 1982 at Hamden, CT.
Height 5' 11", Weight 190. Batted left. Threw right.
Manager: Baltimore IL 1933-34.

Year	Club	League	POS	G	AB	R	H	2B	3B	HR	RBI	SB	BA
1920	New Haven	Eastern	OF	118	423	56	114	16	8	2	55	14	.270
1921	Newark	Int	OF	160	569	100	175	23	21	15	74	27	.308
1922	Philadelphia	American	OF	99	300	36	69	10	5	1	20	6	.230
1923	Philadelphia	American	OF	95	287	41	73	9	1	1	19	4	.254
1924	Milwaukee	A A	OF	147	490	72	142	17	10	14	80	11	.290
1925	Kansas City	A A	OF	144	500	65	133	25	11	10	85	7	.266
1926	New Haven	Eastern	OF	132	484	84	166	24	11	8	-	21	.343
1927	Kansas City	A A	OF	102	357	55	117	19	6	3	74	11	.328
1928	Kansas City	A A	OF	73	244	31	58	11	1	2	29	2	.238
	St. Louis	American	OF	47	168	35	61	13	4	2	18	2	.363
1929	St. Louis	American	OF	125	441	62	112	26	6	2	51	5	.254
1930	Baltimore	Int	OF	168	661	133	222	45	7	21	113	4	.336
1931	Baltimore	Int	OF	73	253	39	66	13	3	8	39	1	.261
	Minneapolis	A A	OF	65	251	51	93	20	6	11	70	5	.371
1932	Baltimore	Int	OF	162	583	131	185	31	5	37	135	17	.317
1933	Baltimore	Int	OF	128	435	91	123	11	3	15	66	8	.283
1934	Balt/Buff	Int	OF	115	403	92	115	21	4	7	64	7	.285
1935	Buffalo	Int	OF	124	404	67	120	19	7	5	75	3	.297
1936	Buffalo	Int	OF	139	522	115	186	45	10	23	111	3	.356
1937	Buffalo	Int	OF	35	101	12	32	7	1	1	15	0	.317
	Boston	National	OF	9	12	0	1	0	0	0	0	0	.083
1938	Baltimore	Int	OF	16	50	21	21	4	0	6	14	2	.420
1939	Baltimore	Int	OF	22	56	11	16	2	0	2	12	2	.286
	Majors			**375**	**1208**	**174**	**316**	**58**	**16**	**6**	**108**	**17**	**.262**
	Minors			**1923**	**6786**	**1226**	**2084**	**353**	**114**	**190**	**1111**	**145**	**.307**

ROBERTO MENDEZ (NAVARRO)

Born May 6, 1947 at San Blas, Sinaloa, Mexico.
Height 5' 8", Weight 160. Batted right. Threw right.

Year	Club	League	POS	G	AB	R	H	2B	3B	HR	RBI	SB	BA
1965	Fresnill	Mex Cent	SS	143	533	124	154	15	7	21	89	22	.289
	Jalisco	Mexican	SS	9	28	8	14	1	1	0	7	2	.500
1966	Orizaba	Mex SE	SS-P	84	296	45	107	9	1	5	36	26	.361
	Jalisco	Mexican	SS	9	15	4	3	0	0	0	1	0	.200
1967	Jalisco	Mexican	SS	136	493	71	162	21	8	1	43	5	.329
1968	Jalisco	Mexican	SS-OF	135	472	78	131	9	4	0	31	9	.278
1969	Jalisco	Mexican	SS-OF	141	447	72	130	12	7	1	36	8	.291
1970	Jalisco	Mexican	SS	150	545	97	172	38	7	1	41	8	.316
1971	Jalisco	Mexican	2B-SS	147	497	85	152	18	3	3	51	21	.306
1972	Jalisco	Mexican	2B-C	100	335	49	86	11	2	2	45	3	.257
1973	Jalisco	Mexican	2B-SS	126	463	91	146	19	6	2	59	3	.315
1974	Jalisco	Mexican	2B	124	472	62	131	11	3	2	28	3	.278
1975	Jalisco	Mexican	2B	127	443	72	125	17	2	1	35	8	.282
1976	Durango	Mexican	2B	128	465	86	135	16	2	4	40	4	.290
1977	Durango	Mexican	2B	149	571	80	165	16	4	2	53	6	.289
1978	Durango	Mexican	2B	139	514	96	166	15	6	0	53	3	.323
1979	Durango	Mexican	2B	127	475	72	132	22	4	1	36	8	.278

Year	Club	League	POS	G	AB	R	H	2B	3B	HR	RBI	SB	BA
1980	Campeche	Mex #1	2B-SS	82	315	33	86	13	0	1	21	5	.273
1981	Aguila	Mexican	2B	123	426	49	113	15	1	0	18	4	.265
1982	Aguila	Mexican	2B	60	133	16	29	4	2	0	12	1	.218
1983	MC Tigers	Mexican	2B	39	85	8	12	2	0	0	5	1	.141
1984	MC Tigers	Mexican	2B-3B	5	7	2	1	0	0	0	0	1	.143
		Minors		**2283**	**8030**	**1300**	**2352**	**284**	**70**	**47**	**740**	**151**	**.293**

CHRISTOBAL RIGOBERTO "MINNY" MENDOZA (AIZPURU)
Born November 16, 1936 at Havana, Cuba.
Height 6', Weight 180. Batted right. Threw right.

Year	Club	League	POS	G	AB	R	H	2B	3B	HR	RBI	SB	BA
1954	Greater Miami	Fla Int	SS	3	2	0	1	0	0	0	0	0	.500
	Nogales	Ariz-Tex	SS	101	436	89	141	35	2	16	79	6	.323
1955	Portsmouth	Piedmont	3B	129	467	65	124	18	4	3	52	4	.266
1956	Havana	Int	3B	4	12	0	1	0	1	0	0	0	.083
	Nuevo Laredo	Mexican	3B-SS	103	318	40	70	12	1	1	27	10	.220
1957	Albuquerque	Western	SS	21	77	10	14	3	1	1	8	0	.182
	Wausau	Northern	SS	100	409	56	94	17	6	5	43	7	.230
1958	Missoula	Pioneer	OF-3B	23	85	10	23	3	1	0	11	0	.271
1959	Missoula	Pioneer	3B	126	487	105	**174**	**32**	9	12	94	8	.357
1960	Charlotte	Sally	2B	138	516	71	152	21	8	2	43	0	.295
1961	Charlotte	Sally	2-3-S	139	536	62	151	16	5	1	41	7	.282
1962	Vancouver	P C	3B	113	366	39	95	12	1	3	35	3	.260
1963	Charlotte	Sally	3B	84	319	47	91	10	4	0	29	9	.285
1964	Charlotte	Southern	OF-3B	125	473	67	143	19	2	8	47	7	.302
1965	Charlotte	Southern	S-3-2	141	549	64	151	20	4	5	42	12	.275
1966	Charlotte	Southern	3B	128	501	68	140	15	1	1	34	29	.279
1967	Charlotte	Southern	S-2-3	134	528	62	157	21	1	0	40	16	.297
1968	Charlotte	Southern	3B-SS	139	545	85	**165**	**35**	3	4	67	30	.303
1969	Denver	A A	SS-3B	139	**582**	97	**194**	23	2	0	48	4	.333
1970	Minnesota	American	3B-2B	16	16	2	3	0	0	0	2	0	.188
	Evansville	A A	3B-2B	84	314	37	87	14	0	2	16	8	.277
1971	Charlotte	Southern	3-S-2	131	516	80	**163**	18	3	1	55	9	**.316**
1972	Charlotte	Southern	3B-2B	135	516	51	128	18	2	2	41	5	.248
1973	Monterrey	Mexican	3B-2B	42	153	22	43	4	1	0	16	2	.281
		Majors		**16**	**16**	**2**	**3**	**0**	**0**	**0**	**2**	**0**	**.188**
		Minors		**2282**	**8707**	**1227**	**2502**	**366**	**62**	**67**	**868**	**176**	**.287**

CONKLYN WELLS "AL" MERIWETHER
Born June 19, 1918 at Island Grove, FL.
Height 6', Weight 189. Batted left. Threw left.

Year	Club	League	POS	G	AB	R	H	2B	3B	HR	RBI	SB	BA
1939	Easton	E Shore	P	40	67	7	12	2	0	1	9	0	.179
1940	Augusta	Sally	P	2	3	0	1	0	1	0	1	0	.333
	Akron	Mid Atl	P	2	0	0	0	0	0	0	0	0	.000
	Amsterdam	Can-Amer	P	32	50	11	18	1	0	2	8	0	.360
1941	Joplin	West A	P	9	18	4	5	0	2	0	4	0	.278
	Easton	E Shore	P	22	59	7	19	3	2	2	5	0	.322
1942	Norfolk	Piedmont	P	5	3	1	1	0	0	0	0	0	.333
	Sanford	Bi-St	OF-P	66	206	29	62	11	5	8	46	0	.301
1943					Military Service								

Year	Club	League	POS	G	AB	R	H	2B	3B	HR	SB	BA
1944	Allentown	Inter-St	P	32	70	8	22	6	1	0	10	0	.314
1945	Allentown	Inter-St	OF-P	71	257	48	91	17	6	13	64	2	.354
	Rochester	Int	P	3	2	1	1	0	1	0	0	0	.500
	Columbus	A A	P	15	14	0	6	1	1	0	4	0	.429
1946	Houston	Texas	1B	14	52	2	17	2	0	0	3	0	.327
	Lufkin	E Texas	1B	110	417	68	133	25	4	21	96	2	.319
1947	Lubbock	WTNM	1B	9	38	8	14	5	3	1	12	0	.368
	Texarkana	Big St	P-OF	41	76	10	23	2	0	5	16	0	.303
1948	Greenville	Big St	1B	134	529	101	172	40	2	31	151	1	.325
1949	Greenville	Big St	1B	139	538	97	151	37	0	27	108	3	.281
1950	Richmond	Piedmont	1B	43	159	19	28	4	1	6	20	0	.176
	Lake Charles	Gulf Cst	1B	62	222	44	78	14	0	24	69	0	.351
1951	Galveston	Gulf Cst	1B	105	409	76	127	27	0	25	112	1	.311
	Crowley	Evang	1B	38	153	34	57	8	0	19	51	1	.373
1952	Crowley	Evang	1B	118	412	97	138	25	0	**33**	123	3	.335
1953	Crowley	Evang	1B	134	525	104	160	21	1	**42**	**134**	3	.305
1954	Tallahassee	Fla Int	1B	94	346	54	97	14	1	14	74	1	.280
	Valdosta	Ga-Fla	1B	38	135	19	30	3	1	6	26	1	.222
	Minors			**1378**	**4760**	**849**	**1463**	**268**	**32**	**280**	**1146**	**18**	**.307**

FRANK METZ

Manager: San Antonio TL 1912; Sioux City WL 1920-21 & 23.

Year	Club	League	POS	G	AB	R	H	2B	3B	HR	SB	BA
1905	Waco	Texas	1B-C	110	390	24	77	13	3	1	9	.197
1906	Dallas	Texas	C-1B	17	52	7	12	1	1	0	3	.231
1907						No record available						
1908	Charlotte	Carolina	C-O-1	25	90	11	21	3	2	0	0	.233
1909	Muskogee	West A	1B	113	447	63	123	**47**	3	5	21	.275
	Springfield	III	1B	28	96	10	18	1	2	0	3	.188
1910	Lynn	New Eng	1B-OF	124	438	53	103	23	5	2	24	.235
	CorpChristi	SW Texas	C-O-1	21	68	1	9	1	1	0	4	.132
1911	San Antonio	Texas	1B	141	519	84	148	25	6	**22**	27	.285
1912	San Antonio	Texas	1B	142	530	86	**171**	**33**	7	**21**	22	**.323**
1913	Indianapolis	A A	1B	146	526	62	155	23	12	6	14	.295
1914	Indianapolis	A A	1B	169	621	99	184	19	9	4	24	.296
1915	Indianapolis	A A	1B	155	551	72	164	22	5	3	19	.298
1916	Sioux City	Western	1B	129	496	87	157	27	4	4	13	.317
1917	Joplin	Western	1B	127	479	63	137	32	5	1	13	.286
1918	Joplin	Western	1B	65	249	31	70	13	4	4	9	.281
1919						Did not play in O. B.						
1920	Sioux City	Western	1B-OF	141	528	73	158	**53**	1	2	2	.299
1921	Sioux City	Western	1B	167	621	114	229	62	1	20	5	.369
1922	Sioux City	Western	1B	166	642	114	231	65	3	20	8	.360
1923	SCity/St. Jo	Western	1B	161	577	89	198	53	4	14	8	.343
	Minors			**2147**	**7920**	**1143**	**2365**	**516**	**78**	**129**	**228**	**.299**

●

Catcher Jim McGuire, who had been returned to the Minors for more seasoning, hit three home runs for Toronto against Hamilton in the International Association September 2, 1889. He would return to the Majors the next season and finish with a record 26 seasons as a player in 1912.

WILLIAM FRANCIS MIZEUR

Born June 22, 1897 at Nokomis, IL. Died August 27, 1976 at Decatur, IL.
Height 6', Weight 180. Batted left. Threw right.
Manager: Cedar Rapids WL 1934.

Year	Club	League	POS	G	AB	R	H	2B	3B	HR	RBI	SB	BA
1922	Fulton	Kitty	OF	53	207	32	69	12	13	4	-	3	.333
1923	Bay City	Mich-Ont	OF	132	**531**	81	171	33	11	3	63	13	.322
	St. Louis	American	PH	1	1	0	0	0	0	0	0	0	.000
1924	Terre Haute	III	OF	119	452	87	148	25	12	11	70	8	.327
	St. Louis	American	PH	1	1	0	0	0	0	0	0	0	.000
1925	Terre Haute	III	OF	124	462	95	155	30	14	16	-	11	.335
	Tulsa	Western	OF	14	48	12	18	6	1	3	-	0	.375
1926	Terre Haute	III	OF	136	504	83	163	27	16	14	-	7	.323
1927	Peoria	III	OF	139	526	**125**	**186**	32	**19**	23	128	11	.354
1928	Mobile/LR	South A	OF	29	84	10	19	5	2	0	8	2	.226
	Springfield	III	OF	89	331	55	108	33	6	6	51	14	.326
1929	Springfield	III	OF	117	421	87	139	26	10	16	100	6	.330
1930	Springfield	III	OF	115	425	92	146	29	12	11	87	8	.344
1931	Spring/Quin	III	OF	113	423	71	129	24	5	5	73	8	.305
1932	Cedar Rapids	Miss Val	OF	116	444	76	160	30	11	7	**86**	9	**.360**
1933	Peoria	Miss Val	OF	115	428	123	141	34	12	20	116	28	.329
1934	Cedar Rapids	Western	OF	118	450	78	141	28	8	13	91	1	.313
1935	CR/Rock Is	Western	OF	57	208	26	49	13	5	6	43	2	.236
		Majors		**2**	**2**	**0**	**0**	**0**	**0**	**0**	**0**	**0**	**.000**
		Minors		**1586**	**5944**	**1133**	**1942**	**387**	**157**	**158**	**916**	**131**	**.327**

PETER G. MONAHAN

Born February 20, 1902 at Cincinnati, OH.
Height 5' 10", Weight 175. Batted left. Threw left.
Manager: Sioux City WL 1937 & 39; Sioux City Neb St 1938; Topeka West A 1940.

Year	Club	League	POS	G	AB	R	H	2B	3B	HR	RBI	SB	BA
1921	Kitchener	Mich-Ont	1B	7	17	1	4	0	0	0	0	2	.235
1922	Lex/Paris	Blue Gr	1B	23	113	15	31	5	0	3	-	1	.274
1923	Paris	Blue Gr	1B	85	327	56	95	19	5	7	-	5	.291
1924	Paris	Blue Gr	1B	93	371	81	133	18	7	19	-	6	.358
1925	Albany	Eastern	1B	10	32	5	4	1	0	0	2	0	.125
	Fairmont	Mid Atl	1B	100	395	77	137	14	**13**	12	-	12	.347
1926	Baltimore	Int	1B-OF	124	453	85	140	28	10	11	94	11	.309
1927	Jersey City	Int	1B	128	434	50	128	16	1	8	59	6	.295
1928	Buff/Roch	Int	1B	123	444	71	125	17	5	9	55	6	.282
1929	Indianapolis	A A	1B	169	636	107	188	37	4	11	100	18	.296
1930	Indianapolis	A A	1B	141	531	82	157	25	5	6	62	6	.296
1931	Indian/KC	A A	1B	143	541	90	163	26	8	6	83	8	.301
1932	Kansas City	A A	1B	145	522	79	156	27	4	7	86	15	.299
1933	Kansas City	AA	1B	38	131	19	33	2	1	0	12	4	.252
	Chat/Atlanta	South A	1B	64	214	39	56	10	3	5	43	3	.262
1934	Tulsa	Texas	1B	4	8	1	2	0	0	0	1	0	.250
	Knoxville	South A	1B	19	66	5	16	3	0	1	10	0	.242
	Rock Island	Western	1B	110	416	80	118	21	8	7	47	13	.284
1935	Sioux City	Western	1B	107	401	42	111	23	1	8	47	16	.277
1936	Sioux City	Western	1B	123	450	58	122	18	1	10	61	4	.271
1937	Sioux City	Western	1B	113	410	67	121	24	1	8	60	4	.295

Year	Club	League	POS	G	AB	R	H	2B	3B	HR	RBI	SB	BA
1938	Sioux City	Neb St	1B	118	405	103	140	21	8	**19**	101	15	.346
1939	Sioux City	Western	1B	115	391	102	133	20	6	15	106	18	.340
1940	Topeka	West A	1B	128	471	107	149	32	4	14	103	5	.316
		Minors		**2230**	**8179**	**1422**	**2462**	**407**	**95**	**186**	**1132**	**178**	**.301**

JOHN ALLEN MONROE
Born August 24, 1898 at Farmersville, TX. Died June 19, 1956 at Conroe, TX.
Height 5' 8", Weight 160. Batted left. Threw right.
Manager: Little Rock SA 1934.

Year	Club	League	POS	G	AB	R	H	2B	3B	HR	RBI	SB	BA
1920	Beaumont	Texas	2B	147	521	84	151	27	**11**	1	48	28	.290
1921	NY/Phil	National	2B	60	154	17	41	4	2	2	11	2	.266
1922	New Orleans	South A	OF-2B	10	20	1	1	0	1	0	3	0	.050
	Houston	Texas	3B	36	82	3	25	6	1	1	12	1	.305
1923	Houston	Texas	2-O	51	210	37	62	14	2	3	26	4	.295
1924	Houston	Texas	2B	125	491	80	148	25	14	3	67	8	.301
1925	Omaha	Western	2B	142	591	141	208	43	10	14	-	20	.352
1926	Sacramento	P C	2B	200	779	122	230	52	10	13	97	26	.295
1927	Sacramento	P C	2B	162	592	112	175	38	7	4	70	12	.296
1928	Sacramento	P C	2B	171	731	124	235	45	4	10	84	14	.321
1929	Sacramento	P C	2B	146	589	93	198	34	9	6	58	13	.336
1930	Mission	P C	2B	188	689	158	241	39	2	28	106	7	.350
1931	Mission/Port	P C	2B	158	**607**	141	220	41	4	7	64	15	.362
1932	Portland	P C	2B	118	415	98	136	27	3	5	59	11	.328
1933	Portland	P C	2B	152	576	126	186	33	6	7	62	20	.323
1934	Kansas City	A A	2B	6	16	2	6	1	0	0	3	0	.375
	Little Rock	South A	2B	64	217	33	63	7	5	0	26	6	.290
		Majors		**60**	**154**	**17**	**41**	**4**	**2**	**2**	**11**	**2**	**.266**
		Minors		**1876**	**7126**	**1355**	**2285**	**432**	**89**	**102**	**785**	**185**	**.321**

FELIPE ANGEL MONTEMAYOR
Born February 7, 1939 at Monterrey, Nuevo Leon, Mexico.
Height 6' 2", Weight 185. Batted left. Threw left.

Year	Club	League	POS	G	AB	R	H	2B	3B	HR	RBI	SB	BA
1948	Monterrey	Mexican	OF	44	91	13	31	5	2	0	13	1	.341
1949	Monterrey	Mexican	OF	84	312	70	103	19	3	6	62	18	.330
1950	Mexicali	Sunset	OF	122	505	125	161	30	13	20	119	9	.319
1951	New Orleans	South A	OF-1B	144	491	84	136	21	11	5	60	14	.277
1952	New Orleans	South A	OF	123	433	80	122	15	13	11	69	4	.282
1953	Pittsburgh	National	OF	28	55	5	6	4	0	0	2	0	.109
	New Orleans	South A	OF	76	259	55	61	7	8	16	50	6	.236
1954	New Orleans	South A	OF	137	489	96	151	30	6	24	92	2	.309
1955	Pittsburgh	National	OF	36	95	10	20	1	3	2	8	1	.211
	Charleston	A A	OF	30	99	16	24	4	1	1	17	0	.242
	New Orleans	South A	OF	34	106	15	17	6	0	3	15	1	.160
1956	MC Tigers	Mexican	OF	117	407	86	122	23	10	22	84	12	.300
1957	MC Tigers	Mexican	O-1-P	109	329	77	97	17	7	16	62	2	.295
1958	St. Paul	A A	OF-1B	132	340	55	72	14	5	13	41	5	.212
1959	Victoria	Texas	OF-1B	30	44	12	14	2	0	0	13	1	.318

Year	Club	League	POS	G	AB	R	H	2B	3B	HR	RBI	SB	BA
	NL/MC Reds	Mexican	OF-1B	80	260	44	69	14	4	12	56	3	.265
1960	MC Reds	Mexican	OF	28	98	28	31	9	1	5	22	0	.316
	San Antonio	Texas	1B-OF	88	263	37	65	10	2	13	44	4	.247
1961	MC Reds/Ag	Mexican	O-1-P	109	365	72	109	19	11	12	70	3	.299
1962	Aguila	Mexican	O-1-P	128	405	89	108	15	3	19	57	4	.267
1963	Reynosa	Mexican	OF-1B	97	303	45	91	18	6	9	53	2	.300
1964	Monterrey	Mexican	OF	26	61	6	14	1	0	0	9	1	.230
1965	Monterrey	Mexican	OF-1B	123	411	68	122	17	1	26	73	1	.297
1966	Monterrey	Mexican	1B-OF	66	167	23	42	5	0	6	32	0	.251
1967	Campeche	Mex SE	OF-1B	99	319	75	120	30	6	10	71	11	.376
1968	Campeche	Mex SE	1B	16	49	8	11	3	0	2	8	0	.224
	Majors			**64**	**150**	**15**	**26**	**5**	**3**	**2**	**10**	**1**	**.173**
	Minors			**2042**	**6606**	**1279**	**1893**	**334**	**113**	**251**	**1192**	**104**	**.287**

ANDRES MORA (IBARRA)

Born May 25, 1955 at Rio Bravo, Coahuila, Mexico.
Height 6', Weight 180. Bats right. Throws right.
Ranks fourth on minor league career home run list

Year	Club	League	POS	G	AB	R	H	2B	3B	HR	RBI	SB	BA
1971	Zacatecas	Mex Cent	OF	56	137	22	42	8	4	1	29	1	.307
	P Penasco	Mex N	OF	78	316	47	90	12	5	3	23	2	.285
1972	Saltillo	Mexican	OF	2	1	0	0	0	0	0	0	0	.000
1973	W Palm Bch	Fla St	OF	8	21	1	0	0	0	0	0	0	.000
1974	Saltillo	Mexican	OF	132	444	56	138	17	6	14	77	4	.311
1975	Saltillo	Mexican	OF	133	492	82	151	18	7	35	109	2	.307
1976	Baltimore	American	OF	73	220	18	48	11	0	6	25	1	.218
	Rochester	Int	OF	18	67	17	22	6	0	6	15	0	.328
1977	Rochester	Int	OF	45	183	31	55	13	2	11	45	0	.301
	Baltimore	American	OF-3B	77	233	32	57	8	2	13	44	0	.245
1978	Rochester	Int	OF	23	88	15	20	3	1	4	10	1	.227
	Baltimore	American	OF	76	229	21	49	8	0	8	14	0	.214
1979	Saltillo	Mexican	OF	114	421	79	145	31	5	23	102	3	.344
1980	Cleveland	American	OF	9	18	0	2	0	0	0	0	0	.111
	Saltillo	Mex #1	OF	45	160	25	48	8	0	8	42	1	.300
	Saltillo	Mex #2	OF	35	110	19	32	4	0	3	21	0	.291
1981	Saltillo	Mexican	1B	124	437	65	138	17	3	23	93	3	.316
1982	Saltillo/NL	Mexican	OF-1B	126	413	72	119	16	2	25	80	12	.288
1983	Nuevo Laredo	Mexican	OF	118	401	64	122	14	0	19	75	6	.304
1984	Nuevo Laredo	Mexican	OF	113	426	86	163	36	1	32	95	9	.383
1985	Nuevo Laredo	Mexican	1B	127	456	98	164	25	2	41	110	2	.360
1986	Nuevo Laredo	Mexican	1B	122	420	86	149	20	3	33	117	2	.355
1987	Nuevo Laredo	Mexican	1B	114	419	87	154	24	0	38	123	0	.368
1988	Nuevo Laredo	Mexican	1B	85	299	51	92	13	1	21	67	2	.308
1989	Monterrey Ind	Mexican	1B-OF	119	427	55	135	15	1	20	81	0	.316
1990	Mont Ind/NL	Mexican	1B	121	422	54	129	19	1	16	68	2	.306
1991	Nuevo Laredo	Mexican	1B	117	413	65	121	11	0	28	96	0	.293
	Majors			**235**	**700**	**71**	**156**	**27**	**2**	**27**	**83**	**1**	**.223**
	Minors			**1975**	**6973**	**1177**	**2229**	**330**	**44**	**404**	**1478**	**52**	**.320**

FREDERICK WILLIAM MULLER

Born December 21, 1907 at Newark, CA. Died October 20, 1976 at Davis, CA.
Height 5' 10", Weight 170. Batted right. Threw right.

Attended the University of California. Had 6 hits in 6 at bats for Toledo May 7, 1939.

Year	Club	League	POS	G	AB	R	H	2B	3B	HR	RBI	SB	BA
1928	Seattle	P C	3B-SS	139	468	51	108	24	8	8	37	5	.231
1929	Seattle	P C	2-S-3	125	436	43	111	12	4	10	37	1	.255
1930	Seattle	P C	2B-SS	144	467	57	128	24	7	13	59	6	.274
1931	Seattle	P C	2B-SS	182	687	82	193	43	6	15	105	8	.281
1932	Seattle	P C	2B	185	682	116	192	49	8	**38**	121	15	.282
1933	Seattle	P C	2B	83	294	63	96	15	6	20	66	5	.327
	Boston	American	2B	15	48	6	9	1	1	0	3	1	.188
	Montreal	Int	3B-2B	49	149	23	36	9	1	1	15	2	.242
1934	Boston	American	3B-2B	2	1	1	0	0	0	0	0	0	.000
	Newark	Int	3B	91	297	48	87	14	7	16	64	2	.293
1935	Oakland	P C	2B	150	556	72	148	32	4	13	109	9	.266
1936	Seattle	P C	2B	157	561	94	171	32	7	**30**	105	11	.305
1937	Seattle	P C	2B	161	559	67	161	32	7	26	111	6	.288
1938	Seattle	P C	2B	170	627	101	186	33	7	20	110	4	.297
1939	Toledo	A A	3B	126	454	51	112	18	3	20	78	1	.247
1940	Portland	P C	2B	68	244	17	57	10	0	3	31	0	.234
		Majors		**17**	**49**	**7**	**9**	**1**	**1**	**0**	**3**	**1**	**.184**
		Minors		**1830**	**6481**	**885**	**1786**	**347**	**75**	**233**	**1048**	**75**	**.276**

WILLIAM "BADE" MYERS

Manager: Playing manager, 1903-13, 15; Muskegon Central 1916; Richmond Central 1917.

Year	Club	League	POS	G	AB	R	H	2B	3B	HR	SB	BA
1896	Jackson	Inter-St	C	41	162	39	55	-	-	-	-	.340
1897	Toledo	Inter-St	1B	126	462	114	190	**45**	3	12	8	**.411**
1898	Toledo	Inter-St	1B	152	588	89	146	34	1	11	8	.248
1899	Toledo	Inter-St	1B-C	129	439	82	124	17	0	3	2	.282
1900	Dayton	Inter-St	1B-C	130	469	59	128	20	4	9	9	.273
1901	Dayton	West A	1B	122	448	74	140	15	5	4	14	.313
1902	Columbus	A A	1B	74	282	36	75	14	0	0	7	.266
1903	Ft. Wayne	Central	1B	131	482	89	158	-	-	-	-	.328
1904	Ft. Wayne	Central	1B	132	486	77	149	19	9	4	17	.307
1905	FW/Canton	Central	1B	101	381	41	92	16	4	2	11	.241
1906	Canton	Central	1B	126	437	47	108	15	4	1	24	.247
1907	Canton	Central	1B	131	453	48	115	18	6	2	18	.254
1908	Dayton	Central	1B	129	482	47	139	18	6	1	18	.288
1909	Dayton	Central	1B	109	385	37	93	11	1	0	11	.242
1910	Quincy	Cent A	1B	91	311	20	81	16	0	1	10	.260
1911	Quincy	III	1B	124	483	54	136	12	1	3	3	.282
1912	Quincy	III	1B	88	294	26	87	13	1	0	4	.296
1913	Canton	Inter-St	1B	71	281	34	90	14	0	2	3	.320
1914				No record available								
1915	Ft. Wayne	Central	1B	16	24	5	6	1	0	0	2	.250
		Minors		**2023**	**7349**	**1018**	**2112**	**298**	**45**	**55**	**169**	**.287**

JUAN NAVARRETE (SANCHEZ)
Born September 22, 1953 at Gomez Palacio, Durango, Mexico
Height 6' 1", Weight 175. Batted left. Threw right.
Manager: Saltillo Mexican 1983 and 1991.

Year	Club	League	POS	G	AB	R	H	2B	3B	HR	RBI	SB	BA
1970	Saltillo	Mexican	3B-SS	11	9	1	1	0	0	0	0	0	.111
1971	Zacatecas	Mex Cent	SS-3B	72	281	49	91	8	1	6	46	3	.324
	Saltillo	Mexican	S-3-2	31	88	17	23	1	3	0	8	2	.261
1972	W. Palm Bch	Fla St	SS	118	383	32	86	10	2	0	20	12	.225
1973	Quebec City	Eastern	2B-SS	119	354	41	100	11	2	0	22	19	.282
1974	Memphis	Int	2B-SS	109	292	34	66	4	3	0	18	4	.226
1975	Memphis	Int	SS-2B	119	346	34	80	1	6	1	25	8	.231
1976	Denver	A A	2-3-S	77	245	29	71	5	6	0	30	9	.290
	Quebec City	Eastern	SS	52	179	24	49	4	2	2	11	9	.274
1977	Denver	A A	2B-SS	113	401	53	103	13	5	0	37	4	.257
1978	Saltillo	Mexican	2B-SS	126	466	79	159	18	5	3	59	17	.341
1979	Saltillo	Mexican	2B-SS	136	521	110	185	15	4	3	61	40	.355
1980	Saltillo	Mex #1	2B	96	367	57	121	10	4	4	46	19	.330
	Saltillo	Mex #2	2B	37	142	22	51	1	3	0	17	7	.359
1981	Saltillo	Mexican	2-S-3	105	378	60	123	17	4	0	28	31	.325
1982	Saltillo	Mexican	2B	110	397	70	136	13	2	3	33	18	.343
1983	Saltillo	Mexican	2B	118	419	60	138	9	1	0	40	21	.329
1984	Saltillo	Mexican	2B	115	469	78	139	17	2	1	51	26	.296
1985	Saltillo	Mexican	2B	131	511	85	156	20	2	4	85	5	.305
1986	Saltillo	Mexican	2B	130	517	92	174	29	3	3	52	19	.337
1987	Saltillo	Mexican	2B-SS	120	458	86	154	21	5	6	55	10	.336
1988	Saltillo	Mexican	2B	104	419	58	131	12	3	1	44	6	.313
1989	Salt/Mont Ind	Mexican	2-3-1-S	105	391	59	124	11	2	4	34	6	.317
1990	Monterrey Ind	Mexican	3B-2B	132	504	71	164	24	4	3	55	9	.325
		Minors		**2386**	**8537**	**1301**	**2625**	**274**	**74**	**44**	**877**	**304**	**.307**

ALBERT RICHARD NEIL
Born August 18, 1925 at San Diego, CA.
Height 6', Weight 195. Batted right. Threw right.

Year	Club	League	POS	G	AB	R	H	2B	3B	HR	RBI	SB	BA
1947	Pocatello	Pioneer	OF	99	356	72	99	11	10	17	78	13	.278
	W. Frankfort	Ill St	OF	26	97	14	21	3	1	2	20	4	.216
1948	Pocatello	Pioneer	OF	123	518	123	202	43	13	25	151	7	**.390**
1949	Pocatello	Pioneer	OF	69	209	33	56	14	4	2	29	4	.268
	Winst-Salem	Carolina	OF	57	209	35	62	15	4	9	45	1	.297
1950	Knoxville	Tri-St	OF	149	522	107	160	31	10	33	146	8	.307
1951	Spartanburg	Tri-St	OF	140	509	114	165	36	6	44	154	5	.324
1952	Reading	Eastern	OF	15	42	8	13	3	0	1	10	0	.310
	Wichita	Western	OF	119	391	78	103	28	0	18	86	0	.263
1953	Wichita Falls	Big St	OF	137	519	126	185	43	4	39	137	1	**.356**
1954	Schenectady	Eastern	OF	14	37	7	12	3	0	1	8	0	.324
	Knoxville	Tri-St	OF	102	356	77	116	18	6	22	97	5	.326
		Minors		**1050**	**3765**	**794**	**1194**	**248**	**58**	**213**	**961**	**48**	**.317**

ORVILLE BURLIN "HANK" NESSELRODE
Born July 30, 1917 at Parkersburg, WV.
Height 6' 3-1/2", Weight 190. Batted right. Threw right.

Year	Club	League	POS	G	AB	R	H	2B	3B	HR	RBI	SB	BA
1939	South Boston	Bi-St	OF	60	236	42	82	21	5	14	53	1	.347
1940	Winst-Salem	Piedmont	OF	11	43	9	9	3	1	2	9	0	.209
	South Boston	Bi-St	OF	86	336	86	124	20	6	**25**	94	11	.369
	OK City	Texas	OF	16	64	6	17	3	1	0	9	0	.266
1941	Salina	West A	OF	27	94	9	19	3	2	0	7	0	.202
	Charleston	Sally	OF	5	17	2	4	1	1	0	2	0	.235
	Sanford	Bi-St	OF	49	181	27	58	12	2	5	28	3	.320
1942-45							Military Service						
1946	Sanford	Tobac St	OF	114	449	95	159	28	9	**30**	**150**	5	.354
1947	Sanford	Tobac St	OF	121	477	121	168	32	3	**32**	**166**	22	.352
1948	Sanford	Tobac St	OF	**141**	549	119	199	**46**	4	**27**	**159**	17	.362
	Minors			**630**	**2446**	**516**	**839**	**169**	**34**	**135**	**677**	**59**	**.343**

FRANK NESSER
Born June 3, 1889 at Columbus, OH. Died January 1, 1953 at Columbus, OH.
Height 6' 1", Weight 245. Batted right. Threw right.
One of 6 brothers, all of whom played pro football.
Manager: Lima Ohio St 1911.

Year	Club	League	POS	G	AB	R	H	2B	3B	HR	RBI	SB	BA
1910	Lima	Ohio St	1B	119	439	61	119	20	14	6	-	33	.271
1911	Lima	Ohio St	1B	128	494	76	165	29	**25**	3	-	23	.334
1912	Lima	Ohio St	1B	126	494	73	170	30	17	10	-	36	.344
1913	Pittsfield	East A	1B	7	25	4	6	1	1	0	-	2	.240
	Chillicotte	Ohio St	1B	135	515	83	178	26	13	19	-	25	.346
1914	Chillicotte	Ohio St	1B	137	507	91	163	32	7	13	-	16	.321
1915	Greensboro	N Carol	OF	85	318	33	85	25	7	5	-	15	.267
1916	Winst-Salem	N Carol	OF	115	427	73	136	28	3	13	94	26	.319
1917-19							Did not play in O. B.						
1920	Columbus	A A	OF	4	11	2	0	0	0	0	0	0	.000
	Chattanooga	South A	OF	5	19	0	2	0	0	0	-	0	.105
	Peoria	III	OF-1B	105	388	52	116	20	6	3	61	23	.299
1921	Saginaw	Mich-Ont	OF	113	449	**90**	**173**	35	12	4	80	31	**.385**
	Minors			**1079**	**4086**	**638**	**1313**	**246**	**105**	**76**	**235**	**230**	**.321**

PAUL FRANCIS OWENS
Born February 7, 1924 at Salamanca, NY.
Height 6' 3", Weight 185. Batted right. Threw right.
Manager: Olean Pony 1955-57; Bakersfield Calif 1958-59; Philadelphia Phillies 1972 and 1983-84.
Hit in 38 consecutive games in 1951. This is the Pony League record.
Currently assistant to the president of the Philadelphia Phillies.

Year	Club	League	POS	G	AB	R	H	2B	3B	HR	RBI	SB	BA
1951	Olean	Pony	1B	111	459	129	187	32	9	17	101	17	**.407**
1952	Winst-Salem	Carolina	1B-3B	136	535	98	181	34	7	11	105	15	.338
1953-54							Did not play in O. B.						
1955	Olean	Pony	1B-3B	126	457	105	177	30	6	9	86	22	.387

Year	Club	League	POS	G	AB	R	H	2B	3B	HR	RBI	SB	BA
1956	Olean	Pony	1B-OF	114	399	87	147	34	3	9	76	6	**.368**
1957	Olean	NY-Penn	1B	107	369	90	150	30	2	13	88	14	**.407**
1958	Bakersfield	Calif	1B	31	98	11	25	2	4	0	14	1	.255
1959	Bakersfield	Calif	1B	1	3	1	1	0	0	0	1	0	.333
		Minors		**626**	**2320**	**521**	**868**	**162**	**31**	**59**	**471**	**75**	**.374**

STANLEY FRANCIS PALYS

Born May 1, 1930 at Blakely, PA.
Height 6' 2", Weight 190. Batted right. Threw right.

Year	Club	League	POS	G	AB	R	H	2B	3B	HR	RBI	SB	BA
1950	Carbondale	N Atl	OF-3-2	113	406	93	129	24	6	11	77	4	.318
1951						Military Service							
1952	Terre Haute	III	OF	99	363	58	98	28	8	8	74	3	.270
1953	Schenectady	Eastern	OF	6	21	1	4	0	0	0	3	0	.190
	Spokane	West Int	OF	128	487	111	161	35	5	22	95	4	.331
	Philadelphia	National	OF	2	2	0	0	0	0	0	0	0	.000
1954	Philadelphia	National	OF	2	4	0	1	0	0	0	0	0	.250
	Syracuse	Int	OF	23	75	10	14	2	0	3	9	1	.187
	Schenectary	Eastern	OF	93	323	62	102	20	5	14	56	2	.316
1955	Phil/Cinci	National	1B-OF	94	274	37	66	17	0	8	38	2	.241
1956	Cincinnati	National	OF	40	53	5	12	0	0	2	5	0	.226
1957	Nashville	South A	OF	134	493	**116**	177	34	6	24	112	5	**.359**
1958	Charleston	A A	OF	129	444	70	128	28	4	11	60	2	.288
1959	Charleston	A A	OF	49	103	11	29	3	0	1	10	0	.282
	Corpus Christi	Texas	OF	43	127	16	46	4	1	4	31	0	.362
1960	Birmingham	South A	OF	147	540	101	**200**	43	13	28	116	2	**.370**
1961	Birmingham	South A	OF	139	492	110	164	33	7	13	**114**	2	.333
1962	Hawaii	P C	OF	148	554	111	184	32	3	**33**	91	3	.332
1963	Hawaii	P C	OF-1B	143	491	63	150	21	0	17	73	2	.305
1964	Tokyo Orions	Jap Pac	OF	129	505	52	143	33	1	17	70	3	.283
1965	Tokyo Orions	Jap Pac	OF	104	380	53	104	21	2	25	69	3	.274
1966	Tokyo Orions	Jap Pac	OF	113	395	41	104	15	1	18	69	3	.263
1967	Tokyo Orions	Jap Pac	OF	100	245	21	68	11	1	6	42	1	.278
		Majors		**138**	**333**	**42**	**79**	**17**	**0**	**10**	**43**	**2**	**.237**
		Minors		**1394**	**4919**	**933**	**1586**	**307**	**58**	**189**	**921**	**28**	**.322**
		Japan		**446**	**1525**	**167**	**419**	**80**	**5**	**66**	**250**	**10**	**.275**

CLARENCE MCKAY "ACE" PARKER

Born May 17, 1912 at Portsmouth, VA.
Height 6', Weight 180. Batted right. Threw right.
Manager: Portsmouth Piedmont 1946-48; Durham Carolina 1949-52.
Hit HR in first O.B. AB April 30, 1937 for Philadelphia A's.
All-American football player at Duke. Played in NFL for Brooklyn, 1937-41; Boston, 1945; New York, 1946. Led league in passing in 1938. Inducted into Pro Football Hall of Fame in 1972.
Broke leg while with Syracuse in 1940. Broke ankle while with Portsmouth in 1941.
Baseball coach at Duke University from 1953 through 1965.

Year	Club	League	POS	G	AB	R	H	2B	3B	HR	RBI	SB	BA
1937	Philadelphia	American	S-2-O	38	94	8	11	0	1	2	13	0	.117
	Atlanta	South A	O-3-1	25	73	9	20	4	3	1	11	0	.274
	Portsmouth	Piedmont	3B	21	70	13	17	3	0	4	16	1	.243

Year	Club	League	POS	G	AB	R	H	2B	3B	HR	RBI	SB	BA
1938	Philadelphia	American	S-3-2	56	113	12	26	5	0	0	12	1	.230
1939	Portsmouth	Piedmont	SS	116	445	90	135	25	6	16	64	14	.303
1940	Syracuse	Int	SS	16	51	12	20	3	0	2	9	2	.392
1941	Portsmouth	Piedmont	SS	10	38	7	11	1	0	0	5	1	.289
1942-45							Military Service						
1946	Portsmouth	Piedmont	S-O	92	375	63	124	13	9	0	40	4	**.331**
1947	Portsmouth	Piedmont	O-S-2	130	534	114	168	34	4	6	53	7	.315
1948	Portsmouth	Piedmont	OF	99	313	54	69	11	3	3	22	2	.220
1949	Durham	Carolina	O-3	83	298	56	89	20	2	1	44	3	.299
1950	Durham	Carolina	O-3-S	89	287	37	80	12	0	1	24	0	.279
1951	Durham	Carolina	OF	36	104	10	28	1	1	0	10	0	.269
1952	Durham	Carolina	O-P	2	5	1	0	0	0	0	1	0	.000
		Majors		**94**	**207**	**20**	**37**	**5**	**1**	**2**	**25**	**1**	**.179**
		Minors		**719**	**2593**	**466**	**761**	**127**	**28**	**34**	**299**	**34**	**.293**

HAROLD ROBERT PATCHETT
Born May 10, 1912 at Flint, MI. Died April 7, 1978 at El Cajon, CA.
Height 5' 11", Weight 170. Batted left. Threw right.
BA degree from Adrian College where he lettered for 4 years in football, basketball and baseball and 2 years in track.
Switch hit in 1932 and then gave it up.

Year	Club	League	POS	G	AB	R	H	2B	3B	HR	RBI	SB	BA
1932	Moline	Miss Val	3B	116	470	**90**	154	18	10	7	54	**35**	.328
1933	Shreveport	Dixie	O-3-2	94	396	86	135	22	4	0	39	31	.341
	Beaumont	Texas	3B	22	77	11	17	1	0	0	9	4	.221
1934	Muskogee	West A	OF	39	165	37	59	5	3	2	20	17	.358
	Beaumont	Texas	OF	97	375	61	111	16	12	0	26	16	.296
1935	St. Joseph	Western	OF	94	377	80	121	18	5	5	43	23	.321
	Tulsa	Texas	OF	31	118	17	27	8	0	0	11	3	.229
1936	Tulsa	Texas	OF	147	547	100	167	35	11	4	58	12	.305
1937	San Diego	P C	OF	169	689	105	211	38	8	8	66	21	.306
1938	San Diego	P C	OF	166	668	98	202	38	12	3	57	10	.302
1939	San Diego	P C	OF	160	610	83	177	24	7	0	32	6	.290
1940	San Diego	P C	OF	166	686	109	195	28	5	0	51	9	.284
1941	San Diego	P C	OF	168	622	78	184	21	8	0	60	25	.296
1942	San Diego	P C	OF	172	663	83	191	23	5	0	43	8	.288
1943	San Diego	P C	OF	141	522	63	148	12	**15**	1	49	25	.284
1944	San Diego	P C	OF	128	426	49	117	10	5	1	56	19	.275
1945	Oak/Seattle	P C	OF	157	580	85	178	21	6	0	47	19	.307
1946	Seattle	P C	OF	109	238	24	58	5	0	0	14	6	.244
		Minors		**2176**	**8229**	**1259**	**2452**	**343**	**116**	**31**	**735**	**289**	**.298**

LESLIE EARL PEDEN
Born September 17, 1923 at Azle, TX.
Height 6' 1-1/2", Weight 212. Batted right. Threw right.
Attended Texas A&M.
Manager: Des Moines WL 1954-55; Little Rock SA 1958; Shreveport SA 1959-61; Portland PCL 1962-63; Quincy Midwest 1964; Wenatchee NWest 1965; Tacoma PCL 1966.

Year	Club	League	POS	G	AB	R	H	2B	3B	HR	RBI	SB	BA
1947	Des Moines	Western	3B-1B	124	486	107	157	33	7	18	106	5	.323

Year	Club	League	POS	G	AB	R	H	2B	3B	HR	RBI	SB	BA
1948	Nashville	South A	C-3B	4	3	0	0	0	0	0	0	0	.000
	Fayetteville	Tri-St	C-2B	107	386	72	131	26	2	24	98	3	.339
1949	Des Moines	Western	C-O-3	127	471	74	147	29	3	22	102	2	.312
1950	Springfield	Int	C	85	268	32	80	14	0	8	41	0	.299
1951	Los Angeles	P C	C	117	402	42	100	15	0	11	54	1	.249
1952	Los Angeles	P C	C	153	527	62	147	18	1	18	71	0	.279
1953	Washington	American	C	9	28	4	7	1	0	1	1	0	.250
	Los Angeles	P C	C	100	340	33	91	16	2	11	55	0	.268
1954	Des Moines	Western	C-3-O	131	445	86	138	30	1	26	91	0	.310
1955	Des Moines	Western	3B-C	52	155	24	45	11	0	5	34	0	.290
	Shreveport	Texas	C	33	92	11	23	6	0	3	12	1	.250
1956	Shreveport	Texas	C	137	464	61	131	22	1	23	88	2	.282
1957	Little Rock	South A	C-3B	134	431	59	128	21	0	15	81	0	.297
1958	Little Rock	South A	C-3B-P	133	458	67	153	29	3	26	88	1	.334
1959	Shreveport	South A	C-OF	82	237	38	71	10	0	10	34	0	.300
1960	Shreveport	South A	C	83	217	31	71	14	0	11	46	2	.327
1961	Shreveport	South A	C	73	184	21	52	12	0	7	31	0	.283
1962	Portland	P C	3B-P	47	111	10	39	7	0	6	24	0	.351
1963	Port/SD	P C	C-1-O	50	76	6	19	4	1	4	15	0	.250
1964	Quincy	Midwest	P	15	24	6	5	2	0	1	4	0	.208
	Majors			**9**	**28**	**4**	**7**	**1**	**0**	**1**	**1**	**0**	**.250**
	Minors			**1787**	**5777**	**842**	**1728**	**319**	**21**	**249**	**1075**	**17**	**.299**

ALONSO THOMAS PERRY
Born April 14, 1923 at Birmingham, AL.
Height 6' 3", Weight 200. Batted left. Threw right.
Dominican was a summer league 1951-54.

Year	Club	League	POS	G	AB	R	H	2B	3B	HR	RBI	SB	BA
1948	Birmingham	Neg Amer	1B	31	80	7	26	4	0	2	12	0	.325
1949	Oakland	P C	P-1B	12	15	0	3	0	0	0	1	0	.200
1950	Birmingham	Neg Amer	1B	73	294	80	92	14	7	14	64	18	.313
1951	Syracuse	Int	1B	9	18	3	5	0	0	0	3	0	.278
	Licey	Dominican	1B	25	90	27	36	4	1	9	32	10	.400
1952	Licey	Dominican	1B	45	162	29	53	9	1	11	38	5	.327
1953	Licey	Dominican	1B	56	229	40	67	11	4	**11**	53	**16**	.293
1954	Licey	Dominican	1B	42	146	29	49	11	1	8	29	6	.336
1955	MC Reds	Mexican	1B	92	365	76	137	24	**15**	21	**122**	5	.375
1956	MC Reds	Mexican	1B	123	451	**103**	**177**	**33**	13	**28**	118	10	**.392**
1957	MC Reds	Mexican	1B	121	466	**96**	**164**	32	6	22	**107**	15	.352
1958	MC Reds	Mexican	1B-P	115	417	93	152	30	4	22	85	5	.365
1959	MC Reds	Mexican	1B-P	127	459	93	153	29	9	12	94	7	.333
1960-61			Did not play in O. B.										
1962	Monterrey	Mexican	1B	124	468	91	149	28	5	16	**105**	4	.318
1963	Monterrey	Mexican	1B	130	496	96	175	27	6	17	90	5	.353
	Minors			**853**	**3155**	**651**	**1115**	**203**	**58**	**138**	**725**	**51**	**.353**
	Negro Lg			**104**	**374**	**87**	**118**	**18**	**7**	**16**	**76**	**18**	**.316**
	Dominican Lg			**168**	**627**	**125**	**205**	**35**	**7**	**39**	**152**	**37**	**.327**

EDGAR EVERETT PICK
Born May 7, 1899 at Attleboro, MA. Died May 13, 1967 at Santa Maria, CA.
Height 6', Weight 185. Batted left and right. Threw right.

Year	Club	League	POS	G	AB	R	H	2B	3B	HR	RBI	SB	BA
1922	Hutchinson	SWestern	3B	49	161	23	42	10	1	4	-	1	.261
1923	Hutchinson	SWestern	OF	131	502	109	175	37	15	21	-	23	.349
	Cincinnati	National	OF	9	8	2	3	0	0	0	2	0	.375
1924	Cincinnati	National	OF	3	2	0	0	0	0	0	0	0	.000
	Hutchinson	West A	OF-1B	46	163	38	47	12	4	8	28	5	.288
	St.Petersburg	Fla St	OF	39	134	28	31	2	3	5	-	2	.231
	Kansas City	A A	OF	11	40	9	15	4	2	0	5	0	.375
1925	Kansas City	A A	SS-OF	148	538	110	175	23	24	10	104	15	.325
1926	Kansas City	A A	OF-3B	161	580	109	194	33	17	14	109	18	.334
1927	Kansas City	A A	3B	39	142	29	51	6	4	2	29	3	.359
	Chicago	National	3-O-2	54	181	23	31	5	2	2	15	0	.171
1928	Milwaukee	A A	O-S-1	165	593	123	175	34	14	14	112	14	.295
1929	Milwaukee	A A	O-1-3-S	144	509	84	150	26	15	14	105	6	.295
1930	Milw/KC	A A	OF-1B	150	538	114	167	30	14	8	97	19	.310
1931	Kansas City	A A	OF	165	672	125	214	**58**	14	9	128	19	.318
1932	Kansas City	A A	OF	163	616	111	212	39	15	7	121	8	.344
1933	Kansas City	A A	OF	65	230	34	67	13	2	3	31	1	.291
		Majors		**66**	**191**	**25**	**34**	**5**	**2**	**2**	**17**	**0**	**.178**
		Minors		**1476**	**5418**	**1046**	**1715**	**327**	**144**	**119**	**869**	**134**	**.317**

LAVERN JACK PIERCE
(Known by middle name.)
Born June 2, 1948 at Laurel, MS.
Height 6', Weight 210. Batted left. Threw right.

Manager: Leon Mexican 1986.

Led all minor league in home runs in 1986. Ranks 8th on minor league career home run list. Switch hit on a few occasions early in career.

Year	Club	League	POS	G	AB	R	H	2B	3B	HR	RBI	SB	BA
1970	Magic Val	Pioneer	1B-C	70	281	44	79	16	1	9	58	1	.281
1971	Kinston	Carolina	1B	136	465	80	136	29	1	20	81	3	.292
1972	Savannah	Southern	1B	138	479	78	140	29	4	23	103	10	.292
1973	Richmond	Int	1-C-2	124	411	55	101	14	1	14	68	4	.246
	Atlanta	National	1B	11	20	0	1	0	0	0	0	0	.050
1974	Jalisco	Mexican	1B	113	379	91	116	23	4	28	87	6	.306
	Atlanta	National	1B	6	9	1	1	0	0	0	0	0	.111
1975	Detroit	American	1B	53	170	19	40	6	1	8	22	0	.235
	Evansville	A A	1B	36	132	26	37	7	0	9	25	0	.280
1976	Puebla	Mexican	1B	132	486	90	161	20	1	**36**	**118**	1	.331
1977	Nankai	JapPac	1B-OF	95	291	30	66	9	1	13	39	1	.227
1978	San Jose	P C	1B	77	275	44	90	20	1	10	61	2	.327
	Puebla	Mexican	1B	32	121	12	24	4	0	3	11	1	.198
1979	Spokane	P C	1B-3B	133	472	64	132	27	4	16	90	1	.280
1980	Salt/Ctz	Mex #1	1B	97	331	50	88	21	0	17	75	2	.266
	Coatz.	Mex #2	1B	36	128	18	31	5	0	**7**	18	1	.242
1981	Coatz.	Mexican	1B	124	422	52	112	19	2	18	78	2	.265
1982	Aguasc.	Mexican	1B	123	438	65	118	22	2	17	74	1	.269
1983	Ca/Vr/Sal	Mexican	1B	111	378	40	93	13	1	15	51	2	.246

Year	Club		League	POS	G	AB	R	H	2B	3B	HR	RBI	SB	BA
1984	Leon		Mexican	1B	115	437	98	159	22	1	35	117	1	.364
1985	Leon		Mexican	1B	128	440	104	137	16	0	40	118	1	.311
1986	Leon		Mexican	1B	128	475	111	181	27	1	**54**	148	3	.381
1987	L/MC Tigers		Mexican	1B	102	376	73	104	18	0	24	89	3	.277
	Majors				**70**	**199**	**20**	**42**	**6**	**1**	**8**	**22**	**0**	**.211**
	Minors				**1955**	**6926**	**1195**	**2039**	**352**	**24**	**395**	**1470**	**45**	**.294**
	Japan				**95**	**291**	**30**	**66**	**9**	**1**	**13**	**39**	**1**	**.227**

ALFRED FREDERICK JOSEPH PLATTE
Born April 13, 1890 at Grand Rapids, MI. Died August 29, 1976 at Grand Rapids, MI.
Height 5' 7", Weight 160. Batted left. Threw left.

Year	Club	League	POS	G	AB	R	H	2B	3B	HR	RBI	SB	BA
1910	Cadillac	Mich St	OF	87	308	45	86	14	9	2	-	9	.279
1911	Cadillac	Mich St	OF	113	442	102	180	28	10	2	-	23	.339
1912	Cadillac	Mich St	OF	92	365	55	134	18	10	4	-	**42**	**.367**
	Providence	Int	OF	24	94	16	25	1	3	0	-	2	.266
1913	Providence	Int	OF	120	441	83	135	8	8	3	-	32	.306
	Detroit	American	OF	7	18	1	2	1	0	0	0	0	.111
1914	Providence	Int	OF	**156**	**597**	128	**190**	16	23	5	-	31	.318
1915	Louisville	A A	OF	79	302	56	97	13	12	2	-	15	.321
1916	Louisville	A A	OF	129	382	72	106	15	13	2	-	12	.277
1917	Louisville	A A	OF	22	58	12	12	3	0	0	-	0	.207
	Chattanooga	South A	OF	42	149	28	32	2	3	1	-	9	.215
1918	Kansas City	A A					Military Service						
1919	Kansas City	A A					Voluntarily Retired						
1920	Kansas City	A A	OF	10	35	4	9	1	0	1	3	0	.257
	Omaha	Western	OF	145	545	94	171	41	11	15	-	14	.314
1921	Peoria	III	OF	137	488	86	145	28	14	13	76	7	.297
1922	Peoria	III	OF	124	450	72	162	25	**23**	11	-	8	**.360**
1923	Peoria	III	OF	137	490	80	152	26	8	11	-	9	.310
1924	Peoria	III	OF	134	481	99	152	30	12	15	**98**	10	.316
1925	Peoria	III	OF	108	380	81	115	20	6	5	-	9	.303
1926	Peoria	III	OF	37	138	25	39	4	1	6	-	3	.283
	Dubuque	Miss Val	OF	24	84	15	29	8	3	1	-	3	.345
	Elmira	NY-Penn	OF	35	113	11	42	4	4	0	17	2	.372
	Majors			**7**	**18**	**1**	**2**	**1**	**0**	**0**	**0**	**0**	**.111**
	Minors			**1755**	**6342**	**1164**	**1983**	**305**	**173**	**99**	**194**	**240**	**.313**

HARLIN WELTY POOL
Born March 12, 1908 at Lakeport, CA. Died February 15, 1963 at Rodeo, CA.
Height 5' 10", Weight 195. Batted left. Threw right.

Year	Club	League	POS	G	AB	R	H	2B	3B	HR	RBI	SB	BA
1930	Phoenix	Ariz St	C-OF	65	230	60	94	14	5	9	52	6	.409
1931	Oakland	P C	OF-C	81	136	23	40	12	2	1	22	1	.294
1932	Oakland	P C	C	15	22	1	5	0	1	0	2	1	.227
1933	Oakland	P C	OF	165	630	103	219	48	10	5	126	21	.348
1934	Oakland	P C	OF	50	170	20	56	11	6	0	25	4	.329
	Cincinnati	National	OF	99	358	38	117	22	5	2	50	3	.327
1935	Cincinnati	National	OF	28	68	8	12	6	2	0	11	0	.176
	Toronto	Int	OF-1B	76	228	34	75	8	3	3	38	0	.329
1936	Toronto	Int	OF	77	278	37	80	16	4	2	33	1	.288

	Oakland	P C	OF	62	221	31	87	21	3	0	43	1	.394
1937	Seattle	P C	OF	136	458	64	153	33	5	6	65	2	.334
1938	Dallas	Texas	OF	154	566	60	187	34	4	1	66	4	**.330**
1939	San Francisco	P C	OF	3	7	2	4	0	0	0	1	0	.571
	Majors			**127**	**426**	**46**	**129**	**28**	**7**	**2**	**61**	**3**	**.303**
	Minors			**884**	**2946**	**435**	**1000**	**197**	**43**	**27**	**473**	**41**	**.339**

JOHN CALVIN POWERS
Born July 8, 1929 at Birmingham, AL.
Height 6' 1", Weight 195. Batted left. Threw right.

Year	Club	League	POS	G	AB	R	H	2B	3B	HR	RBI	SB	BA
1949	Valley	Ga-Ala	OF	62	226	60	72	14	4	6	36	12	.319
	Gadsden	SEastern	OF	75	272	49	79	14	8	11	51	5	.290
1950	Waco	Big St	OF	144	541	124	168	24	6	**39**	135	5	.311
1951	Charleston	Sally	OF-1B	139	501	88	128	34	5	17	88	6	.255
1952-53					Military Service								
1954	Hollywood	P C	1B-3B	5	12	2	2	1	0	0	2	0	.167
	New Orleans	South A	OF	106	366	75	97	13	9	23	74	3	.265
1955	New Orleans	South A	OF-1B	93	342	65	76	14	3	21	53	2	.222
	Williamsport	Eastern	OF-1B	32	105	25	32	5	2	8	24	1	.305
	Pittsburgh	National	OF	2	4	0	1	0	0	0	0	0	.250
1956	New Orleans	South A	OF-1B	153	574	**131**	179	32	12	**39**	116	2	.312
	Pittsburgh	National	OF	11	21	0	1	0	0	0	0	0	.048
1957	Columbus	Int	OF-1B	127	476	73	140	16	11	29	95	3	.294
	Pittsburgh	National	OF-2B	20	35	7	10	3	0	2	8	0	.286
1958	Pittsburgh	National	OF	57	82	6	15	1	0	2	2	0	.183
1959	Cincinnati	National	OF	43	43	8	11	2	1	2	4	0	.256
1960	Balt/Clev	American	OF	18	30	5	4	1	1	0	0	0	.133
	Columbus	Int	OF	104	380	62	105	14	2	24	56	0	.276
1961	Columbus	Int	OF	128	397	71	96	15	2	19	51	3	.242
1962	Columbus	Int	OF	114	323	56	69	9	3	15	48	1	.214
1963	Buffalo	Int	OF	53	140	22	34	7	0	8	22	1	.243
	Tacoma	P C	OF	11	35	1	9	0	0	0	5	0	.257
1964	Columbus	Int	OF	81	263	51	70	13	0	21	52	1	.266
1965	Columbus	Int	OF	107	301	40	65	9	4	18	48	4	.216
	Majors			**151**	**215**	**26**	**42**	**7**	**2**	**6**	**14**	**0**	**.195**
	Minors			**1534**	**5254**	**995**	**1421**	**234**	**71**	**298**	**956**	**49**	**.270**

GEORGE WILLIAM QUELLICH
Born February 10, 1903 at Johnsville, CA. Died August 31, 1958 at Johnsville, CA.
Height 6' 1", Weight 180. Batted right. Threw right.
Collected 15 consecutive hits from August 9th to 12th, 1929.

Year	Club	League	POS	G	AB	R	H	2B	3B	HR	RBI	SB	BA
1923	Portland	P C	PH	3	3	1	1	0	0	0	0	0	.333
	Moline	III	OF	12	50	6	13	0	1	1	-	0	.260
	Martinsburg	Blue Rdg	OF-3B	82	305	53	94	24	1	8	-	5	.308
1924	Grand Rapids	Mich-Ont	OF	87	301	52	105	17	8	9	72	9	.349
	Rochester	Int	OF	50	153	35	52	11	4	10	42	1	.340
1925	Rochester	Int	OF-1B	126	386	77	115	20	12	19	72	5	.298
1926	Roch/Balt	Int	OF	113	372	71	110	16	3	17	76	5	.296
1927	Balt/Read	Int	OF	116	385	69	121	36	4	18	69	5	.314

1928	Reading	Int	OF	140	477	85	153	33	7	19	97	6	.321
1929	Reading	Int	OF	162	577	97	200	36	1	31	130	10	.347
1930	Reading	Int	OF	97	377	69	122	26	6	9	76	4	.324
1931	Read/New	Int	OF	140	532	93	178	40	8	20	111	3	.335
	Detroit	American	OF	13	54	6	12	5	0	1	11	1	.222
1932	Hollywood	P C	OF	47	175	27	47	10	1	5	30	1	.269
	Albany	Int	OF	105	355	51	111	26	5	9	53	1	.313
1933	Albany	Int	OF	10	17	1	5	2	0	0	2	0	.294
	St. Paul	A A	OF	4	16	2	3	1	0	0	2	0	.188
	Dallas	Texas	OF	15	56	6	13	5	0	0	5	0	.232
	Henderson	Dixie	OF	74	298	77	101	21	3	15	85	1	.339
1934	Oakland	P C	OF	2	4	2	1	0	0	0	0	0	.250
		Majors		**13**	**54**	**6**	**12**	**5**	**0**	**1**	**11**	**1**	**.222**
		Minors		**1385**	**4839**	**874**	**1545**	**324**	**64**	**190**	**922**	**56**	**.319**

EARL WELLINGTON RAPP

Born May 20, 1921 at Corunna, MI. Died February 13, 1992 at Swedesboro, NJ.
Height 6' 2", Weight 195. Batted left. Threw right.

Year	Club	League	POS	G	AB	R	H	2B	3B	HR	RBI	SB	BA
1940	Wausau	Northern	OF	62	212	35	67	15	0	6	42	6	.316
1941	Oneonta	Can-Amer	OF	37	144	19	40	3	5	0	17	5	.278
	Jamestown	Pony	OF	67	259	60	88	20	6	5	51	7	.340
1942	Hagerstown	Inter-St	OF	137	482	60	137	21	11	8	75	**19**	.284
	Buffalo	Int	OF	9	22	3	4	1	0	0	3	0	.182
1943-45					Military Service								
1946	Williamsport	Eastern	OF	64	235	47	78	16	5	5	43	12	.332
	Buffalo	Int	OF	62	204	46	66	13	2	5	38	8	.324
1947	Buffalo	Int	OF	137	439	86	129	28	3	16	80	12	.294
1948	Seattle	P C	OF	168	564	88	168	36	6	17	96	10	.298
1949	Detroit/Chi	American	OF	20	54	3	14	1	1	0	11	1	.259
	Oakland	P C	OF	97	340	76	117	24	3	15	86	6	.344
1950	Oakland	P C	OF	181	639	133	222	49	8	24	145	7	.347
1951	Oakland	P C	OF	97	357	66	115	15	8	10	74	5	.322
	New York	National	PH	13	11	0	1	0	0	0	1	0	.091
	St. Louis	American	OF	26	98	14	32	5	3	2	14	1	.327
1952	StL/Wash	American	OF	76	116	10	26	10	0	0	13	0	.224
1953	San Diego	P C	OF	180	630	104	196	32	7	24	108	11	.311
1954	San Diego	P C	OF	162	566	102	191	37	7	24	111	2	.337
1955	San Diego	P C	OF	169	582	**109**	176	25	6	30	**133**	1	.302
1956	San Diego	P C	OF	122	414	59	124	14	5	9	65	3	.300
1957	SD/Port	P C	OF	83	205	27	57	7	2	3	19	1	.278
	Louisville	A A	OF	17	50	5	9	2	0	1	5	0	.180
1958					Did not play in O. B.								
1959	Nashville	South A	OF	18	50	11	15	1	0	1	8	0	.300
		Majors		**135**	**279**	**27**	**73**	**16**	**4**	**2**	**39**	**2**	**.262**
		Minors		**1869**	**6394**	**1136**	**1999**	**359**	**84**	**203**	**1199**	**115**	**.313**

GEORGE REGGIS "REG" RAWLINGS
Born July 13, 1890 at Washington D.C. Died July 6, 1954 at Martinsburg, WV.
Height 6', Weight 165. Batted right. Threw right.
Went to spring training with Philadelphia A's in 1925.

Year	Club	League	POS	G	AB	R	H	2B	3B	HR	SB	BA
1915	Martinsburg	Blue Rdg	OF	71	280	49	91	16	5	2	13	.325
1916	Martinsburg	Blue Rdg	OF	102	366	62	102	17	6	7	14	.279
1917	Martinsburg	Blue Rdg	OF	99	**390**	64	118	21	4	10	13	.303
1918-19					Military Service							
1920	Martinsburg	Blue Rdg	OF	98	366	49	111	18	2	9	13	.303
1921	Martinsburg	Blue Rdg	OF	95	361	77	128	23	3	17	15	.355
1922	Martinsburg	Blue Rdg	OF	99	**394**	82	**146**	19	4	26	17	**.371**
1923	Martinsburg	Blue Rdg	OF	96	**386**	104	**145**	28	6	25	16	**.376**
1924	Martinsburg	Blue Rdg	OF	99	**401**	78	**152**	31	1	21	17	**.379**
1925	Martinsburg	Blue Rdg	OF	90	337	65	113	21	1	18	11	.335
1926	Martinsburg	Blue Rdg	OF	96	366	68	117	16	3	**19**	12	.320
1927	Martinsburg	Blue Rdg	OF	95	350	75	123	17	7	12	10	.351
1928	Martinsburg	Blue Rdg	OF	90	322	37	83	19	1	6	10	.258
1929	Hagerstown	Blue Rdg	OF	112	408	77	131	22	4	11	17	.321
	Minors			**1242**	**4727**	**887**	**1560**	**268**	**47**	**183**	**178**	**.330**

ANDREW JACKSON REESE
Born February 7, 1904 at Tupelo, MS. Died January 10, 1966 at Tupelo, MS.
Height 5' 11", Weight 180. Batted right. Threw right.
Attended Vanderbilt University. In 1925 played under name of Bynaum. Set Southern Association career records with 1641 hits and 320 doubles.
Manager: Greenville CSL 1940.

Year	Club	League	POS	G	AB	R	H	2B	3B	HR	RBI	SB	BA
1925	Tupelo	Tri-St	OF	105	**425**	**102**	**144**	21	**13**	9	-	35	.339
1926	Memphis	South A	OF	144	544	91	167	27	22	6	102	20	.307
1927	New York	National	1B-OF	97	355	43	94	14	2	4	21	5	.265
1928	New York	National	IF-OF	109	406	61	125	18	4	6	44	7	.308
1929	New York	National	2-3-O	58	209	36	55	11	3	0	21	8	.263
1930	New York	National	OF-3B	67	172	26	47	4	2	4	25	1	.273
	Bridgeport	Eastern	-	25	88	18	22	3	1	1	18	5	.250
1931	Oakland	P C	OF-3B	55	188	23	51	12	2	4	28	3	.271
	Memphis	South A	2B	84	328	64	112	27	10	6	55	10	.341
1932	Memphis	South A	1B-2B	150	593	126	199	37	7	13	121	33	.336
1933	Memphis	South A	1B	148	565	107	183	42	17	4	93	12	.324
1934	Memphis	South A	1B	152	594	99	167	36	10	9	**108**	12	.281
1935	Memphis	South A	1B-2B	140	554	74	184	32	8	6	71	29	.332
1936	Memphis	South A	3-2-1	128	438	52	125	24	7	4	67	5	.285
1937	Memphis	South A	1B	151	558	73	170	32	10	0	92	12	.305
1938	Memphis	South A	1B	141	535	72	178	38	13	7	100	5	.333
1939	Memphis	South A	1B	131	479	77	154	24	12	8	55	4	.322
1940	Greenville	Cottn St	1B	128	497	97	168	35	5	12	76	8	.338
1941	Gadsden	SEastern	1B-2B	53	164	27	45	13	0	5	28	3	.274
1942	Knoxville	South A	-	11	18	4	3	1	0	0	3	0	.167
	Meridian	SEastern	1B-2B	77	206	17	52	12	0	2	26	0	.252
	Majors			**331**	**1142**	**166**	**321**	**47**	**11**	**14**	**111**	**21**	**.281**
	Minors			**1823**	**6774**	**1123**	**2124**	**416**	**137**	**96**	**1043**	**196**	**.314**

FRANK REIGER
Born April 24, 1895 at Garber, OK. Died September 5, 1925 at Camden, SC.
Height 6', Weight 190. Batted right. Threw right.

Attended Oklahoma A & M College.

Served in the US Army from 1917 to 1919.

Hit 3 consecutive home runs in a game against Springfield on June 5, 1921.

Killed in a highway accident, along with team manager Emil Huhn, while travelling with the team after a game at Charlotte on September 5, 1925.

Year	Club	League	POS	G	AB	R	H	2B	3B	HR	RBI	SB	BA
1921	Enid	West A	C-OF	133	446	125	139	26	7	**20**	-	11	.312
1922	Enid	West A	OF	120	479	125	188	**39**	6	**31**	-	6	.392
1923	Enid	West A	OF-C	**148**	574	**123**	179	48	3	34	-	12	.312
1924	Bartlesville	West A	O-1-C	149	546	130	179	36	11	32	133	6	.328
	Little Rock	South A	OF	10	37	11	15	5	1	1	11	2	.405
1925	Augusta	Sally	C-1-O	121	448	74	157	23	7	23	95	7	.350
		Minors		**681**	**2530**	**588**	**857**	**177**	**35**	**141**	**239**	**44**	**.339**

WILLIAM JOSEPH RHIEL
Born August 16, 1900 at Youngstown, OH. Died August 16, 1946 at Youngstown, OH.
Height 5' 11", Weight 175. Batted right. Threw right.

Performed unassisted triple play for Portland against Seattle September 21, 1930.

Manager: Warren Pa St 1940.

Year	Club	League	POS	G	AB	R	H	2B	3B	HR	RBI	SB	BA
1926	Greenville	Sally	2-S-O-P	151	583	147	225	30	**19**	23	111	9	**.386**
1927	Atlanta	South A	2B-OF	149	588	110	202	25	19	8	124	14	.344
1928	Atlanta	South A	2B-OF	136	502	67	165	21	10	6	82	6	.329
1929	Brooklyn	National	2B-OF	76	205	27	57	9	4	4	25	0	.278
1930	Boston	National	2B	20	47	3	8	4	0	0	4	0	.170
	Portland	P C	2B	109	423	72	147	30	2	7	79	4	.348
1931	Portland	P C	2B	165	674	129	233	**53**	10	7	112	7	.346
1932	Detroit	American	2-3-S	84	250	30	70	13	3	3	38	2	.280
1933	Detroit	American	2-3-S	19	17	1	3	0	1	0	1	0	.176
	Toledo	A A	OF	30	97	10	20	5	1	0	8	1	.206
1934	Montreal	Int	OF-2B	103	284	43	83	18	4	5	61	2	.292
1935	Montreal	Int	OF	58	124	22	48	10	2	3	19	1	.387
1936	Montreal	Int	OF	99	279	40	85	16	3	3	38	1	.305
		Majors		**199**	**519**	**61**	**138**	**26**	**8**	**7**	**68**	**2**	**.266**
		Minors		**1000**	**3554**	**640**	**1208**	**208**	**70**	**62**	**634**	**45**	**.340**

KENNETH FRANKLIN RICHARDSON
Born May 2, 1915 at Orleans, IN. Died December 7, 1987 at Woodland Hills, CA.
Height 5' 10-1/2", Weight 187. Batted right. Threw right.

Manager: Victoria Gulf States 1976; Newark NY-Penn 1978; Butte Pioneer 1979-81.

Year	Club	League	POS	G	AB	R	H	2B	3B	HR	RBI	SB	BA
1934	Los Angeles	P C	3B	24	54	6	15	4	0	0	3	1	.278
1935	Des Moines	Western	3B	5	19	2	5	0	1	0	4	0	.263
	Ponca City	West A	3B	125	454	70	121	30	7	6	79	23	.267
1936	Ponca City	West A	2B	144	550	132	174	43	20	18	132	**47**	.316
1937	Moline	III	2B	64	239	54	64	18	4	8	-	16	.268

	Los Angeles	P C	2B-3B	70	258	43	57	12	1	7	19	5	.221
1938	Jersey City	Int	2B	54	143	23	33	7	3	1	13	1	.231
	Chattanooga	South A	INF	18	66	7	16	2	0	1	9	0	.242
	Minneapolis	A A	3B	22	61	3	12	2	0	1	8	1	.197
1939	Williamsport	Eastern	2B-3B	130	427	100	131	27	3	27	89	7	.307
1940	Williamsport	Eastern	OF	124	430	77	117	21	1	15	65	5	.272
1941	Williamsport	Eastern	OF	132	434	85	116	23	4	11	67	7	.267
1942	Philadelphia	American	O-3-1	6	15	1	1	0	0	0	0	0	.067
	Williamsport	Eastern	OF-3B	122	391	64	105	20	2	8	58	10	.269
1943	Hollywood	P C	2B-OF	111	310	41	80	15	2	6	38	4	.258
1944	Hollywood	P C	2-3-O	159	536	66	135	25	6	7	62	7	.252
1945	Hollywood	P C	2B-OF	157	469	74	141	25	1	14	85	11	.301
1946	Philadelphia	National	2B	6	20	1	3	1	0	0	2	0	.150
	Hollywood	P C	3B	73	236	35	58	11	4	5	37	5	.246
1947			Did not play in O. B.										
1948	Seattle	P C	1B	65	135	13	30	5	1	1	21	1	.222
1949	Spokane	West Int	3B-2B	126	426	108	138	29	1	24	117	16	.324
1950	Riverside	Sunset	3B-1B	126	407	114	115	22	3	12	80	16	.283
1951	Spokane	West Int	3B	126	435	108	140	30	8	12	108	21	.322
1952	San Francisco	P C	3B	6	19	2	3	0	0	0	2	0	.158
	Yakima	West Int	3B-OF	45	126	21	35	7	2	1	13	9	.278
	Tucson	Ariz-Tex	3B	44	158	39	56	14	2	7	39	10	.354
1953	Lewiston	West Int	3B	133	458	102	138	27	0	15	106	5	.301
1954	Vancouver	West Int	3B	117	406	81	119	21	1	14	100	6	.293
1955	El Paso	WTNM	3B	14	44	6	14	3	0	1	11	1	.318
	Majors			**12**	**35**	**2**	**4**	**1**	**0**	**0**	**2**	**0**	**.114**
	Minors			**2336**	**7691**	**1476**	**2168**	**443**	**77**	**222**	**1365**	**235**	**.282**

VIRGIL DONALD RICHARDSON
Born December 25, 1919 at South Bend, NE.
Height 6', Weight 190. Batted right and left. Threw left.
Manager: Pampa WTNM 1951.

Year	Club	League	POS	G	AB	R	H	2B	3B	HR	RBI	SB	BA
1939	Salina	West A	1B	2	7	0	0	0	0	0	0	0	.000
	Mitchell	Western	1B-OF	118	418	76	131	17	9	7	81	3	.313
1940	Opelous/Ray	Evang	OF-1B	41	166	22	27	2	2	0	5	5	.163
	Worthington	Western	1B	52	164	32	50	6	2	4	26	5	.305
	OK City	Texas	1B	1	4	0	0	0	0	0	0	0	.000
1941	Topeka	West A	1B-OF	131	447	71	121	28	4	6	64	14	.271
1942	Topeka	West A	1B	135	470	87	130	25	10	11	73	7	.277
1943-45			Did not play in O. B.										
1946	Pampa	WTNM	1B	136	504	149	171	41	7	26	132	9	.339
1947	Montgomery	SEAstern	1B	43	156	27	45	15	0	4	35	0	.288
	Lubbock	WTNM	1B	99	368	107	124	31	1	29	113	4	.337
1948	Lubbock	WTNM	1B	136	506	152	201	48	6	38	196	6	.397
1949	Pampa	WTNM	1B	138	479	102	146	35	2	19	95	5	.305
1950	Pampa	WTNM	1B	143	524	137	173	39	3	33	151	4	.330
1951	Pampa	WTNM	1B	140	488	99	158	46	1	25	128	8	.324
1952	Clovis	WTNM	1B	140	518	119	153	36	2	21	115	9	.295
1953	Clovis	WTNM	1B	139	497	139	164	38	1	27	127	7	.330
1954	Clovis	WTNM	1B	131	455	96	135	35	6	12	99	1	.297
	Minors			**1725**	**6171**	**1415**	**1929**	**442**	**56**	**262**	**1440**	**87**	**.313**

DONALD LESTER RICHMOND
Born October 27, 1919 at Gillett, PA. Died May 24, 1981 at Elmira, NY.
Height 6' 01", Weight 175. Batted left. Threw right.
Manager Batavia NY-Penn 1957-58.

Year	Club	League	POS	G	AB	R	H	2B	3B	HR	RBI	SB	BA
1940	Batavia	Pony	3B	107	446	108	147	23	12	6	63	**36**	.330
1941	Willilamsport	Eastern	3B	139	531	61	**169**	22	5	1	59	6	.318
	Philadelphia	American	3B	9	35	3	7	1	1	0	5	0	.200
1942-45				Military Service									
1946	Toronto	Int	3B	117	390	38	114	22	1	4	45	7	.292
	Philadelphia	American	3B	16	62	3	18	3	0	1	9	1	.290
1947	Philadelphia	American	3B-2B	19	21	2	4	1	1	0	4	0	.190
	Birmingham	South A	OF	49	194	42	63	11	3	7	31	7	.325
1948	Toledo	A A	3B	146	496	80	150	28	3	13	75	8	.302
1949	Balt/Roch	Int	3B	116	432	70	130	14	1	8	65	4	.301
1950	Rochester	Int	3B	140	573	**126**	**191**	31	11	18	99	6	**.333**
1951	St. Louis	National	3B	12	34	3	3	1	0	1	4	0	.088
	Rochester	Int	3B	105	412	71	144	31	5	5	49	4	**.350**
1952	Rochester	Int	3B-OF	145	578	91	**190**	**40**	8	6	62	3	.329
1953	Rochester	Int	3B	139	552	101	172	33	8	15	89	9	.312
1954	Roch/Syra	Int	OF	123	415	62	123	22	6	7	50	4	.296
1955	Syracuse	Int	OF	89	225	37	69	6	4	0	20	3	.307
1956	Miami	Int	3B	21	57	4	13	3	0	1	7	1	.228
	Birmingham	South A	OF-3B	69	250	30	76	16	3	1	29	1	.304
1957	Batavia	NY-Penn	OF	73	160	41	61	15	1	6	40	2	.381
		Majors		**56**	**152**	**11**	**32**	**6**	**2**	**2**	**22**	**1**	**.211**
		Minors		**1578**	**5711**	**962**	**1812**	**317**	**71**	**98**	**783**	**101**	**.317**

DAVID LEONARD ROBERTS
Born June 30, 1933 at Panama City, Panama.
Height 6', Weight 172. Batted left. Threw left.

Year	Club	League	POS	G	AB	R	H	2B	3B	HR	RBI	SB	BA
1952	Porterville	SW Int	OF	80	290	98	91	15	4	10	40	20	.314
1953	Grand Forks	Northern	1B-OF	125	465	89	125	20	1	15	88	13	.269
1954	Aberdeen	Northern	1B	135	499	114	148	28	7	33	114	27	.297
1955	San Antonio	Texas	1B	153	488	71	113	22	6	14	84	10	.232
1956	San Antonio	Texas	1B-OF	147	539	109	148	28	9	7	67	6	.275
1957	Vancouver	P C	PH	1	1	0	0	0	0	0	0	0	.000
	Knoxville	Sally	OF-1B	44	153	24	46	6	2	5	22	1	.301
	S.A./Austin	Texas	1B-OF	99	347	50	89	12	4	5	36	7	.256
1958	Austin	Texas	1B	148	521	96	153	19	6	20	61	4	.294
1959	Louisville	A A	OF-1B	133	385	59	97	20	2	10	50	5	.252
1960	Sacramento	P C	1B	9	37	6	9	3	1	1	4	0	.243
	Austin	Texas	1B-OF	55	205	40	63	13	2	9	41	2	.307
	Dal-Ft.Worth	A A	1B	71	235	26	56	7	2	4	18	3	.238
1961	Jacksonville	Sally	1B-OF	77	266	50	84	18	2	8	29	2	.316
	Houston	A A	OF	41	130	20	27	5	1	3	21	0	.208
1962	OK City	A A	OF-1B	133	481	86	155	**38**	8	15	96	3	.322
	Houston	National	OF-1B	16	53	3	13	3	0	1	10	0	.245
1963	OK City	P C	OF-1B	151	507	82	137	24	5	16	86	1	.270
1964	OK City	P C	OF-1B	38	132	32	49	17	3	5	30	0	.371
	Houston	National	OF-1B	61	125	9	23	4	1	1	7	0	.184

1965	OK City	P C	OF-1B	144	493	102	157	20	6	**38**	114	8	.318
1966	Pittsburgh	National	1B	14	16	3	2	1	0	0	0	0	.125
	Columbus	Int	OF-1B	119	408	67	111	14	2	26	83	0	.272
1967	Sankei	Jap Cent	OF-1B	126	459	72	124	26	2	28	89	2	.270
1968	Sankei	Jap Cent	OF-1B	128	456	82	135	12	2	40	94	4	.296
1969	Sankei	Jap Cent	OF-1B	116	424	72	135	18	0	37	95	5	.318
1970	Yakult	Jap Cent	OF-1B	124	420	43	100	22	0	19	52	1	.238
1971	Yakult	Jap Cent	1B	128	452	63	121	20	1	33	76	8	.268
1972	Yakult	Jap Cent	1B	120	383	55	106	21	1	22	63	2	.277
1973	Yakult	Jap Cent	1B	36	115	13	29	5	2	2	16	0	.252
	Kintetsu	Jap Pac	1B	36	65	3	14	0	0	2	7	0	.215
	Majors			**91**	**194**	**15**	**38**	**8**	**1**	**2**	**17**	**0**	**.196**
	Minors			**1903**	**6582**	**1221**	**1858**	**329**	**73**	**244**	**1084**	**112**	**.282**
	Japan			**814**	**2774**	**403**	**764**	**124**	**8**	**183**	**492**	**22**	**.275**

Dave Roberts

HECTOR ANTONIO RODRIGUEZ (ORDENANA)
Born June 13, 1920 at Villa Alquizar, Cuba.
Height 5' 8", Weight 165. Batted right. Threw right.
Manager in 1964-65-66.

Year	Club	League	POS	G	AB	R	H	2B	3B	HR	RBI	SB	BA
1943	Mexico City	Mexican	3B	90	395	68	127	19	4	0	34	22	.322
1944	NY Cubans	Neg. Nat.	3B	34	130	29	31	3	3	0	8	6	.238
1945	Tampico	Mexican	3B	92	374	76	122	13	14	0	47	17	.326
1946	Tampico	Mexican	3B	99	412	78	132	11	8	3	32	29	.320
1947	Tampico	Mexican	3B	123	504	91	147	13	8	1	51	36	.292

122

Year	Club	League	POS	G	AB	R	H	2B	3B	HR	RBI	SB	BA
1948	Tamp/Vera	Mexican	3B	87	338	63	96	15	6	2	41	12	.289
1949	San Luis Pot	Mexican	3B	52	135	20	39	5	0	2	17	1	.289
1950	Veracruz	Mexican	3B	20	85	17	28	2	2	1	12	4	.329
1951	San Luis Pot	Mexican	3B	62	253	51	78	7	0	5	30	0	.308
	Montreal	Int	3B	153	609	105	184	28	10	8	95	26	.302
1952	SLP/MC/Mon	Mexican	3B	72	280	36	71	10	4	2	27	1	.309
	Chicago	American	3B	124	407	55	108	14	0	1	40	7	.265
1953	Syracuse	Int	3B-SS	148	527	90	159	21	7	4	62	12	.302
1954	Toronto	Int	SS-3B	147	535	105	164	22	3	4	43	8	.307
1955	Toronto	Int	SS	146	560	99	162	31	8	9	57	7	.289
1956	Toronto	Int	SS	150	524	73	143	17	3	4	40	8	.273
1957	Toronto	Int	SS	147	528	53	152	19	7	2	62	2	.288
1958	Toronto	Int	SS-OF	128	456	54	104	11	2	3	34	5	.228
1959	Toronto	Int	S-3-O	132	414	48	106	16	3	6	30	3	.256
1960	San Diego	P C	SS	134	446	52	117	9	3	0	42	8	.262
1961	San Diego	P C	3B-SS	100	300	33	88	15	3	0	33	3	.293
1962	MC Reds	Mexican	3B-SS	96	321	37	89	18	7	0	29	5	.277
1963	MC Reds	Mexican	SS-3B	113	379	45	111	16	4	3	54	3	.293
1964	Campeche	Mex S. E.	SS-3B	88	320	38	89	9	9	1	37	8	.278
1965	SL Potosi	Mex. Cent.		Manager, did not play									
1966	Tabasco	Mex. S. E.	3B	30	95	11	30	4	3	0	16	0	.316
		Majors		**124**	**407**	**55**	**108**	**14**	**0**	**1**	**40**	**7**	**.265**
		Minors		**2223**	**8120**	**1235**	**2351**	**308**	**114**	**51**	**852**	**224**	**.290**
		Negro Lg		**34**	**130**	**29**	**31**	**3**	**3**	**0**	**8**	**6**	**.238**

HILARIO OSCAR RODRIGUEZ (MOYO)
(Known by middle name.)
February 17, 1931 at Cabo Rojo, Puerto Rico
Height 5' 11-1/2", Weight 175 Batted right. Threw right.
Manager: Carmen Mexican SE 1969.

Year	Club	League	POS	G	AB	R	H	2B	3B	HR	RBI	SB	BA
1951	Middlesboro	Mtn St	2-1-3-O	93	374	85	104	13	3	6	50	11	.278
1952	Middlesboro	Mtn St	O-2-3	119	445	89	129	26	7	4	82	27	.290
1953	Middlesboro	Mtn St	OF-3B	94	352	96	135	21	11	10	79	22	.384
	Longview	Big St	OF	29	87	13	28	4	0	1	11	3	.322
1954	Waco	Texas	OF-1B	125	424	80	118	12	4	8	57	19	.278
1955	Waco	Texas	O-3-1	134	505	94	162	35	8	4	85	6	.321
1956	Waco	Texas	3-O-1	134	508	97	151	36	6	11	93	4	.297
1957	MC Tigers	Mexican	3-C-O	109	382	62	107	15	9	8	63	4	.280
1958	MC Tig/Yuc	Mexican	3B-OF	114	401	71	116	13	8	14	62	9	.289
1959	Vera/NL	Mexican	C-3B	145	532	97	167	33	4	22	90	4	.314
1960	Puebla	Mexican	C-O-3	140	485	102	167	28	2	26	105	1	.344
1961	Puebla	Mexican	3-O-C	125	445	94	135	17	9	22	85	4	.303
1962	Puebla	Mexican	O-3B	95	356	63	133	20	2	15	59	5	.374
1963	Puebla	Mexican	O-3B	122	462	82	158	31	6	17	73	1	.342
1964	Puebla	Mexican	O-3B	129	498	103	181	37	9	18	107	4	.363
1965	Puebla	Mexican	O-C-3	130	486	82	155	30	7	15	90	1	.319
1966	Puebla	Mexican	OF-C	136	496	103	**165**	**35**	2	13	74	4	.333
1967	Reynosa	Mexican	3-1-O	134	492	86	175	**42**	5	14	89	5	.356
1968	Reynosa	Mexican	3-1-C	137	451	51	126	27	2	9	82	2	.279
1969	Reynosa	Mexican	OF-1B	32	100	15	23	6	1	2	16	1	.230
	Carmen	Mex S.E.	3-O-1	65	204	27	66	12	1	5	38	3	.324
		Minors		**2341**	**8485**	**1592**	**2701**	**493**	**106**	**244**	**1490**	**140**	**.318**

RAY ROHWER
(Correct first name was Ray and had no middle name.)
Born June 5, 1895 at Dixon, CA. Died January 24, 1988 at Davis, CA.
Height 5' 10", Weight 155. Batted left. Threw left.
Brother of Claude, minor league player.

Graduated from the University of California in 1920.

Collected 25 hits in 40 AB during a 7 day period from May 24 through May 30, 1927. He scored 12 runs, knocked in 21 runs and had 5 doubles and 4 HR.

Year	Club	League	POS	G	AB	R	H	2B	3B	HR	RBI	SB	BA
1921	Pittsburgh	National	OF	30	40	6	10	3	2	0	6	0	.250
1922	Pittsburgh	National	OF	53	129	19	38	6	3	3	22	1	.295
1923	Seattle	P C	OF	179	655	125	213	30	20	37	135	12	.325
1924	Seattle	P C	OF	176	644	120	209	42	15	33	155	11	.325
1925	Portland	P C	OF	177	677	139	226	44	3	40	153	12	.334
1926	Port/Sacra	P C	OF	168	565	99	148	25	2	28	107	14	.262
1927	Sacramento	P C	OF	133	422	70	141	32	4	14	95	11	.334
1928	Sacramento	P C	OF	142	478	76	138	34	2	10	84	13	.289
1929	Sacramento	P C	OF	149	495	76	127	29	7	11	70	8	.257
1930	Sacramento	P C	OF	124	392	56	117	27	6	13	83	6	.298
1931	Sacramento	P C	OF	110	356	40	88	24	2	10	47	5	.247
	Majors			**83**	**169**	**25**	**48**	**9**	**5**	**3**	**28**	**1**	**.284**
	Minors			**1358**	**4684**	**801**	**1407**	**287**	**61**	**196**	**929**	**92**	**.300**

HARRY ROSENBERG
Born June 22, 1909 at San Francisco, CA.
Height 5' 10", Weight 180. Batted right. Threw right.
Brother of Lou, major league player.

Year	Club	League	POS	G	AB	R	H	2B	3B	HR	RBI	SB	BA
1930	Missions	P C	OF	70	239	60	88	19	2	11	53	3	.368
	New York	Naitonal	OF	9	5	1	0	0	0	0	0	0	.000
1931	Newark	Int	OF	21	67	13	19	3	1	0	6	1	.284
	Bridgeport	Eastern	OF	71	277	51	91	17	9	2	40	11	.329
	Indianapolis	A A	OF	35	112	15	37	10	1	0	-	3	.330
1932	Indianapolis	A A	OF	144	516	69	164	27	6	7	79	6	.318
1933	Indianapolis	A A	OF	44	146	20	41	8	2	2	20	2	.281
	Ft. Worth	Texas	OF	75	274	50	89	17	7	4	34	3	.325
1934	Indianapolis	A A	OF	126	450	74	148	18	11	2	65	2	.329
1935	Sacramento	P C	OF	151	567	95	201	27	16	10	80	15	.354
1936	Missions	P C	OF	172	668	103	223	33	15	3	99	11	.334
1937	Missions	P C	OF	162	612	92	202	32	11	10	76	7	.330
1938	Portland	P C	OF	154	575	75	184	37	8	4	82	12	.320
1939	Portland	P C	OF	172	646	103	214	45	5	8	95	5	.331
1940	Portland	P C	OF	177	659	91	207	28	6	4	70	10	.314
1941	Hollywood	P C	OF	120	420	58	120	31	2	1	55	9	.286
1942					Did not play in O. B.								
1943	San Francisco	P C	OF	26	94	11	34	4	1	0	18	0	.362
	Majors			**9**	**5**	**1**	**0**	**0**	**0**	**0**	**0**	**0**	**.000**
	Minors			**1720**	**6322**	**980**	**2062**	**356**	**103**	**68**	**872**	**100**	**.326**

JOHN WILLIAM JOSEPH "BUNNY" ROSER

Born November 15, 1901 at St. Louis, MO. Died May 6, 1979 at Rocky Hill, CT.
Height 5' 11", Weight 175. Batted left. Threw left.
Manager Gloversville-Johnstown Can Amer 1938; Bradford Pony 1939.

Year	Club	League	POS	G	AB	R	H	2B	3B	HR	RBI	SB	BA
1920	Mineral Wells	W Texas	OF	57	202	25	63	9	5	0	-	5	.312
1921	Chattanooga	South A		On suspended list									
1922	St.Petersburg	Fla St	OF	114	419	89	131	20	17	**10**	-	10	.313
	Boston	National	OF	32	113	13	27	3	4	0	16	2	.239
1923	Wor/Pitts	Eastern	OF	129	496	88	155	41	16	18	-	4	.313
1924	Worcester	Eastern	OF	148	543	119	179	28	9	**38**	-	9	.330
1925	Baltimore	Int	OF	117	353	75	107	16	4	25	77	0	.303
1926	Birmingham	South A	OF	44	143	32	44	8	3	2	25	1	.308
	Williamsport	NY-Penn	OF	58	187	28	49	8	5	0	34	3	.262
1927	Bridgeport	Eastern	OF	149	538	114	178	36	17	20	111	5	.331
1928	Ft. Worth	Texas	PH	1	1	0	0	0	0	0	0	0	.000
	Hartford	Eastern	OF	150	579	113	187	45	7	**27**	106	4	.323
1929	Hartford	Eastern	OF-1B	**155**	568	109	173	37	3	25	118	11	.305
1930	Hartford	Eastern	OF	55	199	30	66	14	2	7	30	1	.332
	Harrisburg	NY-Penn	OF-1B	68	233	42	66	10	10	7	54	3	.283
1931	Rich/Norfolk	Eastern	OF-1B	137	496	68	145	33	4	10	73	6	.292
1932	Norfolk	Eastern	OF	12	31	6	8	0	1	0	3	0	.258
	Harrisburg	NY-Penn	OF	1	4	0	1	0	0	0	0	0	.250
1933				Did not play in O. B.									
1934	Hartford	NEastern	1B	97	338	55	111	26	6	14	-	6	.328
1935-37				Did not play in O. B.									
1938	Glov/Johns	Can-Amer	1-O-P	95	283	61	98	11	2	10	56	1	.346
1939	Bradford	Pony	1B	1	2	0	1	1	0	0	2	0	.500
		Majors		**32**	**113**	**13**	**27**	**3**	**4**	**0**	**16**	**2**	**.239**
		Minors		**1588**	**5615**	**1054**	**1762**	**343**	**111**	**213**	**689**	**69**	**.314**

EWELL ALBERT "REB" RUSSELL

Born April 12, 1889 at Jackson, MS. Died September 30, 1973 at Indianapolis, IN.
Height 5' 11", Weight 185. Batted left. Threw left.
Won 81 games as a major league pitcher, with 22 wins in 1913. Shifted to outfield in 1919.

Year	Club	League	POS	G	AB	R	H	2B	3B	HR	RBI	SB	BA
1912	Bonham	Tex-Okla	P	28	78	14	23	2	1	0	-	8	.295
	Ft. Worth	Texas	P	13	20	3	6	0	0	0	-	1	.300
1913	Chicago	American	P	52	106	9	20	5	3	0	7	0	.189
1914	Chicago	American	P	43	64	6	17	1	1	0	7	0	.266
1915	Chicago	American	P	45	86	11	21	2	3	0	7	1	.244
1916	Chicago	American	P	56	91	9	13	2	0	0	6	1	.143
1917	Chicago	American	P	39	68	5	19	3	3	0	9	0	.279
1918	Chicago	American	P	27	50	2	7	3	0	0	3	0	.140
1919	Chicago	American	P	1	0	0	0	0	0	0	0	0	.000
	Minneapolis	A A	OF-P	92	364	51	97	13	4	9	-	2	.266
1920	Minneapolis	A A	OF-P	85	298	46	101	22	8	6	41	5	.339
1921	Minneapolis	A A	OF-P	146	549	118	202	35	18	33	132	9	.368
1922	Minneapolis	A A	OF	77	245	53	81	17	8	17	63	3	.331
	Pittsburgh	National	OF	60	220	51	81	14	8	12	75	4	.368

Year	Club	League	POS	G	AB	R	H	2B	3B	HR	RBI	SB	BA
1923	Pittsburgh	National	OF	94	291	49	84	18	7	9	58	3	.289
1924	Columbus	A A	OF-1B	150	531	105	180	36	16	25	116	4	.339
1925	Columbus	A A	OF	146	493	109	157	22	13	30	131	6	.318
1926	Indianapolis	A A	OF-1B	119	376	79	121	16	10	14	61	4	.322
1927	Indianapolis	A A	OF	128	431	80	166	34	4	10	96	8	**.385**
1928	Indianapolis	A A	OF-1B	109	328	60	102	21	3	17	55	2	.311
1929	Indianapolis	A A	OF	41	92	10	24	3	1	5	-	1	.261
	Quincy	III	OF	63	230	45	79	16	7	13	60	4	.343
1930	Mob/Chat	South A	1B-OF	92	320	60	96	14	7	16	80	5	.300
	Quincy	III	1B	25	84	20	26	6	1	4	19	1	.310
	Majors			**417**	**976**	**142**	**262**	**48**	**25**	**21**	**172**	**9**	**.268**
	Minors			**1314**	**4439**	**853**	**1461**	**257**	**101**	**199**	**854**	**63**	**.329**

Ewell "Reb" Russell

ROBERT ALOYSIUS "JOE" SCHMIDT
Born June 9, 1918 at Belleville, IL.
Height 5' 10-1/2", Weight 190. Batted right. Threw right.
Manager: Newnan 1949 & 1950; Mount Vernon 1953.
Led all minor leagues with a .441 batting average in 1939.

Year	Club	League	POS	G	AB	R	H	2B	3B	HR	RBI	SB	BA
1937	Grand Island	Neb St	3B	29	112	18	32	5	4	3	26	4	.286
1938	Grand Island	Neb St	3B	15	56	9	9	1	1	0	6	2	.161
	Duluth	Northern	OF-3B	71	232	39	67	16	0	8	51	1	.289
1939	Duluth	Northern	3B-OF	120	440	**114**	**194**	29	9	**31**	**133**	17	**.441**
1940	Portsmouth	Mid Atl	3B-2B	126	480	82	153	24	3	15	94	15	.319
1941	Mobile	SEastern	3B	120	443	76	135	37	2	7	80	10	.305

1942-45			Military Service									
1946	Anniston	SEastern	3B-OF	119	433	94	138	19	10	19	76	6	.319
1947	Anniston	SEastern	OF-3B	117	456	102	152	29	9	18	103	10	.333
1948	Anniston	SEastern	OF	15	55	11	18	5	0	2	8	0	.327
1949	Newnan	Ga-Ala	2B	123	455	102	140	21	4	17	108	13	.308
1950	Newnan	Ga-Ala	2B	113	409	100	130	31	3	13	100	20	.318
1951	Fargo-Moor	Northern	3B	79	281	53	69	20	3	11	53	4	.246
1952	Keokuk	III	OF	120	460	76	138	19	3	11	96	8	.300
1953	Mt Vernon	Miss-O V	2B	109	408	88	146	29	9	12	103	6	.358
1954	Paris	Miss-O V	1B-2B	123	460	105	155	30	14	22	125	11	.337
		Minors		**1399**	**5180**	**1069**	**1676**	**315**	**74**	**189**	**1162**	**127**	**.324**

JOHN THOMAS SHEEHAN

Born April 15, 1893 at Chicago, IL. Died May 29, 1987 at West Palm Beach, FL.
Height 5' 8-1/2", Weight 165. Batted both. Threw right.

Manager: Winnipeg Northern 1916; Winnipeg W Canada 1919-20; Elmira NY-Penn 1928;
Columbus SEL 1932; Wheeling MAL, 1933-34; Peoria III 1935.

Year	Club	League	POS	G	AB	R	H	2B	3B	HR	RBI	SB	BA
1912	Zanesville	Central	3B	48	162	28	42	7	2	1	-	4	.259
1913	Zanesville	Inter-St	3B	73	266	27	62	6	8	0	-	16	.233
	Fon du Lac	Wis-Ill	SS	56	208	32	54	13	0	0	-	8	.260
1914	Twin Cities	Wis-Ill	SS	94	346	50	92	11	2	5	-	30	.266
1915	Ft. Wayne	Central	3B	93	360	43	108	9	2	0	-	19	.300
1916	Winnipeg	Northern	SS	121	460	80	131	21	5	2	-	42	.285
1917	Oakland	P C	SS	104	350	30	76	7	1	0	-	19	.217
1918				Did not play in O. B.									
1919	Winnipeg	W Canada	SS	100	359	69	92	10	9	1	-	17	.256
1920	Winnipeg	W Canada	SS	99	342	52	121	18	5	1	50	34	.354
	Brooklyn	National	SS-3B	3	5	0	2	1	0	0	0	0	.400
1921	Brooklyn	National	2-S-3	5	12	2	0	0	0	0	0	0	.000
	Buffalo	Int	SS-3B	127	486	103	120	18	8	1	-	29	.247
1922	Buffalo	Int	SS	151	532	96	148	24	8	1	58	24	.278
1923	Buffalo	Int	SS	138	472	87	147	27	3	2	52	9	.311
1924	Newark	Int	SS	150	542	110	166	30	8	3	55	24	.306
1925	Providence	Int	SS-2B	162	564	102	159	26	13	7	71	15	.282
1926	Rochester	Int	2-S-3	128	467	81	137	23	6	2	66	14	.293
1927	Jersey City	Int	3-2-S	76	289	32	66	9	2	0	19	2	.228
	San Francisco	P C	2B	45	144	21	35	7	0	0	15	2	.243
1928	Elmira	NY-Penn	2B-SS	110	399	60	115	14	3	0	33	9	.288
1929	Atlanta	South A	2B	150	548	91	163	33	6	2	58	12	.297
1930	Atlanta	South A	2B	156	580	142	185	43	11	1	59	13	.319
1931	Atlanta	South A	2B	126	448	92	120	7	2	1	34	12	.268
1932	Columbus	SEastern	2B	32	104	37	36	3	2	0	20	6	.346
	Knoxville	South A	2B	114	416	82	111	20	5	2	39	16	.267
1933	Wheeling	Mid Atl	3B	85	299	56	78	14	3	2	27	7	.261
1934	Wheeling	Mid Atl	3B	10	27	7	4	1	1	0	0	0	.148
		Majors		**8**	**17**	**2**	**2**	**1**	**0**	**0**	**0**	**0**	**.118**
		Minors		**2548**	**9170**	**1610**	**2568**	**401**	**115**	**34**	**656**	**383**	**.280**

CHARLES ARTHUR "ART" SHIRES

Born August 13, 1907 at Milford, MA. Died July 13, 1967 at Italy, TX.
Height 6' 1", Weight 195. Batted left. Threw right.

A legendary exhibitionist and brawler who fought with his manager, players, and others. He had a brief but well publicized experiment as a pro wrestler and boxer in Chicago in the 1929-30 off-season. Commissioner Landis halted his boxing career after six bouts, one with Chicago Bear's center George Trafton on December 16, 1929.

Year	Club	League	POS	G	AB	R	H	2B	3B	HR	RBI	SB	BA
1926	Waco	Texas	1B	104	368	46	103	22	2	5	36	8	.280
1927	Waco	Texas	1B	156	558	74	170	19	8	8	83	17	.305
1928	Waco	Texas	1B	106	379	74	120	16	6	11	55	22	.317
	Chicago	American	1B	33	123	20	42	6	1	1	11	0	.341
1929	Chicago	American	1B	100	353	41	110	20	7	3	41	4	.312
1930	Chi/Wash	American	1B	75	212	25	64	10	1	2	27	3	.302
1931	Milwaukee	A A	1B	157	623	120	**240**	45	8	11	131	8	.385
1932	Boston	National	1B	82	298	32	71	9	3	5	30	1	.238
1933	Columbus	A A	1B	44	176	35	55	12	1	5	30	2	.313
	Rochester	Int	1B	59	195	31	54	10	3	2	24	2	.277
1934	Fort Worth	Texas	1B	138	512	63	147	33	5	1	71	4	.287
1935	Harrisburg	NY-Penn	1B	63	205	28	50	5	2	1	30	3	.244
	Majors			**290**	**986**	**118**	**287**	**45**	**12**	**11**	**109**	**8**	**.291**
	Minors			**827**	**3016**	**471**	**939**	**162**	**35**	**44**	**460**	**66**	**.311**

SYLVESTER ADAM SIMON

Born December 14, 1897 at Evansville, IN. Died February 28, 1973 at Chandler, IN.
Height 5' 10-1/2", Weight 170. Batted right. Threw right.

Son-in-law of Charles Knoll (see record elsewhere in this section).

Manager: Quincy III 1932.

Lost part of left hand in accident after 1926 season when he ran hand into saw at factory in Evansville, IN. Thumb, part of palm and little finger were all that remained of hand. Devised a special glove and a mechanical grip for use when batting.

Year	Club	League	POS	G	AB	R	H	2B	3B	HR	RBI	SB	BA
1920	Ludington	Central	O-3-2	74	260	23	55	7	3	2	-	9	.212
1921					Did not play in O. B.								
1922	Bay City	Mich-Ont	3B	130	477	71	149	20	18	0	79	31	.312
1923	San Antonio	Texas	3B	140	519	96	167	29	11	12	116	11	.322
	St. Louis	American	PH	1	1	0	0	0	0	0	0	0	.000
1924	St. Louis	American	3B-SS	22	32	5	8	1	1	0	6	0	.250
1925	Tulsa	Western	3B-2B	106	408	90	147	28	4	22	-	17	.360
1926	Milwaukee	A A	3B	107	357	57	110	19	7	5	59	14	.308
1927	Evansville/Qu	III	3B	55	179	31	50	5	2	6	35	10	.279
1928	Beaumont	Texas	3B	2	8	1	1	0	0	0	0	0	.125
	Ft. Wayne	Central	3B	81	300	54	108	20	5	19	-	18	.360
1929	Erie	Central	3B	119	453	105	153	25	5	30	97	30	.338
1930	Nashville	South A	3B	14	36	6	9	2	0	1	5	2	.250
	Ft. Wayne	Central	3B	95	390	93	142	31	9	15	95	20	.364
1931	Elmira/Bing	NY-Penn	3B	9	24	3	6	0	0	0	1	2	.250
	Bloomington	III	3B	99	392	71	125	12	16	4	78	33	.319
1932	Quincy	III	3B	41	126	22	37	8	0	3	-	13	.294
	Majors			**23**	**33**	**5**	**8**	**1**	**1**	**0**	**6**	**0**	**.242**
	Minors			**1072**	**3929**	**723**	**1259**	**206**	**80**	**119**	**565**	**210**	**.320**

Fred Muller
(Record on page 108.)

Andy Reese
(Record on page 118.)

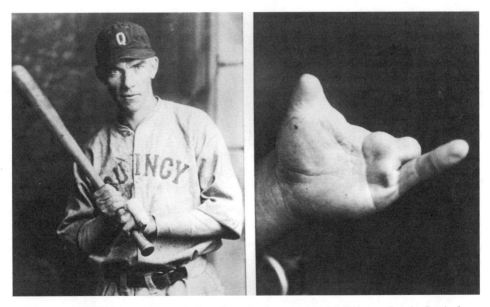

The extent of Sylvester Simon's handicap is shown at right. The mechanical grip he used for batting is demonstrated at left. Simon was able to hit 30 homers in 119 games

EMANUEL CARR SMITH
(Known by middle name)
Born April 8, 1901 at Kernersville, NC. Died April 14, 1989 at Miami, FL.
Height 6', Weight 175. Batted right. Threw right.
Manager: Tri Cities BiState 1934.

Year	Club	League	POS	G	AB	R	H	2B	3B	HR	RBI	SB	BA
1923	Raleigh	Piedmont	O-1-P	112	440	107	184	28	25	24	137	4	.418
	Washington	American	OF	5	9	0	1	1	0	0	1	0	.111
1924	Washington	American	OF	5	10	1	2	0	0	0	0	0	.200
	Chat/Memp	South A	OF	91	344	65	111	24	6	6	69	8	.323
1925	Columbus	A A	OF	4	3	0	0	0	0	0	0	0	.000
	Winst-Salem	Piedmont	OF	98	344	70	111	27	13	11	74	7	.323
1926	Rochester	Int	OF	20	62	11	15	2	1	1	14	0	.242
	Wilson	Virginia	OF	57	208	41	73	16	2	4	30	8	.351
	Winst-Salem	Piedmont	OF	40	140	21	42	5	8	3	22	5	.300
1927	Terre Haute	III	OF	132	480	77	150	22	18	9	88	19	.313
1928	Norfolk	Virginia	OF	42	155	41	54	13	2	5	-	1	.348
	Selma	SEastern	OF	37	125	12	29	5	2	0	14	1	.232
	Greensboro	Piedmont	OF-1B	44	162	37	60	14	1	7	37	0	.370
1929	Williamsport	NY-Penn	OF	139	534	105	179	22	17	15	94	11	.335
1930	Williamsport	NY-Penn	OF	139	539	75	172	35	15	16	113	13	.319
1931	Norfolk	Eastern	OF	137	562	85	192	39	8	10	101	8	.342
1932	Richmond	Eastern	OF	54	214	50	82	19	9	4	32	0	.383
1933	Richmond	Piedmont	OF	41	175	32	58	11	5	3	30	2	.331
	Jersey City	Int	OF	4	10	0	0	0	0	0	0	0	.000
	Williamsport	NY-Penn	OF	86	322	36	95	20	9	1	49	1	.295
1934	Tri-Cities	Bi-St	OF	25	106	27	41	10	1	12	-	0	.387
1935	Danville	Bi-St	OF	15	53	9	14	5	1	0	-	7	.264
1936-41				Did not play in O. B.									
1942				Military Service									
1943	Norfolk	Piedmont	OF	104	356	27	85	10	1	0	39	1	.239
1944	Norfolk	Piedmont	OF	64	217	17	51	11	1	0	20	0	.235
		Majors		**10**	**19**	**1**	**3**	**1**	**0**	**0**	**1**	**0**	**.158**
		Minors		**1485**	**5551**	**945**	**1798**	**338**	**145**	**131**	**963**	**96**	**.324**

MORRIS HIRSCH "MOSES" SOLOMON
Born December 8, 1990 at New York, NY. Died June 25, 1966 at Miami, FL.
Height 5' 9-1/2", Weight 180. Batted left. Threw left.
Set minor league HR record with 49 in 1923. This broke the record (45) of Perry Werden, Minneapolis WL, held since 1895.

Year	Club	League	POS	G	AB	R	H	2B	3B	HR	RBI	SB	BA
1921	Vancouver	P C Int	1B-OF	115	422	73	132	19	8	13	-	13	.313
1922	Vanc/Tac	P C Int	1B	19	76	10	23	3	1	0	-	2	.303
1923	Hutchinson	SWestern	1B-OF	134	527	143	222	40	15	49	-	12	.421
	New York	National	OF	2	8	0	3	1	0	0	1	0	.375
1924	Toledo	A A	1B	5	21	0	3	0	1	0	1	0	.143
	Pitt/Brid/Wat	Eastern	1B-OF	142	555	65	169	37	11	5	-	7	.305
1925	Toledo	A A	PH	2	2	0	0	0	0	0	0	0	.000
	Hartford/Alba	Eastern	OF-1B	133	511	61	149	31	8	2	-	11	.292
1926	Albany	Eastern	OF-1B	144	545	64	164	36	11	1	-	11	.301
1927	Albany	Eastern	OF	153	589	72	158	43	9	7	91	15	.268

130

1928	Albany	Eastern	1B-OF	41	101	18	31	7	2	1	17	1	.307
1929	Canton	Central	1B	12	43	5	11	1	1	0	2	2	.256
		Majors		**2**	**8**	**0**	**3**	**1**	**0**	**0**	**1**	**0**	**.375**
		Minors		**900**	**3392**	**511**	**1062**	**217**	**67**	**78**	**111**	**74**	**.313**

JESUS MARTIN SOMMERS (LOPEZ)
Born November 11, 1949 at Guayamas, Sonora, Mexico
Height 5' 11", Weight 175. Bats right. Throws right.
Son of Lonnie Summers (different spelling of last name), former Negro League and minor league catcher.

Year	Club	League	POS	G	AB	R	H	2B	3B	HR	RBI	SB	BA
1966	SanLuisPotose	Mex Cent	SS-OF	28	98	8	23	3	0	0	12	1	.235
1967					Did not play in O. B.								
1968	Ciudad Mad	Mex Cent	3-O-C	89	306	48	76	9	1	11	45	5	.248
1969	Ciudad Mad	Mex Cent	OF-2B	17	56	5	10	0	1	1	9	0	.179
	Penasco	Mex North	O-S-3	89	354	72	118	24	5	10	53	19	.333
1970	Carmen	Mex SE	3B-2B	20	73	9	16	4	0	2	9	3	.219
	Yucatan	Mexican	3-O-2	92	265	27	66	8	1	3	22	3	.249
1971	Yucatan	Mexican	3B	12	42	5	11	1	1	0	8	0	.262
1972	Yucatan	Mexican	3B	37	128	17	34	3	1	2	22	2	.266
1973	Yucatan	Mexican	3B-SS	**135**	446	66	130	16	3	9	58	18	.291
1974	Puebla	Mexican	3B-2B	136	469	62	130	22	5	11	61	15	.277
1975	Puebla	Mexican	3-2-S	91	318	38	92	17	2	2	32	4	.289
1976	Puebla	Mexican	3B	**137**	**538**	81	157	26	3	15	79	2	.292
1977	Aguascal	Mexican	3B	142	517	71	138	22	5	9	74	10	.267
1978	Aguascal	Mexican	3B-1B	145	504	89	153	23	12	6	55	11	.304
1979	Tampico	Mexican	3B-1B	122	467	60	131	18	1	10	43	9	.281
1980	Tol/MC Reds	Mex #1	3B-1B	93	350	59	108	12	6	10	65	3	.309
1981	MC Reds	Mexican	3B-1B	119	430	63	136	22	4	3	55	8	.316
1982	Tabasco	Mexican	3-S-2	121	399	36	111	20	2	3	41	7	.278
1983	MC R/Leon	Mexican	1B-3B	104	367	43	81	11	2	10	48	3	.221
1984	Leon	Mexican	3-1-2	109	425	95	139	18	1	27	101	4	.327
1985	Leon	Mexican	3B	114	415	81	120	22	2	19	83	4	.289
1986	Leon	Mexican	1B-3B	116	450	100	160	30	2	18	86	7	.356
1987	Leon	Mexican	3-1-2	118	444	81	156	34	2	20	114	4	.351
1988	Leon	Mexican	3B-1B	124	457	68	146	26	1	10	75	0	.319
1989	Torreon	Mexican	1B	129	484	85	151	28	1	19	84	5	.312
1990	Torreon	Mexican	1B	84	285	34	79	14	0	6	43	1	.277
1991	Jalisco	Mexican	1B	114	411	57	115	17	3	9	81	2	.280
		Minors		**2637**	**9498**	**1460**	**2787**	**450**	**67**	**245**	**1458**	**150**	**.293**

EDWARD LEE STEVENS
Born January 12, 1925 at Galveston, TX.
Height 6' 1", Weight 190. Batted left. Threw left.

Year	Club	League	POS	G	AB	R	H	2B	3B	HR	RBI	SB	BA
1941	Big Spring	WTNM	1B	117	462	81	125	24	6	13	74	10	.271
1942	Lamesa	WTNM	1B	64	281	67	103	18	9	13	79	1	.367
	Johnstown	Pa St A	1B	46	176	28	48	10	3	3	21	2	.273
1943					Did not play in O.B.								
1944	Montreal	Int	1B	153	543	77	147	37	4	16	102	5	.271
1945	Montreal	Int	1B	110	401	64	124	19	6	19	95	5	.309
	Brooklyn	National	1B	55	201	29	55	14	3	4	29	0	.274

Year	Team	League	Pos	G	AB	R	H	2B	3B	HR	RBI	SB	AVG
1946	Brooklyn	National	1B	103	310	34	75	13	7	10	60	2	.242
1947	Brooklyn	National	1B	5	13	0	2	1	0	0	0	0	.154
	Montreal	Int	1B	133	458	89	133	22	4	27	108	5	.290
1948	Pittsburgh	National	1B	128	429	47	109	19	6	10	69	4	.254
1949	Pittsburgh	National	1B	67	221	22	58	10	1	4	32	1	.262
1950	Pittsburgh	National	1B	17	46	2	9	2	0	0	3	0	.196
	Indianapolis	A A	1B	61	198	26	52	3	2	5	27	0	.263
1951	Indianapolis	A A	1B	152	575	55	150	21	7	12	91	0	.261
1952	Toronto	Int	1B	155	554	87	154	31	7	26	**113**	4	.278
1953	Toronto	Int	1B	151	520	82	146	20	5	19	92	6	.281
1954	Toronto	Int	1B	155	552	99	161	24	6	27	**113**	4	.292
1955	Toronto	Int	1B	66	236	35	65	7	1	7	42	3	.275
1956	Toronto	Int	1B	140	506	65	125	12	1	21	73	1	.247
1957	Charleston	A A	1B	105	370	46	84	20	2	16	45	1	.227
	Rochester	Int	1B	40	139	25	38	5	0	12	25	0	.273
1958	Rochester	Int	1B	123	415	54	109	23	3	14	47	2	.263
1959	Dallas	Texas	1B	17	55	7	15	6	0	1	9	1	.273
	Atlan/Chat	South A	1B	60	204	21	47	11	1	4	23	1	.230
1960				Did not play in O. B.									
1961	Mobile	South A	1B	17	44	4	12	2	0	2	8	0	.273
	Majors			**375**	**1220**	**134**	**308**	**59**	**17**	**28**	**193**	**7**	**.252**
	Minors			**1865**	**6689**	**1012**	**1838**	**315**	**67**	**257**	**1187**	**51**	**.275**

Ed Stevens

GEORGE FREDERICK STUMPF
Born December 15, 1910 at New Orleans, LA.
Height 5' 8", Weight 155. Batted left. Threw left.
Manager: New Iberia Evang 1948.

Year	Club	League	POS	G	AB	R	H	2B	3B	HR	RBI	SB	BA
1929	BR/Monroe	Cottn St	OF	109	379	67	102	23	4	11	-	7	.269
1930	Mobile	South A	OF	139	520	74	161	19	10	4	41	9	.310
1931	Nashville	South A	OF	37	144	21	37	5	0	2	13	3	.257
	Quincy	III	OF	100	417	**100**	148	31	**17**	10	74	11	.355
	Boston	American	OF	7	28	2	7	1	1	0	4	0	.250
1932	Boston	American	OF	79	169	18	34	2	2	1	18	1	.201
1933	Reading	NY-Penn	OF	125	474	89	156	35	12	6	93	16	.329
	Boston	American	OF	22	41	8	14	3	0	0	5	4	.341
1934	Kansas City	A A	OF	131	514	68	152	26	13	3	65	6	.296
1935	Kansas City	A A	OF	150	580	84	187	32	13	3	105	16	.322
1936	Kansas City	A A	OF	130	489	69	141	22	8	5	62	15	.288
	Chicago	American	OF	10	22	3	6	1	0	0	5	0	.273
1937	Kansas City	A A	OF	137	523	81	140	27	10	6	58	1	.268
1938	St. Paul	A A	OF	151	582	104	161	25	10	9	51	9	.277
1939	St. Paul	A A	OF	147	536	82	148	33	7	6	55	9	.276
1940	St. Paul	A A	OF	149	532	69	145	26	5	1	53	9	.273
1941	St. Paul	A A	OF	144	472	43	120	18	6	1	51	6	.254
1942	St. Paul	A A	OF	38	124	11	22	4	2	0	6	1	.177
1943	Columbus	A A	OF	112	402	59	104	10	4	5	24	1	.259
1944	Columbus	A A	OF	144	554	118	156	36	4	19	68	3	.282
1945	Columbus	A A	OF	2	7	2	1	1	0	0	0	0	.143
1946	Columbus	A A	OF	18	64	7	18	0	0	2	9	0	.281
	Houston	Texas	OF	10	39	4	10	1	1	0	9	0	.281
1947	New Orleans	South A	OF	130	471	100	141	30	5	9	68	2	.299
1948	New Iberia	Evang	OF	113	431	91	138	25	10	13	86	2	.320
	Majors			**118**	**260**	**31**	**61**	**7**	**3**	**1**	**32**	**5**	**.235**
	Minors			**2216**	**8254**	**1343**	**2388**	**429**	**141**	**115**	**991**	**126**	**.289**

CHARLES R. SWAIN
Born August 16, 1882 at Palo Alto, CA. Died November 5, 1918 at Oakland, CA.
Height 6'-1/2", Weight 202. Batted right. Threw right.
Led minor leagues in HR in 1913 with 39 while playing in 2 leagues.
Lost a leg in December 1914 while working for telephone company in San Francisco, CA.

Year	Club	League	POS	G	AB	R	H	2B	3B	HR	SB	BA
1904	San Francisco	P C	SS	3	12	0	1	0	0	0	0	.083
1905	Spokane	Pac Nat	O-3-1	35	119	11	25	2	3	1	4	.210
	Spokane	NWestern	OF	36	134	16	28	1	8	1	5	.209
1906	Spokane	NWestern	OF	85	318	44	97	15	9	4	15	.305
1907	Spokane	NWestern	OF	132	448	84	107	22	**20**	2	35	.239
1908	Butte	NWestern	OF	137	494	87	132	18	**18**	13	24	.267
1909	Tacoma/Van	NWestern	OF	165	580	71	147	18	12	8	29	.253
1910	Vancouver	NWestern	OF	146	543	**88**	136	14	8	**11**	17	.250
1911	Vancouver	NWestern	OF	115	392	73	121	34	6	8	12	.309
1912	Sacramento	P C	OF	133	426	64	122	26	6	11	21	.286
1913	Victoria	NWestern	OF-2B	141	499	**112**	164	**42**	6	**34**	23	.329
	Sacramento	P C	OF	33	110	16	31	4	2	5	7	.282
1914	Seattle	NWestern	OF	**157**	546	89	169	**43**	14	**12**	24	.310
	Minors			**1318**	**4621**	**755**	**1280**	**239**	**112**	**110**	**216**	**.277**

DOUGLAS JOHN "POCO" TAITT

Born August 3, 1902 at Bay City, MI. Died December 12, 1970 at Portland, OR.
Height 6', Weight 176. Batted left. Threw right.

Manager: Pocatello Utah-Idaho 1926; Tyler E Texas 1938; Monroe CSL 1938-41; Tyler E Texas 1946; Alexander City Ga-Ala 1947.

Year	Club	League	POS	G	AB	R	H	2B	3B	HR	RBI	SB	BA
1925	Raleigh	Piedmont	OF	45	168	23	49	11	6	1	18	2	.292
	Los Angeles	P C	OF	63	143	19	38	12	0	1	18	0	.266
1926	Pocatello	Utah-Ida	OF-1B	108	417	110	154	24	10	19	-	22	.369
	Los Angeles	P C	OF	23	70	15	21	3	0	0	2	1	.300
1927	Nashville	South A	OF	135	500	110	175	36	10	18	108	13	.350
1928	Boston	American	OF	143	482	51	144	28	14	3	61	13	.299
1929	Boston/Chi	American	OF	73	189	17	39	11	0	0	18	0	.206
1930	Dallas	Texas	OF	98	388	67	133	35	2	8	76	13	.343
	LR/Atlanta	South A	OF	59	228	34	75	7	5	2	35	2	.329
1931	Atlanta	South A	OF	120	470	86	174	21	**19**	6	89	9	.370
	Philadelphia	National	OF	38	151	13	34	4	2	1	15	0	.225
1932	Philadelphia	National	OF	4	2	0	0	0	0	0	1	0	.000
	Indianapolis	A A	OF	137	526	70	158	29	11	9	89	9	.300
1933	Hollywood	P C	OF	103	378	56	127	26	3	15	67	3	.336
1934	Syra/Balt	Int	OF	45	143	20	44	12	0	3	23	0	.308
	Nashville	South A	OF	72	265	43	92	14	3	12	54	2	.347
1935	Nashville	South A	OF	142	546	91	**194**	31	9	**17**	87	14	.355
1936	Nashville	South A	OF	151	581	123	194	38	9	**20**	**132**	6	.334
1937	Memphis	South A	OF	58	193	36	60	15	1	2	28	4	.311
	Williamsport	NY-Penn	OF	78	276	47	85	14	4	2	35	2	.308
1938	Tyler	E Texas	OF	41	124	20	39	11	2	3	23	3	.315
	Shreveport	Texas	OF	1	3	0	0	0	0	0	0	0	.000
	Monroe	Cottn St	OF	68	218	57	78	15	3	2	60	11	.358
1939	Monroe	Cottn St	OF	111	365	72	120	29	7	9	75	7	.329
1940	Monroe	Cottn St	OF	76	213	37	60	13	2	3	37	8	.282
1941	Monroe	Cottn St	OF	44	98	14	33	7	0	4	27	3	.337
1942-43					Did not play in O. B.								
1944	Port/Sac	P C	OF	5	12	0	3	0	0	0	1	0	.250
1945		'			Did not play in O. B.								
1946	Tyler	E Texas	OF	39	86	11	24	6	0	2	14	1	.279
1947	Alex City	Ga-Ala	1B-OF	52	94	7	20	3	1	0	12	1	.213
	Majors			**258**	**824**	**81**	**217**	**43**	**16**	**4**	**95**	**13**	**.263**
	Minors			**1874**	**6505**	**1168**	**2150**	**412**	**107**	**158**	**1110**	**136**	**.331**

JOE CEPHUS TAYLOR

Born March 2, 1926 at Chapman, AL.
Height 6' 1", Weight 195. Batted right. Threw right.

Year	Club	League	POS	G	AB	R	H	2B	3B	HR	RBI	SB	BA
1951	Farnham	Provincl	OF	43	172	25	62	9	1	10	29	1	.360
1952	St. Hyacinthe	Provincl	OF	120	483	102	149	**35**	4	25	112	16	.308
1953	Williamsport	Eastern	OF	78	284	38	92	9	2	10	44	14	.324
	Ottawa	Int	OF	70	243	42	76	16	3	7	45	4	.313
1954	Ottawa	Int	OF	131	462	71	149	24	4	23	79	4	.323
	Philadelphia	American	OF	18	58	5	13	1	1	1	8	0	.224
1955	Colum/Tor	Int	OF	55	203	44	58	10	1	12	38	2	.286
	Portland	P C	OF	73	271	38	80	18	4	10	55	2	.295

Year	Club	League	POS	G	AB	R	H	2B	3B	HR	RBI	SB	BA
1956	Seattle	P C	OF	150	484	79	126	32	0	24	89	5	.260
1957	Seattle	P C	OF	115	394	70	120	15	4	22	72	3	.305
	Cincinnati	National	OF	33	107	14	28	7	0	4	9	0	.262
1958	Omaha	A A	OF	43	148	28	40	10	0	10	34	4	.270
	St. Louis	National	OF	18	23	2	7	3	0	1	3	0	.304
	Baltimore	American	OF	36	77	11	21	4	0	2	9	0	.273
1959	Vancouver	P C	OF	110	401	70	117	25	2	23	77	10	.292
	Baltimore	American	OF	14	32	2	5	1	0	1	2	0	.156
1960	Seattle	P C	OF	145	526	104	153	26	7	30	94	7	.291
1961	San Diego	P C	OF	132	441	69	118	22	4	26	74	0	.268
1962	Hawa/Van	P C	OF	109	353	35	87	15	0	13	37	2	.246
1963	Pueb/MC T	Mexican	OF	122	418	82	129	23	3	19	76	4	.309
	Majors			**119**	**297**	**34**	**74**	**16**	**1**	**9**	**31**	**0**	**.249**
	Minors			**1496**	**5283**	**897**	**1556**	**289**	**39**	**264**	**955**	**78**	**.295**

HERBERT MARX THOMAS
Born May 26, 1902 at Sampson City, FL. Died December 4, 1991 at Starke, FL.
Height 5' 4-1/2", Weight 157. Batted right. Threw right.
Manager: Palatka Fla St 1938; Ft. Lauderdale Fla E C 1940-42; West Palm Beach Fla Int 1946.

Year	Club	League	POS	G	AB	R	H	2B	3B	HR	RBI	SB	BA
1922	Jacksonville	Fla St	O-SS	112	426	80	127	19	14	4	-	24	.298
1923	Day Beach	Fla St	SS-O	74	297	50	115	13	5	0	-	11	**.387**
1924	Boston	National	OF	32	127	12	28	4	1	1	8	5	.220
	Clearwater	Fla St	OF	94	388	63	134	32	8	3	-	22	.345
1925	Boston	National	2B	5	17	2	4	0	1	0	0	0	.235
	Worcester	Eastern	2B-SS	126	524	121	177	33	5	4	-	54	.338
1926	Providence	Eastern	2B	153	620	125	202	38	12	3	-	35	.326
1927	Boston/NY	National	2B	37	91	13	20	7	2	0	7	2	.220
1928	Buffalo	Int	2B-SS	154	571	82	186	34	7	10	89	6	.326
1929	Toledo	A A	2B	46	159	19	37	5	2	0	-	9	.233
	Buffalo	Int	2B	91	385	73	130	17	3	14	64	6	.338
1930	Buff/New	Int	2-S-3	168	677	116	218	43	13	19	131	6	.322
1931	Newark	Int	S-2-3	133	479	66	132	34	4	6	49	0	.276
1932	Montreal	Int	S-2-3	142	506	68	155	36	7	5	72	3	.306
1933	Albany/JC	Int	2B-SS	74	258	32	54	19	0	1	20	2	.209
	Harrisburg	NY-Penn	2B	33	120	16	35	7	0	0	13	0	.292
1934	Lima	Central	3B-SS	8	27	2	4	1	1	0	1	0	.148
1935				Did not play in O. B.									
1936	Jack/Aug	Sally	2B-OF	94	343	52	95	18	4	0	36	7	.277
1937				Did not play in O. B.									
1938	Palatka	Fla St	2B-OF	52	148	25	37	5	0	0	12	2	.250
1939				Did not play in O. B.									
1940	Ft. Lauder	Fla E C	2B	102	389	65	137	25	1	0	38	6	.352
1941	Ft. Lauder	Fla E C	2B	55	220	49	68	13	2	2	33	6	.309
	Greenville	Ala St	3B	41	112	17	32	5	1	0	15	1	.286
1942	WP Beach	Fla E C	-	8	27	6	5	0	0	0	1	3	.185
	Majors			**74**	**235**	**27**	**52**	**11**	**4**	**1**	**15**	**7**	**.221**
	Minors			**1760**	**6676**	**1127**	**2080**	**397**	**89**	**71**	**574**	**203**	**.312**

CHESTER JULIUS "CHICK" TOLSON
Born May 3, 1895 at Washington D.C. Died April 16, 1965 at Washington D.C.
Height 6', Weight 185. Batted right. Threw right.

Year	Club	League	POS	G	AB	R	H	2B	3B	HR	RBI	SB	BA
1922	Norfolk	Virginia	1B	1	3	0	0	0	0	0	0	0	.000
1923	Salisbury	E Shore	1B	57	228	57	81	14	2	27	-	5	.355
1924	Charlotte	Sally	1B	127	493	91	168	27	16	22	111	6	.341
1925	Nashville	South A	1B	140	537	110	194	44	15	19	143	5	.361
	Cleveland	American	1B	3	12	0	3	0	0	0	0	0	.250
1926	Chicago	National	1B	57	80	4	25	6	1	1	8	0	.313
1927	Chicago	National	1B	39	54	6	16	4	0	2	17	0	.296
1928	Los Angeles	P C	1B	149	501	89	176	30	7	28	108	1	.351
1929	Los Angeles	P C	1B	134	487	96	175	30	2	28	122	1	.359
	Chicago	National	1B	32	109	13	28	5	0	1	19	0	.257
1930	Chicago	National	1B	13	20	0	6	1	0	0	1	1	.300
	Minneapolis	A A	1B	28	113	30	35	8	2	8	35	0	.310
1931	Minneapolis	A A	PH	1	1	0	0	0	0	0	0	0	.000
	Baltimore	Int	1B	7	24	5	8	1	0	2	7	0	.333
	Nashville	South A	1B	26	88	10	30	4	0	0	8	0	.341
1932	Atlanta	South A	1B	4	17	1	3	1	0	0	2	0	.176
		Majors		144	275	23	78	16	1	4	45	1	**.284**
		Minors		674	2492	489	870	159	44	134	536	18	**.349**

LEONARD W. TUCKER
Born November 18, 1929 at Mounds, IL.
Height 6' 2", Weight 195 Batted right. Threw left.
Graduate of Fresno State College with degree in Physical Education.
Entered U. S. Air Force in 1947 for 4-year hitch.
Achieved highest level ever reached in Organized Baseball in steals and homers with totals of 47 and 51 in 1956.
First Negro to sign in St. Louis Cardinal organization when he signed a Fresno contract on May 26, 1953.
Went to spring training with Washington in 1958. Hit 2 HR in one inning vs. Yucatan on 8/28/58.

Year	Club	League	POS	G	AB	R	H	2B	3B	HR	RBI	SB	BA
1953	Fresno	Calif	OF	97	379	79	108	13	9	11	55	16	.285
1954	Peoria	III	OF	130	474	120	139	25	2	23	89	47	.293
1955	Peoria	III	1B-OF	121	479	99	138	22	5	26	72	31	.288
1956	Pampa	SWestern	OF-P	140	565	181	228	40	13	51	181	47	**.404**
1957	NLaredo/Vera	Mexican	OF-1B	48	177	28	54	6	2	8	38	8	.305
1958	Poza Rica	Mexican	1B-OF	109	421	81	138	28	8	21	64	29	.328
1959	Miami	Int	1B	18	39	6	5	0	0	0	1	1	.128
	Charlotte	Sally	OF-1B	16	60	8	15	2	0	3	13	2	.250
	Van/Port	P C	OF	43	119	15	26	6	1	2	15	6	.218
1960	Yakima	NWestern	1B	132	469	126	158	25	5	24	117	48	.337
1961	Yakima	NWestern	OF	50	164	36	48	6	3	11	43	3	.293
1962	Modesto	Calif	1B-OF	94	347	78	102	19	3	30	101	7	.294
1963	Modesto	Calif	1B	92	353	67	115	16	2	26	113	12	.326
		Minors		1090	4046	924	1274	208	53	236	902	257	**.315**

JOSE VIDAL (NICOLAS)
Born April 3, 1940 at Batey Lechugas, Dominican Republic.
Height 6', Weight 190. Batted right. Threw right.

Year	Club	League	POS	G	AB	R	H	2B	3B	HR	RBI	SB	BA
1958	Hastings	Neb St	OF	21	61	4	12	3	1	0	7	2	.197
1959	Dubuque	Midwest	OF-3B	85	284	42	61	14	1	11	41	6	.215
1960	Hobbs	Soph	OF	93	363	85	124	20	6	17	81	20	.342
1961	Burlington	III	OF	96	320	54	75	10	0	13	37	9	.234
1962	Grand Forks	Northern	OF-P	32	109	26	26	1	0	4	22	2	.239
	Burlington	Midwest	OF	28	110	21	30	3	3	3	25	1	.273
1963	Reno	Calif	O-3-P	139	512	126	174	31	3	**40**	**162**	14	**.340**
1964	Charleston	Eastern	OF-3B	44	155	22	43	3	5	3	26	4	.277
1965	Portland	P C	OF	141	495	73	129	26	5	21	86	17	.261
1966	Portland	P C	OF	115	403	65	118	19	8	15	57	14	.293
	Cleveland	American	OF	17	32	4	6	1	1	0	3	0	.188
1967	Portland	P C	OF	69	230	43	70	14	7	12	42	4	.304
	Cleveland	American	OF	16	34	4	4	0	0	0	0	0	.118
1968	Cleveland	American	OF-1B	37	54	5	9	0	0	2	5	3	.167
	Portland	P C	OF	44	146	27	48	5	4	12	31	1	.329
1969	Seattle	American	OF	18	26	7	5	0	1	1	2	1	.192
	Syracuse	Int	OF-3B	86	231	30	49	8	2	7	35	10	.212
1970	Syracuse	Int	OF	73	195	36	51	7	2	7	22	6	.262
1971	Toledo	Int	OF-1B	28	58	7	10	0	0	2	10	0	.172
	Nish Lions	Jap Pac	OF	39	122	6	27	6	0	2	9	6	.221
1972	Tampico	Mexican	OF	121	404	86	120	26	1	32	79	6	.297
1973	Tampico	Mexican	O-1-3	116	391	74	120	12	2	23	101	15	.307
1974	Yucatan	Mexican	OF	130	416	58	109	15	0	14	53	3	.262
1975	Poza Rica	Mexican	OF-1B	131	454	62	117	21	3	15	71	5	.258
		Majors		**88**	**146**	**20**	**24**	**1**	**2**	**3**	**10**	**4**	**.164**
		Minors		**1592**	**5337**	**941**	**1486**	**238**	**53**	**251**	**988**	**139**	**.278**
		Japan		**39**	**122**	**6**	**27**	**6**	**0**	**2**	**9**	**6**	**.221**

IRVING J. WALDRON
Born January 21, 1876 at Hillside, NY. Died July 22, 1944 at Worcester, MA.
Batted right. Threw right.

Year	Club	League	POS	G	AB	R	H	2B	3B	HR	SB	BA
1895	Pawtucket	NEastern	OF	106	452	124	159	42	7	4	**84**	.352
1896	Pawtucket	NEastern	OF	107	484	**137**	**182**	41	6	7	55	.376
1897	Milwaukee	Western	OF	4	13	3	4	0	0	0	3	.308
	St. Joseph	West A	OF	112	458	117	162	35	11	5	51	**.354**
1898	Milwaukee	Western	OF	137	510	100	132	12	4	7	50	.259
1899	Milwaukee	Western	OF	115	484	98	161	21	9	0	40	.333
1900	Milwaukee	American	OF	139	**579**	92	170	29	8	1	34	.294
1901	Milw/Wash	American	OF	141	**598**	102	186	22	9	0	20	.311
1902	Kansas City	Western	OF	132	553	99	178	24	12	3	21	.322
1903	Kansas City	Western	OF	123	503	98	156	18	10	1	17	.310
1904	San Francisco	P C	OF	215	888	131	245	38	9	1	48	.276
1905	San Francisco	P C	OF	196	763	103	213	23	7	1	43	.279
1906	San Francisco	P C	OF	11	33	12	10	0	2	0	5	.303
1907	Kansas City	AA	OF	114	423	47	117	10	6	0	16	.277
1908	Denver	Western	OF	149	562	85	148	12	7	2	27	.263

Year	Club	League	POS	G	AB	R	H	2B	3B	HR	RBI	SB	BA
1909	Lincoln	Western	OF	150	609	99	183	22	10	1	21		.300
1910	Linc/Denver	Western	OF	103	369	60	98	12	3	1	15		.266
	Utica/Scrant	NY St	OF	26	94	14	23	1	2	0	3		.245
1911	Meridian	Cottn St	OF	74	286	50	80	19	4	0	28		.280
	Majors			**141**	**598**	**102**	**186**	**22**	**9**	**0**	**20**		**.311**
	Minors			**2013**	**8063**	**1469**	**2421**	**359**	**117**	**34**	**561**		**.300**

NED WALDROP

Born October 3, 1922 at Rutherfordton, NC.
Height 6' 3", Weight 215. Batted left. Threw right.
Manager: Fulton Kitty 1955.

Year	Club	League	POS	G	AB	R	H	2B	3B	HR	RBI	SB	BA
1948	Forest City	W Carol	OF	88	362	69	124	26	8	17	107	6	.343
1949	Charlotte	Tri-St	OF	26	96	13	26	5	3	2	12	0	.271
	Fulton	Kitty	1B	79	311	66	98	14	2	22	82	2	.315
1950	Fulton	Kitty	1B	118	458	104	**150**	32	8	**28**	**130**	5	.328
1951	Fulton	Kitty	1B	116	442	95	144	27	3	12	97	21	.326
1952	Fulton	Kitty	1B	112	459	108	163	**37**	5	8	103	36	.355
1953	Fulton	Kitty	1B	105	431	93	149	27	7	14	108	8	.346
1954	Fulton	Kitty	1B	116	474	114	**180**	36	2	22	159	1	.380
1955	Fulton	Kitty	1B	73	266	46	74	18	2	4	48	6	.278
	Minors			**833**	**3299**	**708**	**1108**	**222**	**40**	**129**	**846**	**85**	**.336**

FRANK GRAY "PIGGY" WARD

Born April 16, 1867 at Chambersburg, PA. Died October 24, 1912 at Altoona, PA.
Height 5' 9-1/2", Weight 196. Threw right.
Holds Major league record for most times reaching base in a 9-inning game with 8 on June 18, 1893 (2-1B, 5-BB, 1-HBP).

Year	Club	League	POS	G	AB	R	H	2B	3B	HR	SB	BA
1883	Philadelphia	National	3B	1	5	0	0	0	0	0	-	.000
1884	St. Paul	NWestern	SS	4	14	0	1	0	0	0	-	.071
1885-86				Did not play in O. B.								
1887	Johnstown	Pa St	1B	15	65	16	17	1	2	1	0	.262
1888	Allentown	Central	2B	30	120	18	32	1	0	0	28	.267
1889	New Orleans	Southern	2B	30	133	34	40	5	3	1	11	.301
	Philadelphia	National	2B-OF	7	25	0	4	1	0	0	1	.160
	Hamilton	Int-St A	2B	50	201	34	62	5	3	0	37	.308
1890	Galveston	Texas	2B	42	176	46	62	9	**6**	0	**28**	.352
	Spokane	Pac NW	2B-OF	71	302	**97**	111	17	10	4	54	**.368**
1891	Sacramento	Calif	2-O-3	47	180	50	57	7	3	1	27	.317
	Spokane	NWestern	OF-IF	12	51	8	21	3	3	0	8	.412
	Minneapolis	West A	1B	54	207	56	74	10	0	1	30	.357
	Pittsburgh	National	OF	6	18	3	6	0	0	0	3	.333
1892	Milwaukee	Western	2-3-S	51	211	49	65	14	5	2	**39**	.308
	Baltimore	National	O-2-S	56	186	28	54	6	5	1	10	.290
1893	New Orleans	Southern	OF-1B	30	119	47	40	8	2	0	26	.336
	Balt/Cinci	National	OF-1B	53	199	55	54	5	4	0	31	.271
	Alt/Harris	Pa St	2B-OF	19	76	23	28	4	3	0	6	.368
1894	Washington	National	2B-OF	98	347	86	105	11	7	0	41	.303
1895	Scranton	Eastern	2-O-1	104	419	93	156	23	5	1	26	**.372**
1896	Scrant/Tor	Eastern	2-O-1	104	409	83	126	24	7	2	27	.308

1897	Lancaster	Atlantic	2B-OF	131	525	105	147	30	7	1	45	.280
1898	Lancaster	Atlantic	2B	129	515	90	144	19	7	2	59	.280
1899	Lancaster	Atlantic	2B	94	**381**	82	**136**	**29**	15	2	37	.357
	Mansfield	Inter-St	2B	42	150	23	37	7	1	0	1	.247
1900	Worc/Hart	Eastern	2B	48	185	34	44	8	2	1	12	.238
	Binghamton	NY St	2B	42	152	25	37	12	4	0	3	.243
1901						Did not play in O. B.						
1902	Butte	Pac NW	2B	118	473	85	**157**	24	**12**	1	**51**	**.332**
1903	Butte	Pac NW	2B	126	496	97	157	36	4	1	46	.317
1904	Butte	Pac NW	2B	90	375	84	128	22	6	2	40	.341
	Birmingham	South A	2B	16	55	8	19	0	1	0	5	.345
1905	Charleston	Sally	2B	44	146	5	20	2	0	0	7	.137
		Majors		**221**	**780**	**172**	**223**	**23**	**16**	**1**	**86**	**.286**
		Minors		**1543**	**6136**	**1292**	**1918**	**320**	**111**	**22**	**653**	**.313**

JAMES ALBERT WARNER
Born September 23, 1923 at Panama Canal Zone.
Height 6', Weight 194. Batted right. Threw right.

Year	Club	League	POS	G	AB	R	H	2B	3B	HR	RBI	SB	BA
1942	Fresno	Calif	OF	67	265	56	74	11	5	6	**48**	15	.279
	Columbus	Sally	OF	17	56	4	7	0	0	0	1	0	.125
	Springfield	West A	OF	10	22	1	3	0	0	0	2	0	.136
	Pocatello	Pioneer	OF	25	106	8	30	4	1	1	18	0	.283
1943-45						Military Service							
1946	Sacramento	P C	OF	3	11	1	3	0	0	0	2	0	.273
	Wenatchee	West Int	OF	122	480	106	140	31	2	25	97	21	.292
1947	Sacramento	P C	OF	97	180	39	38	5	1	4	26	7	.211
1948	Sacramento	P C	OF	51	186	22	38	7	2	4	16	0	.204
	Grand Rapids	Central	OF	60	198	47	56	11	1	12	57	6	.283
1949	Sacramento	P C	OF	17	33	4	7	0	0	1	5	0	.212
	Wenatchee	West Int	OF	138	542	**152**	167	38	5	**43**	123	36	.308
1950	Tri-Cities	West Int	OF	145	548	**143**	182	33	5	20	131	32	.332
1951	Modesto	Calif	OF	147	571	**145**	182	41	2	35	137	28	.319
1952	Mod/Visalia	Calif	OF	131	484	109	146	28	2	26	118	19	.302
1953	Little Rock	South A	OF-3B	7	26	3	5	1	0	1	3	0	.192
	Wichita Falls	Big St	OF	132	466	92	121	20	3	32	104	19	.260
1954	Harlingen	Big St	OF-P	63	234	52	71	12	1	17	53	7	.303
	Port Arthur	Evang	OF	33	125	29	39	9	0	5	27	6	.312
	Decatur	Miss-O V	OF	45	173	35	54	8	3	8	49	9	.312
		Minors		**1310**	**4706**	**1048**	**1363**	**259**	**33**	**240**	**1017**	**205**	**.290**

ARTHUR JOHN "BUTCH" WEIS
Born March 2, 1903 at St. Louis, MO.
Height 5' 11", Weight 180. Batted left. Threw left.

Year	Club	League	POS	G	AB	R	H	2B	3B	HR	RBI	SB	BA
1920	Rock Island	III	P-OF	41	108	4	12	0	0	1	6	0	.111
1921	Springfield	West A	OF	124	488	80	137	30	8	4	-	24	.281
1922	Chicago	National	PH	2	2	2	1	0	0	0	0	0	.500
	St. Paul	A A	OF	27	45	9	13	4	0	0	9	1	.289
	Wichita Falls	Texas	OF	22	78	18	26	5	1	0	11	2	.333

Year	Club	League	POS	G	AB	R	H	2B	3B	HR	RBI	SB	BA
1923	Chicago	National	OF	22	26	2	6	1	0	0	2	0	.231
	Wichita Falls	Texas	OF	91	320	52	98	24	4	2	46	17	.306
1924	Wichita Falls	Texas	OF	126	499	97	188	40	8	11	96	4	**.377**
	Chicago	National	OF	39	133	19	37	8	1	0	23	4	.278
1925	Chicago	National	OF	67	180	16	48	5	3	2	25	2	.267
1926	Los Angeles	P C	OF	157	543	87	172	36	8	7	80	3	.317
1927	Los Angeles	P C	OF	161	527	101	167	47	9	13	77	4	.317
1928	Mission	P C	OF	35	113	14	31	10	0	1	19	1	.274
	Little Rock	South A	OF	100	336	49	110	17	7	3	54	8	.327
1929	Birmingham	South A	OF	148	510	105	176	25	11	7	90	17	**.345**
1930	Birmingham	South A	OF	153	573	113	192	24	18	13	109	6	.335
1931	Birmingham	South A	OF	154	566	132	209	33	14	20	122	8	.369
1932	Louisville	A A	OF	137	470	77	120	26	5	11	74	0	.255
1933	Atl/Knox/Bir	South A	OF	97	341	48	88	13	3	11	58	3	.258
1934	Birmingham	South A	OF	146	494	82	160	25	7	11	79	5	.324
1935	Ft. Worth	Texas	OF	159	556	84	184	39	3	9	83	2	**.331**
1936	Ft. Worth	Texas	OF	50	170	22	51	10	2	2	23	0	.300
	Toledo	A A	OF	30	111	17	30	8	0	1	9	2	.270
1937					Did not play in O. B.								
1938	St. Paul	A A	OF	56	160	16	34	4	1	5	21	0	.213
	Majors			**130**	**341**	**39**	**92**	**14**	**4**	**2**	**50**	**6**	**.270**
	Minors			**2014**	**7008**	**1207**	**2198**	**420**	**109**	**132**	**1066**	**107**	**.314**

STANLEY AARON WENTZEL
Born January 13, 1917 at Lorane, PA.
Height 6' 1", Weight 200. Batted right. Threw right.
Manager: Burlington/Graham Carolina 1953-54; Waco Big St 1955; Clinton Midwest 1956-58.

Year	Club	League	POS	G	AB	R	H	2B	3B	HR	RBI	SB	BA
1940	Logan	Mtn St	OF	126	**521**	118	164	29	8	**26**	97	6	.315
1941	Logan	Mtn. St	OF	103	402	81	125	27	6	23	82	3	.311
1942	Logan	Mtn. St	OF	88	352	71	113	24	3	13	71	15	.321
	Canton	Mid Atl	OF	33	106	10	29	7	0	0	11	3	.274
1943	Hartford	Eastern	OF	144	572	89	167	28	5	5	59	12	.292
1944	Hartford	Eastern	OF	127	465	81	150	31	2	**9**	88	23	.323
1945	Indianapolis	A A	OF	154	574	102	184	35	11	14	103	30	.321
	Boston	National	OF	4	19	3	4	0	1	0	6	1	.211
1946	Indianapolis	A A	OF	154	565	94	169	30	3	12	79	20	.299
1947	Indianapolis	A A	OF	118	377	59	94	18	5	2	37	4	.249
1948	New Orleans	South A	OF	151	**582**	76	180	39	13	3	96	7	.309
1949	New Orleans	South A	OF	145	506	86	149	26	7	9	88	7	.294
1950	New Orleans	South A	OF	151	538	87	169	34	6	14	99	8	.314
1951	New Orleans	South A	OF	146	527	85	163	31	4	17	83	13	.309
1952	New Orleans	South A	OF	97	243	36	64	11	3	4	36	0	.263
1953	Burl-Graham	Carolina	OF	122	415	55	101	18	4	12	72	19	.243
1954	Burl-Graham	Carolina	OF	128	468	77	149	25	8	20	108	6	.318
1955	Waco	Big St	OF-1B	123	435	76	132	21	1	26	87	5	.303
1956	Clinton	Midwest	1B	120	420	81	126	28	3	14	116	3	.300
1957	Clinton	Midwest	1B	15	18	0	3	0	0	0	0	0	.167
	Majors			**4**	**19**	**3**	**4**	**0**	**1**	**0**	**6**	**1**	**.211**
	Minors			**2245**	**8086**	**1364**	**2431**	**462**	**92**	**223**	**1412**	**184**	**.301**

LEWIS WHISTLER
(Correct family name was Wissler.)
Born March 10, 1868 at St. Louis, MO. Died December 30, 1959 at St. Louis, MO.
Height 5' 10-1/2", Weight 178. Threw right.

Manager Chattanooga Mobile 1895; Springfield 1897 & 1898; Syracuse 1899; Schenectady 1899, 1900 & 1902; Chattanooga 1901; Montgomery 1903; Memphis 1904 & 1905.

Year	Club	League	POS	G	AB	R	H	2B	3B	HR	SB	BA
1887	Wichita	Kan St	1B-OF	21	97	24	33	8	3	3	1	.340
	Wichita	Western	INF-OF	25	100	13	32	6	2	1	0	.320
1888	SA/Houston	Texas	1B	35	124	18	27	6	0	5	1	.218
	Hous/Galves	Tex So	1B	29	98	18	16	2	1	2	4	.163
1889	Evansville	Cent Int-St	1B	116	437	91	121	26	10	22	19	.277
1890	Washington	Atl A	1B	82	305	60	80	11	4	10	27	.262
	New York	National	1B	45	170	27	49	9	7	2	8	.288
1891	New York	National	INF-OF	72	265	39	65	8	7	4	4	.245
1892	Balt/Louis	National	1-2-O	132	494	74	114	10	13	7	26	.231
1893	Louis/StL	National	1B-OF	23	85	10	19	2	1	0	1	.224
	Albany	Eastern	1B	36	144	44	49	3	4	4	4	.340
1894	New Orleans	Southern	1-S-2	67	248	58	63	8	4	3	18	.254
1895	Chat/Mobile	Southern	1B	71	267	72	108	20	2	8	23	.404
1896	Detroit	Western	1B	128	507	99	145	23	7	5	9	.286
1897	Detroit	Western	1B	46	167	40	48	10	6	2	6	.287
	Springfield	Inter-St	1B	67	256	53	80	13	1	10	9	.313
1898	Springfield	Inter-St	1B	128	491	80	163	37	6	9	21	.332
1899	Syracuse	Eastern	1B	16	56	4	9	0	0	0	2	.161
	Schenectady	NY St	1B	62	232	45	93	20	3	4	18	.401
	Wheeling	Inter-St	1B	7	25	1	3	0	0	0	0	.120
1900	Schenectady	NY St	1B	102	387	62	122	34	13	9	18	.315
1901	Chattanooga	Southern	1B	120	456	68	157	31	3	1	12	.344
1902	Schenectady	NY St	1B	101	374	64	118	25	0	2	15	.316
1903	Montgomery	South A	1B	111	426	63	130	27	5	18	5	.305
1904	Memphis	South A	1B	48	177	25	41	5	0	2	2	.232
1905	Memphis	South A	1B	105	381	32	89	11	2	0	7	.234
		Majors		**272**	**1014**	**150**	**247**	**29**	**28**	**13**	**39**	**.244**
		Minors		**1523**	**5755**	**1034**	**1727**	**326**	**76**	**120**	**221**	**.300**

JOHN WALLACE WHITE
Born January 19, 1878 at Indianapolis, IN. Died September 30, 1963 at Indianapolis, IN.
Height 5' 6", Weight - Batted right. Threw right.

Year	Club	League	POS	G	AB	R	H	2B	3B	HR	SB	BA
1895	Jack/Quincy	West A	OF-3B	82	337	57	90	13	10	2	12	.267
	Indianapolis	Western	2B	1	4	1	3	0	0	0	0	.750
1896	Burlington	West A	O-S-3	68	283	68	93	15	4	4	38	.329
	Indian/Minn	Western	OF-SS	49	192	35	49	10	2	6	3	.255
1897	Toronto	Eastern	OF	118	506	103	158	16	7	5	50	.312
1898	Buffalo	Eastern	OF	124	524	91	144	12	6	0	30	.275
1899	Buffalo/GR	Western	O-2-S	106	439	54	113	14	4	1	30	.257
1900	Cleveland	American	OF-SS	19	72	11	20	2	0	0	4	.278
	Syracuse	Eastern	OF	100	393	59	103	18	7	3	36	.262
1901	Syracuse	Eastern	OF	22	85	12	24	2	0	2	6	.282
1902	Toronto	Eastern	OF	119	461	80	118	16	6	2	33	.256
1903	Toronto	Eastern	OF	125	492	79	154	11	8	0	36	.313

1904	Boston	National	OF	1	5	1	0	0	0	0	0	.000
	Toronto	Eastern	OF	134	509	70	141	26	11	1	29	.277
1905	Toronto	Eastern	OF	137	515	64	142	13	**14**	1	33	.276
1906	Tor/Buff	Eastern	OF	131	472	59	122	12	6	1	21	.258
1907	Buffalo	Eastern	OF	116	425	67	123	13	6	0	25	.289
1908	Buffalo	Eastern	OF	137	457	59	135	16	6	6	35	.295
1909	Buffalo	Eastern	OF	153	568	72	159	17	12	2	20	.280
1910	Buffalo	Eastern	OF	146	487	58	133	13	5	0	25	.273
1911	Buffalo	Eastern	OF	105	312	38	85	17	5	0	9	.272
1912	Syracuse	NY St	OF	131	468	61	135	13	2	1	18	.288
1913	Syracuse	NY St	OF	24	95	10	31	5	0	0	2	.326
	Majors			**1**	**5**	**1**	**0**	**0**	**0**	**0**	**0**	**.000**
	Minors			**2147**	**8096**	**1208**	**2275**	**274**	**121**	**37**	**495**	**.281**

SOLOMON "SOL" WHITE

Born June 12, 1868 at Bellaire, OH. Died 1955 at New York, NY.
Height 5' 9", Weight 170. Batted right. Threw right.

Although he played only briefly in five seasons in Organized Baseball, this black player's batting average was uniformly high (.356). He began his professional play in May 1887 with the Pittsburgh Keystones in the National Colored Baseball League, which was in O.B. He batted .308 in seven games before the circuit collapsed. When not in OB, he played with the top black teams of his era, including the Cuban Giants, NY Gorhams, Page Fence Giants, Cuban X-Giants, and Columbia Giants of Chicago. He co-founded the Philadelphia Giants and played with them 1902-09. He managed the Lincoln Giants in 1911 and the Boston Giants in 1912. In 1924 he managed the Cleveland Browns in the Negro National League. In 1907 he published *History of Colored Baseball*.

Year	Club	League	POS	G	AB	R	H	2B	3B	HR	SB	BA
1887	Pittsburgh	Nat. Col.	2B	7	39	5	12	3	0	0	5	.308
	Wheeling	Ohio St	3B	53	232	53	86	13	4	4	10	.371
1888				Did not play in O. B.								
1889	Phil Gorhams	Mid Sts	2B-P	31	108	20	35	5	1	0	8	.324
1890	York C Gnts	E. Int-St	2B-3B	54	236	78	84	14	5	2	28	.356
1891	Ansonia C Gts	Conn	2B	4	16	3	6	1	0	1	0	.375
1892-94				Did not play in O. B.								
1895	Fort Wayne	W. Int-St	2B	10	52	15	20	6	2	0	3	.385
	Minors			**159**	**683**	**174**	**243**	**42**	**12**	**7**	**54**	**.356**

HARRISON P. WICKEL

Born September 21, 1910 at Reading, PA. Died March 25, 1989 at Sherman Oaks, CA.
Height 6', Weight 165. Batted right. Threw right.

Graduated from Ohio State Univ. in 1935.
Manager: West Plains and Caruthersville NE Ark 1936; Caruthersville NE Ark 1937; New Iberia Evang 1938; Daytona Beach, Fla St 1938; Williamson Mtn St 1939-41; Columbus Sally 1942; Decatur Ill 1946.

Year	Club	League	POS	G	AB	R	H	2B	3B	HR	RBI	SB	BA
1935	Springfield	West A	O-S-1	77	273	55	82	16	6	0	32	10	.300
1936	WPlains/Car	NE Ark	SS	99	374	68	114	16	6	11	68	5	.305
1937	Caruthersvl.	NE Ark	SS	107	405	78	124	30	2	12	**124**	4	.306
1938	New Iberia	Evang	2B	106	397	61	121	8	7	16	51	4	.305
	Daytona Bch	Fla St	2B	34	131	28	43	8	5	3	30	6	.328

Year	Club	League	POS	G	AB	R	H	2B	3B	HR	RBI	SB	BA
1939	Williamson	Mtn St	SS-2B	126	446	108	164	36	6	23	**142**	8	.368
1940	Williamson	Mtn St	SS	123	445	103	142	31	14	2	129	27	.319
1941	Williamson	Mtn St	SS	127	500	116	178	**53**	6	20	**147**	12	.356
1942	Columbus	Sally	SS-OF	100	311	43	78	12	5	2	36	3	.251
1943-45					Military Service								
1946	Decatur	III	-	31	45	6	12	4	0	0	5	0	.267
		Minors		**930**	**3327**	**666**	**1058**	**214**	**57**	**89**	**764**	**79**	**.318**

FRED "PAP" WILLIAMS

Born July 17, 1913 at Meridian, MS.
Height 6' 1", Weight 200. Batted right. Threw right.

Manager Grand Forks Northern 1940; Winnipeg Northern 1941; Meridian SEastern 1946; Greenville Coast Pl 1949; Waycross Ga-Fla 1951-52; Crestview Ala-Fla 1954; Vicksburg CSL 1955.

Year	Club	League	POS	G	AB	R	H	2B	3B	HR	RBI	SB	BA
1935	Colum/Cleve	E Dixie	1B	137	554	99	**187**	26	**22**	7	111	15	.338
1936	Greenville	Cottn St	1B-OF	129	558	98	186	**39**	11	10	105	9	.333
1937	Jack/Merid	SEastern	1B-OF	137	533	80	**175**	**39**	5	4	73	24	.328
	Memphis	South A	1B	15	46	5	16	3	0	0	3	1	.348
1938	Sav/Green	Sally	OF-1B	70	273	41	68	10	4	1	21	6	.249
1939	Savannah	Sally	1B	18	69	8	23	2	1	0	14	0	.333
	Greenwood	Cottn St	1B-3B	5	18	3	2	0	0	1	1	0	.111
1940	Grand Forks	Northern	1B	124	487	71	156	24	9	6	82	5	.320
1941	Winnipeg	Northern	1B	112	447	74	131	27	5	9	96	13	.293
1942-44					Did not play in O. B.								
1945	Wilkes-Barre	Eastern	1B	49	180	17	48	5	3	4	26	3	.267
	Cleveland	American	1B	16	19	0	4	0	0	0	0	0	.211
1946	Meridian	SEastern	1B	132	504	84	162	31	3	15	97	12	.321
1947	Meridian	SEastern	1B	128	503	76	152	31	6	10	100	6	.302
1948	Kinston/RMt	Coast Pl	1B	135	563	122	205	35	8	24	134	8	.364
1949	Greenville	Coast Pl	1B	136	490	86	164	31	1	15	**122**	31	.335
1950	Borger	WTNM	1B	123	474	115	175	48	3	33	133	16	.369
1951	Waycross	Ga-Fla	1B	120	465	64	137	19	4	0	79	16	.295
1952	Waycross	Ga-Fla	1B	113	399	27	98	18	1	0	53	6	.246
1953					Did not play in O. B.								
1954	Crestview	Ala-Fla	1B	113	429	81	173	27	2	7	111	**44**	.403
1955	Vicksburg	Cottn St	1B	90	270	33	91	16	0	5	37	2	.337
		Majors		**16**	**19**	**0**	**4**	**0**	**0**	**0**	**0**	**0**	**.211**
		Minors		**1886**	**7262**	**1184**	**2349**	**431**	**88**	**151**	**1398**	**217**	**.323**

MARVIN WILLIAMS

Born February 12, 1923 at Houston, TX.
Height 6', Weight 195.
Batted right. Threw right.

Manager: Chihuahua Ariz-Tex 1952. One of first Negro managers in 20th century O.B.

Year	Club	League	POS	G	AB	R	H	2B	3B	HR	RBI	SB	BA
1944	Philadelphia	Neg Nat		40	154	30	52	8	3	4	32	2	.338
1945	Philadelphia	Neg Nat		15	56	15	22	1	3	4	13	1	.393
	Mexico City	Mexican	OF	51	221	53	80	18	6	10	51	7	.362
1946-47					No records available								

Year	Team	League	Pos	G	AB	R	H	2B	3B	HR	RBI	SB	AVG
1948	Mexico City	Mexican	OF	78	302	65	100	12	11	14	50	8	.331
1949	Jalisco	Mexican	OF	3	12	4	7	1	0	1	4	0	.583
	Philadelphia	Neg Nat					No records available						
1950	Sacramento	P C	2B	38	120	18	30	4	1	6	21	3	.250
	Cleveland	Neg Nat		22	84	14	21	4	1	0	10	1	.250
1951	Mexico City	Mexican	OF	81	296	58	95	18	5	12	64	8	.321
1952	Chihuahua	Ariz-Tex	2B	117	397	136	159	27	9	**45**	131	10	**.401**
1953	Laredo	Gulf Cst	OF	23	86	14	24	7	3	3	14	0	.279
	Mexico City	Mexican	2B	40	153	37	57	12	3	2	29	11	.373
1954	Vancouver	West Int	2B	119	456	114	164	32	9	20	90	15	**.360**
1955	Seattle	P C	1B	35	117	20	27	6	2	5	22	1	.231
	Columbia	Sally	3B	97	351	70	115	18	7	16	84	1	.328
1956	Tulsa	Texas	1-2-3-O	144	534	102	172	36	7	26	111	1	.322
1957	Tulsa	Texas	3-O-2-1	134	466	53	118	23	3	8	76	2	.253
1958	Tulsa	Texas	1B	144	524	76	154	33	3	19	88	2	.294
1959	MC T/MC R	Mexican	1B-OF	109	378	76	117	14	2	**29**	**109**	1	.310
	Victoria	Texas	PH	5	5	2	2	0	0	1	2	0	.400
1960	Vict/SA	Texas	1-3-O	94	297	52	83	13	2	17	54	0	.279
1961	Vict/R.G.Val	Texas	1B-3B	116	354	55	98	16	2	10	71	2	.277
	Minors			**1428**	**5069**	**1005**	**1602**	**290**	**75**	**244**	**1071**	**72**	**.316**
	Negro Lg			**77**	**294**	**59**	**95**	**13**	**7**	**8**	**55**	**4**	**.323**

George Wilson

GEORGE WASHINGTON WILSON

Born August 30, 1925 at Cherryville, NC.
Height 6' 1", Weight 188. Batted left. Threw right.
Manager: Shelby W Carol 1960; Statesville W Carol 1961.

Year	Club	League	POS	G	AB	R	H	2B	3B	HR	RBI	SB	BA
1942	Owensboro	Kitty	OF	48	**206**	42	65	13	3	2	33	2	.316
	Statesville	N Car St	OF	63	266	48	89	14	1	6	42	1	.335
	Canton	Mid Atl	OF	5	18	2	6	1	0	0	1	0	.333
1943-45					Military Service								
1946	Durham	Carolina	OF	123	453	91	148	34	12	16	121	9	.327
1947	Roanoke	Piedmont	OF	141	**577**	**124**	**206**	**45**	12	16	**136**	8	.357
1948	Birmingham	South A	OF	127	469	115	157	25	11	27	102	6	.335
1949	Louisville	A A	OF	141	528	90	141	28	1	17	67	7	.267
1950	Louisville	A A	OF	126	380	68	104	19	2	17	82	2	.274
1951	Birmingham	South A	OF	143	489	100	159	29	8	29	112	2	.325
1952	Chicago	American	OF	8	9	0	1	0	0	0	1	0	.111
	New York	National	OF-1B	62	112	9	27	7	0	2	16	0	.241
1953	New York	National	PH	11	8	0	1	0	0	0	0	0	.125
	Minneapolis	A A	OF	118	461	93	145	32	3	**34**	94	1	.315
1954	Minneapolis	A A	OF	136	474	**110**	143	29	7	27	92	5	.302
1955	Minneapolis	A A	OF	140	541	115	166	33	3	31	99	4	.307
1956	New York	National	OF	53	68	5	9	1	0	1	2	0	.132
	New York	American	OF	11	12	1	2	0	0	0	0	0	.167
1957	Denver	A A	OF	122	399	85	119	23	8	14	92	3	.298
1958	Denver	A A	OF	124	395	65	118	26	3	12	66	0	.299
1959	Rochestr	Int	OF	89	233	37	63	7	2	12	36	0	.270
1960	Shelby	W Carol	OF-P	49	102	22	39	7	0	10	39	1	.382
1961	Statesville	W Carol	OF-P	17	18	2	6	0	0	1	6	1	.333
1962	Denver	A A	OF	72	96	8	27	3	0	4	26	0	.281
1963	Nishitetsu	Jap Pac	OF	127	369	43	94	12	0	20	67	5	.255
1964	Nishitetsu	Jap Pac	OF	98	255	28	67	11	0	7	40	0	.263
	Majors			**145**	**209**	**15**	**40**	**8**	**0**	**3**	**19**	**0**	**.191**
	Minors			**1784**	**6105**	**1217**	**1901**	**368**	**76**	**275**	**1246**	**52**	**.311**
	Japan			**225**	**624**	**71**	**161**	**23**	**0**	**27**	**107**	**5**	**.258**

JOHN THOMAS "LONG TOM" WINSETT

Born November 24, 1909 at McKenzie, TN.
Height 6' 2", Weight 190. Batted left. Threw right.
Hit 21 home runs during month of June, 1936. Hit two homers in AA All-Star game July 8, 1936.

Year	Club	League	POS	G	AB	R	H	2B	3B	HR	RBI	SB	BA
1929	Merid/LC	Cottn St	OF	22	95	11	27	4	1	4	-	0	.284
	Mobile	South A	OF	78	301	40	104	11	8	7	57	1	.346
1930	Boston	American	OF	1	1	0	0	0	0	0	0	0	.000
	St. Paul	A A	OF	7	5	2	1	0	0	0	0	0	.200
	Dallas	Texas	OF	4	16	0	2	1	0	0	0	0	.125
	Mobile	South A	OF	74	254	43	76	18	6	8	38	2	.299
1931	Boston	American	OF	64	76	6	15	1	0	1	7	0	.197
1932	Buffalo	Int	OF	109	365	66	128	15	6	18	81	6	.351
1933	Boston	American	OF	6	12	1	1	0	0	0	0	0	.083
	Montreal	Int	OF	114	315	47	89	14	5	18	61	2	.282
1934	Rochester	Int	OF	112	343	61	122	20	**13**	21	74	3	.356
1935	St. Louis	National	OF	7	12	2	6	1	0	0	2	0	.500
	Columbus	A A	OF	108	368	91	128	29	5	20	90	3	.348

1936	Columbus	A A	OF	141	536	**144**	190	34	9	**50**	**154**	6	.354
	Brooklyn	National	OF	22	85	13	20	7	0	1	18	0	.235
1937	Brooklyn	National	OF-P	118	350	32	83	15	5	5	42	3	.237
1938	Brooklyn	National	OF	12	30	6	9	1	0	1	7	0	.300
	Jersey City	Int	OF	132	433	69	112	20	7	20	75	4	.259
1939	Jersey City	Int	OF	3	4	1	1	0	0	0	0	0	.250
	Sacramento	P C	OF	22	79	13	20	3	1	3	15	1	.253
	Columbus	A A	OF	67	221	37	58	11	3	14	50	2	.262
1940	Houston	Texas	OF	139	443	82	133	29	13	18	82	3	.300
1941	Rochester	Int	OF	15	50	4	8	2	0	0	3	0	.160
	New Orleans	South A	OF	109	375	70	115	27	9	16	67	3	.307
1942	New Orleans	South A	OF	73	267	36	71	13	4	3	39	1	.266
1943-45						Military Service							
	Majors			**230**	**566**	**60**	**134**	**25**	**5**	**8**	**76**	**3**	**.237**
	Minors			**1329**	**4470**	**817**	**1385**	**251**	**90**	**220**	**886**	**37**	**.310**

Long Tom Winsett twists himself into a pretzel on this swing.

BURNIS "BILL" WRIGHT
Born June 6, 1914 at Milan, TN.
Height 6' 5", Weight 230. Batted both. Threw right.

Year	Club	League	POS	G	AB	R	H	2B	3B	HR	RBI	SB	BA
1932	Nashville	Neg So	OF	12	40	-	12	1	1	0	-	2	.300
1933	Nashville	Neg. Nat	OF	21	78	-	19	2	2	0	-	0	.244
1934	Nashville	Neg Nat	OF	12	50	-	6	0	1	3	-	2	.120
1935	Columbus	Neg Nat	OF	21	82	-	20	1	0	2	-	4	.244
1936	Washington	Neg Nat	OF	21	74	-	25	2	5	1	-	2	.338
1937	Washington	Neg Nat	OF	31	100	-	41	4	2	7	-	0	**.410**
1938	Baltimore	Neg Nat	OF	22	81	-	19	2	0	0	-	3	.235
1939	Baltimore	Neg Nat	OF	27	99	-	40	1	3	3	-	2	.404
1940	Santa Rosa	Mexican	OF	87	350	94	126	30	10	8	67	29	.360
1941	Mexico City	Mexican	OF	100	387	98	151	25	9	17	85	26	**.390**
1942	Baltimore	Neg Nat	OF	44	163	-	53	8	2	1	-	2	.325
1943	Mexico City	Mexican	OF	88	352	65	129	25	5	13	70	21	.366
1944	Mexico City	Mexican	OF	87	334	59	112	24	7	10	60	14	.335
1945	Baltimore	Neg Nat	OF	44	165	-	62	12	5	3	-	5	.376
1946	Mexico City	Mexican	OF	85	316	47	95	11	8	5	52	17	.301
1947	Mexico City	Mexican	OF	79	249	36	76	10	4	3	38	13	.305
1948	Monterrey	Mexican	-	66	258	47	86	16	3	0	32	12	.333
1949	Torreon/MC	Mexican	-	74	293	46	81	14	3	7	43	3	.276
1950	Mexico City	Mexican	-	63	248	75	73	10	1	2	31	5	.300
1951	NLaredo/MC	Mexican	-	30	104	23	38	10	2	2	25	4	.365
1952-54					No records available								
1955	Aguascal.	Cent Mex	-	68	250	49	75	12	3	3	40	6	.300
1956	Aguascal.	Cent Mex	-	79	297	48	102	8	3	8	45	7	.343
		Minors		**905**	**3438**	**646**	**1146**	**195**	**58**	**78**	**588**	**157**	**.333**
		Negro Lg		**255**	**932**	**-**	**297**	**33**	**21**	**20**	**-**	**22**	**.319**

ELMER ELLSWORTH YOTER
Born June 26, 1900 at Plainfield, PA. Died July 26, 1966 at Camp Hill, PA.
Height 5' 7", Weight 155. Batted right. Threw right.
Had 6 hits in 6 at bats for Minneapolis September 2, 1929.
Manager: Danville III 1932; Wilkes-Barre NYPL 1933-36; Portsmouth Piedmont 1937; Greenwood SCL 1938; Gloversville-Johnston Can-Amer 1939; Danville-Schoolfield Bi-State 1941-42; Scranton EL 1945-46; Toronto IL 1947; Marion Ohio-Ind 1950-51; Roanoke Piedmont 1953; Albany EL 1953; Greensboro Carolina 1955; Corning Pony 1956; Corning NYPL 1957-58; Waterloo Midwest 1959; Winston-Salem Carolina 1961.

Year	Club	League	POS	G	AB	R	H	2B	3B	HR	RBI	SB	BA
1921	Norfolk	Virginia	SS	115	435	103	133	32	6	5	-	30	.306
	Philadelphia	American	PH	3	3	0	0	0	0	0	0	0	.000
1922	Portsmouth	Virginia	SS-3B	121	466	**98**	136	23	**10**	**13**	-	40	.292
1923	Petersburg	Virginia	S-3-O	123	477	78	146	27	2	13	64	20	.306
1924	Saginaw	Mich-Ont	3B-OF	115	406	70	137	32	14	3	64	31	.337
	Cleveland	American	3B	19	66	3	18	1	1	0	7	0	.273
1925	Indianapolis	A A	3-2-O	141	484	86	148	18	11	2	63	26	.306
1926	Indianapolis	A A	3B	167	605	87	171	25	12	4	65	15	.283
1927	Indianapolis	A A	3B	114	452	89	140	22	10	6	60	13	.310
	Chicago	National	3B	13	27	2	6	1	1	0	5	0	.222
1928	Chicago	National	3B	1	0	0	0	0	0	0	0	0	.000
	Minneapolis	A A	3B-SS	143	566	112	182	32	13	2	45	13	.322

1929	Minneapolis	A A	3B-SS	167	**687**	148	218	50	7	4	65	31	.317
1930	Minn/Colum	A A	3B	142	562	110	178	30	8	4	49	24	.317
1931	Colum/Indian	A A	3B	89	342	71	103	16	3	2	40	10	.301
1932	Danville	III	3B	25	80	13	18	0	1	0	-	0	.225
	Houston	Texas	3B	45	169	32	42	6	2	0	10	7	.249
1933	Wilkes-Barre	NY-Penn	3B	139	469	53	126	13	8	1	48	27	.269
1934	Wilkes-Barre	NY-Penn	3B	121	445	85	136	23	9	1	71	12	.306
1935	Wilkes-Barre	NY-Penn	3B	131	444	78	117	20	6	2	58	14	.264
1936	Scranton	NY-Penn	3B	116	414	78	121	14	11	1	43	11	.292
1937	Portsmouth	Piedmont	3B	117	403	68	97	20	5	1	44	12	.241
1938	Greenwood	Cottn St	3B	121	366	83	109	20	6	0	57	15	.298
1939	Gloversville	Can-Amer	3B	55	170	34	47	11	1	3	25	5	.276
1940						Did not play in O. B.								
1941	Dan-School	Bi-St	OF	50	130	21	36	8	2	2	25	5	.277
1942	Dan-School	Bi-St	3B-OF	61	151	25	40	10	1	2	22	2	.265
		Majors		**36**	**96**	**5**	**24**	**2**	**2**	**0**	**12**	**0**	**.250**
		Minors		**2418**	**8723**	**1622**	**2581**	**452**	**148**	**71**	**918**	**363**	**.296**

Louis LeRoy, the American Indian who won 239 games in the Minors. One was a no-hitter for St. Paul over Indianapolis on July 27, 1910

Pitchers

ANDRES AYON (GARCIA)
Born October 22, 1940 at Havana, Cuba.
Height 5' 10", Weight 170. Threw right. Batted right.
Led Mexican League in wins and winning percentage in 1967 and 1972.
Manager: Sabinas Mexican 1971.

Year	Club	League	G	IP	W	L	H	R	ER	BB	SO	ERA
1957	Wausau	Northern	39	144	8	13	149	98	79	71	115	4.94
1958	Visalia	Calif	35	212	18	8	192	109	80	111	184	3.40
1959	Havana	Int	5	9	0	1	11	10	6	5	9	6.00
	Savannah	Sally	10	56	3	4	47	24	20	32	50	3.21
	Topeka	III	26	144	12	4	143	80	59	71	159	3.69
1960	Havana/JC	Int	52	114	5	6	102	47	38	49	82	3.00
1961	Jersey City	Int	60	97	6	6	93	43	37	39	81	3.43
1962	Macon	Sally	55	112	8	4	96	55	45	46	93	3.62
1963	Macon	Sally	25	59	5	3	59	39	23	19	66	3.51
1964	Puebla	Mexican	30	150	16	5	131	54	49	57	106	2.94
1965	Puebla	Mexican	43	214	17	12	226	115	99	81	125	4.16
1966	Puebla	Mexican	34	199	16	12	207	96	80	81	106	3.62
1967	Jalisco	Mexican	42	237	**25**	6	243	100	88	50	81	3.34
1968	Jalisco	Mexican	38	231	13	13	248	107	82	59	82	3.19
	Seattle	P C	1	1	0	1	3	4	1	1	2	9.00
1969	Jalisco	Mexican	36	231	20	12	216	99	66	72	94	2.57
1970	Jalisco	Mexican	31	176	11	14	205	85	68	51	58	3.48
1971	Sabinas/Salt	Mexican	24	147	12	6	121	28	20	34	68	1.22
1972	Saltillo	Mexican	42	200	**22**	3	185	79	70	55	106	3.15
1973	Salt/Puebla	Mexican	21	116	11	6	121	48	40	21	62	3.10
1974			Did not play in O. B.									
1975	Cordoba	Mexican	10	51	2	5	55	28	22	18	24	3.88
1976	Nuevo Laredo	Mexican	3	22	1	2	20	12	7	12	7	2.86
1977	Nuevo Laredo	Mexican	5	25	2	1	29	11	9	16	14	3.24
1978			Did not play in O. B.									
1979	Nuevo Laredo	Mexican	3	18	1	1	15	5	5	10	9	2.50
		Minors	**670**	**2965**	**234**	**148**	**2917**	**1376**	**1093**	**1061**	**1783**	**3.32**

EDWIN C. BRYAN
Born March 26, 1900 at Belleville, IL.
Height 6' 1", Weight 180. Threw right. Batted left.
Pitched 8-0 win over Oakland June 6, 1930 in first night game in PCL.
Set PCL season record for hits allowed with 441 in 1933.

Year	Club	League	G	IP	W	L	H	R	ER	BB	SO	ERA
1921	Dallas	Texas	3	4	0	0	7	5	4	1	2	9.00
	Min. Wells	Tex-Okla	25	179	11	10	113	56	-	43	105	-
1922	Greenville	E Texas	24	190	19	3	155	56	-	43	101	-

	Dallas	Texas	12	49	2	3	54	31	24	15	10	4.41
1923	Dallas	Texas	30	157	8	11	196	103	81	55	36	4.64
	Greenville	E Texas	4	25	1	2	23	11	10	7	18	3.60
1924	Dallas	Texas	4	19	1	2	22	14	12	7	6	5.68
	Texarkana	E Texas	16	125	8	4	111	42	-	28	42	-
	Vernon	P C	24	173	13	5	168	77	63	42	34	3.28
1925	Vernon	P C	45	251	9	18	310	167	137	59	72	4.91
1926	Missions	P C	49	194	7	10	223	108	73	46	41	3.39
1927	Missions	P C	43	164	8	7	219	106	94	49	45	5.16
1928	Miss/Sea	P C	34	191	8	11	243	123	100	51	48	4.71
1929	Sacramento	P C	48	328	20	12	401	188	161	80	79	4.42
1930	Sacramento	P C	38	250	18	12	304	133	117	67	84	4.21
1931	Sacramento	P C	44	280	14	18	348	152	134	60	71	4.31
1932	Sacramento	P C	40	271	19	13	295	126	114	55	59	3.79
1933	Sacramento	P C	43	318	21	17	441	200	182	54	78	5.15
1934	Portland	P C	42	309	11	24	367	175	121	81	77	3.52
1935	Port/Sea	P C	54	259	15	19	341	176	123	62	54	4.27
1936	Tulsa	Texas	10	54	4	5	75	35	30	20	19	5.00
	Minors		**632**	**3790**	**217**	**206**	**4416**	**2084**	**1580**	**925**	**1081**	**4.31**

CHARLES WILLIAM CHECH
Born April 27, 1879 at Madison, WI. Died January 31, 1938 at Los Angeles, CA.
Height 5' 11-1/2", Weight 190. Threw right. Batted right.
Attended University of Wisconsin.

Year	Club	League	G	IP	W	L	H	R	ER	BB	SO	ERA
1899	Milwaukee	Western	16	-	5	9	-	-	-	35	18	-
1900	Cleveland	American	5	35	0	2	48	26	-	10	3	-
1901	St. Paul	Western	25	199	15	9	158	68	-	41	78	-
1902	St. Paul	A A	36	293	15	19	316	161	-	66	64	-
1903	St. Paul	A A	48	326	24	9	299	131	-	75	142	-
1904	St. Paul	A A	35	311	27	8	250	103	-	64	152	-
1905	Cincinnati	National	39	268	14	15	300	139	86	77	79	2.89
1906	Cincinnati	National	11	66	1	4	59	30	17	24	17	2.32
	Toledo	A A	23	180	9	11	164	81	-	26	63	-
1907	Toledo	A A	39	314	25	11	286	120	-	67	134	-
1908	Cleveland	American	27	166	11	7	136	51	32	34	51	1.73
1909	Boston	American	17	107	7	5	107	51	35	27	40	2.94
	St. Paul	A A	16	111	5	9	91	-	-	19	38	-
1910	St. Paul	A A	49	299	19	15	295	122	-	77	99	-
1911	St. Paul	A A	46	234	11	13	262	118	-	60	69	-
1912	Los Angeles	P C	50	360	25	14	-	137	-	80	118	-
1913	Los Angeles	P C	42	305	18	20	295	121	-	86	84	-
1914	Los Angeles	P C	46	297	20	16	258	132	95	82	72	2.88
1915	L.A./Vernon	P C	34	228	12	14	240	99	83	46	60	3.28
1916-17					No records available							
1918	Vernon	P C	20	141	9	7	128	40	33	18	24	2.11
	Majors		**94**	**607**	**33**	**31**	**602**	**271**	**170**	**162**	**187**	**2.52**
	Minors		**530**	**3633**	**239**	**186**	**3090**	**1459**	**211**	**852**	**1218**	**-**

ROBERT M. COUCHMAN
Born 1888 at Urbana, OH. Died June, 1948 at Springfield, OH.
Height 6', Weight 185. Threw right. Batted right.
Manager: San Antonio TL 1927; Coleman W Texas 1928.

Year	Club	League	G	IP	W	L	H	R	ER	BB	SO	ERA
1909	Bay City	S Mich	32	-	13	19	-	-	-	-	-	-
1910	St. Paul	A A	1	1	0	0	3	3	-	1	0	-
	Rock Island	III	37	299	24	14	221	97	-	83	205	-
1911	Los Angeles	P C	13	73	2	6	-	53	-	28	15	-
	Rock Island	III	3	12	0	0	-	5	-	5	3	-
1912	Quincy/Decat	III	18	125	5	11	144	-	-	31	50	-
	Hannibal	Cent A	16	134	9	5	137	51	-	18	84	-
1913	Akron	Inter-St	22	161	11	7	138	58	-	44	70	-
	Davenport	III	12	93	5	6	83	41	-	62	63	-
1914	Montreal	Int	30	214	12	12	222	116	-	58	56	-
1915	Montreal	Int	1	8	0	1	11	7	-	2	3	-
	Little Rock	South A	33	230	15	13	218	88	-	61	68	-
1916	Little Rock	South A	33	180	8	16	197	98	-	43	52	-
	Galveston	Texas	13	90	7	3	84	-	15	30	51	1.50
1917	Galveston	Texas	12	70	2	8	57	30	16	18	23	2.06
	Richmond	Central	26	177	9	12	182	78	57	42	62	2.90
1918						Military Service						
1919	Galveston	Texas	45	335	12	18	286	108	80	77	96	2.15
1920	Galveston	Texas	37	309	18	17	216	124	96	48	97	2.80
1921	Gal/San Ant	Texas	41	314	20	15	329	136	119	65	109	3.41
1922	San Antonio	Texas	40	253	17	17	278	122	103	44	81	3.66
1923	San Antonio	Texas	43	261	15	17	294	146	108	68	77	3.72
1924	San Antonio	Texas	37	225	16	11	265	112	99	53	49	3.96
1925	San Antonio	Texas	33	176	10	10	188	107	88	64	43	4.50
1926	San Antonio	Texas	31	254	15	14	261	95	72	62	50	2.55
1927	San Antonio	Texas	16	102	3	10	139	62	55	29	10	4.85
1928	Coleman	W Texas	2	12	1	1	-	-	-	4	4	-
		Minors	**627**	**4108**	**249**	**263**	**3953**	**1737**	**908**	**1040**	**1421**	**-**

HOWARD OLIVER CRAGHEAD
Born May 25, 1908 at Selma, CA. Died July 15, 1962 at San Zieloe, CA.
Height 6' 2", Weight 200. Threw right. Batted right.

Year	Club	League	G	IP	W	L	H	R	ER	BB	SO	ERA
1926	Oakland	P C	20	83	2	3	78	40	30	33	37	3.25
1927	Ogden	Utah-Ida	9	65	4	4	73	32	29	28	60	4.02
	Oakland	P C	24	100	4	4	104	46	38	41	49	3.42
1928	Oakland	P C	39	282	18	13	283	122	107	104	147	3.41
1929	Oakland	P C	52	298	21	12	321	158	134	128	**190**	4.05
1930	Oakland	P C	47	343	21	22	342	156	139	125	199	3.65
1931	Oakland	P C	36	229	13	15	233	117	106	100	156	4.17
	Cleveland	American	4	6	0	0	8	4	4	2	2	6.00
1932	Toledo	A A	41	253	18	15	292	157	-	98	112	-
1933	Cleveland	American	11	17	0	0	19	13	12	10	2	6.35
	Toledo	A A	21	119	5	9	154	87	78	44	45	5.90
1934	Seattle	P C	46	280	16	21	339	162	135	110	145	4.34
1935	Seattle	P C	39	276	18	16	316	149	125	101	120	4.08
1936	Seattle/San D	P C	40	235	16	12	233	109	94	83	109	3.60
1937	San Diego	P C	42	245	16	13	265	100	89	74	119	3.27

1938	San Diego	P C	47	271	18	18	279	132	86	79	138	2.86
1939	San Diego	P C	34	203	11	16	239	121	107	56	94	4.74
1940	San Diego	P C	38	175	8	14	205	104	95	74	66	4.89
		Majors	**15**	**23**	**0**	**0**	**27**	**17**	**16**	**12**	**4**	**6.26**
		Minors	**575**	**3457**	**209**	**207**	**3756**	**1792**	**1392**	**1278**	**1786**	**3.91**

WILLIAM GEORGE "WHEEZER" DELL
Born June 11, 1887 at Tuscarora, NV. Died August 24, 1966 at Independence, CA.
Height 6' 4", Weight 210. Threw right. Batted right.
Led PCL with 7 shutouts in 1920.

Year	Club	League	G	IP	W	L	H	R	ER	BB	SO	ERA
1909	Butte	Intermtn	11	65	5	4	69	49	-	29	37	-
1910	Edmonton	W Canada	32	225	16	10	-	-	-	119	166	-
1911				No record available								
1912	Butte	Union A	48	-	20	12	-	-	-	-	-	-
	St. Louis	National	3	2	0	0	3	3	3	3	0	13.50
1913	Seattle	NWestern	43	313	20	19	258	144	-	116	231	-
1914	Seattle	NWestern	43	335	21	13	235	93	-	116	182	-
1915	Brooklyn	National	40	215	11	10	166	80	56	100	94	2.34
1916	Brooklyn	National	32	155	8	9	143	52	39	43	76	2.26
1917	Brooklyn	National	17	58	0	4	55	35	24	25	28	3.72
1918	Vernon	P C	27	208	14	7	170	54	39	74	78	1.69
1919	Vernon	P C	50	352	25	16	303	109	93	99	162	2.38
1920	Vernon	P C	54	370	27	15	368	145	123	126	123	2.99
1921	Vernon	P C	49	336	**28**	14	311	142	110	112	134	2.95
1922	Vernon	P C	49	369	23	17	328	149	130	104	143	3.17
1923	Vernon/Sea	P C	39	236	12	11	276	146	106	72	88	4.04
1924	Seattle	P C	38	183	9	14	215	141	113	86	74	5.56
1925	Atlanta	South A	28	148	10	10	179	83	66	38	44	4.01
1926	Beaumont	Texas	4	22	1	2	30	20	17	10	8	6.95
		Majors	**92**	**430**	**19**	**23**	**367**	**170**	**122**	**171**	**198**	**2.55**
		Minors	**515**	**3162**	**231**	**164**	**2742**	**1275**	**797**	**1101**	**1470**	**3.23**

CARROLL PHILLIP DIAL
Born August 20, 1925 at Altus, OK.
Height 5' 11", Weight 160. Threw right. Batted right.
Good hitting pitcher who also played outfield. Batted .366 in 104 games in 1954.

Year	Club	League	G	IP	W	L	H	R	ER	BB	SO	ERA
1947	Bartlesville	KOM	38	233	**22**	8	205	122	86	84	214	**3.32**
1948	Waco	Big St	34	216	13	11	247	148	103	95	116	4.29
1949	Waco	Big St	5	16	2	1	6	4	-	12	14	-
	Saginaw	Central	16	84	3	6	103	59	44	41	37	4.71
	Lamesa	WTNM	8	23	0	2	29	29	22	13	20	8.61
1950	Paris	E Texas	10	61	5	4	67	41	38	31	39	5.61
	Sherman-Den	Big St	31	168	9	10	181	114	86	83	96	4.61
1951	Pampa	WTNM	49	257	22	15	292	201	**172**	123	**174**	6.02
1952	Clovis	WTNM	38	269	**27**	10	322	167	152	111	170	5.09
1953	Clovis	WTNM	48	**308**	**28**	11	320	209	146	135	243	4.27
1954	Clovis	WTNM	44	258	**25**	12	241	157	127	98	**234**	4.43
1955	Pampa	WTNM	**50**	**296**	20	15	301	177	117	114	171	**3.56**

1956	Pampa	SWest	12	83	5	6	113	61	46	23	63	4.99
	Shreveport	Texas	20	51	2	5	60	38	35	29	17	6.18
1957	Wichita Falls	Big St	5	8	0	2	-	-	4	-	-	4.50
	Minors		**408**	**2331**	**183**	**118**	**2487**	**1527**	**1178**	**992**	**1608**	**4.58**

EDWARD ALEXANDER DONALDS
Born June 22, 1885 at Bidwell, OH. Died July 3, 1950 at Columbus, OH.
Height 5' 11", Weight 180. Threw right. Batted right.
His won-lost record for 1913-14 was 60-12.

Year	Club	League	G	IP	W	L	H	R	ER	BB	SO	ERA
1911	Lima	Ohio St	35	-	18	15	-	-	-	-	-	-
1912	Portsmouth	Ohio St	36	-	24	11	-	-	-	-	-	-
	Cincinnati	National	1	4	1	0	7	2	2	0	1	4.50
1913	Portsmouth	Ohio St	40	-	**30**	8	-	-	-	-	-	-
1914	Waco	Texas	42	304	**30**	4	218	91	-	62	134	-
1915	Waco	Texas	39	286	18	12	268	95	-	44	124	-
1916	Waco	Texas	36	264	17	11	242	-	68	60	111	2.32
1917	Waco	Texas	45	277	17	11	242	84	73	58	120	2.37
1918	Waco	Texas	24	172	11	8	165	69	53	41	84	2.77
1919	Waco	Texas	23	192	11	11	179	67	56	54	76	2.63
1920			Did not play in O. B.									
1921	Houston	Texas	32	225	17	9	227	100	80	55	70	3.20
1922	Houston	Texas	13	98	3	9	120	61	52	21	19	4.78
	Evansville	III	18	136	9	6	131	45	36	19	24	2.38
1923	Evansville	III	34	215	14	14	239	107	-	58	70	-
	Majors		**1**	**4**	**1**	**0**	**7**	**2**	**2**	**0**	**1**	**4.50**
	Minors		**417**	**2169**	**219**	**129**	**2031**	**719**	**418**	**472**	**832**	**-**

GARY REESE FORTUNE
Born October 11, 1894 at High Point, NC. Died September 23, 1955 at Washington, DC.
Height 5' 11-1/2", Weight 176. Threw right. Batted both.
Pitched doubleheader shutout (both 9 inning games) against New Haven on August 29, 1919; winning 1-0 and 3-0.

Year	Club	League	G	IP	W	L	H	R	ER	BB	SO	ERA
1914	Asheville	N Carol	19	113	5	5	91	59	-	45	56	-
1915	Asheville	N Carol	47	309	22	10	241	115	-	98	209	-
1916	New London	Eastern	30	239	19	7	-	-	-	87	159	-
	Philadelphia	National	1	5	0	1	2	2	2	4	3	3.60
1917	New London	Eastern	21	146	5	10	135	59	46	67	72	2.84
1918	New London	Eastern	18	142	13	2	97	27	-	44	77	-
	Philadelphia	National	5	31	0	2	41	30	28	19	10	8.13
1919	Pittsfield	Eastern	**41**	304	24	9	227	95	-	**96**	182	-
1920	Springfield	Eastern	6	54	6	0	42	18	-	11	33	2.33
	Boston	American	14	42	0	2	46	32	27	23	10	5.79
1921	Toronto	Int	34	219	14	15	207	116	88	122	120	3.62
1922	Toronto	Int	1	2	0	0	3	3	-	2	0	-
	Springfield	Eastern	30	240	18	9	230	92	67	75	121	2.51
1923	Springfield	Eastern	43	**328**	22	12	358	183	144	132	120	3.95
1924	Springfield	Eastern	35	286	**23**	9	275	130	119	91	118	3.74
1925	Springfield	Eastern	34	264	14	15	268	130	97	84	120	3.31
1926	Asheville	Sally	12	73	5	2	86	38	27	18	26	3.33

	Springfield	Eastern	14	90	5	5	87	45	42	30	28	4.20
1927	Springfield	Eastern	34	240	12	16	263	127	103	82	76	3.86
1928	Springfield	Eastern	34	263	19	12	301	122	108	84	74	3.70
1929	Hartford	Eastern	27	170	8	12	209	115	87	84	70	4.61
1930	New Haven	Eastern	7	33	3	2	47	30	-	21	8	-
		Majors	**20**	**78**	**0**	**5**	**89**	**64**	**57**	**46**	**23**	**6.58**
		Minors	**487**	**3515**	**237**	**152**	**3167**	**1504**	**928**	**1273**	**1669**	**-**

WHEELER BISHOP "MOOSE" FULLER

Born January 19, 1893 at Ceredo, WV. Died August 5, 1943 at Albany, NY.
Height 5' 11-1/2", Weight 180. Threw right. Batted right.
Was a spitball pitcher.

Year	Club	League	G	IP	W	L	H	R	ER	BB	SO	ERA
1913	Law/New Bed	New Eng	33	-	11	14	-	-	-	-	-	-
1914	Lawrence	New Eng	38	-	18	17	-	-	-	-	-	-
1915	Lawrence	New Eng	34	-	15	10	-	-	-	-	-	-
1916	Law/New Lon	Eastern	31	235	16	12	202	-	-	48	109	-
1917	Lawrernce	Eastern	18	123	10	4	95	33	25	20	44	1.83
1918		Military Service										
1919	Shreveport	Texas	6	51	4	1	46	16	-	13	20	-
1920	Waterbury	Eastern	26	190	9	11	187	74	-	25	77	2.66
1921	Waterbury	Eastern	36	304	20	14	274	110	69	55	150	2.04
1922	Waterbury	Eastern	43	317	19	20	302	146	105	53	118	2.98
1923	Waterbury	Eastern	36	250	12	17	301	125	89	35	75	3.20
1924	Waterbury	Eastern	35	248	17	13	258	97	73	43	73	2.65
1925	Waterbury	Eastern	44	263	20	15	291	133	88	50	88	3.01
1926	Albany	Eastern	32	228	16	10	246	109	69	24	81	2.72
1927	Albany	Eastern	42	260	22	11	280	115	90	48	88	3.12
1928	Albany	Eastern	40	219	13	13	240	113	98	52	63	4.03
1929	Albany	Eastern	28	125	8	8	157	90	74	46	42	5.33
		Minors	**522**	**2813**	**230**	**190**	**2879**	**1161**	**780**	**512**	**1028**	**-**

RALPH GARCIA

Born December 14, 1948 at Los Angeles, CA.
Height 6', Weight 195. Threw right. Batted right.
Seventh on career minor league strikeout list.

Year	Club	League	G	IP	W	L	H	R	ER	BB	SO	ERA
1970	Tri-City	NWest	2	7	0	1	9	10	3	9	16	3.86
	Lodi	Calif	13	84	3	6	78	46	39	53	108	4.18
1971	Lodi	Calif	26	179	11	12	140	92	73	115	199	3.67
1972	Hawaii	P C	29	177	8	8	192	100	87	83	157	4.42
	San Diego	National	3	5	0	0	4	1	1	3	3	1.80
1973	Hawaii	P C	22	127	6	10	118	81	69	79	119	4.89
1974	Hawaii	P C	21	116	7	5	104	67	60	65	122	4.66
	San Diego	National	8	10	0	0	15	8	7	7	9	6.30
1975	Alexandria	Texas	16	116	7	6	102	58	47	58	79	3.65
1976	Juarez	Mexican	25	155	11	8	143	60	52	73	122	3.02
1977	Juarez	Mexican	20	167	14	5	104	47	33	55	114	1.78
1978	Juarez	Mexican	18	141	5	10	127	56	46	38	114	2.94
1979	Juarez	Mexican	29	261	20	6	199	61	49	60	**222**	**1.69**
1980	Juarez	Mex #1	17	130	10	3	107	37	33	31	112	2.28
	Juarez	Mex #2	8	75	**6**	0	59	14	10	11	**47**	1.20

1981	Juarez	Mexican	26	212	**20**	5	176	58	43	42	**187**	1.83
1982	Juarez	Mexican	28	208	**19**	8	165	70	53	52	177	2.29
1983				Did not play in O. B.								
1984	Juarez	Mexican	28	225	16	9	244	121	99	72	184	3.96
1985	Torreon	Mexican	12	80	4	4	98	62	51	42	63	5.74
1986	Saltillo	Mexican	28	198	11	13	210	134	123	72	155	5.59
1987				Did not play in O. B.								
1988	Aguascalient	Mexican	27	183	11	10	176	111	92	78	152	4.52
		Majors	**11**	**15**	**0**	**0**	**19**	**9**	**8**	**10**	**12**	**4.80**
		Minors	**395**	**2841**	**189**	**129**	**2551**	**1285**	**1062**	**1088**	**2449**	**3.36**

HARRY RAY GARDNER
Born July 1, 1887 at Quincy, MI. Died August 2, 1961 at Canby, OR.
Height 6' 2", Weight 180. Threw right. Batted right.

Year	Club	League	G	IP	W	L	H	R	ER	BB	SO	ERA
1909	Boise	Intermtn	3	22	1	1	18	15	-	9	18	-
1910	Vancouver	NWest	35	288	22	13	199	76	-	97	201	-
1911	Pittsburgh	National	13	42	1	1	39	25	21	20	24	4.50
1912	Pittsburgh	National	1	1	0	0	3	6	0	1	0	0.00
	St. Paul	A A	31	181	12	10	203	108	-	84	81	-
1913	St. Paul	A A	44	245	11	11	233	126	-	91	98	-
1914	St. Paul	A A	42	265	6	25	276	159	124	102	116	4.21
1915	St. Paul/KC	A A	48	246	13	14	282	126	100	62	94	3.66
1916	Kansas City	A A	2	5	0	0	8	6	6	1	1	10.80
	Lincoln	Western	38	272	17	14	290	-	97	58	138	3.21
1917	Gr Falls/Tac	NWest	23	184	12	8	161	84	-	69	108	-
	Portland	P C	22	124	7	6	122	48	29	33	24	2.10
1918	Sacramento	P C	27	195	12	8	183	69	48	34	78	2.22
1919	Sacra/Sea	P C	29	168	10	12	165	76	62	44	56	3.32
1920	Seattle	P C	46	279	20	15	263	119	78	54	115	2.52
1921	Seattle	P C	41	291	18	12	310	136	95	75	115	2.94
1922	Seattle	P C	42	287	17	15	301	141	104	73	128	3.26
1923	Seattle	P C	41	305	22	12	314	127	105	59	98	3.10
1924	Portland	P C	16	99	5	6	139	83	59	29	33	5.36
		Majors	**14**	**43**	**1**	**1**	**42**	**31**	**21**	**21**	**24**	**4.40**
		Minors	**530**	**3456**	**205**	**182**	**3467**	**1499**	**907**	**974**	**1502**	**-**

SALVADOR MICHAEL GLIATTO
Born May 7, 1902 at Chicago IL.
Height 5' 8", Weight 150. Threw right. Batted both.
Manager: Greenville E Texas 1946.

Year	Club	League	G	IP	W	L	H	R	ER	BB	SO	ERA
1927	Terre Haute	III	36	238	19	11	199	106	81	99	86	3.06
1928	Terre Haute	III	29	205	14	9	217	105	93	52	90	4.08
1929	Terre Haute	III	40	248	17	12	247	105	82	68	79	2.98
1930	New Orleans	South A	20	120	10	6	117	61	49	43	31	3.68
	Cleveland	American	8	15	0	0	21	15	11	9	7	6.60
1931	New Orleans	Sally	45	281	20	15	308	129	119	63	91	3.81
1932	New Orleans	Sally	44	208	8	19	254	138	118	75	52	5.11
1933	Dallas	Texas	32	184	14	10	153	94	76	72	88	3.72
1934	Dallas	Texas	41	226	12	11	236	123	101	90	96	4.02

Year	Club	League	G	IP	W	L	H	R	ER	BB	SO	ERA
1935	Dallas	Texas	43	257	15	15	234	108	76	68	108	2.66
1936	Dallas	Texas	35	204	13	9	227	97	77	53	84	3.40
1937	St. Paul	A A	37	94	1	3	133	85	77	42	39	7.37
1938	Dallas	Texas	40	268	18	16	259	120	103	75	108	3.46
1939	Dallas	Texas	38	214	14	16	225	113	82	58	92	3.45
1940	Dallas	Texas	26	158	12	8	155	67	48	30	77	2.73
1941	Dallas	Texas	42	268	21	10	262	102	81	47	117	2.72
1942	Dallas	Texas	31	185	7	14	170	70	63	52	81	3.06
1943-45				Did not play in O.B.								
1946	Greenville	E Texas	39	186	11	10	208	99	79	29	89	3.82
1947-48				Did not play in O.B.								
1949	Greenville	Big St	34	102	7	7	103	54	41	29	44	3.62
		Majors	**8**	**15**	**0**	**0**	**21**	**15**	**11**	**9**	**7**	**6.60**
		Minors	**652**	**3646**	**233**	**201**	**3707**	**1776**	**1446**	**1045**	**1452**	**3.57**

OSCAR M. GRAHAM

Born July 20, 1878 at Plattsmouth, NE. Died October 15, 1931 at Moline IL.
Height 6' 1/2". Threw left. Batted left.

Hit 49 batters in 1903.

Year	Club	League	G	IP	W	L	H	R	ER	BB	SO	ERA
1901	Omaha	Western	17	134	6	10	133	87	-	57	72	-
	Rock Island	III	13	101	1	8	100	81	-	44	84	-
1902	Omaha	Western	36	270	16	17	258	136	-	128	160	-
	Oakland	P C	16	-	6	9	117	-	-	22	29	-
1903	Oakland	P C	59	489	27	28	474	285	-	228	133	-
1904	Oakland	P C	46	380	19	23	462	192	-	124	157	-
1905	Oakland	P C	60	500	28	25	414	184	-	191	210	-
1906	Oakland	P C	52	-	24	24	-	-	-	-	-	-
1907	Washington	American	20	104	4	9	116	66	46	29	44	3.98
	Minneapolis	A A	12	102	7	4	93	36	-	34	51	-
1908	Minneapolis	A A	20	111	8	5	104	54	-	33	53	-
1909	Indianapolis	A A	40	254	15	15	218	102	-	93	118	-
1910	Ind/Mil	A A	27	156	8	10	124	60	-	52	55	-
1911	Milwaukee	A A	7	43	1	3	42	20	-	15	15	-
	Wheeling	Central	24	187	10	11	162	75	-	65	88	-
1912	Wheeling	Central	32	259	19	8	227	91	-	80	122	-
1913	Wheeling	Inter-St	19	159	8	9	158	61	-	43	78	-
	Battle Creek	S. Mich		No record available								
1914	Wichita	Western	3	13	0	2	22	16	-	3	5	-
	TH/Evans	Central	32	227	10	14	240	108	-	69	118	-
1915	Moline	III	27	206	16	8	151	65	36	67	108	1.57
1916	Moline	III	38	277	23	12	249	103	71	109	111	2.31
1917	Moline	III	19	124	9	6	127	65	41	41	52	2.98
	Joplin	Western	19	134	9	6	104	-	20	37	46	1.34
1918				Did not play in O. B.								
1919	Moline/Rock	III	10	72	3	3	70	42	32	35	27	4.00
		Majors	**20**	**104**	**4**	**9**	**116**	**66**	**46**	**29**	**44**	**3.98**
		Minors	**628**	**4198**	**273**	**260**	**4049**	**1863**	**200**	**1570**	**1892**	**-**

HOWARD WATTERSON GREGORY
Born November 18, 1886 at Hannibal, MO. Died May 30, 1970 at Tulsa, OK.
Height 6', Weight 175. Threw right. Batted left.
Manager: Wichita WL 1922-26; Topeka WL 1931.

Year	Club	League	G	IP	W	L	H	R	ER	BB	SO	ERA
1909	Springfield	West A	28	-	10	14	-	-	-	58	128	-
1910	Joplin	West A	25	-	18	3	-	-	-	52	115	-
1911	St. Louis	American	3	7	0	1	11	5	4	4	1	5.14
	Oakland	P C	33	201	16	10	-	81	-	60	64	-
1912	Oakland	P C	37	274	18	14	-	109	-	80	98	-
1913	Oakland/LA	P C	37	187	5	16	232	123	-	75	50	-
1914	Sacramento	P C	46	249	13	14	290	124	76	80	67	2.75
1915	Salt Lake City	P C	39	204	13	11	220	121	97	81	65	4.28
1916	Salt Lake City	P C	7	48	2	4	51	24	20	18	5	3.75
	Lincoln	Western	40	277	14	13	286	-	100	69	85	3.25
1917	Lincoln	Western	39	319	23	8	304	-	77	60	86	2.17
1918				Military Service								
1919	Sioux C/Wich	Western	42	295	18	14	290	141	-	50	103	-
1920	Wichita	Western	45	320	25	13	325	140	-	47	93	-
1921	Wichita	Western	48	304	22	13	275	152	-	45	63	-
1922	Wichita	Western	41	302	22	12	366	164	-	45	57	-
1923	Wichita	Western	24	148	7	7	182	89	-	34	25	-
1924	Wichita	Western	33	204	12	12	270	152	-	33	44	-
1925	Wichita	Western	32	181	9	7	245	125	-	47	36	-
		Majors	**3**	**7**	**0**	**1**	**11**	**5**	**4**	**4**	**1**	**5.14**
		Minors	**596**	**3513**	**247**	**185**	**3336**	**1545**	**370**	**934**	**1184**	**-**

HERBERT SILAS HALL
Born June 5, 1894 at Steelville, IL. Died July 3, 1970 at Fresno, CA.
Height 6' 4", Weight 220. Threw right. Batted both.

Year	Club	League	G	IP	W	L	H	R	ER	BB	SO	ERA
1913	LB/Pas/SB	S Calif	29	214	15	11	202	125	-	-	-	-
1914	Modesto	Calif St	3	21	1	2	22	10	-	6	12	-
	Racine	Wis-Ill	10	77	4	4	77	36	-	17	47	-
1915	Phoenix	RG Val A	24	174	14	8	156	79	-	51	99	-
	Topeka	Western	13	72	6	3	72	30	21	23	26	2.63
1916	Topeka	Western	49	313	16	20	323	-	105	109	134	3.02
1917	Kansas City	A A	1	1	0	1	2	3	3	2	1	27.00
	Joplin	Western	52	343	23	16	307	-	89	106	159	2.34
1918	Detroit	American	3	6	0	0	12	11	10	7	1	15.00
	Joplin	Western	6	51	3	3	41	19	12	26	31	2.12
	Kansas City	A A	17	113	7	4	84	27	19	46	43	1.51
1919	Kansas City	A A	49	296	21	16	298	150	124	141	86	3.77
1920-21				Did not play in O. B.								
1922	Los Angeles	P C	3	8	0	0	14	7	6	2	0	6.75
	Denver	Western	46	275	15	20	321	181	-	74	107	-
1923	Denver	Western	46	289	14	21	392	218	-	85	108	-
1924	Denver	Western	57	315	26	13	388	193	-	87	154	-
1925	Denver	Western	52	261	23	14	325	170	-	110	135	-
1926	Denver	Western	56	341	29	15	385	186	-	96	137	-
1927	Denver	Western	44	234	12	15	278	151	-	66	81	-
1928	Denver	Western	13	57	1	5	81	45	-	17	17	-
		Majors	**3**	**6**	**0**	**0**	**12**	**11**	**10**	**7**	**1**	**15.00**
		Minors	**570**	**3455**	**230**	**191**	**3768**	**1630**	**379**	**1064**	**1377**	**-**

LUKE DANIEL "HOT POTATO" HAMLIN
Born July 3, 1906 at Terris Center, MI. Died February 18, 1978 at Clare, MI.
Height 6' 1", Weight 170. Threw right. Batted left.
Manager: Leesburg Fla St 1949.

Year	Club	League	G	IP	W	L	H	R	ER	BB	SO	ERA
1928	Hanover	Blue Rdg	23	173	12	6	158	67	39	67	123	2.03
1929	Fort Smith	West A	35	248	20	9	253	122	67	88	146	2.43
1930	Evansville	III	31	213	18	7	213	96	76	77	148	3.21
1931	Evansville	III	1	9	1	0	4	1	1	2	12	1.00
	Beaumont	Texas	34	228	14	13	229	108	88	83	138	3.47
1932	Beaumont	Texas	37	221	20	10	190	78	68	63	96	2.77
1933	Toronto	Int	39	261	21	13	261	107	101	83	127	3.48
	Detroit	American	3	17	1	0	20	11	9	10	10	4.76
1934	Detroit	American	20	75	2	3	87	48	45	44	30	5.40
1935	Milwaukee	A A	30	178	8	14	202	94	80	46	90	4.04
1936	Milwaukee	A A	44	273	19	14	316	143	116	69	159	3.82
1937	Brooklyn	National	39	186	11	13	183	96	74	48	93	3.58
1938	Brooklyn	National	44	237	12	15	243	111	97	65	97	3.68
1939	Brooklyn	National	40	270	20	13	255	115	109	54	88	3.63
1940	Brooklyn	National	33	182	9	8	183	77	62	34	91	3.07
1941	Brooklyn	National	30	136	8	8	139	75	64	41	58	4.24
1942	Pittsburgh	National	23	112	4	4	128	58	49	19	38	3.94
1943	Toronto	Int	31	227	21	8	186	72	54	46	108	2.14
1944	Philadelphia	American	29	190	6	12	204	94	79	38	58	3.74
1945	Toronto	Int	30	215	16	11	216	92	77	53	99	3.22
1946	Toronto	Int	26	193	12	10	209	90	78	41	98	3.64
1947	Toronto	Int	24	195	15	6	166	65	48	52	99	**2.22**
1948	Toronto	Int	21	147	6	10	161	81	63	28	69	3.86
1949	Lakeland	Fla Int	15	86	3	8	101	53	46	19	18	4.81
	Leesburg	Fla St	8	72	5	3	46	15	10	6	34	1.25
1950	Saginaw	Central	9	46	2	5	70	39	28	8	18	5.48
	Majors		**261**	**1405**	**73**	**76**	**1442**	**685**	**588**	**353**	**563**	**3.77**
	Minors		**438**	**2985**	**213**	**147**	**2981**	**1323**	**1040**	**831**	**1582**	**3.14**

GEORGE B. HARPER
Born August 17, 1866 at Milwaukee, WI. Died December 11, 1931 at Stockton, CA.
Height 5' 10", Weight 165. Threw right. Batted right.
Ranks 6th on minor league career strikeout list. Leading strike-out hurler of 19th century.
Manager: Stockton Calif 1900; Stockton Calif St 1914. Umpire: California Lg 1901.

Year	Club	League	G	IP	W	L	H	R	ER	BB	SO	ERA
1886	Oshkosh	NWestern	24	206	10	14	180	153	-	51	151	-
1887	LaCrosse	NWestern	4	33	3	1	51	39	12	16	10	3.27
	Omaha	Western	7	62	3	4	87	52	19	28	18	2.76
1888	Oak/Stock	Calif	23	194	12	11	139	138	33	78	153	1.53
1889	Stockton	Calif	39	-	21	18	312	218	75	**159**	212	-
1890	Sacramento	Calif	**70**	**596**	**41**	26	**483**	352	81	**272**	**396**	1.22
1891	San Jose	Calif	**80**	**704**	47	**32**	**555**	417	75	**348**	313	**0.96**
1892	San Jose	Calif	78	697	37	38	617	323	94	247	**232**	**1.21**
1893	Stockton	Calif	37	315	15	21	333	254	75	158	116	2.14
1894	Detroit	Western	8	64	2	6	102	92	53	45	16	7.45
	Nashville	Southern	13	101	8	3	102	71	30	48	44	2.67
	Philadelphia	Naitonal	12	86	6	6	128	84	51	49	24	5.34

1895	Rochester	Eastern	48	395	24	21	461	288	99	146	233	2.26
1896	Scranton	Eastern	11	96	6	5	104	73	21	34	36	1.97
	Brooklyn	National	16	86	4	8	106	72	53	39	22	5.55
1897	Scranton	Eastern	31	262	13	16	273	210	65	151	112	2.23
1898	Stockton	Calif	1	6	0	1	5	4	0	1	9	0.00
	Roch/Ott	Eastern	31	256	13	17	246	143	-	100	75	-
	Stockton	P C	3	28	2	0	15	2	1	7	12	0.32
1899	Wat/Oak/Sac	Calif	35	311	19	13	218	109	-	85	213	-
1900	Stockton	Calif	35	287	13	18	246	147	74	112	126	2.32
		Majors	**28**	**172**	**10**	**14**	**234**	**156**	**104**	**88**	**46**	**5.44**
		Minors	**578**	**4613**	**289**	**265**	**4529**	**3085**	**807**	**2086**	**2477**	**1.72**

BUNN HEARN

Born May 21, 1891 at Chapel Hill, NC. Died October 10, 1959 at Wilson, NC.
Height 5' 11-1/2'', Weight 190. Threw left. Batted left.

Manager: Wilson Virginia 1926-27; Winston-Salem Piedmont 1928 & 31; Henderson Piedmont 1929.

Year	Club	League	G	IP	W	L	H	R	ER	BB	SO	ERA
1910	Wilson	E Carol	28	203	16	10	128	41	-	38	162	-
	St. Louis	National	5	39	1	3	49	22	22	16	14	5.08
1911	St. Louis	National	2	3	0	0	7	4	4	0	1	12.00
	Louisville	A A	22	124	2	11	146	82	-	38	52	-
1912	Omaha	Western	3	10	0	1	14	7	-	2	5	-
	Springfield	III	39	306	27	11	268	103	-	38	197	-
1913	New York	National	2	13	1	1	13	6	4	7	8	2.77
	Toronto	Int	34	222	11	11	214	90	-	41	97	-
1914	Toronto	Int	36	243	13	13	234	130	-	78	136	-
1915	Pittsburgh	Federal	29	176	6	11	187	73	64	37	49	3.27
1916	New London	Eastern	30	263	22	7	176	-	-	44	121	-
1917	Toronto	Int	37	310	23	9	292	-	70	62	133	2.03
1918	Boston	National	17	126	5	6	119	43	35	29	30	2.50
1919		Did not play in O. B.										
1920	Boston	National	11	43	0	3	54	34	27	11	9	5.65
	Toronto	Int	14	99	8	4	112	47	38	14	45	3.45
1921	Wilson	Virginia	21	165	12	7	170	-	-	18	75	-
1922	Wilson	Virginia	28	203	17	8	197	-	-	20	107	-
1923	Wilson	Virginia	30	211	14	10	218	87	65	43	88	2.77
1924	Wilson	Virginia	24	183	11	11	188	76	64	34	54	3.15
1925	Wilson	Virginia	32	234	13	12	287	123	103	38	61	3.96
1926	Wilson	Virginia	32	218	19	10	218	79	65	25	74	2.68
1927	Wilson	Virginia	24	166	11	8	202	93	73	24	41	3.96
1928	Winst-Salem	Piedmont	24	167	13	9	170	73	61	26	64	3.29
1929	Henderson	Piedmont	7	37	1	5	55	26	-	5	11	-
	York	NY-Penn	9	55	4	2	66	33	28	12	16	4.58
1930	York/Harris	NY-Penn	28	156	9	12	187	91	80	23	27	4.62
1931	Wins-Salem	Piedmont	8	56	1	5	84	53	-	9	18	-
		Majors	**66**	**400**	**13**	**24**	**429**	**182**	**156**	**100**	**111**	**3.51**
		Minors	**510**	**3631**	**247**	**176**	**3626**	**1234**	**647**	**632**	**1584**	**-**

CLARENCE T. "CACK" HENLEY
Born 1885 at Sacramento, CA. Died July 9, 1929 at Sacramento, CA.
Height 6' 1", Weight 184. Threw right. Batted right.
Pitched Organized Baseball's longest shutout, a 24-inning 1-0 win for San Francisco over Jimmy Wiggs of Oakland, June 8, 1909.

Year	Club	League	G	IP	W	L	H	R	ER	BB	SO	ERA
1904	Sacramento	Calif	-	-	3	1	-	-	-	-	-	-
1905	San Francisco	P C	49	431	24	19	346	156	-	100	173	-
1906	San Francisco	P C	8	-	4	4	-	-	-	-	-	-
	Pueblo	Western	13	114	8	5	142	66	-	34	45	-
	Sacramento	Calif	2	17	0	2	18	8	-	3	7	-
1907	San Francisco	P C	**56**	-	24	15	-	134	-	103	197	-
1908	San Francisco	P C	54	-	20	18	-	147	-	84	151	-
1909	San Francisco	P C	46	-	31	10	-	90	-	71	188	-
1910	San Francisco	P C	57	-	**34**	19	-	127	-	76	224	-
1911	San Francisco	P C	45	321	17	14	-	121	-	76	158	-
1912	San Francisco	P C	45	324	14	23	-	134	-	54	161	-
1913	San Francisco	P C	40	253	15	15	242	97	-	56	106	-
1914	Venice	P C	37	269	17	13	249	110	83	59	109	2.78
1915	Vernon	P C	42	276	15	21	252	120	85	50	96	2.77
		Minors	**494**	**2005**	**223**	**178**	**1249**	**1310**	**168**	**766**	**1615**	**-**

CARMEN PROCTOR HILL
Born October 1, 1895 at Royalton, MN. Died January 1, 1990 at Indianapolis, IN.
Height 6' 1", Weight 185. Threw right. Batted right.

Year	Club	League	G	IP	W	L	H	R	ER	BB	SO	ERA
1914	Warren	Inter-St				No record available						
1915	Youngstown	Central	37	291	19	12	248	95	74	86	146	2.29
	Pittsburgh	National	8	47	2	1	42	9	6	13	24	1.15
1916	Pittsburgh	National	2	6	0	0	11	10	6	5	5	9.00
	Rochester	Int	35	258	14	16	227	-	55	98	129	1.92
1917	Birmingham	South A	42	220	26	12	253	102	78	85	109	3.19
1918	Birmingham	South A	18	130	7	9	125	45	-	37	39	-
	Kansas City	A A	5	33	3	1	25	9	7	8	10	1.91
	Pittsburgh	National	6	44	2	3	24	11	6	17	15	1.23
1919	Pittsburgh	National	4	5	0	0	12	5	5	1	1	9.00
	Indianapolis	A A	26	182	14	9	188	74	59	52	64	2.92
1920-21				Did not play in O. B.								
1922	Indianapolis	A A	35	210	15	12	214	91	76	66	93	3.26
	New York	National	8	28	2	1	33	15	15	5	6	4.82
1923	Indianapolis	A A	44	263	12	21	331	181	144	72	100	4.93
1924	Indianapolis	A A	45	213	17	14	235	121	94	56	66	3.97
1925	Indianapolis	A A	37	251	16	15	237	130	109	61	100	3.91
1926	Indianapolis	A A	39	264	21	7	274	110	95	59	106	3.24
	Pittsburgh	National	6	40	3	3	42	17	15	9	8	3.38
1927	Pittsburgh	National	43	278	22	11	260	125	100	80	95	3.24
1928	Pittsburgh	National	36	237	16	10	229	110	93	81	73	3.53
1929	Pitt/St. Lou	National	30	88	2	3	104	51	43	43	29	4.40
1930	St. Louis	National	4	15	0	1	12	12	12	13	8	7.20
	Minneapolis	A A	36	128	8	9	174	102	86	42	54	6.05
1931	Rochester	Int	37	220	18	12	191	93	74	61	94	3.03
1932	Colum/Minn	A A	42	183	12	13	252	128	-	66	45	-
		Majors	**147**	**788**	**49**	**33**	**769**	**365**	**301**	**267**	**264**	**3.44**
		Minors	**478**	**2846**	**202**	**162**	**2974**	**1281**	**951**	**849**	**1155**	**3.38**

HAROLD ASHLEY HILLIN
(Known by middle name.)
Born September 7, 1904 at Mt. Calm, TX.
Height 6' 2", Weight 195. Threw right. Batted both.
Set Texas League season record with 31 wins in 1937; League Most Valuable Pitcher in 1934 and Most Valuable Player in 1937.

Year	Club	League	G	IP	W	L	H	R	ER	BB	SO	ERA
1927	Palestine	LoneStar	26	167	13	8	161	72	43	77	80	2.32
	Wichita Falls	Texas	2	15	0	2	18	12	12	13	2	7.20
1928	Abilene	W Texas	35	218	11	14	236	133	97	99	128	4.00
1929	Spartanburg	Sally	42	305	18	16	281	141	112	123	104	3.30
1930	Wichita Falls	Texas	26	88	6	4	105	66	44	53	38	4.50
1931	Wichita Falls	Texas	37	251	12	17	243	113	87	85	73	3.12
1932	Milwaukee	A A	50	254	15	15	332	183	142	99	59	5.03
1933	Milwaukee	A A	50	204	4	15	264	159	136	102	81	6.00
1934	San Antonio	Texas	47	295	**24**	12	332	143	120	87	137	3.66
1935	San Antonio	Texas	48	275	14	18	279	127	118	91	88	3.86
1936	San Antonio	Texas	44	211	11	20	233	112	96	77	84	4.09
1937	Ok City	Texas	**62**	302	**31**	10	271	104	79	95	120	**2.35**
1938	Ok City	Texas	50	275	**23**	10	276	119	91	90	70	2.98
1939	Okla City	Texas	40	147	4	13	173	85	61	69	58	3.73
1940	Fort Worth	Texas	47	215	11	17	265	143	117	79	60	4.90
1941	Fort Worth	Texas	7	25	0	0	36	17	13	7	9	4.68
1942-46			Did not play in O. B.									
1947	Waco	Big St	19	111	4	10	140	87	68	47	41	5.51
		Minors	**632**	**3358**	**201**	**201**	**3645**	**1816**	**1436**	**1293**	**1232**	**3.85**

ROY WESLEY HITT
Born June 22, 1884 at Carleton, NE. Died February 8, 1956 at Pomona, CA.
Height 5' 10", Weight 200. Threw left. Batted left.

Year	Club	League	G	IP	W	L	H	R	ER	BB	SO	ERA
1903	Oakland	P C	3	14	1	0	9	6	-	19	8	-
1904	Los Ang/SF	P C	2	9	0	2	14	10	-	4	3	-
1905	Fresno	Calif	11	-	4	7	-	-	-	-	-	-
	San Francisco	P C	42	346	24	14	245	99	-	122	218	-
1906	San Francisco	P C	50	-	31	12	-	-	-	-	-	-
1907	Cincinnati	National	21	153	6	10	143	72	58	56	63	3.41
1908	Columbus	A A	10	46	4	2	54	27	-	13	10	-
1909	Vernon	P C	47	-	15	29	-	143	-	114	197	-
1910	Vernon	P C	49	-	26	18	-	105	-	98	135	-
1911	Vernon	P C	45	290	21	15	-	121	-	77	125	-
1912	Vernon	P C	42	314	21	12	-	127	-	92	149	-
1913	Venice	P C	53	320	22	15	310	116	-	73	142	-
1914	Venice	P C	46	364	25	18	306	104	83	116	152	2.05
1915	Vernon	P C	46	258	15	11	257	89	72	56	88	2.51
1916	Vernon	P C	4	8	0	1	7	2	0	4	2	0.00
		Majors	**21**	**153**	**6**	**10**	**143**	**72**	**58**	**56**	**63**	**3.41**
		Minors	**450**	**1969**	**209**	**156**	**1202**	**949**	**155**	**788**	**1229**	**-**

BERLYN DALE HORNE
Born April 12, 1899 at Bachman, OH. Died February 3, 1983 at Franklin, OH.
Height 5' 9", Weight 155. Threw right. Batted right.

Year	Club	League	G	IP	W	L	H	R	ER	BB	SO	ERA
1917	Jacksonville	Sally	25	177	11	11	161	74	-	74	93	-
1918		Military Service										
1919	Battle Creek	Mich-Ont	34	245	19	9	239	107	71	62	119	2.61
1920	Battle Creek	Mich-Ont	33	223	8	15	242	-	76	67	114	3.07
1921	Port H/Sarnia	Mich-Ont	33	233	16	13	208	-	85	111	97	3.28
1922	Port H/Sarnia	Mich-Ont	16	104	6	7	135	-	51	41	44	4.41
1923	Saginaw	Mich-Ont	27	149	7	8	186	90	64	62	63	3.87
1924	Saginaw	Mich-Ont	22	132	11	4	134	67	41	51	57	2.80
	Rochester	Int	20	112	3	11	127	71	57	51	30	4.58
1925	Rochester	Int	40	252	13	12	282	142	108	97	93	3.86
1926	Rochester	Int	42	241	15	16	269	144	114	87	111	4.26
1927	Rochester	Int	37	199	18	10	212	117	106	82	67	4.79
1928	Jersey City	Int	44	266	16	17	258	146	89	140	137	3.01
1929	Chicago	National	11	23	1	1	24	20	13	21	6	5.09
	Los Angeles	P C	9	49	5	4	63	35	33	24	27	6.06
1930	Los Angeles	P C	31	175	13	7	185	100	87	107	98	4.47
1931	Jersey City	Int	7	46	2	4	43	24	-	20	15	-
	Indianapolis	A A	30	136	9	9	149	87	68	61	66	4.50
1932	Indianapolis	A A	4	10	1	0	12	9	-	4	4	-
	Knoxville	South A	9	33	2	1	40	30	29	30	12	7.91
	Scranton	NY-Penn	7	44	2	4	42	24	-	18	10	-
	Omaha	Western	7	58	3	3	68	36	-	23	23	-
1933	Oakland/Sac	P C	23	142	9	7	140	63	55	50	86	3.49
1934	Sac/Missions	P C	44	114	7	7	116	88	55	38	52	4.34
1935	Miss/Holly	P C	39	174	13	7	196	97	77	50	73	3.98
1936	San Diego	P C	38	164	7	14	183	110	80	78	76	4.39
1937	Seattle	P C	26	64	1	3	69	35	32	36	40	4.50
	Wenatchee	West Int		Less than 45 innings								
1938	Yakima/Van	West Int	29	184	12	8	220	108	80	58	108	3.91
	Majors		**11**	**23**	**1**	**1**	**24**	**20**	**13**	**21**	**6**	**5.09**
	Minors		**676**	**3726**	**229**	**211**	**3979**	**1804**	**1458**	**1522**	**1715**	**3.87**

EDWARD CHARLES HOVLIK
Born August 20, 1891 at Cleveland, OH. Died March 19, 1955 at Painesville, OH.
Height 6', Weight 180. Threw right. Batted right.

Year	Club	League	G	IP	W	L	H	R	ER	BB	SO	ERA
1913	Charleston	Ohio St	36	-	24	11	-	-	-	-	-	-
1914	Waterbury	East A	28	-	14	10	155	83	-	113	109	-
1915	Erie	Central	30	223	16	10	170	86	60	108	154	2.42
	New Orleans	South A	5	23	1	1	26	15	-	20	15	-
1916	St. Joseph	Western	41	287	16	18	263	-	104	155	176	3.26
1917	St. Joseph	Western	28	173	12	10	137	78	-	87	108	-
	Vernon	P C	25	178	6	15	177	110	84	92	63	4.25
1918	Wichita	Western	22	172	13	6	136	47	35	67	128	1.83
	Washington	American	8	28	2	1	25	10	4	10	10	1.29
1919	Washington	Ameican	3	6	0	0	12	10	8	9	3	12.00
	Minneapolis	A A	32	208	10	18	202	113	82	96	91	3.55
1920	Minneapolis	A A	28	128	4	5	107	53	45	75	50	3.16

1921	St. Joseph	Western	40	300	16	16	320	191	-	128	139	-
1922	St. Joseph	Western	44	268	18	12	313	163	-	108	142	-
1923	Wichita	Western	47	310	23	17	347	196	-	120	161	-
1924	Wichita	Western	47	317	20	17	341	191	-	139	144	-
1925	Wichita	Western	49	231	11	18	311	215	-	110	76	-
1926	Beaumont	Texas	29	159	9	8	173	91	68	58	50	3.85
1927	Beumont	Texas	5	24	0	1	40	27	24	14	6	9.00
	Bloom/Quin	III	30	192	11	13	212	126	112	80	70	5.25
	Majors		**11**	**34**	**2**	**1**	**37**	**20**	**12**	**19**	**13**	**3.18**
	Minors		**566**	**3193**	**224**	**206**	**3430**	**1785**	**614**	**1570**	**1682**	**-**

THOMAS L. HUGHES

Born January 28, 1884 at Coal Creek, CO. Died November 1, 1961 at Los Angeles, CA.
Height 6' 2", Weight 180. Threw right. Batted right.
Pitched no-hit games for NY AL in 1910 and Boston NL in 1916.

Year	Club	League	G	IP	W	L	H	R	ER	BB	SO	ERA
1904	Pitt/Topeka	Mo Val	47	-	10	26	-	-	-	86	172	-
1905	Topeka	West A	45	-	15	20	-	-	-	79	233	-
1906	Atlanta	South A	37	282	25	5	198	67	-	60	143	-
	New York	American	3	15	1	0	11	8	7	1	5	4.20
1907	New York	American	4	27	2	0	16	9	8	11	10	2.67
	Montreal	Eastern	36	262	14	17	215	106	-	96	131	-
1908	Newark	Eastern	30	247	16	9	170	73	-	61	161	-
1909	New York	American	24	119	7	8	109	42	35	37	69	2.65
1910	New York	American	23	152	7	9	153	77	59	37	64	3.49
1911	Rochester	Eastern	28	217	15	12	201	91	-	62	132	-
1912	Rochester	Int	35	239	17	10	239	106	-	74	122	-
1913	Rochester	Int	32	239	15	13	222	104	-	74	146	-
1914	Rochester	Int	33	262	17	9	205	76	-	77	182	-
	Boston	National	2	17	1	0	14	7	5	4	11	2.65
1915	Boston	National	50	280	16	14	208	88	66	58	171	2.12
1916	Boston	National	40	161	16	3	121	46	42	51	97	2.35
1917	Boston	National	11	74	5	3	54	21	16	30	40	1.95
1918	Boston	National	3	18	0	2	17	8	7	6	9	3.50
1919	Los Angeles	P C	1	5	1	0	4	1	-	4	1	-
1920	Los Angeles	P C	23	94	7	4	78	49	38	42	47	3.64
1921	Los Angeles	P C	36	241	14	14	203	87	76	89	130	2.84
1922	Los Angeles	P C	31	231	17	9	212	95	79	88	95	3.08
1923	Los Angeles	P C	36	235	14	16	265	129	112	93	88	4.29
1924	Los Angeles	P C	31	208	12	14	229	129	108	99	73	4.67
1925	Los Angeles	P C	23	89	5	4	88	41	39	38	36	3.94
1926	Little Rock	South A	18	57	0	3	66	46	39	28	20	6.16
	Beau/San Ant	Texas	20	117	5	9	112	61	50	64	63	3.85
	Majors		**160**	**863**	**55**	**39**	**703**	**306**	**245**	**235**	**476**	**2.56**
	Minors		**542**	**3025**	**219**	**194**	**2707**	**1261**	**541**	**1214**	**1975**	**-**

WILLIAM ELMER JACOBS

Born August 10, 1892 at Salem, MO. Died February 10, 1958 at Salem MO.
Threw right. Batted right. Height 6', Weight 165.
Led PCL in shutouts 1928 and 1929.

Year	Club	League	G	IP	W	L	H	R	ER	BB	SO	ERA
1912	Clint/Kanka	Ill-Mo	36	265	14	19	243	125		83	149	
1913	Burlington	Cent	43	317	20	19	301	162		71	**230**	
1914	Philadelphia	National	14	51	1	3	65	39	27	20	17	4.76
1915	Albany	NY St	38		10	16	216	102		77	118	
1916	Pittsburgh	National	34	153	6	10	151	70	50	38	46	2.94
1917	Pittsburgh	National	38	227	6	19	214	87	71	76	58	2.81
1918	Pitts/Phil	National	26	146	9	6	122	57	48	56	35	2.96
1919	Phil/StL	National	34	214	9	16	231	96	79	69	68	3.32
1920	St.Louis	National	23	78	4	8	91	56	45	33	21	5.19
1921	Seattle	PC	41	292	19	14	311	140	119	87	124	3.67
1922	Seattle	PC	48	306	23	17	336	141	119	65	95	3.50
1923	Seattle	PC	44	312	24	10	333	138	109	91	143	3.14
1924	Chicago	National	38	190	11	12	181	93	79	72	50	3.74
1925	Chicago	National	18	56	2	3	63	37	32	22	19	5.14
	Los Angeles	PC	15	121	9	5	112	49	37	24	50	2.75
1926	Los Angeles	PC	40	278	20	12	254	98	68	69	103	**2.20**
1927	Chicago	American	25	74	2	4	105	49	38	37	22	4.62
1928	San Fransisco	PC	37	277	22	8	277	98	79	64	**159**	**2.57**
1929	San Fransisco	PC	38	290	21	11	324	145	112	63	130	3.48
1930	San Fransisco	PC	38	275	17	13	335	151	119	81	120	3.89
1931	San Fransisco	PC	30	217	12	11	236	113	96	51	78	3.98
1932	Memp/Knox	South A	24	129	9	8	150	77	68	49	23	4.74
		Majors	**250**	**1189**	**50**	**81**	**1223**	**584**	**469**	**423**	**336**	**3.55**
		Minors	**472**	**3079**	**220**	**163**	**3428**	**1539**	**926**	**875**	**1522**	**3.34**

EARL JOHNSON

Born November 1, 1896 at Fairmont, WV.
Height 6', Weight 185. Threw right. Batted right.

Year	Club	League	G	IP	W	L	H	R	ER	BB	SO	ERA
1920	Cedartown	Ga St	36	252	20	8	238	106	-	40	124	-
1921	Rochester	Int	9	44	3	3	61	30	21	6	11	4.30
1922	Hartford	Eastern	41	259	19	14	232	113	79	62	112	2.75
1923	Hartford	Eastern	45	251	16	10	214	120	79	58	104	2.83
1924	Hartford	Eastern	46	305	20	12	268	96	77	79	99	2.27
1925	Hartford	Eastern	50	350	23	17	321	120	95	70	147	2.44
1926	Hart/Albany	Eastern	39	197	16	17	296	145	112	75	81	5.12
1927	Albany	Eastern	41	307	23	10	303	110	99	64	98	2.90
1928	Albany	Eastern	45	276	21	8	274	104	84	45	67	2.74
1929	Albany	Eastern	45	286	21	13	353	157	137	66	73	4.31
1930	Albany	Eastern	19	110	8	4	134	67	58	28	33	4.75
	W-B/York	NY-Penn	20	123	9	8	152	78	65	30	67	4.76
1931	York	NY-Penn	35	255	19	13	294	116	96	51	126	3.39
1932	York	NY-Penn	37	206	14	12	215	99	77	60	89	3.36
1933	Wilkes-Barre	NY-Penn	34	221	20	10	221	89	70	61	62	2.85
1934	Wilkes-Barre	NY-Penn	13	85	5	7	106	49	46	17	15	4.87
1935	Wilkes-Barre	NY-Penn	44	221	11	13	267	121	110	50	42	4.48
		Minors	**599**	**3748**	**268**	**179**	**3949**	**1720**	**1305**	**862**	**1350**	**3.36**

CLAUDE ALFORD JONNARD
Born November 23, 1897 at Nashville, TN. Died August 27, 1959 at Nashville, TN.
Height 6' 1", Weight 165. Threw right. Batted right.
Twin brother of Clarence James Jonnard, pro-player 1917-36.

Year	Club	League	G	IP	W	L	H	R	ER	BB	SO	ERA
1917	Talladega	Ga-Ala	3	31	2	0	26	10	-	10	16	-
	Nashville	South A	5	23	1	2	24	17	12	5	13	4.70
1918	Nashville	South A	12	81	3	6	95	-	-	38	34	-
1919	Nashville	South A	34	270	13	19	230	92	70	71	134	2.33
1920	Nashville/LR	South A	47	283	13	17	246	118	-	74	129	-
1921	Little Rock	South A	**58**	**347**	22	19	336	139	89	146	**234**	2.31
	New York	National	1	4	0	0	4	0	0	0	7	0.00
1922	Indianapolis	A A	9	75	7	1	63	25	18	24	41	2.16
	New York	National	33	96	6	1	96	45	41	28	44	3.84
1923	New York	National	**45**	96	4	3	105	45	35	35	45	3.28
1924	New York	National	34	90	4	5	80	33	24	24	40	2.40
1925	Toledo	A A	47	**333**	22	**19**	319	155	125	126	127	3.38
1926	St. Louis	American	12	36	0	2	46	27	24	24	13	6.00
	Milwaukee	A A	22	163	9	9	160	77	64	67	71	3.53
1927	Milwaukee	A A	44	282	22	14	297	162	131	**136**	176	4.18
1928	Milwaukee	A A	41	299	20	11	301	136	109	85	**150**	3.28
1929	Chicago	National	12	28	0	1	41	27	23	11	11	7.39
	Indianapolis	A A	13	108	6	5	96	42	35	43	58	2.92
1930	Indianapolis	A A	34	232	11	17	285	164	147	85	122	5.70
1931	Milwaukee	A A	43	240	11	15	281	163	138	91	**130**	5.18
1932	Louisville	A A	40	249	18	15	294	150	-	91	135	-
1933	Louisville	A A	20	48	1	7	72	49	43	29	25	8.06
1934	Fort Worth	Texas	24	173	8	14	169	93	73	46	80	3.80
1935	Fort Worth	Texas	33	222	13	16	229	120	84	73	91	3.41
1936	Fort W/Dallas	Texas	22	69	4	4	93	44	40	30	26	5.22
	Longview	E Texas	6	43	2	2	54	25	18	9	19	3.77
1937	Galveston	Texas	37	135	7	5	105	77	52	88	46	3.47
1938	Shreveport	Texas	3	4	0	0	1	-	-	1	2	-
1939	Joplin	West A	15	57	4	1	58	16	-	16	36	-
1940	Amarillo	W Tex-N. Mex	4	16	0	1		-	-	-	-	-
-												
	Majors		**137**	**350**	**14**	**12**	**372**	**177**	**147**	**122**	**160**	**3.78**
	Minors		**616**	**3783**	**219**	**219**	**3834**	**1874**	**1248**	**1384**	**1895**	**-**

CHARLES SAMUEL "RUBE" KISSINGER
(Correct family name is Kisinger.)
Born December 13, 1876 at Adrian, MI. Died July 14, 1941 at Huron, OH.
Height 6', Weight 190. Threw right. Batted right.

Year	Club	League	G	IP	W	L	H	R	ER	BB	SO	ERA
1901	Toledo	West A	1	9	0	1	12	7	-	3	3	-
1902	Detroit	American	5	43	2	3	48	20	15	14	7	3.14
1903	Detroit	American	16	119	7	9	118	58	39	27	33	2.95
	Toronto	Eastern	19	161	11	7	107	34	-	29	119	-
1904	Buffalo	Eastern	38	289	24	11	258	95	-	55	132	-
1905	Buffalo	Eastern	39	317	20	15	289	145	-	82	157	-
1906	Buffalo	Eastern	38	319	23	12	273	113	-	61	171	-
1907	Buffalo	Eastern	34	254	15	10	205	86	-	63	113	-

Year	Club	League	G	IP	W	L	H	R	ER		BB	SO	ERA
1908	Buffalo	Eastern	34	256	16	14	193	87	-		61	117	-
1909	Buffalo	Eastern	44	309	18	19	271	100	-		74	125	-
1910	Buffalo/JC	Eastern	34	237	16	7	172	81	-		68	110	-
1911	Jersey City	Eastern	35	182	7	13	179	90	-		53	93	-
1912	Memphis	South A	31	267	14	17	237	102	-		62	161	-
1913	Memphis	South A	32	243	13	14	218	106	-		71	139	-
1914	Atlanta/NO	South A	28	209	13	9	167	60	-		55	111	-
1915	Nashville	South lA	28	218	14	11	181	73	-		81	77	-
1916	New Orleans	South A	2	12	1	0	14	14	-		10	2	-
		Majors	**21**	**162**	**9**	**12**	**166**	**78**	**54**		**41**	**40**	**3.00**
		Minors	**437**	**3282**	**205**	**160**	**2776**	**1193**	**-**		**828**	**1630**	**-**

FREDERICK AUGUSTUS KLOBEDANZ
Born June 13, 1871 at Waterbury, CT. Died April 12, 1940 at Waterbury, CT.
Height 5' 11", Weight 190. Threw left. Batted left.
Because of his batting ability, also played first base and outfield. Hit .377 and .357 for Fall River in 1895 and 1896.

Year	Club	League	G	IP	W	L	H	R	ER	BB	SO	ERA
1892	Portland	New Eng	29	244	18	10	233	139	55	59	150	2.03
1893	Port/Lew/Dov	New Eng	26	200	10	13	235	175	107	88	95	4.82
1894	Fall River	New Eng	24	203	14	7	187	109	42	64	105	1.86
1895	Waterbury	Conn St	2	17	0	2	36	33	-	4	5	-
	Fall River	New Eng	39	321	27	11	325	159	73	110	124	2.05
1896	Fall River	New Eng	34	280	26	6	298	159	79	78	132	2.54
	Boston	National	10	81	6	4	69	41	27	31	26	3.00
1897	Boston	National	38	309	26	7	344	193	158	125	92	4.60
1898	Boston	National	35	271	19	10	281	170	117	99	51	3.89
1899	Boston	National	5	33	1	4	39	23	18	9	8	4.91
	Worcester	Eastern	26	200	16	8	221	128	79	59	95	3.56
1900	Worcester	Eastern	42	337	21	17	360	181	-	56	93	-
1901	Worcester	Eastern	37	298	18	15	340	170	-	61	108	-
1902	Lawrence	New Eng	39	320	26	10	268	114	46	77	185	1.29
	Boston	National	1	8	1	0	9	1	1	2	4	1.13
1903	Lawrence	New Eng	26	204	11	13	198	111	53	34	116	2.34
1904	Law/New Bed	New Eng	44	375	18	23	391	200	74	58	159	1.78
1905	New Bedford	New Eng	20	153	11	7	150	76	-	30	64	-
1906	New Bedford	New Eng	32	244	18	10	243	115	-	51	141	-
1907	New Bedford	New Eng	4	34	1	1	29	12	-	10	16	-
1908	Brockton	New Eng	4	26	0	3	30	17	13	5	12	4.50
		Majors	**89**	**702**	**53**	**25**	**742**	**428**	**321**	**266**	**181**	**4.12**
		Minors	**428**	**3456**	**235**	**156**	**3544**	**1898**	**621**	**844**	**1600**	**-**

LOUIS PAUL LEROY
Born February 18, 1879 at Red Springs, WI. Died October 10, 1944 at Shawano, WI.
Height 5' 10", Weight 180. Threw right. Batted right.
Leroy was a Seneca Indian who attended the Carlisle Indian School in Pennsylvania.

Year	Club	League	G	IP	W	L	H	R	ER	BB	SO	ERA
1902	Buffalo	Eastern	20	-	13	5	-	-	-	37	54	-
1903	Buffalo	Eastern	18	-	6	4	81	-	-	24	55	-
1904	Montreal	Eastern	31	245	14	10	207	104	-	57	87	-
1905	Montreal	Eastern	32	250	18	12	198	106	-	53	166	-

Fred Klobedanz   **Rube Kissinger**

Carmen Hill and Lee Meadows were a "spectacular" pitching duo for the pennant-winning Pirates in 1927. It was then rare for any player to wear glasses. Hill won 22 games and Meadows 19. (Hill's record is on page 160.)

Year	Club	League	G	IP	W	L	H	R	ER	BB	SO	ERA
	New York	American	3	24	1	1	26	14	10	1	9	3.75
1906	New York	American	11	45	3	0	33	18	11	12	28	2.20
	Montreal	Eastern	21	177	6	14	177	99	-	53	87	-
1907	St. Paul	A A	40	302	14	22	327	-	-	80	133	-
1908	St. Paul	A A	49	332	16	21	321	160	-	69	144	-
1909	St. Paul	A A	57	372	20	17	291	107	-	72	179	-
1910	Boston	American	1	4	0	0	6	8	5	2	3	11.25
	St. Paul	A A	46	268	14	16	221	91	-	53	89	-
1911	St. Paul	A A	60	300	18	23	315	159	-	80	131	-
1912	St. Paul	A A	44	277	20	10	297	142	-	51	117	-
1913	St. Paul/Ind	A A	44	235	11	20	251	122	-	50	90	-
1914	Indianapolis	A A	44	201	12	5	226	101	73	50	54	3.27
1915	Salt Lake City	P C	30	143	6	9	165	86	63	50	55	3.97
	St. Paul	A A	11	57	3	2	52	21	19	16	24	3.00
1916	Springfield	Eastern	23	137	10	8	134	-	-	45	39	-
	Muskegon	Central	8	47	3	3	52	19	10	12	14	1.91
1917	Joplin	Western	1	3	0	1	6	4	-	1	1	-
	La Crosse	Cent A	20	129	10	7	101	46	39	30	35	2.72
1918	St. Paul	A A	3	19	0	2	23	9	8	8	8	3.79
	Seattle	P C Int	14	108	7	5	94	45	-	31	61	-
1919						No record available						
1920	Mitchell	S Dak	26	200	18	6	207	103	-	45	79	-
	Majors		**15**	**73**	**4**	**1**	**65**	**40**	**26**	**15**	**40**	**3.21**
	Minors		**642**	**3802**	**239**	**222**	**3746**	**1524**	**212**	**967**	**1702**	**-**

RAY WALTER LINDSAY
Born December 5, 1907 at Sevier County, TN.
Height 6' 1", Weight 175. Threw right. Batted right.
Had impressive ratio of strikeouts to walks for career, 1904 to 490.

Year	Club	League	G	IP	W	L	H	R	ER	BB	SO	ERA
1937	Newton/Con	N Car St	20	157	11	7	146	62	57	38	152	3.27
1938	Thomasville	N Car St	34	245	19	9	210	98	74	70	**247**	2.72
1939	Thomasville	N Car St	35	**271**	22	10	234	91	57	35	**237**	**1.89**
1940	Thomasville	N Car St	38	**270**	**20**	11	279	91	58	48	**269**	1.93
1941	Thomasville	N Car St	34	240	17	13	233	118	78	49	189	2.93
1942-45					Military Service							
1946	Lexington	N Car St	14	114	9	4	112	43	29	19	105	2.29
	Martinsville	Carolina	10	51	2	3	61	41	-	13	18	-
1947	Martinsville	Carolina	32	219	11	17	231	122	90	70	168	3.70
1948	Newton/Con	W Carol	36	**263**	**21**	9	**262**	153	122	69	**255**	4.17
1949	Newton/Con	W Carol	35	231	17	11	222	116	91	58	200	3.55
1950	Newton/Con	W Carol			Did not play							
1951	Newton/Con	W Carol	6	39	4	1	40	14	11	12	36	2.54
1952	Hickory	W Carol	4	33	1	3	34	22	19	9	28	5.18
	Minors		**298**	**2133**	**154**	**98**	**2064**	**971**	**686**	**490**	**1904**	**2.97**

GROVER CLEVELAND LOWDERMILK

Born January 15, 1885 at Sanborn, IN. Died March 31, 1968 at Odin, IL.
Height 6' 4", Weight 190. Threw right. Batted right.
Brother of Louis Lowdermilk, former O. B. pitcher.
Struck out a minor league season record 465 batters in 1907.

Year	Club	League	G	IP	W	L	H	R	ER	BB	SO	ERA
1907	Decatur	III	1	9	0	1	11	12	-	2	7	-
	Mattoon	East Ill	44	**388**	**33**	10	179	62	40	116	**458**	0.93
1908	Decatur	III	32	217	12	10	131	85	-	124	183	-
1909	St. Louis	National	7	29	0	2	28	27	20	30	14	6.21
	Decatur	III	10	78	5	4	41	16	-	42	48	-
1910	Springfield	III	45	334	25	9	211	101	-	141	209	-
1911	St. Louis	National	11	33	0	1	37	27	27	33	15	7.36
1912	Louisville	A A	43	271	17	16	229	128	-	141	155	-
	Chicago	National	2	13	0	1	17	18	14	14	8	9.69
1913	Louisville	A A	51	304	20	14	235	104	-	137	**197**	-
1914	Louisville	A A	42	284	18	16	224	110	90	159	**254**	2.85
1915	St. Louis/Det	American	45	250	13	18	200	126	90	157	148	3.24
1916	Detroit/Clev	American	11	52	1	5	52	33	18	48	28	3.12
	Portland	P C	7	38	1	4	26	25	16	25	18	3.79
1917	Columbus	A A	50	355	25	14	254	97	67	128	**250**	**1.70**
	St. Louis	American	3	19	2	1	16	6	3	4	9	1.42
1918	St. Louis	American	13	80	2	6	74	44	28	38	25	3.15
1919	St. Louis/Chi	American	27	109	5	5	101	46	31	47	49	2.56
1920	Chicago	American	3	5	0	0	9	4	4	5	0	7.20
	Minneapolis	A A	31	223	14	12	337	112	74	**151**	119	2.99
1921	Minneapolis	A A	25	166	11	9	149	107	77	117	128	4.17
1922	Columbus	A A	7	32	0	2	29	20	-	27	15	-
		Majors	**122**	**590**	**23**	**39**	**534**	**331**	**235**	**376**	**296**	**3.58**
		Minors	**388**	**2699**	**181**	**121**	**2056**	**979**	**364**	**1310**	**2041**	**-**

WILLIAM FRANCIS LUDOLPH

Born January 21, 1900 at San Francisco, CA. Died April 7, 1952 at Oakland, CA.
Height 6' 1", Weight 170. Threw right. Batted right.

Year	Club	League	G	IP	W	L	H	R	ER	BB	SO	ERA
1921	San Francisco	P C	4	18	1	0	15	12	6	9	6	3.00
	Sioux Falls	Dakota	18	157	11	5	98	52	34	80	90	1.95
1922	Sioux Falls	Dakota	19	151	12	6	102	55	37	52	84	2.21
1923	Sioux Falls	S Dak	13	101	8	3	75	43	25	47	65	2.23
	Bay City	Mich-Ont	11	86	9	1	69	28	20	37	54	2.09
1924	Vernon	P C	26	138	7	10	148	91	71	36	45	4.63
	Detroit	American	3	6	0	0	5	3	3	2	1	4.50
1925	Vernon	P C	42	266	13	12	287	125	108	89	60	3.65
1926	Missions	P C	43	253	15	13	259	125	107	88	85	3.81
1927	Missions	P C	41	238	9	20	287	145	133	72	74	5.03
1928	Missions	P C	8	49	2	4	57	24	18	17	12	3.31
	Little Rock	South A	29	189	12	10	236	111	99	63	43	4.71
1929	Birmingham	South A	36	239	21	8	260	106	96	69	71	3.62
1930	Birmingham	South A	33	210	14	9	253	125	110	74	40	4.71
1931	Oakland	P C	39	184	10	12	229	126	101	50	72	4.94
1932	Oakland	P C	38	271	16	14	269	112	83	62	99	2.76
1933	Oakland	P C	38	262	19	9	277	121	90	59	74	**3.09**

1934	Oakland	P C	37	231	16	12	262	112	102	53	58	3.97
1935	Oakland	P C	37	283	20	13	309	109	97	40	74	3.08
1936	Oakland	P C	33	250	21	6	230	84	75	45	80	2.70
1937	Oakland	P C	12	99	7	4	85	31	27	24	35	2.45
		Majors	**3**	**6**	**0**	**0**	**5**	**3**	**3**	**2**	**1**	**4.50**
		Minors	**557**	**3675**	**243**	**171**	**3807**	**1737**	**1439**	**1066**	**1221**	**3.52**

JAPHET MONROE "RED" LYNN

Born December 27, 1913 at Kenney, TX. Died October 27, 1977 at Bellville, TX.
Height 6', Weight 162. Threw right. Batted right.
Led Minors with 32 wins in 1937.
Manager: Lubbock WTNM 1954

Year	Club	League	G	IP	W	L	H	R	ER	BB	SO	ERA
1934	Huntington	Mid Atl	26	145	10	7	140	70	56	52	98	3.48
	Springfield	Central	3	22	1	2	29	20	-	13	13	-
1935	Asheville	Piedmont	9	49	3	4	56	44	29	26	25	5.33
	Jacksonville	W Dixie	23	168	10	7	151	89	61	50	106	3.27
1936	Columbus	Sally	33	162	14	7	190	110	87	78	92	4.83
	Huntington	Mid Atl	8	44	3	3	39	26	25	27	28	5.11
1937	Jacksonville	E Texas	**56**	**340**	**32**	13	274	132	100	**143**	233	**2.65**
1938	Columbus	A A	**50**	175	8	11	173	112	86	78	104	4.42
1939	Detroit	American	4	8	0	1	11	8	8	3	3	9.00
	New York	National	26	50	1	0	44	21	17	21	22	3.06
1940	New York	National	33	42	4	3	40	21	18	24	25	3.86
1941	Jersey City	Int	30	109	6	7	111	56	50	56	60	4.13
1942	Los Angeles	P C	43	211	12	13	172	89	73	67	108	3.11
1943	Los Angeles	P C	36	248	21	8	218	77	68	64	110	2.47
1944	Chicago	National	22	84	5	4	80	41	38	37	35	4.07
1945		Military Service										
1946	Los Angeles	P C	41	271	17	16	200	85	84	**123**	165	2.79
1947	Los Angeles	P C	42	273	16	16	251	112	102	110	145	3.36
1948	Los Angeles	P C	42	244	19	10	236	108	101	114	131	3.73
1949	L.A./Port	P C	37	194	10	18	203	104	100	95	85	4.64
1950	Portland	P C	41	239	14	10	218	105	94	92	117	3.54
1951	Portland	P C	41	192	13	12	190	97	80	87	68	3.75
1952	Port/Holly	P C	39	121	9	6	130	65	57	56	30	4.24
1953	Hollywood	P C	53	143	10	4	158	78	59	63	42	3.71
1954	Lubbock	WTNM	6	29	1	3	32	21	13	9	27	4.03
	Beaumont	Texas	8	25	0	3	36	21	19	9	12	6.84
1955		Did not play in O.B.										
1956	Bakersfield	Calif	24	140	12	9	162	95	79	52	72	5.08
	Salt Lake City	Pioneer	5	42	3	2	51	23	19	10	29	4.07
		Majors	**85**	**184**	**10**	**8**	**175**	**91**	**81**	**85**	**85**	**3.96**
		Minors	**696**	**3586**	**244**	**191**	**3420**	**1739**	**1442**	**1474**	**1900**	**3.64**

●

Three future Hall of Fame members led the Minneapolis Millers to an 11-0 victory over Columbus May 1, 1951. Hoyt Wilhelm pitched the shutout at Nicollet Field and hit a two-run double. Third baseman Ray Dandridge collected four hits, including a home run, and youhg Willie Mays had three hits and made a spectacular catch and throw in center field.

JOHN WALTER MAILS
(Known by middle name.)
Born October 1, 1895 at San Quentin, CA. Died July 5, 1974 at San Francisco, CA.
Height 6', Weight 200.Threw left. Batted left.
Manager: Eugene Far West 1951.

Year	Club	League	G	IP	W	L	H	R	ER	BB	SO	ERA
1914	Seattle	NWestern	14	45	2	2	29	18	-	32	24	-
1915	Seattle	NWestern	39	348	24	18	275	133	-	154	250	-
	Brooklyn	National	2	5	0	1	6	5	2	5	3	3.60
1916	Brooklyn	National	11	17	0	1	15	7	7	9	13	3.71
1917	Portland	P C	7	49	3	2	28	14	12	37	18	2.20
1918						Military Service						
1919	Seat/Sacra	P C	47	301	19	17	265	116	105	99	134	3.14
1920	Sacramento	P C	43	292	18	17	228	140	104	187	105	3.21
	Cleveland	American	9	63	7	0	54	18	13	18	25	1.86
1921	Cleveland	American	34	194	14	8	210	103	85	89	87	3.94
1922	Cleveland	American	26	104	4	7	122	69	61	40	54	5.28
1923	Oakland	P C	49	356	23	18	338	141	117	125	206	2.96
1924	Oakland	P C	56	382	24	22	388	198	158	140	190	3.72
1925	St. Louis	National	21	131	7	7	145	78	67	58	49	4.60
1926	St. Louis	National	1	1	0	1	2	1	0	1	1	0.00
	Syracuse	Int	10	44	1	2	52	29	22	26	17	4.50
	San Francisco	P C	27	176	9	13	207	106	82	54	54	4.19
1927	San Francisco	P C	40	217	11	11	240	123	106	75	102	4.40
1928	San Francisco	P C	45	277	20	12	316	151	122	101	152	3.96
1929	San Francisco	P C	38	250	15	16	306	152	135	103	119	4.86
1930	Portland	P C	39	234	11	16	259	138	114	112	144	4.38
1931	Portland	P C	37	212	13	13	234	136	118	140	124	5.01
1932	Chattanooga	South A	33	198	17	9	203	101	89	78	86	4.05
1933	Kansas City	A A	24	140	9	8	148	69	59	58	79	3.79
1934	San Francisco	P C	30	167	4	13	189	79	77	62	74	4.15
1935	San Francisco	P C	16	41	3	1	52	26	22	19	16	4.83
1936	San Francisco	P C	8	10	0	0	21	17	-	10	5	-
		Majors	**104**	**515**	**32**	**25**	**554**	**281**	**235**	**220**	**232**	**4.11**
		Minors	**602**	**3739**	**226**	**210**	**3778**	**1887**	**1442**	**1612**	**1899**	**3.89**

LEON ALLEN MANGUM
Born May 24, 1898 at Durham, NC. Died July 9, 1974 at Lima, OH.
Height 6' 1", Weight 187. Threw right. Batted right.

Year	Club	League	G	IP	W	L	H	R	ER	BB	SO	ERA
1920	Albany	Eastern	25	175	8	11	169	72	57	61	70	2.93
	Portsmouth	Virginia	8	63	5	3	49	21	12	13	30	1.71
1921	Wichita Falls	Texas	1	7	0	0	13	6	-	0	4	-
	St. Joseph	Western	28	180	12	11	182	76	-	34	76	-
	Minneapolis	A A	12	70	8	1	71	33	25	29	22	3.21
1922	Minneapolis	A A	24	103	5	5	131	70	59	42	37	5.16
	St. Joseph	Western	17	109	5	7	126	62	-	32	39	-
1923	Minneapolis	A A	11	51	4	2	48	27	25	19	17	4.41
	St. Joseph	Western	32	216	12	11	262	116	-	60	77	-
1924	Minneapolis	A A	31	182	14	7	170	83	72	53	57	3.56
	Chicago	American	13	47	1	4	69	43	37	25	12	7.09
1925	Chicago	American	7	15	1	0	25	24	13	6	6	7.80

Year	Club	League	G	IP	W	L	H	R	ER	BB	SO	ERA
	Reading	Int	26	165	9	8	190	87	71	46	53	3.87
1926	Portland	P C	53	328	19	20	354	162	140	88	106	3.84
1927	Buffalo	Int	35	238	21	7	255	98	88	40	67	3.33
1928	New York	National	1	3	0	0	6	5	5	5	1	15.00
	Buffalo	Int	30	231	15	11	263	89	73	38	73	2.84
1929	Buffalo	Int	35	208	15	13	263	122	109	39	57	4.72
1930	Buff/Newark	Int	38	222	10	19	287	145	124	49	70	5.03
1931	Newark	Int	35	225	14	9	252	104	96	47	55	3.84
1932	Montreal	Int	19	146	10	7	177	73	57	25	46	3.51
	Boston	National	7	10	0	0	17	8	6	0	3	5.40
1933	Boston	National	25	84	4	3	93	33	31	11	28	3.32
1934	Boston	National	29	94	5	3	127	67	60	23	28	5.74
1935	Boston	National	3	5	0	0	6	2	2	2	0	3.60
	Montreal	Int	22	110	3	5	128	78	67	37	36	5.48
1936	Syracuse	Int	36	222	10	15	250	122	103	43	71	4.18
1937	Syracuse/JC	Int	29	132	7	14	168	86	77	26	42	5.25
1938	W-B/Wmp	Eastern	15	53	1	5	66	29	22	4	19	3.74
	Clinton	III	7	43	3	3	66	25	-	8	13	-
	Majors		**85**	**258**	**11**	**10**	**343**	**182**	**154**	**72**	**78**	**5.37**
	Minors		**569**	**3479**	**210**	**194**	**3940**	**1786**	**1277**	**833**	**1137**	**3.93**

JOHN HOWARD MERRITT

(Known by middle name.)
Born October 12, 1894 at Tupelo, MS. Died November 3, 1955 at Tupelo, MS.
Height 5' 10", Weight 165. Threw left. Batted right.
Played part of one game in outfield for NY Giants in 1913.

Year	Club	League	G	IP	W	L	H	R	ER	BB	SO	ERA
1913	Clarksdale	Cottn St	22	155	6	13	138	60	-	22	123	-
	Knoxville	Appalach	12	88	8	3	70	18	-	23	49	-
	New York	National		Played outfield in one game								
1914	Memphis	South A	36	285	17	12	268	109	-	72	117	-
1915	Memphis	South A	48	311	20	15	313	126	-	83	114	-
1916	Memp/Chatt	South A	35	212	9	18	217	126	-	69	75	-
	San Antonio	Texas	5	42	1	1	29	14	-	19	14	-
1917	Chattanooga	South A	44	307	20	14	241	109	-	86	108	-
1918	Chattanooga	South A	19	137	7	9	130	69	-	27	42	-
	St. Paul	A A	10	66	6	3	60	20	11	13	30	1.50
1919	St. Paul	A A	42	258	19	9	245	105	75	59	113	2.62
1920	St. Paul	A A	47	291	21	10	285	107	85	81	106	2.63
1921	St. Paul	A A	48	287	19	14	290	137	120	117	115	3.76
1922	St. Paul	A A	38	164	9	9	177	112	92	87	72	5.05
1923	St. Paul	A A	51	310	20	11	318	142	116	94	120	3.37
1924	St. Paul	A A	47	277	19	17	333	163	144	86	99	4.68
1925	St. Paul	A A	47	160	6	13	196	104	85	60	42	4.78
1926	Atl/Mobile	South A	33	136	8	12	171	100	88	52	36	5.82
	Minors		**584**	**3486**	**215**	**183**	**3481**	**1621**	**816**	**1050**	**1375**	**-**

OTTO MERZ
Born 1889, at Red Bend, IL.
Height 5' 11-1/2'', Weight 180. Threw right. Batted right.

Year	Club	League	G	IP	W	L	H	R	ER	BB	SO	ERA
1910	Springfield	III	3	18	2	1	10	2	2	5	8	1.00
	Decatur	North A	18	-	9	6	-	-	-	-	-	-
	Newark	Ohio St	12	-	6	3	-	-	-	-	-	-
	Indianapolis	A A	9	69	4	1	67	32	-	26	26	-
1911	Indianapolis	A A	41	215	11	11	218	104	-	59	90	-
1912	Indianapolis	A A	44	280	9	25	274	142	-	81	95	-
1913	Indianapolis	A A	53	272	15	14	258	119	-	90	108	-
1914	Indianapolis	A A	48	214	20	19	311	136	91	88	78	3.83
1915	Indianapolis	A A	35	164	6	10	164	88	61	62	47	3.35
1916	Omaha	Western	36	250	18	11	242	-	68	59	105	2.45
1917	Omaha	Western	43	335	26	14	316	-	89	67	127	2.39
1918	Omaha	Western	15	110	6	6	82	35	21	36	25	1.72
1919	Omaha	Western	15	89	5	5	85	48	-	20	37	-
1920	Des Moines	Western	35	237	11	18	237	114	-	50	70	-
1921	Des Moines	Western	46	305	18	21	330	150	-	100	80	-
1922	Des Moines	Western	36	269	14	17	322	180	-	69	94	-
1923			Did not play in O. B.									
1924	Memphis	South A	41	246	20	6	242	112	87	73	66	3.18
1925	Memphis	South A	41	234	13	15	280	158	116	69	61	4.46
1926	Birmingham	South A	21	83	5	3	100	57	43	32	26	4.66
	Quincy	III	10	63	4	4	64	20	16	13	32	2.29
1927	Quincy	III	27	167	8	11	186	86	79	49	51	4.26
1928	Hattiesburg	Cottn St	6	40	3	3	49	22	17	8	8	3.83
1929	Columbus	SEastern	29	190	13	9	179	80	56	61	45	2.65
1930	Colum/Mont	SEastern	22	126	3	10	162	81	60	32	29	4.29
		Minors	**686**	**3976**	**249**	**243**	**4178**	**1766**	**806**	**1149**	**1308**	**-**

GEORGE EARL MILSTEAD
Born June 26, 1903 at Cleburne, TX. Died August 9, 1977 at Cleburne, TX.
Height 5' 10'', Weight 144. Threw left. Batted left.
Manager: Wichita Falls WTNM 1942; Henderson E Texas 1949; Lake Charles Gulf Cst 1950.

Year	Club	League	G	IP	W	L	H	R	ER	BB	SO	ERA
1921	Bonham	Tex-Okla	9	44	1	5	23	18	-	17	14	-
1922	Bonham	Tex-Okla	15	109	5	9	105	51	-	38	66	-
	Houston	Texas	13	73	1	5	74	46	37	35	26	4.56
1923	Decatur	III	7	25	1	3	30	22	-	16	9	-
	Sapulpa	SWestern	4	32	1	1	-	-	-	14	20	-
	Marshall	E Texas	20	157	9	8	122	66	-	43	139	-
1924	Marshall	E Texas	12	95	7	4	78	43	-	36	71	-
	Chicago	National	13	30	1	1	41	25	20	13	6	6.00
1925	Chicago	National	5	21	1	1	26	12	7	8	7	3.00
	Los Angeles	P C	27	72	2	4	88	57	45	35	32	5.63
1926	Chicago	National	18	55	1	5	63	30	22	24	14	3.60
1927	Toledo	A A	44	215	16	11	247	122	91	69	64	3.81
1928	Toledo	A A	18	37	0	2	57	36	-	13	15	-
	Birmingham	South A	11	41	3	2	49	-	17	16	16	3.73
	Balt/Buff	Int	4	24	0	3	30	20	-	10	4	-
1929	Nashville	SouthA	42	234	16	12	263	103	98	52	66	3.77

Year	Club	League	G	IP	W	L	H	R	ER	BB	SO	ERA
1930	Nashville	South A	38	223	12	13	272	157	138	86	90	5.57
1931	Nashville	South A	43	246	11	24	344	196	161	95	72	5.89
1932	Nashville	South A	3	12	1	1	16	11	-	7	1	-
	Albany	Int	38	225	10	17	269	121	114	77	93	4.56
1933	Albany/Buff	Int	41	187	5	14	224	130	111	67	69	5.34
1934	Buffalo	Int	30	149	10	8	179	90	81	48	44	4.89
1935	Fort Worth	Texas	35	213	9	18	214	100	79	75	82	3.34
1936	Tulsa	Texas	36	224	13	12	247	133	112	82	81	4.50
1937	Tulsa	Texas	34	180	14	9	188	82	68	67	86	3.40
1938	Tulsa	Texas	32	163	12	15	210	97	79	51	69	4.36
1939	Tulsa	Texas	35	200	10	12	207	91	78	47	62	3.51
1940	Tulsa/Ok City	Texas	5	8	1	1	14	10	8	2	6	9.00
1941	Fort Worth	Texas	2	1	0	0	2	1	-	0	1	-
	Cheyenne	Western	25	217	19	5	210	77	55	26	111	2.28
1942	WFalls/Pampa	WTNM	14	98	4	8	119	73	39	13	67	3.58
1943-46		Did not play in O. B.										
1947	Dallas	Texas	7	22	1	1	26	10	9	4	6	3.68
	Greenville	Big St	18	140	10	6	162	71	58	26	35	3.73
1948	Texarkana	Big St	27	82	8	5	91	50	38	25	16	4.17
	Gladewater	LoneStar	14	111	7	5	148	68	55	23	33	4.46
1949	Ballinger	Longhorn	3	7	1	1	7	4	4	6	3	5.14
	Henderson	E Texas	29	140	9	5	157	65	48	39	55	3.09
1950	Lake Charles	Gulf Cst	5	20	2	0	27	16	5	6	14	2.25
		Majors	**36**	**106**	**3**	**7**	**130**	**67**	**49**	**45**	**27**	**4.16**
		Minors	**740**	**4026**	**231**	**249**	**4499**	**2237**	**1628**	**1266**	**1638**	**4.20**

JOHN JOSEPH PAPPALAU

Born April 3, 1895 at Albany, NY. Died May 12, 1944 at Albany, NY.
Height 6', Weight 175. Threw right. Batted right.

Year	Club	League	G	IP	W	L	H	R	ER	BB	SO	ERA
1897	Cleveland	National	2	12	0	1	22	16	14	6	3	10.50
	GRapids/Milw	Western	20	167	8	11	232	187	70	73	39	3.77
1898	Springfield	Eastern	36	287	17	14	321	173	-	72	69	-
1899	Springfield	Eastern	40	336	19	21	356	221	-	102	78	-
1900	Springfield	Eastern	38	336	19	18	407	253	-	96	70	-
1901	Worcester	Eastern	35	290	17	17	320	171	-	66	65	-
1902	Worc/Tor	Eastern	27	216	12	12	206	99	-	53	42	-
1903	Worc/Mont	Eastern	28	224	9	13	246	143	-	42	87	-
1904	Montreal	Eastern	35	289	18	14	273	127	-	77	79	-
1905	Montreal	Eastern	35	290	13	20	310	140	-	59	124	-
1906	Montreal	Eastern	29	260	15	13	208	105	-	73	75	-
1907	Rochester	Eastern	36	291	14	19	327	133	-	67	111	-
1908	Binghamton	NY St	28	223	11	13	182	74	-	33	77	-
1909	Binghamton	NY St	34	273	16	14	257	102	-	35	92	-
1910	Binghamton	NY St	31	270	14	14	245	127	-	47	96	-
1911	Binghamton	NY St	32	253	14	15	238	91	-	45	83	-
1912	Troy	NY St	33	276	18	6	247	88	-	43	73	-
1913	Troy/W-B/Alb	NY St	13	100	4	8	100	56	-	27	19	-
1914	Albany	NY St	8	70	3	3	66	43	-	18	16	-
		Majors	**2**	**12**	**0**	**1**	**22**	**16**	**14**	**6**	**3**	**10.50**
		Minors	**538**	**4451**	**241**	**245**	**4541**	**2333**	**70**	**1028**	**1295**	**-**

ANTONIO POLLORENA (OSUNA)
Born April 17, 1947 at Los Mochis, Sinaloa, Mexico.
Height 5' 7", Weight 180. Threw right. Batted right.

Year	Club	League	G	IP	W	L	H	R	ER	BB	SO	ERA
1965	Fresnillo	Mex Cent	39	116	6	5	112	69	61	55	55	4.73
	Jalisco	Mexican	2	10	2	0	10	2	2	2	1	1.80
1966	Jalisco	Mexican	35	102	3	4	112	49	43	30	52	3.79
1967	Orizaba	Mex SE	16	95	5	5	91	55	40	36	55	3.79
	Jalisco	Mexican	17	41	1	0	59	20	18	14	25	3.95
1968	Jalisco	Mexican	37	193	16	10	174	75	64	63	100	2.98
1969	Jalisco	Mexican	42	203	13	12	197	76	61	51	109	2.70
1970	Jalisco	Mexican	27	154	10	5	151	59	49	39	79	2.86
1971	Jalisco	Mexican	19	70	3	5	75	36	28	30	30	3.60
	SLP	Mex Cent	3	14	0	2	15	10	5	6	10	3.21
1972	Torreon	Mexican	39	208	10	16	214	111	79	73	148	3.42
1973	Torreon	Mexican	31	177	10	11	169	73	52	36	113	2.64
1974	Torreon	Mexican	38	260	25	7	225	82	63	67	183	2.18
1975	Torreon	Mexican	35	254	20	11	236	79	67	50	136	2.37
1976	Torreon	Mexican	32	252	20	9	214	77	69	52	117	2.46
1977	Torreon	Mexican	32	252	20	11	247	95	72	44	129	2.57
1978	Torreon	Mexican	28	189	15	8	181	70	54	34	91	2.57
1979	Lag/Leon	Mexican	15	108	5	8	116	56	53	19	48	4.42
1980	Saltillo	Mex #1	24	172	10	12	189	67	60	43	109	3.14
	Saltillo	Mex #2	6	46	2	2	41	16	14	8	31	2.74
1981	Saltillo	Mexican	26	184	14	9	198	67	58	34	112	2.84
1982	Saltillo	Mexican	27	185	11	9	193	75	72	41	87	3.50
1983	Saltillo	Mexican	23	166	12	7	153	57	45	37	83	2.44
1984	Saltillo	Mexican	16	90	5	5	128	70	67	18	23	6.70
1985	U Laguna	Mexican	23	139	6	9	184	79	65	27	65	4.21
		Minors	**632**	**3680**	**244**	**182**	**3684**	**1525**	**1261**	**909**	**1991**	**3.08**

RAYMOND LEE PRIM
Born December 30, 1906 at Salitpa, AL.
Height 6', Weight 178. Threw left. Batted right.

Year	Club	League	G	IP	W	L	H	R	ER	BB	SO	ERA
1928	Alexandria	Cottn St	20	115	4	11	147	74	-	29	50	-
1929			Did not play in O. B.									
1930	Greensboro	Piedmont	24	124	6	6	152	101	86	33	57	6.24
1931	Greens/Dur	Piedmont	34	204	16	7	207	110	-	71	110	-
	Baltimore	Int	1	8	0	1	14	6	-	0	1	-
1932	York	NY-Penn	19	129	8	8	161	77	67	38	50	4.67
	Youngstown	Central	5	31	0	4	40	22	-	5	16	-
1933	Albany	Int	38	187	14	10	198	88	71	66	70	3.42
	Washington	American	2	14	0	1	13	6	5	2	6	3.21
1934	Washington	American	8	15	0	2	15	11	11	8	3	6.60
	Albany	Int	23	89	4	6	105	57	50	31	45	5.06
1935	Albany	Int	9	42	2	4	47	24	22	7	12	4.71
	Philadelphia	National	29	73	3	4	110	54	47	15	27	5.79
1936	Minneapolis	A A	1	0	0	0	1	0	0	1	0	0.00
	Los Angeles	P C	29	161	13	8	186	84	80	48	69	4.47
1937	Los Angeles	P C	39	293	21	13	317	151	121	59	176	3.72
1938	Los Angeles	P C	31	230	17	10	243	99	84	42	126	3.29

Year	Club	League	G	IP	W	L	H	R	ER	BB	SO	ERA
1939	Los Angeles	P C	39	280	20	17	302	128	111	43	107	3.57
1940	Los Angeles	P C	38	240	18	11	227	78	69	69	110	2.59
1941	Los Angeles	P C	36	255	16	15	261	102	81	38	119	2.86
1942	Los Angeles	P C	39	277	21	10	265	83	76	39	121	2.47
1943	Chicago	National	29	60	4	3	67	24	17	14	27	2.55
1944	Los Angeles	P C	41	286	22	10	238	75	54	40	139	1.70
1945	Chicago	National	34	165	13	8	142	58	44	23	88	2.40
1946	Chicago	National	14	23	2	3	28	17	15	10	10	5.87
1947	Los Angeles	P C	9	39	2	3	42	15	11	8	14	2.54
		Majors	**116**	**350**	**22**	**21**	**375**	**170**	**139**	**72**	**161**	**3.57**
		Minors	**475**	**2990**	**204**	**154**	**3153**	**1374**	**983**	**667**	**1392**	**3.36**

FRANCISCO RAMIREZ (ZAVALA)
Born March 9, 1928 at San Luis Potosi, Mexico.
Height 5' 10", Weight 175. Threw right. Batted right.

Year	Club	League	G	IP	W	L	H	R	ER	BB	SO	ERA
1950	San Luis Pot	Mexican	24	108	3	5	88	-	32	51	62	2.67
1951	San Luis Pot	Mexican	39	192	13	10	209	-	82	81	94	3.84
1952	SLP/Mex. C.	Mexican	49	223	10	17	230	127	104	115	122	4.20
1953	Mexicali	Ariz-Tex	12	94	9	3	95	45	37	29	89	3.54
1954	Mexicali	Ariz-Tex	48	**264**	18	9	282	134	103	69	**193**	3.51
1955	Houston	Texas	7	18	0	1	24	9	7	3	19	3.50
	Mexicali	Ariz-Tex	34	205	10	8	232	95	67	51	175	**2.94**
1956	MC Reds	Mexican	41	**232**	**20**	3	194	69	58	49	**148**	**2.25**
1957	Havana	Int	11	41	2	2	47	19	18	10	19	3.95
	MC Reds	Mexican	25	67	4	4	62	33	28	25	30	3.76
1958	MC Reds	Mexican	35	214	17	10	238	101	93	56	90	3.91
1959	Mex Reds	Mexican	**47**	**294**	17	12	**310**	126	106	65	139	3.24
1960	MC Reds	Mexican	43	**236**	**17**	13	**279**	149	126	78	100	4.81
1961	MC R/Mont	Mexican	36	**228**	9	**18**	258	122	106	48	135	4.18
1962	Monterrey	Mexican	33	**227**	18	9	**254**	103	91	64	113	3.61
	San Luis Pot	Mex Cent	4	29	2	1	26	13	9	8	11	2.79
1963	Monterrey	Mexican	33	241	14	13	**275**	**125**	**111**	47	140	4.15
1964	Monterrey	Mexican	21	135	9	10	144	90	72	30	71	4.80
1965	Monterrey	Mexican	35	236	13	11	232	100	87	42	144	3.32
1966	Monterrey	Mexican	30	154	8	11	170	78	71	39	62	4.15
1967	Monterrey	Mexican	35	229	12	13	230	90	70	51	111	2.75
1968	Jalisco	Mexican	2	9	0	2	13	7	4	4	4	4.00
	Poza Rica/Car	Mex SE	12	92	6	4	64	29	27	16	68	2.64
1969	Campeche	Mex SE	27	154	8	12	162	64	46	21	82	2.69
1970	MC Reds	Mexican	4	7	0	0	7	5	1	1	6	1.29
	Tampico	Mex Cent	5	28	3	0	18	9	1	3	18	0.32
		Minors	**692**	**3958**	**242**	**201**	**4143**	**1742**	**1557**	**1057**	**2245**	**3.54**

VICENTE ROMO (NAVARRO)
Born April 12, 1943 at Santa Rosalia, Baja Calif, Mexico.
Height 6', Weight 185. Threw right. Batted right.
Older brother of Enrique Romo, former major league hurler. Compiled impressive minor league career ERA of 2.70.

Year	Club	League	G	IP	W	L	H	R	ER	BB	SO	ERA
1962	Aguascal	Mex Cent	24	133	8	9	146	88	66	54	88	4.47
1963	MC Tigers	Mexican	33	199	12	10	192	84	72	74	126	3.26
1964	MC Tigers	Mexican	31	195	16	8	205	93	81	74	158	3.74
1965	Portland	P C	28	66	2	5	56	39	33	41	51	4.50
1966	MC Tigers	Mexican	38	220	17	7	199	77	59	93	206	2.41
1967	Portland	P C	25	104	3	11	106	58	48	55	76	4.15
1968	Los Angeles	National	1	1	0	0	1	1	0	0	0	0.00
	Portland	P C	10	57	4	3	57	26	20	17	42	3.16
	Cleveland	American	40	83	5	3	43	15	15	33	54	1.63
1969	Clev/Boston	American	55	135	8	10	123	54	47	53	96	3.13
1970	Boston	American	48	108	7	3	115	51	49	43	71	4.08
1971	Chicago	American	45	72	1	7	52	27	27	37	48	3.38
1972	Chicago	American	28	52	3	0	47	19	19	18	46	3.29
1973	San Diego	National	49	88	2	3	85	43	36	46	51	3.68
1974	San Diego	National	54	71	5	5	78	47	36	37	26	4.56
1975	Cordoba	Mexican	22	161	13	6	149	60	47	32	101	2.63
1976	Cordoba	Mexican	25	176	11	9	150	67	49	38	113	2.51
1977	Cordoba	Mexican	31	211	16	9	186	72	57	46	157	2.43
1978	Cordoba	Mexican	32	218	13	11	205	80	61	39	137	2.52
1979	Coatzacoal	Mexican	32	206	14	13	191	59	45	41	127	1.97
1980	Coatzacoal	Mex #1	21	169	10	8	123	48	35	40	147	1.86
	Coatzacoal	Mex #2	8	59	5	3	40	12	8	15	47	1.22
1981	Coatzacoal	Mexican	29	219	16	6	161	50	34	55	159	**1.40**
1982	Coatzacoal	Mexican	8	58	7	0	41	12	10	12	63	1.55
	Los Angeles	National	15	36	1	2	25	12	12	14	24	3.00
1983	MC Tigers	Mexican	26	181	14	6	160	57	50	33	119	2.49
1984	MC Reds	Mexican	22	141	10	6	143	70	54	40	110	3.45
1985	Cordoba	Mexican	14	60	4	2	42	18	14	13	49	2.10
1986	Cordoba/Yuc	Mexican	11	63	4	2	61	27	25	15	38	3.57
	Majors		**335**	**646**	**32**	**33**	**569**	**269**	**241**	**281**	**416**	**3.36**
	Minors		**470**	**2896**	**199**	**134**	**2613**	**1097**	**868**	**827**	**2114**	**2.70**

JESSE HOWARD "ANDY" RUSH
Born December 26, 1889 at Longton, KS. Died March 16, 1969 at Fresno, CA.
Height 6' 3", Weight 180. Threw right. Batted right.

Year	Club	League	G	IP	W	L	H	R	ER	BB	SO	ERA
1914	Hutchinson	Kan St	9	-	4	4	-	-	-	34	51	-
	Tulsa	West A	7	33	2	1	37	23	19	12	30	5.18
1915-20		Did not play in O.B.										
1921	Pars/Musk	SWestern	40	310	22	12	291	115	-	49	174	-
1922	Muskogee	SWestern	33	239	23	5	199	74	50	44	145	1.88
1923	Muskogee	SWestern	32	223	18	7	232	118	-	57	108	-
	Ardmore	West A	5	22	2	1	19	12	-	8	7	-
	Waterbury	Eastern	6	57	4	2	46	21	12	22	23	1.89
1924	Waterbury	Eastern	42	278	22	10	266	96	77	54	127	2.49

Year	Club	League	G	IP	W	L	H	R	ER	BB	SO	ERA
1925	Brooklyn	National	4	10	0	1	16	10	10	5	4	9.00
	Reading	Int	2	12	0	2	19	18	-	9	3	-
	Waterbury	Eastern	37	241	17	7	223	91	75	61	59	2.80
1926	Birmingham	South A	7	26	2	2	28	15	-	12	16	-
	Bridgeport	Eastern	26	211	15	10	216	89	71	59	71	3.03
1927	Bridgeport	Eastern	20	149	10	6	127	29	26	34	44	1.57
1928	Des Moines	Western	34	230	9	17	282	159	-	54	92	-
1929	All/Bridge	Eastern	36	254	23	6	248	114	94	61	97	3.33
1930	Bridgeport	Eastern	44	232	14	16	260	127	103	58	91	4.00
1931	Harrisburg	NY-Penn	42	212	14	9	208	92	72	46	77	3.06
1932	Harr/Hazle	NY-Penn	45	193	11	11	247	125	105	29	57	4.90
	Majors		**4**	**10**	**0**	**1**	**16**	**10**	**10**	**5**	**4**	**9.00**
	Minors		**467**	**2922**	**212**	**128**	**2948**	**1318**	**704**	**703**	**1272**	**-**

NORMAN ROMAINE SHOPE
Born June 14, 1915 at Swannanoa, NC.
Height 5' 11", Weight 168. Threw right. Batted left.

Year	Club	League	G	IP	W	L	H	R	ER	BB	SO	ERA
1937	Martinsville	Bi-St	10	38	0	2	74	70	54	-	19	12.79
	Elizabethton	Appalach	31	177	14	9	163	86	68	66	117	3.46
1938	Elizabethton	Appalach	23	158	11	6	120	52	-	63	88	-
1939	Elizabethton	Appalach	32	229	14	11	202	103	80	97	**154**	3.14
1940	Mayodan	Bi-St	8	56	1	5	65	44	37	31	38	5.95
	Lexington	N Car St	26	192	12	11	210	114	94	69	138	4.41
1941	Lexington	N Car St	23	180	13	5	181	79	58	58	103	2.90
1942	Lexington	N Car St	28	203	14	10	219	114	89	73	150	3.95
1943	Hagers/York	Inter-St	21	170	13	4	170	75	50	64	107	**2.65**
1944	York	Inter-St	32	**258**	**20**	11	229	122	88	86	**239**	3.07
1945	Rochester	Int	28	149	10	6	164	107	84	83	87	5.07
1946	Columbus	Sally	29	189	11	11	198	94	65	48	105	3.10
1947	Lynchburg	Piedmont	36	**253**	14	18	233	131	87	93	144	3.09
1948	Lynchburg	Piedmont	27	223	12	15	207	90	67	53	103	2.70
1949	Omaha	Western	8	26	1	1	27	13	-	14	17	-
	Lynchburg	Piedmont	21	137	10	8	129	60	49	39	82	3.22
1950	Lynchburg	Piedmont	31	192	13	7	192	69	61	61	67	2.86
1951	Pocatello	Pioneer	12	68	3	6	83	51	38	31	26	5.03
	Lynchburg	Piedmont	15	99	4	9	113	60	49	42	44	4.45
1952	Houston	Texas	4	6	0	0	13	7	7	3	0	10.50
	Columbia	Sally	29	116	7	5	101	48	34	50	49	2.64
1953	Charl/Macon	Sally	41	157	7	12	145	59	47	47	61	2.69
1954	Macon/Colum	Sally	45	127	7	1	145	74	64	37	55	4.54
1955	Columbia	Sally	27	45	3	3	51	25	23	15	14	4.60
	Minors		**587**	**3448**	**214**	**176**	**3434**	**1747**	**1293**	**1223**	**2007**	**3.57**

CLAUDE ALFRED THOMAS
Born May 15, 1890 at Stanberry, MO. Died March 6, 1946 at Sulphur, OK.
Height 6' 1", Weight 180. Threw left. Batted left.

Year	Club	League	G	IP	W	L	H	R	ER	BB	SO	ERA
1910	Bartlesville	West A	27	-	16	8	-	-	-	45	140	-
	Kewanee	Carol A	10	57	1	5	60	29	-	10	21	-
1911	Steubenville	Ohio-Pa	21	-	13	8	170	71	-	69	95	-

Year	Club	League	G	IP	W	L	H	R	ER	BB	SO	ERA
1912	Prov/Roch	Int	11	37	0	2	49	35	-	26	15	-
	Wichita	Western	13	73	1	5	102	53	-	35	39	-
1913	Clarksdale	Cottn St	24	155	9	11	177	81	-	20	91	-
1914	Grand Rapids	Central	25	172	8	12	151	75	-	58	85	-
	Des Moines	Western	14	98	5	8	74	33	27	38	43	2.48
1915	Des Moines	Western	48	292	22	13	282	120	68	97	110	2.10
1916	Des Moines	Western	43	290	15	15	289	-	107	92	137	3.32
	Washington	American	7	28	1	2	27	14	13	12	7	4.18
1917	Minneapolis	A A	62	374	20	24	338	157	112	113	108	2.70
1918	Minneapolis	A A	8	29	0	3	48	30	24	14	7	7.45
1919	Wichita	Western	10	72	2	6	55	22	-	14	19	-
	Seattle	P C	33	210	10	16	202	100	69	47	59	2.96
1920	Los Angeles	P C	49	304	21	19	325	139	102	78	72	3.02
1921	Los Angeles	P C	42	225	12	7	271	115	88	46	44	3.52
1922	Los Angeles	P C	45	263	18	11	294	128	87	75	51	2.98
1923	Los Angeles	P C	50	247	9	15	303	150	108	66	44	3.94
1924	Vernon	P C	31	181	10	11	226	115	84	52	37	4.18
1925	Des Moines	Western	44	249	19	6	280	137	-	65	57	-
1926	Des Moines	Western	27	170	12	11	217	113	-	33	26	-
	Majors		**7**	**28**	**1**	**2**	**27**	**14**	**13**	**12**	**7**	**4.18**
	Minors		**637**	**3498**	**223**	**216**	**3913**	**1703**	**876**	**1093**	**1300**	**-**

FAY WESLEY THOMAS

Born October 10, 1904 at Holvrood, KS. Died August 16, 1990 at Chatsworth, CA.
Height 6' 2", Weight 195. Threw right. Batted right.
Won 22 consecutive games for Los Angeles 1933-34. Played football at University of Southern California. First of many USC baseball players to reach major leagues.

Year	Club	League	G	IP	W	L	H	R	ER	BB	SO	ERA
1925	Ottumwa	Miss Val	7	49	3	3	52	27	-	23	47	-
1926	Toledo	A A	10	38	1	1	36	34	-	36	28	-
	New Haven	Eastern	25	173	15	4	109	65	44	79	112	2.29
1927	Buffalo	Int	12	85	3	5	95	44	37	28	45	3.92
	New York	National	9	16	0	0	19	10	6	4	11	3.38
1928	Okla City	Western	7	28	0	2	30	19	-	20	13	-
1929	Baltimore	Int	10	29	0	2	38	27	17	20	15	5.28
	New Haven	Eastern	29	186	13	10	202	119	105	103	128	5.08
1930	Sacramento	P C	52	298	18	20	292	170	131	131	228	3.96
1931	Cleveland	American	16	49	2	4	63	34	28	32	25	5.14
	Oakland	P C	25	163	12	10	159	75	70	59	123	3.87
1932	Oakland	P C	34	255	12	19	216	107	92	93	**196**	3.25
	Brooklyn	National	7	17	0	1	22	15	14	8	9	7.41
1933	Los Angeles	P C	42	300	20	14	364	181	125	104	159	3.75
1934	Los Angeles	P C	41	295	**28**	4	246	98	85	118	**204**	2.59
1935	St. Louis	American	49	147	7	15	165	95	78	89	67	4.78
1936	Los Angeles	P C	28	206	15	10	219	91	71	75	134	3.10
1937	Los Angeles	P C	40	294	23	11	275	124	105	112	181	3.21
1938	Los Angeles	P C	31	200	18	8	196	83	73	68	123	3.29
1939	Los Angeles	P C	35	246	17	13	216	86	75	91	139	2.74
1940	Los Angeles	P C	30	161	6	11	185	87	89	64	77	4.98
1941	Los Angeles	P C	28	154	10	13	168	84	70	65	72	4.09
1942		Did not play in O. B.										
1943	Port/Holly	P C	5	20	0	3	23	12	12	7	3	5.40
	Majors		**81**	**229**	**9**	**20**	**269**	**154**	**126**	**133**	**112**	**4.95**
	Minors		**491**	**3180**	**214**	**163**	**3121**	**1533**	**1201**	**1296**	**2027**	**3.53**

JOHN LAWRENCE TILLMAN
Born October 6, 1893 at Bridgeport, CT. Died April 7, 1964 at Harrisburg, PA.
Height 5' 11", Weight 170. Threw right. Batted both.
Manager: Harrisburg NY-Penn 1929-30.

Year	Club	League	G	IP	W	L	H	R	ER	BB	SO	ERA
1914	New Bedford	Colonial	40	288	21	11	253	-	-	97	185	-
1915	New Bedford	Colonial	31	268	22	6	201	81	-	84	176	-
	St. Louis	American	2	10	1	0	6	2	1	4	6	0.90
1916	Memphis	South A	2	10	0	1	9	8	-	4	5	-
	Houston	Texas	19	110	7	6	95	48	-	42	36	-
1917	Charleston	Sally	23	186	11	10	165	61	-	50	50	-
1918		Military Service										
1919	New Hav/Pitt	Eastern	29	191	14	11	196	79	-	45	43	-
1920	Pittsfield	Eastern	37	211	12	8	238	88	74	79	74	3.16
1921	Pittsfield	Eastern	36	240	16	10	252	94	73	76	81	2.74
1922	Pittsfield	Eastern	37	250	16	15	267	111	86	78	97	3.10
1923	Pitt/Alb/NH	Eastern	36	194	9	14	233	137	92	68	42	4.27
1924	New Haven	Eastern	14	31	0	2	42	33	27	15	6	7.84
1925	Jersey City	Int	3	3	0	0	5	4	-	5	1	-
	York	NY-Penn	20	121	7	5	135	56	48	38	48	3.57
1926	York	NY-Penn	34	248	16	11	253	108	70	74	80	2.54
1927	York	NY-Penn	36	239	16	11	258	129	109	79	58	4.10
1928	Harrisburg	NY-Penn	31	189	10	13	186	96	60	56	54	2.86
1929	Harrisburg	NY-Penn	39	270	21	12	308	139	112	75	67	3.73
1930	Harris/W-B	NY-Penn	33	178	10	13	214	125	99	60	39	5.01
1931	York	NY-Penn	33	212	10	16	233	96	89	73	75	3.78
1932	York/W-B	NY-Penn	6	24	0	2	29	21	-	6	4	-
	Springfield	III	4	22	0	3	40	25	-	12	12	-
1933		Did not play in O. B.										
1934	Manchester	New Eng	25	183	11	8	195	102	-	72	70	-
		Majors	**2**	**10**	**1**	**0**	**6**	**2**	**1**	**4**	**6**	**0.90**
		Minors	**568**	**3668**	**229**	**188**	**3807**	**1641**	**939**	**1188**	**1303**	**-**

JAMES ROY WALKER
(Known by middle name.)
Born March 12, 1893 at Lawrenceburg, TN. Died February 10, 1962 at New Orleans, LA.
Height 6' 1-1/2", Weight 185. Threw right. Batted both.
Holds Southern Association career record with 1240 strikeouts.

Year	Club	League	G	IP	W	L	H	R	ER	BB	SO	ERA
1912	Bristol	Appalach	31	240	17	11	166	61	-	44	203	-
	Cleveland	American	1	2	0	0	0	0	0	2	1	0.00
1913	Toledo	A A	11	54	1	1	64	45	-	33	27	-
	New Orleans	South A	17	127	6	9	123	69	-	56	81	-
1914	New Orleans	South A	32	243	15	11	178	85	-	**107**	**200**	-
1915	New Orleans	South A	10	79	7	2	44	18	-	35	63	-
	Cleveland	American	25	131	5	9	122	73	58	65	57	3.98
1916	New Orleans	South A	39	294	16	14	229	94	-	**118**	**173**	-
1917	New Orleans	South A	36	297	19	11	170	75	54	**162**	**231**	**1.64**
	Chicago	National	2	7	0	1	8	3	3	5	4	3.86
1918	Chicago	National	13	43	1	3	50	27	13	15	20	2.72
1919	Columbus	A A	21	140	10	7	140	69	50	67	95	3.21
	New Orleans	South A	13	82	2	6	62	24	18	29	56	1.98

Year	Club	League										
1920	New Orleans	South A	47	363	**26**	11	281	104	-	93	**237**	-
1921	St. Louis	National	38	171	11	12	194	93	80	53	52	4.21
1922	St. Louis	National	12	32	1	2	34	20	17	15	14	4.78
	New Orleans	South A	19	120	12	1	104	30	21	35	53	1.58
1923	New Orleans	South A	41	296	21	9	274	109	86	94	115	2.61
1924	Milwaukee	A A	36	186	5	13	238	139	123	77	88	5.95
1925	Birmingham	South A	22	107	6	9	128	77	56	51	31	4.71
	Shreveport	Texas	2	5	0	1	9	5	-	3	1	-
	Knoxville	Sally	3	17	0	3	26	16	14	5	10	7.41
	Majors		**91**	**386**	**18**	**27**	**408**	**216**	**171**	**155**	**148**	**3.99**
	Minors		**380**	**2650**	**163**	**119**	**2236**	**1020**	**422**	**1009**	**1664**	-

THOMAS ROYAL "GOAT" WALKER

Born November 5, 1903 at Goshen, AL.
Height 5' 11-1/2", Weight 180. Threw right. Batted right.
Manager: Jacksonville Sally 1938-39.

Year	Club	League	G	IP	W	L	H	R	ER	BB	SO	ERA
1924	Birmingham	South A	13	76	3	7	94	67	51	38	27	6.04
1925	Birmingham	South A	5	13	1	1	13	12	11	14	5	7.62
	Columbia	Sally	Played outfield									
	Marshall	E Texas	7	36	2	4	43	28	-	16	17	-
1926	Montgomery	SEastern	18	127	7	6	141	72	-	39	48	-
1927	Montgomery	SEastern	45	254	17	11	252	108	-	77	90	-
1928	Montgomery	SEastern	34	245	18	8	237	99	84	58	65	3.09
1929	Montgomery	SEastern	41	278	15	13	266	99	77	96	69	2.49
1930	Nashville	South A	Pinch hit in one game									
	Montgomery	SEastern	36	225	13	10	262	128	95	99	64	3.80
1931	San Antonio	Texas	17	42	1	2	55	31	21	20	11	4.50
	York	NY-Penn	2	7	0	1	16	11	-	8	4	-
	Ashe/High Pt	Piedmont	8	52	1	5	69	40	-	22	21	-
1932	High Pt/Ral	Piedmont	27	172	8	12	172	121	100	62	62	5.23
1933-35			Did not play in O.B.									
1936	Jacksonville	Sally	29	227	20	8	220	88	65	53	93	2.58
1937	Jacksonville	Sally	35	278	19	13	265	108	86	59	100	2.78
1938	Jacksonville	Sally	33	236	21	7	267	95	77	41	114	2.94
1939	Jacksonville	Sally	32	219	14	12	213	105	84	52	110	3.45
1940	Montgomery	SEastern	36	262	**22**	10	293	136	108	36	92	3.71
1941	Montgomery	SEastern	37	210	11	14	240	106	91	37	77	3.90
1942	Montgomery	SEastern	30	241	**20**	7	263	92	74	50	82	2.76
1943	Memphis	South A	32	151	10	11	175	93	77	39	41	4.59
1944			Did not play in O. B.									
1945	Memphis	South A	6	39	3	2	45	24	20	15	9	4.62
1946	Selma	SEastern	4	22	1	1	20	5	4	4	4	1.64
1947-48			Did not play in O. B.									
1949	Selma	SEastern	23	123	4	8	153	71	56	28	32	4.10
1950	Selma	SEastern	-	-	0	1	-	-	-	-	-	-
	Minors		**550**	**3535**	**231**	**174**	**3774**	**1739**	**1181**	**963**	**1237**	**3.47**

JOHN MILTON WARHOP

Born July 4, 1884 at Hinton, WV. Died October 4, 1960 at Freeport, IL.
Height 5' 9-1/2", Weight 168. Threw right. Batted right.

Pitched 13 shutouts for Freeport in 1907. In an 11-inning game against Oshkosh on May 14, 1907, he fanned 22 batters. At age 43 on July 14, 1927, he pitched 13-inning 4-3 win over Hartford and scored the deciding run. Also known for giving up the first two major league home runs to Babe Ruth, the opposing hurler, in 1915.

Year	Club	League	G	IP	W	L	H	R	ER	BB	SO	ERA
1906	Freeport	Wis St	35	293	23	7	176	84	-	62	**231**	-
1907	Freeport	Wis St	39	**325**	**30**	6	170	52	-	81	**339**	-
1908	Williamsport	Tri-St	37	305	**29**	7	242	100	-	83	140	-
	New York	American	5	36	1	2	40	21	18	8	11	4.50
1909	New York	American	36	243	13	15	197	84	65	81	95	2.41
1910	New York	American	37	254	14	14	219	108	81	79	75	2.87
1911	New York	American	31	210	12	13	239	120	97	44	71	4.16
1912	New York	American	39	258	10	19	256	120	82	59	110	2.86
1913	New York	American	15	62	4	6	69	42	26	33	11	3.77
1914	New York	American	37	217	8	15	182	75	57	44	56	2.36
1915	New York	American	21	143	7	9	164	74	63	52	34	3.97
1916	Salt Lake City	P C	10	40	1	4	43	32	21	17	9	4.73
1917	Toronto	Int	36	240	15	10	252	68	105	92	75	3.94
1918	Toronto	Int	7	46	4	1	21	21	17	16	27	3.33
1919				Did not play in O. B.								
1920	Norfolk	Virginia	8	74	5	3	64	22	7	18	38	0.85
1921	Norfolk	Virginia	36	255	20	7	234	-	-	51	177	-
1922	Columbia	Sally	30	256	15	13	201	85	71	55	133	2.50
1923-26				Did not play in O. B.								
1927	Bridgeport	Eastern	21	177	11	7	173	67	49	50	44	2.49
1928	Portland	P C	9	12	0	0	6	2	2	7	1	1.50
	Spartansburg	Sally	5	29	2	3	36	22	18	10	3	5.59
	New Haven	Eastern	16	48	0	2	60	34	33	8	13	6.19
		Majors	**221**	**1423**	**69**	**93**	**1366**	**644**	**489**	**400**	**463**	**3.09**
		Minors	**289**	**2100**	**155**	**70**	**1678**	**589**	**323**	**550**	**1230**	-

WILLIAM L. "JIMMY" WHELAN

Born 1880 at San Francisco, CA. Died January 12, 1915 at Sacramento, CA.
Threw right.

Year	Club	League	G	IP	W	L	H	R	ER	BB	SO	ERA
1898	San Francisco	Calif	2	17	1	1	17	15	-	10	11	-
	Stock/Sa/SC	P C	16	137	4	10	108	73	-	40	59	-
1899	Wat/SC	Calif	42	335	17	22	295	160	-	118	126	-
1900	Stockton	Calif	38	320	17	18	276	143	64	92	102	1.80
1901	San Francisco	Calif	67	537	36	23	419	249	124	218	147	2.08
1902	San Francisco	Calif	56	-	30	26	386	-	-	151	157	-
1903	San Francisco	P C	51	443	28	21	404	202	-	145	106	-
1904	San Francisco	P C	59	492	32	23	436	181	-	137	143	-
1905	San Francisco	P C	**65**	512	**32**	25	383	155	-	108	214	-
1906	Montreal	Eastern	30	246	12	17	333	121	-	53	71	-
1907	Williamsport	Tri-St	28	202	14	8	195	90	-	51	51	-
	Oakland	Calif	2	17	1	1	21	8	-	3	9	-
1908	Sacramento	Calif	43	367	31	8	266	83	-	78	147	-
1909	Sacramento	P C	51	-	23	18	-	140	-	82	127	-

1910	Sacramento	P C	44	-	14	22	-	99	-	85	80	-
1911	Tacoma	NWestern	Broke leg, did not play									
1912	Vernon	P C	11	52	2	4	-	34	-	20	12	-
		Minors	**605**	**3677**	**294**	**247**	**3539**	**1753**	**188**	**1391**	**1562**	**-**

RICHARD OLIVER WHITWORTH
Born October 21, 1893 at McDade, TX.
Height 5' 10", Weight 180. Threw right. Batted right.
Pitched record 452 games in Texas League.

Year	Club	League	G	IP	W	L	H	R	ER	BB	SO	ERA
1923	Austin	Texas A	35	212	9	12	190	95	-	50	128	-
1924	Austin	Texas A	35	250	16	9	238	105	-	51	137	-
1925	Austin	Texas A	36	239	17	8	-	-	-	34	113	-
1926	Austin	Texas A	44	275	24	10	218	103	-	58	176	-
	Houston	Texas	2	18	1	1	14	4	3	4	5	1.50
1927	Houston	Texas	43	215	12	12	227	112	94	67	48	3.93
1928	Houston	Texas	26	118	6	4	115	47	44	48	50	3.36
1929	Fort Worth	Texas	39	223	16	12	267	127	102	61	53	4.12
1930	Fort Worth	Texas	48	**261**	20	11	271	138	113	72	96	3.90
1931	Fort Worth	Texas	34	267	18	12	271	107	86	54	87	2.90
1932	Fort Worth	Texas	41	282	17	16	276	112	97	48	66	3.10
1933	Fort Worth	Texas	42	281	15	20	309	152	137	61	74	4.39
1934	Fort Worth	Texas	41	264	14	18	301	153	129	60	44	4.40
1935	Tulsa	Texas	37	147	10	9	159	78	58	28	22	3.55
1936	Okla City	Texas	46	212	15	9	235	94	77	55	49	3.27
1937	OC/Ft. W	Texas	41	140	12	5	175	83	62	29	87	3.99
1938	Ft. W/Dall	Texas	13	49	2	3	53	27	18	12	9	3.31
		Minors	**603**	**3453**	**224**	**171**	**3319**	**1537**	**1020**	**792**	**1244**	**-**

ADRIAN ZABALA (RODRIGUEZ)
Born August 26, 1916 at San Antonio de los Banos, Cuba.
Height 5' 11", Weight 165. Threw left. Batted left.

Year	Club	League	G	IP	W	L	H	R	ER	BB	SO	ERA
1937	Panama City	Ala-Fla	21	143	10	7	96	38	32	61	137	**2.01**
1938	Panama City	Ala-Fla	33	231	11	13	280	155	123	95	143	4.79
1939	Jacksonville	Sally	37	206	13	11	232	115	94	90	93	4.11
1940	Jacksonville	Sally	28	170	9	8	181	86	75	54	91	3.97
1941	Jacksonville	Sally	43	277	20	17	265	125	95	94	173	3.09
1942	Jacksonville	Sally	25	187	16	5	183	70	47	39	91	2.26
	Jersey City	Int	14	75	3	5	72	31	26	30	25	3.12
1943		No record available										
1944	Puebla	Mexican	18	122	10	2	103	-	37	51	53	2.74
1945	Jersey City	Int	28	171	14	7	153	86	61	75	77	3.21
	New York	National	11	43	2	4	46	25	23	20	14	4.81
1946	Puebla	Mexican	43	203	11	14	250	-	111	98	86	4.92
1947	Puebla	Mexican	45	281	19	14	283	-	106	93	85	3.40
1948	Sherbrooke	Provincl	40	-	16	7	-	-	-	-	-	-
1949	Sherbrooke	Provincl	16	110	8	6	93	-	48	29	62	3.93
	New York	National	15	41	2	3	44	28	24	10	13	5.27
1950	Minneapolis	A A	33	130	11	4	151	83	71	54	52	4.92
1951	Minneapolis	A A	49	177	14	12	198	98	78	60	76	3.97

1952	Minneapolis	A A	69	139	14	10	138	58	46	50	65	2.98
1953	Minneapolis	A A	48	97	5	6	108	40	30	33	56	2.78
1954	San Francisco	P C	59	112	11	8	108	61	40	43	43	3.21
1955	San Fran/Oak	P C	10	17	0	2	26	16	11	7	5	5.82
	Jacksonville	Sally	36	74	11	3	65	22	15	25	32	1.82
1956	Jacksonville	Sally	32	56	5	2	58	25	20	14	25	3.21
		Majors	**26**	**84**	**4**	**7**	**90**	**53**	**47**	**30**	**27**	**5.04**
		Minors	**727**	**2978**	**231**	**163**	**3043**	**1109**	**1166**	**1095**	**1470**	**3.52**